D1520299

ARIZONA'S
DEADLIEST
GUNFIGHT

ARIZONA'S DEADLIEST GUNFIGHT

DRAFT RESISTANCE AND TRAGEDY AT THE POWER CABIN, 1918

HEIDI J. OSSELAER

UNIVERSITY OF OKLAHOMA PRESS : NORMAN

Library of Congress Cataloging in Publication Control Number: 2017043089

The paper in this book meets the guidelines for permanence and durability of the Committee on Production Guidelines for Book Longevity of the Council on Library Resources, Inc. ∞

1 2 3 4 5 6 7 8 9 10

CONTENTS

List of Illustrations   vii
Preface   ix
Acknowledgments   xv

1. Origins   3
2. Texas Hill Country   11
3. New Mexico Territory   22
4. Frontier Honor   32
5. Aravaipa Canyon   44
6. The Gila Valley   62
7. The Abandoned Mines   79
8. The Great War   88
9. Shootout at Dawn   104
10. On the Run   122
11. Captured   141
12. On Trial   155
13. The Big House on the Gila   169
14. Clemency   187
15. Redemption   208

Abbreviations   223
Notes   225
Selected Bibliography   267
Index   297

ILLUSTRATIONS

MAP

The Power Family's Southwest   25

FIGURES

Power Family   49

Rattlesnake Canyon   50

Charles Power   56

John Power   57

Tom Power and George Morgan   58

Tom Sisson   84

Ola May Power   105

Frank McBride   115

Martin and Sena Kempton   116

Thomas Kane Wootan   117

Power cabin, 1918   119

Wanted poster   136

John Power in prison, 1918   172

Tom Power in prison, 1918   172

Don Dedera and J. Frank Wootan   203

Tom Power at his parole hearing, 1960   204

Spurs presented to Don Dedera   206

Tom and John Power at Klondyke in 1970   212

Power stamp mill, 2014   220

Power cabin, 2014   220

PREFACE

I guess there have been a thousand stories about us.

Jeff Power found solace in the isolation of the Galiuro Mountains of southeastern Arizona, living in a canyon so remote that it had no official name. It took several years of backbreaking work to cut a trail through some of the toughest country he had ever seen to connect his mine to the nearest road into town, but he had chosen to live there precisely because it was far from civilization. His sons John and Tom had done the bulk of the labor, while Jeff and hired hand Tom Sisson rounded out the road crew. A prospective buyer for his mining claim was due anytime, and after a lifetime of just getting by on the frontier, Jeff Power was certain prosperity was close at hand.

A snowstorm was threatening on the evening of February 9, 1918, delaying his anticipated visitor, but events far from his canyon hideaway also jeopardized Jeff Power's plans. Even in his secluded location he could no longer distance himself or his family from the transformations occurring in American society. His sons were required to register for the draft, but he saw no reason to send them off to fight in a war in Europe he did not believe in, telling a shopkeeper when he made the long trip into the Gila Valley for supplies, "This is your war." Pointing toward his home in the distant canyon, he added, "That country over there is ours; we don't want nothing to do with your war."

———

Sheriff Frank McBride left the Graham County courthouse in Safford on Saturday, February 9, 1918, for the Galiuro Mountains with warrants for the arrests of the four men living at the mining shack owned by Jeff Power. He had a long automobile drive ahead of him from his home in the Gila Valley to the small ranching community of Klondyke, and then several hours on horseback over difficult trails into Rattlesnake Canyon, before he would reach the Power camp. McBride did not think much of the Power brothers, Tom and John, who refused to serve in the military. The sheriff, a devout Mormon, believed every man, woman, and child should pledge their all to the war effort. His religion had taught him that in times of crisis and hardship, sacrificing individual desires while pulling together for the good of the community was the best solution. From his years in law enforcement McBride believed the Aravaipa region, where the Powers lived, was full of people who disregarded the law—poachers, moonshiners, bootleggers, cattle rustlers, and murderers. Gossip was circulating among the residents of the Gila Valley that Jeff Power's daughter, Ola May, who had died recently under suspicious circumstances, had been murdered, perhaps by someone in her own family. McBride was determined to find out what really happened to her and bring the Powers to justice.

———

But Jeff Power never found a buyer for his gold mine and Sheriff Frank McBride never served his warrants, because both men died the next morning in a gun battle that took place at the Power cabin. Two of McBride's deputies, Martin Kempton and Thomas Kane Wootan, also were slain, bringing the death toll to four, the deadliest gunfight in Arizona history. At first glance the shootout reads like something out of a Zane Grey novel or a John Ford Western movie script. *Four armed men surround a lonely mining cabin at dawn. Someone inside, awakened by the commotion, walks out the front door, rifle in hand. One of the men outside the cabin yells, "Throw up your hands!" Firing commences.* But closer examination reveals a far more complicated story in which it is difficult to determine who held the moral high ground.

There are hundreds of books and articles written about the shootout near the OK Corral, where three men died on the streets of Tombstone in 1881, but far less has been written about what happened in 1918 at the cabin owned by Jeff Power, located just sixty miles north of Tombstone.[1] While the setting of the Earp and Clanton-McLaury confrontation fits expectations for a western gunfight—the center of a bustling mining town during Arizona's raucous territorial days—the Power shootout occurred miles from the nearest settlement and after the frontier had closed, when America was on the threshold of becoming a modern society.

By the 1910s, political, social, industrial, and commercial institutions had transformed a nation once filled with unique communities into a formidable federal system, as Richard Slotkin argues, "capable of touching the lives and influencing the behavior of communities in every part of the nation." Even in the newly minted state of Arizona, one of the last frontiers of the American West, industrialization and urbanization were transforming the landscape as people moved from rural homesteads to towns, attracted by such modern conveniences as electricity, indoor plumbing, good roads, and opportunities for advanced education for their children. The country had recently entered the Great War raging in Europe, and the increased power of the federal government affected everyone in 1918, even someone like Jeff Power living in an isolated canyon.[2]

History tends to portray America's entrance into World War I as a time of unity, when few people challenged the war or the nation's enactment of the first large-scale military conscription. Acts of defiance against the draft, such as the Cleburne County War in Arkansas and the Green Corn Rebellion in Oklahoma, are often relegated to the footnotes of that conflict. The Power shootout, probably the deadliest single instance of draft resistance during World War I, should have taken its place long ago among those other, better-documented incidents, but until now it has not received the scholarly attention needed to position it within Great War historiography. This oversight can be attributed to a curious combination of missing documents and wartime censors, who kept accurate coverage of the shootout and subsequent trial from ever reaching the public.

It is difficult to determine what really happened when the four lawmen encountered the Power men and Tom Sisson on that cold dawn in 1918. Impartial judgment and neutral witnesses were in short supply following the gun battle, and each of the four men who lived through it felt the need to defend his actions that day. The sole officer to escape always maintained the Power men and Tom Sisson fired first. The residents of the cabin who survived—brothers Tom and John Power and Sisson—steadfastly asserted that they acted in self-defense when Jeff Power was shot trying to surrender to men who ambushed their home. Even impartial observers struggled to make sense of the killings, which took place in wartime when newspaper coverage and official reports were tinged with hyperpatriotic rhetoric condemning draft evaders like the Power brothers as dangerous enemies of the state.

Prior to and following the deadly exchange, newspaper editors and federal officials alike published outrageous accounts of the Power family based on rumors rather than solid intelligence, even failing to correctly identify family members in official reports. As a frustrated Tom Power later begged reporters, "Spell our name right, please. . . . It's Power, not Powers. I guess there have been a thousand stories about us, but nobody ever asked us how we spell our name."[3] The misspelling of the family name was so ubiquitous, the United States Forest Service later perpetuated the mistake on all trail markers and maps indicating Power landmarks in Rattlesnake Canyon. Although I have corrected the most egregious spelling and typographical errors in quotations where they confuse meaning, I have retained the original misspelling of names, like "Powers," places, and expressions found in newspaper articles, court documents, federal reports, and telegrams. These eccentricities allow the reader to understand that the authors were not always in possession of reliable information or familiar with their subject matter.

After the sensational murder trial many documents related to the case went missing. State and county record keeping in 1918 was haphazard at best, and documents were often misplaced or destroyed in fires or floods. Of course, it is also common for souvenir hunters to abscond with public records about a sensational murder case. Although some of the missing documents related to the Power case, including arrest warrants, trial exhibits, inquest reports, and even court dockets, have reappeared in private collections in recent years, other records, most notably the trial transcripts and much of the correspondence of the federal marshal and the U.S. attorney in charge of the case, remain missing. The pattern became so suspicious that it led some people investigating the case in the 1950s and 1960s to believe that this was not just an act of random theft, but rather a much more systematic attempt to suppress evidence that might have exonerated the Powers and Sisson.[4]

It is not in my nature to believe in grand conspiracy theories, so initially I believed the losses were normal accidents of history. The shorthand notes of the testimony likely vanished because the trial never underwent a formal review, the only legal event that would have mandated their transcription and preservation. The records of the United States attorney for Arizona, Thomas Flynn, were not preserved, because the federal government did not begin to systematically collect federal records until the creation of the National Archives and Records Administration in 1934. While those losses can be explained, the disappearance of the Power correspondence from the United States Marshals' Collection, housed at the Arizona Historical Society in Tucson since 1959, cannot. Arizona marshal Joseph Dillon was known to keep meticulous records, and the collection contains a treasure trove of his letters and telegrams exchanged with the U.S. attorney for Arizona, the Department of Justice, Arizona sheriffs, his own deputies, and others, but items concerned with the Power brothers, the most important case of his tenure, are missing. Two letters Dillon sent to his deputy Frank Haynes were entered as evidence during the trial in 1918, and his telegrams to the U.S. attorney general are preserved in the National Archives, but his personal carbon copies of those messages have vanished, indicating there were indeed parties interested in covering up the truth of this case.[5]

The vacuum created by the missing records and newspaper censors allowed many individuals with an interest in the story to create their own narratives to explain why so many people fought to the death in an obscure canyon. Oral histories handed down from one generation to the next by descendants of the lawmen or the Power family and their surrogates became the foundation for most books and articles about the shootout, but like the child's game of "telephone," in which a message becomes warped through multiple retellings, the shootout evolved over time into many different stories. Conspiracy theories were formulated to explain why documents vanished and why there was so much loss of life during an arrest of men wanted for nonviolent crimes. The resulting shootout historiography is a pastiche of western lore in which the contestants were brought together on a snowy Sunday morning to fight over—depending on which version you read—a gold mine, the love of a woman, water rights, bootleg liquor, or some personal affront, rather than the Power family's defiance of the federal government.[6]

With so many problems in the existing published accounts of the shootout, I decided to start from scratch, relying primarily on public records contemporaneous with events and dipping into the unreliable oral histories, written years later, to flesh out the story only when more objective sources corroborate their substance. I liberally use words such as "alleged," "probably," or "folklore" to alert readers to material that has a tenuous hold on the truth. I resort to those qualifiers more often than I would like.

The Powers were not well educated, so they left behind few personal documents that provide insight into their behavior, but they did leave a long paper trail of civil and criminal court cases, as well as property, tax, and census records that provide context for their actions. I cast my net both wide and deep while collecting information, tracing several generations of Jeff Power's ancestors to determine the ethos that guided this frontier family. When pulled together, the new information creates a more objective view of the Power family, whose members were not the murderous outlaws portrayed by the press and the families of the lawmen, nor did they resemble the tragic victims of greed and corruption found in Power hagiography.

I reconstructed much of the government's case against the Powers from reports held by the United States Department of Justice and the Military Intelligence Division. These records, uncovered and declassified for the first time, combined with correspondence in Arizona Department of Correction records, provide fresh evidence for the actions of the lawmen and refute the prevailing legend that emerged long after the killings that the sheriff and deputies went to the Power cabin under false pretenses to steal the gold mine or take revenge on the Power men. Instead, the lawmen were simply performing their duty to arrest men they believed were criminals, with the full backing of the federal government. However, those records also reveal that much of the information gathered by law enforcement agencies about the Power family was based on faulty intelligence, which means that rumors and wartime histrionics rather than hard evidence fueled this tragedy.

After a century, folklore has encrusted the Power gunfight story like barnacles on the rusting hull of a ship—when you scrape it away in places, little substance is left. I am under no illusion that the entire truth of this story will ever be known. Too many documents remain missing, and misinformation drove this event from start to finish. As Graham County historian Hal Herbert told me, for decades it seemed no one wanted the truth uncovered.[7] However, there exists sufficient material to piece together the motives of the principal players and, once revealed, they allow us to reframe the context for the gun battle. While previous studies have agonized over who ambushed whom at the Power cabin, I believe the central question is: Why did lawmen feel it was necessary to travel for miles into the backwoods in the middle of the night and in the dead of winter to arrest men wanted for nonviolent crimes? We can know that answer when we understand the forces that brought Jeff Power and Frank McBride face-to-face in 1918. Both men were well into middle age and each had experienced his fair share of personal pain and loss. Neither man would have been duped into a gun battle over a mine or a personal grievance, as so many have suggested. Rather, the man who sought seclusion from the world and the sheriff who sought to bring law and order to the canyon were caught up in a much larger battle over what it meant to be an American during World War I. Their story allows us to understand how the animosities created by that war exploded into violence in the most unlikely of places: a mining cabin in the rugged Galiuro Mountains of southeastern Arizona.

ACKNOWLEDGMENTS

Simply put, this book would never have been written without documentary filmmaker Cameron Trejo, who first contacted me in 2012 to ask for assistance in researching the Power shootout story. Although several academic colleagues relayed to me their experiences working with filmmakers who asked them to provide historical analysis for a project and then promptly ignored it, that was never the case during the filming of *Power's War*. Cameron was dedicated to getting to the elusive truth and supported me as I scoured archives in Arizona, Texas, and New Mexico, as well as the federal archives scattered around the country. Long after filming was completed, and as I continued my own research for this book, Cameron generously shared his opinions as well as his contacts with family members, photographs, and interview transcripts for this project. More important, his filmmaker's eye allowed me to understand how this tale is defined by its physical geography.

Before we completed the filming of *Power's War*, Cameron insisted that I accompany his film crew in 2014 on its last expedition into Rattlesnake Canyon. Although I was reluctant to make the difficult, three-day journey on horseback, I am grateful he nudged me, because it allowed me to understand the improbable setting where this story unfolded. The Galiuro Wilderness remains a place far removed from civilization, so Cameron arranged to have three incredible wranglers lead the expedition: Scott Platt (who happens to be a descendant of Dr. William Platt of this story), Preston Alder, and Denver Finch. I cannot thank them enough for risking their own lives and limbs to protect the crew, the equipment, and especially me from rampaging mules, hungry bears, treacherous trails, and the unpredictable elements of the Galiuro Mountains. They provided great grub and campfire stories and memories I will cherish for a lifetime. Steve Porter, a McBride descendant, also accompanied us and documented the journey in photographs that he has generously shared for publication here.

As someone who in the past has focused on women's and political history, I waded into some unfamiliar territory with this project. I benefited tremendously from the insights provided by historians and writers familiar with the story, including Tom Cobb, Marshall Trimble, Cathy Ellis, Barbara Wolfe, and Hal Herbert. Paul Hietter, Mark Weitz, and Eduardo Pagán helped me understand the criminal justice system during this period, and Mark, Eduardo, and Cathy Ellis also provided valuable comments and corrections on an early draft. The late Jeff Robenalt made me aware of how Texas history shaped the Power family, James McBride and John Lacy shared their knowledge of Arizona mining, and Dave Berman and Phil VanderMeer helped me hone my understanding of the political backdrop for the shootout. Many thanks as well to editor Chuck Rankin for his enthusiastic support of the project.

Descendants of the lawmen and the Powers also made substantial contributions, sharing valuable stories, photographs, and documents. On the Power side, Sarah McStotts Oborne, who had no idea her distant relatives were so notorious, helped me trace early generations of the Power family. Morgan family members Patricia Morgan Fuson, Joanne Collins, and Howard Morgan shared their memories, as did Haby descendant Pamela Pollock, whom I happened to meet during a trip to the Greenlee County courthouse, where she works as the clerk of the superior court, the same court where the Power-Sisson trial took place. Wayne Lackner told stories from the time when the Power brothers lived with his family after their release from prison. Wootan and Kempton family descendants Millie Wootan Barnes, Bill Lundquist, and Martin Kempton spent hours providing background information on their relatives, as well as their honest opinions of what they thought happened at the cabin. Robin Willett talked to me about her grandfather Frank Haynes, and Connie Huber and other members of the McBride family have made public many documents belonging to Frank McBride, an invaluable collection that helped me to understand what motivated the sheriff of Graham County. I have no doubt that the descendants of the shootout's participants will disagree with some of my interpretations, but I am indebted to them for their willingness to generously share many of the painful aspects of this story that have haunted their families for generations.

Many thanks to Maxine Bean, who allowed me access to the material she retains from the late Graham County historian William Ryder Ridgway, and to Colleen Cavanaugh DeRose, who made available the investigative work of her late father, Wade Cavanaugh. Don Dedera spent hours talking with me about his role in freeing the Power brothers and shared his personal collection of letters, photographs, and articles. It was clear from our discussions, held sixty years after his first meeting with the Power boys, that those memories still take an emotional toll on Don, and I appreciate that he was so patient with my questions. His memories allowed me to reconstruct what happened to the men after they were incarcerated, a story no less interesting than the shootout itself.

I have long maintained that archivists are the best people, and this project confirmed that opinion. Since this was a transcontinental research project, many individuals whose names I do not even know helped obtain interlibrary loans or steered me in the right direction. Jennifer Albin at NARA Riverside, California, was especially helpful in locating the FBI files pertaining to the Power brothers, and archivists at NARA College Park, Maryland, helped me navigate the labyrinth of their collections. Scott Crago and other archivists at the New Mexico State Records Center and Archives helped me locate materials so I could piece together the Power family's time in New Mexico. In Safford, Arizona, Graham County recorder Wendy John personally hauled enormous ledger books from the basement of her office and explained the county records system, always while wearing a smile on her face. Kudos to the folks at the Grant County clerk's office in Silver City who house and protect an amazingly complete collection of New Mexico public records, which kept me busy for days. Chris Reid of the Pinal County Historical Museum kindly tracked down photos of the Power brothers.

Arizona state archivist Melanie Sturgeon and her incredible staff bent over backward to help me track down every item they hold related to the Power story. Over the years, Melanie has taught me more about archival research than I ever learned in graduate school—she is a treasure. Each of her archivists is a historical supersleuth in his or her own right, but several went above and beyond and helped me brainstorm ideas as well. Wendi Goen assisted me with identifying photographs and encouraged me to "keep pulling the thread" to unravel this story, until the folklore fell by the wayside. Libby Coyner's enthusiasm was infectious, and Laura Palma-Blandford became a Power shootout aficionado, sending me emails whenever she found something that might be of interest.

My husband, Tom, convinced me to take on the Power story when I initially had reservations, read many versions of chapters, listened patiently as I went down conspiracy rabbit holes, offered constructive comments as well as unlimited support, and even helped act out the shootout on dark winter mornings on our back patio. Thanks to our adult children, Shannon and Ryan, my cheerleaders who always freely offer their unfiltered critiques. I would be remiss if I did not thank two individuals who influenced me early in life and are no longer with me: my maternal grandmother, Elsa Warias, who was entranced with the Old West and was reading Karl May Western novels before I was born, and my father, Joseph Donlan, who raised me on a steady diet of Spaghetti Westerns. Both would have loved this story.

ARIZONA'S
DEADLIEST
GUNFIGHT

1

ORIGINS

A gun, a bottle of whiskey, and a pack of cards

Members of the Power family were always hill people. Early generations lived in small and scattered settlements on the rocky, thin soil of the hill country of Kentucky, Arkansas, or Texas, producing barely enough corn to feed themselves and their livestock. The impoverished conditions they lived in and their lack of education inspired outsiders to deride them and their neighbors as "crackers" and "clay eaters" in the nineteenth century, and "hillbillies," "white trash," "rabble," and "low-class" in the twentieth century.[1]

Early generations of Powers were typical of nineteenth-century Americans who engaged in multiple migrations westward across the country, always looking to improve their circumstances. From the time of the American Revolution until just prior to the Civil War, the nation's population doubled every twenty years. There was constant demand for new land, so settlers pushed westward, encroaching on territory held by American Indians and the government of Mexico. In 1790 fewer than one thousand Americans lived west of the Appalachians, but by 1840, more than 7 million, or 40 percent of the nation's population, lived in the West. Members of four generations of the Power family would settle in at least ten different states and territories, often able to scrape together enough cash to buy a small plot of land, but occasionally, when times were tough, resorting to squatting on land they did not own.[2]

The original patriarch of the Power family in America was born in Germany in 1770 and arrived in Pennsylvania as a young man, where he lived for a time before migrating to the newly opened backcountry of Kentucky around the turn of century. Samuel Power was the name of this Pennsylvania "Dutchman," and he was the great-grandfather of Thomas Jefferson "Jeff" Power, who would meet his end during the shootout that took place in the doorway of his mining cabin in Arizona in 1918. Samuel Power and his wife, a native of Virginia whose name is unknown, lived in Kentucky among people from Scotland, Ireland, and northern England—primarily Protestants known as Scotch-Irish—as well as families who had followed the trail forged by pioneer Daniel Boone through the Cumberland Gap from Virginia, Maryland, and the Carolinas.[3]

Samuel Power's son was born somewhere in rural Kentucky in 1809, and this first Power male born in the New World was the first of four successive generations of men named Thomas Jefferson Power. Thomas Jefferson was completing his second term as president of the United States in 1809, and no doubt Samuel and his Virginian wife were eager to honor the president by naming a son after him. Over time the name Thomas Jefferson acquired significant meaning among Americans as a symbol of the virtue of the independent yeoman farmer. President Jefferson set great store by the ability of rural farmers and tradesmen to exercise good judgment in governing, because they held the "earthbound virtue of a simple and uncorrupted people." Passing down the name Thomas Jefferson may have been simply a custom in the family—Samuel and John were names given to male offspring in the family as well—but later events suggest the name Thomas Jefferson may have had special meaning for multiple generations of fiercely independent Power males.[4]

Farmers, artisans, and indentured servants inhabited the region of Kentucky where the first generation of Powers lived. Typically, family members all lived together in a crude, single-room cabin hewn of oak, measuring about fourteen by sixteen feet. Children, hogs, and hounds were abundant, and privies, schoolhouses, and churches were rare. Self-reliance was essential to survival on this frontier, while genteel manners and an education were considered superfluous. Book learning was not a high priority in a subsistence economy, so school attendance among children was intermittent or even nonexistent. Poverty was so universal among these hill folk that it was barely noticed unless they ventured down their mountains into the river bottoms, where they might catch a glimpse of the cotton or tobacco plantations whose harvests benefited from the more fertile alluvial soil and the labor of slaves.[5]

The first Thomas Jefferson Power probably had no formal education, but there is evidence he could read and write, and he was a trained blacksmith, a skill that, when combined with farming, allowed him to provide well for his family.

Sometime in the late 1820s he married a fellow Kentuckian, Mary Lindsay, and their first child, Samuel, was born in 1830 while they were living in Anderson County, located between Lexington and Louisville in what is considered the outer Bluegrass region of Kentucky.[6] The early inhabitants grew corn, wheat, and tobacco, and of necessity, they were hardy folk. They rarely had the means to buy or make coats or shoes, so they often did without them, even in the snow. Child labor was necessary to complete all the tasks at hand. Young boys spent much of their day hunting, fishing, and helping their fathers in the fields, while girls were needed to assist their mothers with the overwhelming domestic chores: cooking, sewing, washing, making candles and soap, and slaughtering animals, as well as caring for the sick and augmenting male labor during the planting and harvest seasons.[7]

Although life was primitive for the early generations of Powers, amusements were abundant. Kentuckians were, and continue to be, "addicted to storytelling, many being expert raconteurs," and subsequent generations of Power men all proved adept at telling tall tales. Liquor too played an important role in their culture. In 1813 the first commercial distillery in Kentucky, located in Anderson County, where the Powers lived, began producing "Old Joe" whiskey, the oldest brand in the state. The people of Kentucky loved their whiskey, as well as horses, games of chance, and their fiddles. As Andrew Jackson noted, "I have never seen a Kentuckian without a gun, a bottle of whiskey, and a pack of cards in my life.'"[8]

As the Power family grew, it moved often. First, in the late 1830s, the Powers moved across the Ohio River to Salem, Indiana, where Thomas's blacksmith skills were well suited for the mills, and where two more sons, Thomas Jefferson Jr. and John May, were born. After six or seven years they moved on to recently annexed Texas, where the first Power daughter, named Mary for her mother, was born in 1846 while the family was crossing the Red River. It is unclear whether the Power family spent time living on the Texas frontier, much of which was still controlled by Comanche Indians. They may have believed this land remained too raw and dangerous for a young family, or they might have heard of new opportunities in Arkansas. Sometime in 1848, the family became among the first settlers in the small town of Witcherville, located close to the western border with what was then called Indian Territory, now known as Oklahoma. Thomas paid cash for forty-one acres in Crawford County and served as county coroner, an indication that he was a trusted member of his community and sufficiently literate to navigate the paperwork required for the position. Two additional daughters were born after the family's arrival in western Arkansas.[9]

Thomas Power's new land was in the Ouachita Mountains, where the soil was rocky. Unlike the Ozark Mountain region of Arkansas, with its abundance of oak and hickory providing rich organic material, the Ouachitas are ridged with pine forest, making the land far less fertile for farming. Residents lived in log cabins with stone chimneys and split-shingle roofs and tended their swine and cleared the land to grow corn, a continuation of the hog-and-hominy existence they brought with them from Kentucky, Tennessee, and other parts of the South. Although it is impossible to know with certainty the Powers' politics or religion, some assumptions can be made based on where and when they lived. As a poor, rural, white southerner, the first Thomas Jefferson Power was probably a Democrat, the party more popular among the small farmers in western Arkansas. He came of age during the presidency of Andrew Jackson, whose party supported western expansion and gave voting rights to almost all white male adult citizens. A central tenet of Jacksonian Democracy was "that individual liberty was constantly threatened by excessive power." The Whig Party rose in opposition to Jacksonian Democrats, but in the South, Whigs were almost always members of the upper class, not marginal farmers or skilled laborers like Thomas Power.[10]

Evangelical religions touched the lives of many residents of Kentucky, southern Indiana, and Arkansas in the early 1800s. Methodist and Baptist ministers held camp meetings that lasted for days and attracted hundreds of worshippers. When the Power family arrived in Witcherville, there were a Baptist church and a Methodist-Episcopalian church in town, but public and private records are silent as to which denomination the Powers belonged. Family folklore reveals that later generations of Power women attended church regularly, while Power men were usually absent from services on the Sabbath, a common pattern found within rural southern families.[11]

Although western Arkansas was a remote frontier when the Powers first arrived, that changed quickly in September 1848, when news of gold discovered in California reached the Arkansas Valley and Fort Smith, the county seat and a military outpost that was well positioned to benefit from the Gold Rush. The Arkansas River remained the major transportation artery in the region, and Fort Smith, the last navigable town on the western Arkansas frontier, lay on its banks. Before long, steamboats arrived filled with would-be Argonauts seeking to organize overland wagon trains to California. The town quickly drew an estimated three thousand prospectors, mostly single men from the South, and the streets were "crowded with California wagons and teams." What had been a backwater community was quickly transformed: a county court system was implemented in 1851, telegraph lines were laid in 1856, and the Butterfield Overland Stage line arrived in 1858, making the town an important stop on the mail line that ran between St. Louis and San Francisco. Thomas Power's blacksmith business thrived as he forged shoes for oxen, mules, and horses and repaired wagon irons for the caravans as they prepared for the journey to California. From his windfall he bought additional farmland worth $150, making him not exactly a wealthy man, but a man of some worth compared to his neighbors, most of whom owned no property at all.[12]

The family spent more than ten years living in Arkansas, watching numerous wagon trains head west. The gold seekers leaving Fort Smith in the early days were primarily young men who often sent back word from California of the difficult conditions in the mining camps, where a lack of sanitation coupled with inadequate food supplies fostered disease. Inflationary prices gobbled up any profits made by day laborers—a gallon of whiskey cost thirty-five cents in Arkansas, while a glass of it cost twenty-five cents in the Golden State. Mining towns were meccas for gamblers, prostitutes, and alcoholics. Mary Power undoubtedly had little interest in bringing her young children into such an unhealthy setting, and so they remained in Arkansas, but by the late 1850s the composition of westward-bound wagon trains in Fort Smith changed.[13] More families were drawn now to farming and grazing land in California or Texas, while others left the South because they were concerned the country might be advancing toward war over slavery. Sometime in the spring of 1860 Thomas and Mary Power, along with their five youngest children, who were between the ages of nine and twenty, embarked on the longest journey of their lives, traveling from Arkansas to California. Sam, their firstborn son, was almost thirty and married and chose not to make the trip west.[14]

The dangers of the trip to California were many. Disease and accidents took the largest tolls, but fear of attacks by outlaws or Indians were also on the minds of travelers. It is not clear which route the Powers took. Most overland expeditions took the northern route out of Arkansas through Utah Territory, while others opted for the southern route through the territories of New Mexico and Arizona, along what is known as the Gila Trail. The southern route was less popular because there were long stretches without water, but the northern route held its own dangers.

In 1857, three years prior to the Power trek, 120 members of the Baker-Fancher wagon train left Fort Smith, headed toward Visalia, California, and were attacked by Mormon settlers and Paiute Indians outside Cedar City in southern Utah, in a valley named Mountain Meadows. It is unclear what precipitated the attack. Some suggest it happened in retaliation for the government crackdown on the Saints, while others believe it was simply a theft of much-needed supplies. Members of the Church of Jesus Christ of Latter-day Saints, led by Brigham Young, had engaged in practices that provoked hostility among non-Mormons, including polygamy, while openly defying federal law. President James Buchanan sent in troops after his appointed officials died mysteriously or returned from the territory reporting that the Mormons were in rebellion. Although the Baker-Fancher party fought off their attackers for five days, they were finally forced to surrender and were then executed. Only seventeen children under the age of seven were spared, and those orphans were returned to Arkansas in the late summer of 1859 to much fanfare. The Power family would have been aware of the dangers on the trail and the Mountain Meadows Massacre before they left Fort Smith for Visalia, and in fact, many years later, Thomas Power's descendants would invoke the massacre after they had their own run-in with Mormons in Arizona.[15]

Despite the dangers of the western journey, the Power family arrived safely in California in the fall of 1860, and Thomas paid cash for 160 acres of farmland just north of Visalia, in Tulare County in the San Joaquin Valley. Visalia was pioneered in 1852 and named by migrants after the town of Visalia in Kentucky, but it was clearly a quite different place. The San Joaquin Valley consists of flat, fertile farmland located on the watershed of creeks and rivers created from the snowmelt of the Sierra Nevada. Here farming was done for profit, not subsistence. Upon his arrival, Power was a man of modest means. His real estate holdings were valued at $640 in 1860, making him one of the poorer, though not the poorest, landholders among his neighbors, but he had managed to save cash from blacksmithing and used it to purchase additional property. During the Civil War his fortunes rose because California was far removed from the battlefields that disrupted commerce in the East, and local farmers like Power profited by providing food for the Union Army. Sometime before 1870 Thomas Power moved his family north to Sonoma County, where he purchased fifty-four acres of farmland on rolling terrain in the community of Analy, just outside Santa Rosa. Before long he was growing three hundred bushels of wheat and hay each year in the sandy loam. He and Mary continued to raise hogs, but now also could afford two horses, a milk cow, and a honey-producing apiary, and in 1870 their operation produced $1,500 in income and their land was worth $2,500, four times what their holdings had been worth a decade earlier. In California, the four youngest Power children all attended school until they were eighteen, a luxury the two oldest sons had not enjoyed growing up in the South. The youngest son, John, soon accumulated enough wealth as a farmer working with his father to allow him to speculate in real estate holdings all over the West.[16]

Although Thomas and Mary and their youngest four children living in California were sheltered from the Civil War, the two older Power boys were thrust into it. The oldest, Sam, remained behind in Arkansas, where inhabitants voted to secede from the Union. The second son, Thomas Jefferson Jr., who had traveled with his parents to the West, volunteered for the First California Cavalry Company and fought for the North. Popularly known as the California Volunteers, the First Regiment under General Edward Canby had driven the Confederate Army out of the New Mexico Territory and into Texas prior to Thomas Jr.'s enlistment in February 1863 at Stockton, California. Private Power was twenty-three years old when he signed up for a three-year term for the Union cause and was assigned to K Company. He spent most of the first year of service in Los Angeles at Drum Barracks, where local authorities believed a Union presence was needed to suppress the Confederate sympathizers among the local population. His outfit left for the New Mexico Territory in the spring of 1864, traveling through Tucson and then on to Fort Union, located in the far northeast corner of the territory.[17]

During the Civil War, Indians controlled much of the southwestern United States, so the greater danger faced by Private Power and his fellow soldiers was not from the Confederate Army, but from the Apache, Kiowa, Comanche, and other tribes which threatened military supply lines. In late November 1864, Brigadier General James Carleton, who had taken command of the First California Cavalry from Canby, decided to take punitive action against the Kiowas and Comanches in the Texas Panhandle, near William Bent's abandoned trading post. Colonel Christopher "Kit" Carson of the First New Mexico Cavalry, an esteemed frontiersman, was placed in charge, and Private Power's Company K saw action in what would become known as the First Battle of Adobe Walls. During this engagement, Carson's troops were greatly outnumbered, but he effectively used howitzers and back fires to save his men from a disastrous outcome that many believed could have rivaled Custer's defeat at Little Bighorn in 1876.[18]

After Adobe Walls, Carson was placed in charge of removing the Navajos from their ancestral home in Canyon de Chelly in the New Mexico Territory, and once again Private Power and Company K came under his command. Soldiers forced the Diné, as the Navajos called themselves, from their ancestral homes, slaughtered their sheep, contaminated their wells, and destroyed their fields, orchards, and food stores. Facing starvation, they turned themselves over to the military, and eventually 8,500 Navajos were taken at gunpoint from Fort Bascom to their new reservation at Bosque Redondo, a journey on foot of 250 miles that is now referred to as the Long Walk of the Navajos. Private Power's Company K escorted approximately 250 Navajo prisoners there in the winter of 1864. Poorly provisioned given the harsh weather, many Navajos, especially the youngest, the oldest, and pregnant women, lost their lives to disease and starvation along the way. Some who were too weak to keep up were shot down by soldiers.[19]

By the time Private Power returned with his unit to Fort Union in early 1865, he had spent days on end with little or no sleep, often with nothing but hardtack and salt pork to eat. At Adobe Walls and on the Long Walk he had witnessed tremendous loss of life, and while most of his unit mustered out in February 1865, Power still had a year left on his enlistment. When the war ended in May 1865, Power would have been eligible to muster out as well under the terms of his enlistment, but instead he found himself under confinement for killing a fellow trooper with a pistol near Fort Larned, Kansas. The homicide was deemed neither justifiable nor excusable by his superiors, and he was transported to Fort Lyon in Colorado for court-martial, but he somehow managed to escape and deserted the Union Army.[20]

Power could not return to California and his family without repercussions, so he headed to his former home of Arkansas instead. There he married and, after the war ended, moved with his wife to Texas, settling just outside Dallas in the early 1870s. In the late 1880s he tried to claim a military pension, but when officials reviewed his record, they refused his request because he had not served out the terms of his enlistment. Power hired an attorney and swore out depositions stating that he had never deserted and had killed no one, offering up the unlikely excuse that someone had knocked him senseless during a robbery and he became separated from his unit when he left for medical assistance. Although the adjutant general did not have sufficient evidence or the witnesses needed to take up the murder charge against Power at that late date, he insisted the private had deserted and rejected his pension claim. We do not know what circumstances caused Power to kill another man and desert the Union Army, but this incident, along with his unsuccessful two-year legal battle to collect a pension he felt was due to him, created bitter feelings toward the military, feelings that he surely shared with other family members, including his own sons, his older brother Sam, and Sam's son Jeff Power.[21]

2

TEXAS HILL COUNTRY

Thieves, outlaws, cut-throats, and desperadoes

To understand how Jeff Power came to die in a gun battle during World War I, it is necessary to examine the world he was born into during the Civil War in the Hill Country of Texas. It is tempting to suggest that his father, Sam, remained in the South when the rest of his family left for California in 1860, because he favored the Southern cause in the coming war. Indeed, family folklore suggests Sam was a soldier in the Confederate Army, even while his brother, Thomas Jr., fought for the North—a classic story of brother versus brother. However, the military records contain no evidence suggesting Sam fought for the South, and it is evident that Sam and Thomas Jr. remained close after the war and were not bitter enemies. More likely, hearing stories about his brother's travails in the Union Army, coupled with Sam's own experiences witnessing the reign of terror that gripped the Hill Country during the war, negatively influenced Sam's attitude toward government in general and conscription in particular, feelings he passed on to his son Jeff.

Sam Power likely remained in Arkansas for personal reasons rather than political beliefs. He was married and his wife, Jane, might have been pregnant. They had married sometime in the mid-1850s, yet there is no record of a birth prior to 1863 when their only child, Thomas Jefferson "Jeff" Power, was born, so Jane likely had trouble carrying previous pregnancies to full term, and they may have chosen not to risk the long, dangerous trip to California. We know almost nothing about Jane's early life except that she was born Martha Jane in Indiana in the early 1840s and her maiden name was probably Smith. Decades later her grandsons told friends they believed her father was Irish and her mother was Cherokee, that Jane was orphaned as a child and first met Sam when the Power family lived in Salem, Indiana, and she married him when she was only thirteen. It is impossible to verify these bits of family history, but they make an intriguing story that helps explain why many years later Jane's grandsons Tom and John Power were branded as "half-breeds" by the press after the shootout at their father's cabin in the Galiuro Mountains of Arizona.[1]

In 1860 Sam and Jane Power were living in a small house in the town of Center, Arkansas, where Sam worked as a blacksmith. Sometime in the next year or two, as war broke out and the citizens of Arkansas voted to leave the Union, the young couple fled west to Gillespie County in the Hill Country of Texas, a dangerous frontier and one of the most pro-Union locations in the Confederate South. Jane and Sam vanished from the public records between 1861 and 1876—not surprising given the state of affairs in the Hill Country at the time. Between the politics of the Civil War and Reconstruction, Indian attacks, and brutal guerrilla warfare among cattle rustlers, local officials faced a number of problems far more important than proper record keeping. The only reason we know the Powers even lived there is because their son Jeff, many years later, told friends and the census enumerator that he was born in February 1863 outside Fredericksburg, in the Hill Country of Texas.[2]

The Texas Hill Country was then and remains today a beautiful land that beckoned settlers. Frederick Law Olmsted, who toured the region about the time Sam and Jane Power moved there, described it as "a rolling sheet of the finest grass, sprinkled thick with bright, many-hued flowers, with here and there a live-oak and an occasional patch of mesquite trees."[3] But beyond the lush landscape lurked many obstacles for would-be farmers, including insufficient rainfall for agriculture, a Native population that refused to relinquish its hold on the land, and local government that was unable to reliably administer the law. More important for the Power family, it was a place where sectional strife pitted neighbor against neighbor.

Among the first Anglos to arrive in the Hill Country were German immigrants, part of a poorly organized immigration company called the Adelsverein, who settled there in the mid-1840s. German aristocrats bought three million acres in the Hill Country sight unseen and relocated poor farmers and tradesmen to the virgin soil. Most who journeyed to Texas were Freethinkers, intellectuals who fought against social injustice and religious tyranny and who fled the Old World when the liberal political revolts of 1848 failed. The early years were difficult and many died from disease, while others were discouraged over questionable title to the land and went elsewhere. Their arrival during the Mexican-American War made their difficult circumstances worse, as soldiers stripped them of desperately needed supplies and equipment.[4]

Despite the numerous hurdles, those early German settlers who stayed and survived built a strong community in the Hill Country. Most of the immigrants lived in Fredericksburg, the Gillespie County seat, located about seventy miles west of Austin, the state capital, or in New Braunfels, which became the Comal County seat. Travelers noted that the region around Fredericksburg had the look of New England farmland, "thrifty and well cared for." The Germans built good schools, Lutheran and Catholic churches, meeting halls, and beer halls. They also clung stubbornly to their customs and language, publishing newspapers in German. Many of the original immigrants never learned to speak English.[5]

Shortly after the arrival of the Germans, many non-slave-owning southerners began to arrive in the Hill Country, settling in rural areas outside Fredericksburg and New Braunfels where the land was inexpensive. But of course these settlers paid the price in other ways. Many were poor white farmers fleeing debt or the law in Appalachia or the Ozark-Ouachita region of Missouri and Arkansas. In the Hill Country they found large tracts of available grassland, plenty of elm and cedar to build their cabins, and abundant fish and game for the taking, but problems also plagued the region.[6] The Germans distanced themselves physically, culturally, and politically from southern settlers, and chose to live in fortified towns to protect themselves from the sporadic attacks by the Comanches, while southerners resided on scattered ranches in "terrible isolation" and constant fear of attack. The Germans looked down upon their southern neighbors, who were slow to build schools and churches and who lived in tiny, filthy cabins where even rudimentary outhouses were a rarity. Outsiders from the north commented on the "'squalid poverty'" and the "'abundance of grog shops'" in those outlying southern settlements.[7]

During the Civil War, politics separated the inhabitants of the region as well. Many Hill Country Germans had left their homeland to avoid mandatory military service and detested the institution of slavery and military conscription. Yet in 1861 they found themselves once again in the middle of those debates on the Texas frontier. Gillespie County residents, dominated by Freethinking Germans, voted overwhelmingly (96 percent) to reject secession from the Union, as did residents of neighboring Mason and Burnet counties. Their pro-Union sentiment was an aberration in Texas, where most of the population dwelled in the state's eastern part and slave-owning cotton planters held sway on the issue of secession.[8]

As historian Claude Elliott notes, the mere fact that Texans voted to secede from the Union in 1861 did not mean they were united concerning the war. He estimates as few as one-third of the state's population sided with the Union, another one-third sided with the Confederate States of America (CSA), and the final third wanted no part of the argument. Even Texas governor Sam Houston fought against secession at the onset and gave only lip service to the CSA once the secession vote was cast. Military conscription was even less popular. Many Southerners strongly believed that military service should be voluntary, and some even questioned whether the draft was constitutional. They viewed it as "an unwarranted extension of the power of the central government, and an action that interfered with the traditional rights of the states to conduct their own affairs." The draft policies of both the North and the South during the Civil War left many loopholes for wealthy men to escape military service, leaving the bulk of the fighting to the poorest citizens. The disparities caused draft riots in the North and widespread disregard for conscription in parts of the South, where "rich man's war, poor man's fight" became a slogan that rallied many draft resisters.[9]

Some men of draft age who opposed secession in the Hill Country moved to California when Texas left the Union in February 1861. Among those who remained behind in Gillespie County were an estimated five hundred men who formed a secret local chapter of the Union Loyalty League. Most members were Germans, but about one-third were native-born Anglos from Southern states. The local loyalty league members initially used nonviolent means—speeches and newspaper articles—to pursue their goal of reuniting Texas with the North, so they provoked little notice. That changed when Jefferson Davis, president of the Confederate States of America, along with the Confederate congress, passed laws requiring residents to profess loyalty to the new government and all white males between eighteen and thirty-five to register for three years of military service. Rebellion in the Hill Country followed when Union loyalists refused to enlist and began to speak out against the draft, even when threatened with death for noncompliance.[10]

By the spring of 1862 many Germans began hiding out in the countryside to avoid conscription. Few Southerners in the area owned slaves, so many had no desire to die in battle for that cause and joined their German neighbors in refusing to serve. In fact, Gillespie County sent very few recruits to battle, since most men opted to "sit out" the war either hiding in the hills or fleeing to Mexico. To the CSA, the residents of Gillespie County were deemed the most determined and belligerent Union loyalists. The Confederate military imposed martial law in Texas as a means to curb disloyalty, and the CSA sent Captain James Duff's

Partisan Ranger Company to the Hill Country to suppress the rebellion. Duff gave residents six days to report to him and take an oath of allegiance to the Confederacy, but few locals showed up and family and neighbors refused to turn one another in. In August 1862, thirty-two German loyalist immigrants attempting to flee to Mexico were killed in a battle with Confederate militiamen, and nine additional men who had been wounded were captured and summarily executed in the aftermath of what historians now call the Battle of the Nueces. After the slaughter, Duff ordered as many as fifty men hanged, and an unknown number of others were later killed for failure to support the war effort. As historian David Johnson describes it, the Hill Country became an area of "savage guerrilla action."[11]

The public record is silent about the actions of Sam Power during the Civil War. He did not serve in the Confederate Army, and his name cannot be found on any of the surviving lists of Union loyalty leagues, though those lists are incomplete. As chapter one relates, he was born in a slaveholding state, Kentucky, which did not secede from the Union, but as a young man he lived in Arkansas, which voted to join the CSA. Neither Sam nor his father or grandfather ever owned slaves, though that did not mean the Power men were necessarily abolitionists. Sam married a woman from the northern state of Indiana, where he had lived as a child, and the couple left Arkansas when the war began and settled in an outpost of Union loyalists located deep in rebel country. Sam's youngest brother, John, was a Republican, the party of Abraham Lincoln and the Union. His other brother, Thomas Jefferson Power Jr., fought for the North. Like many Americans during the Civil War, Sam Power found himself with conflicting allegiances.[12]

It is likely that Sam prioritized family concerns over political debates during the war. Jane Power was pregnant with her son Jeff in 1862 when Duff began his reign of terror in Gillespie County, and considering that they had no family in the area, who would harvest the corn or care for Jane when it was time for the baby to arrive if Sam went off to battle? Perhaps Sam felt it was his duty to take care of his own family first, and like many of his neighbors, he volunteered for the various home guard units formed to protect residents from attack by unionists, rebels, or the Comanches, although his name does not appear on any surviving lists of those volunteers, either. More likely, he hid from Confederate forces.

Of course, it was dangerous to avoid military enlistment. In 1864 a squad of men from William Quantrill's command, notorious in history for the atrocities they committed in Kansas during the war, arrived in Gillespie County and proceeded to the northeastern part of the county, where the Powers lived. They combined forces with recently released members of McCord's Frontier Regiment and created a loose-knit organization of men known as the *hangerbande,* the German term for a band of hangmen or vigilantes. This mob burned buildings and chased down the estimated fifteen hundred draft evaders and deserters living in the area, bringing those they caught to swift justice without the benefit of trial and leaving unknown numbers of men hanging from trees. If Sam was among them, he was fortunate to have escaped such a fate.[13]

Undoubtedly, as Sam's son Jeff grew up in Texas, he heard stories of the horrors of the Civil War told by his parents and his uncle Private Thomas J. Power Jr., who had served on the southwestern frontier. Jeff too would remain caught in the crosshairs of that conflict for the rest of his life. By birth he was a southerner, and as an adult he would live in Texas and communities in the Southwest dominated by former Confederates, yet he was always an outsider because his father and uncles had not supported the Confederate cause. To protect them, Jeff Power's own children grew up hearing false stories that their grandfather Sam had fought for the Confederacy, using his blacksmith skills to construct canon and rifles, and that he stood on a tree stump and declared: "I am a 'Sesesh' and I will fight 'em till I die!" Sam Power, of course, was not a secessionist, but if he, his brother Thomas, or their families in Texas had said otherwise, they would have had endless arguments with their southern neighbors and faced alienation from society, if not outright attack. More important, as Jeff and his sons and nephews reached adulthood, their conflicting allegiances meant they disconnected from partisan politics, which were so woven into southern culture.[14] Like many of their brethren, they viewed the conscription policies of the Civil War as "flawed and fraudulent." The Power brothers would pass on their disgust of mandatory military service to their own sons. Although they lived in different states—Texas, New Mexico, and Arizona—all draft-age male descendants of Sam and Thomas J. Power Jr. failed to comply with the Selective Service Act during World War I.[15]

The Civil War left a lasting impression on the Hill Country of Texas, as well. The war's conclusion did not bring peace to the region; rather, violence continued until the late 1870s, as federal and military officials focused manpower on the problems faced by freed slaves in East Texas, ignoring Hill Country settler pleas for assistance. Republicans elected in the state legislature did little to fortify the western frontier, and even after federal troops returned to local garrisons, they failed to curb outbreaks of Comanche raiding, leading some local residents to question the commitment of both the state and federal government to adequately

protect white settlers. But the Comanches were less of a threat to the local popu-
lace after the war than were displaced southern whites who moved into the Hill
Country to take advantage of the vacuum in local law enforcement.[16]

After the Civil War, as the American appetite for beef increased, the cattle
industry grew exponentially, drawing many stockmen to the lush grasslands of
central Texas to graze their herds. Cattle represented cash to southerners, and
without adequate personnel to police the burgeoning industry, "cow-boys,"
as they were called then, were hired to protect herds. Among these footloose
young men were a number of "thieves, outlaws, cut-throats and desperadoes"
who appeared on the western edge of the Hill Country. With local government
in disarray, law enforcement was unable to contain the violence, and citizens
often were forced to organize to protect their property. As historian Peter R.
Rose has noted, "Whatever the law was west of the Pecos, little of it existed in the
Hill Country and beyond. Rustlers and road agents not only abounded; in some
counties they organized and ruled." Numerous deadly feuds broke out between
families competing for control, so vigilante justice, rather than the rule of law,
prevailed. Historians have long noted that under such conditions, regardless of
the time or place, people living on dangerous frontiers "were alone and resigned to
it," turning them into "a fiercely independent people." The lawlessness in the Hill
Country finally reached such proportions that the Texas legislature was forced to
act, and the Frontier Battalion was created under the newly reconstituted Texas
Rangers to combat the outlaws and the Indians harassing settlers.[17]

With the return of the rule of law in the Hill Country, local government
finally started to function in a more orderly fashion. In 1876, Sam and Jane Power
purchased 640 acres of land about twenty miles northeast of Fredericksburg. They
probably had squatted on the land for some time prior to that, since the previous
owner had fled Texas for California before the war and abandoned the property,
but in the chaos of the war and its aftermath, business transactions were difficult
to conduct. The parcel they bought was located along the waters of Sandy Creek,
in the county's northeast corner, which borders Llano County to the north and
Burnet County to the east. Sam did not have the cash to purchase the property,
so he formed a partnership with his youngest brother, John, in California, and
together they paid $640 for this property bisected by Coal Creek. The acreage
contained both flat and rolling terrain that featured stands of live oak, mesquite,
elm, and of course the ubiquitous grasslands of the Hill Country. The area is
known for its springtime displays of wildflowers, especially the bluebells that
blanket the terrain. Coal Creek runs over solid granite in most places and attracts

an abundance of wildlife that provided meat for the table: whitetail deer, turkey, quail, dove, and duck. Sam and Jane planted enough Indian corn to feed their dozen swine and to provide hominy for the dinner table, and in good years a little was left over to sell at market.[18]

The nearest post office was nine miles away in a tiny village that would become known as Willow City, one of the few Gillespie County communities settled by English-speakers. Most local residents were from the South and reportedly disliked their German neighbors, preferring to travel the extra distance to Austin to trade rather than going into Fredericksburg, where inhospitable German proprietors spoke little or no English. Unlike their German neighbors, the southerners of Willow City were slow to establish schools, churches, and other community services. No school was built in the area until 1881, by which time Jeff Power was eighteen, too old to take advantage. His mother, Jane, could neither read nor write, but his father, Sam, was literate and likely taught Jeff the basic skills he needed to navigate life. Likewise, religion was slow to take root in this community, and it was not until 1885 that the first congregation, a Methodist church, was established. His upbringing in a community without a religious core left Jeff bereft of that form of cultural identity. As an adult he demonstrated little interest in religion, and some more pious neighbors later commented they believed him to be an atheist. His more religious mother disagreed with that notion, jokingly telling friends she knew her son was a believer because when he got sick he always called on God. Jeff would also demonstrate an aversion to partisan politics and this, combined with his lack of religiosity, cut him off from two major avenues for social interaction used by American males in the nineteenth century.[19]

Among the Germans, Willow City had a reputation as a place where outlaws congregated, especially cattle rustlers who preyed on the numerous ranchers in the region. Unlike most of his neighbors, however, Jeff's father took no interest in the highly speculative cattle business, and the only livestock owned by Sam and Jane were a milk cow and three horses. With only one son to help on the farm, Sam did not have sufficient family labor to run a cattle ranch, nor did he seem to have the ambition needed for such an enterprise. He was very different from his father and younger brother, John, in California, or even his other brother, Thomas Jr., who had settled just outside Dallas. All three were hardworking and managed to acquire substantial landholdings during their lifetimes, but Sam showed little interest in farming, preferring to hunt and fish to support his family, and passing those passions on to his son Jeff.[20]

Sam's lack of ambition had a profound effect on his family, and the 1880 agricultural census provides insight into the poverty of the Power family's existence. Even among their struggling neighbors, they were the poorest. Their 320 acres of land was worth only six hundred dollars, and they produced corn on eighteen acres that netted only ten dollars in 1879. After more than two decades of struggling to get by in Texas, Sam's personal life began to unravel. Whether his lack of success led him to drink or alcoholism led to his economic failures, the ultimate outcome was the end of his marriage. On September 8, 1886, Jane had him arrested for disturbing the peace. Having had enough of his drinking, she called the local sheriff to remove her husband from their home. He was found guilty and held in custody for two months until his fines were finally paid by a friend, which indicates that he could not muster the five dollars that he owed the court and Jane had no desire to free him from jail.[21]

During the nineteenth century, alcoholism was an enormous problem, especially among the working poor. Wives suffered if their husbands spent more time in saloons than at work and failed to provide for their families. When men returned home in a drunken rage, women and children often felt their wrath. Many women joined temperance clubs, like the Woman's Christian Temperance Union, which formed in the Midwest in the 1870s and encouraged members to obtain abstinence pledges from their husbands, brothers, or sons, which many did. But women living on isolated farms and ranches of Texas at this early date did not yet have the benefit of a well-developed female community for support. Jane Power seemingly took the situation into her own hands, adroitly using the law to remove her troublesome husband from his own home. This pattern would continue the rest of her life, as she became quite adept at launching court actions to protect her own interests and those of her family.[22]

Despite her small size—Jane was just five feet tall and weighed ninety-six pounds—she was, according to her son, grandchildren, neighbors, and friends, a force to be reckoned with. As Jeff grew to adulthood, he became, as doubtless his father and father's father were before him, an accomplished storyteller, and among his favorite tales was of the time his mother walked into a grogshop in Texas where Sam was drinking and chased him out with a horse whip. Sam climbed a tree to escape her wrath, but his wife found an ax to cut it down. No doubt the story was apocryphal, but it was obviously steeped in the truth of his parents' turbulent marriage. Later on, there would be no stories about Jeff or his own sons getting in drunken brawls. The Power men drank spirits, but they also knew that if they got out of line, there would be hell to pay with Jane. When her temper flared, "she would go on a tongue-lashing spree, which the Power men laughingly termed a 'bender,'" and fear of her anger would keep them in line better than any pledge to temperance. If the Hill Country "was a harsh land" that "bred hard men," as some have suggested, it certainly bred hard women like Jane Power as well.[23]

There is no indication of a formal divorce between Sam and Jane, a proceeding that would have required the payment of legal fees, money the couple did not have to spare. But in June of 1888, Sam and Jane decided to go their separate ways. They sold their land in Gillespie County to Sam's younger brothers, John and Thomas Jr. It is unlikely Sam and Jane would have found a buyer outside the family at that time, since Texas was in the midst of the worst drought in anyone's memory. Much of the region is semiarid, the claylike soil is not well suited for intensive agriculture, and the grassland is fragile. During the drought of the 1880s the soil quickly gave out where fields were plowed and livestock grazed, and the lush grasslands disappeared. Some years there was adequate rainfall to replenish it, but when drought persisted, cattle died on the range and corn withered in the fields. Soil conditions deteriorated so much that many folks in the Hill Country moved west to find new land.[24]

While his parents' marriage unraveled and the local economy declined, twenty-four-year-old Jeff Power embarked on his own adult life. On August 11, 1887, he married nineteen-year-old Martha Morgan, who also had grown up in the Hill Country of Texas. Years later, Jeff loved to tell friends the story of his marriage to the pretty girl everyone called Mattie in a ceremony on a dusty road in Kimble County. "'We was goin' to get married anyway, so when we happened to meet that preacher out that way we just got off our horses and got hitched right 'n the middle of the road.'" There was no church ceremony or family present, just the young couple and the preacher, which suited Jeff, a man who had little interest in society. On February 9, 1889, Mattie and Jeff welcomed their first child, Charles Samuel, into the world.[25]

Jeff was now part of his wife's large, vibrant family—the Morgans, who were quite different from the Powers. Mattie's father, Seebird, was originally from Missouri, and in the 1850s he moved his family to Williamson County in the Hill Country of Texas, where he grew pecans and eventually began to acquire cattle. Those were the early days of the legendary cattle drives in Texas, and Sebe, as he was called, and his wife, Amanda Bybee Morgan, raised a large family of budding ranch hands on the Texas and New Mexico frontiers. Like Sam Power, Sebe Morgan managed to avoid military service during the war in

Texas, but other members of the Morgan family had fought on the rebel side and all were staunch Democrats. With local conditions in Texas for cattle ranching deteriorating rapidly, in 1890 Sebe Morgan and his oldest son, Wiley, convinced Jeff and Mattie Power to join them and a larger exodus of people out of the Hill Country into the New Mexico Territory. Jeff and Mattie packed up their infant son, Charley; Jeff's mother, Jane; and their few meager belongings in a wagon and headed west.[26]

In many ways, doors were closing on Sam Power at this time. In 1888 his father, Thomas, and his mother, Mary, who had prospered in California, both died, and Sam's marriage also ended that year. As Jane and Jeff left him for new opportunities in New Mexico, Sam Power bought several small parcels of land in the town of Oxford, just a few miles north of Sandy Creek in Llano County, where he set up a blacksmithing business.[27] The town had once been a local trade center for both the cattle and cotton business, but by the time Sam moved there, Oxford's heyday was in the past. When he died on April 28, 1900, he was alone, without "kith or kin" in the county to dispose of his few possessions, to pay off the debts incurred during his last illness, and to see to his burial. A German immigrant named John H. Englemann, a farmer and a friend of Sam's, temporarily administered his estate over the next four years until Jane and Jeff were finally located and notified of his death. While he left little in the way of monetary wealth to his son, Sam Power bequeathed a legacy of animosity toward war, forged during his time in Texas.[28]

3

NEW MEXICO TERRITORY

We take a man here and ask no questions.

Jeff and Mattie Power and their family arrived in the New Mexico Territory at a time when the Southwest was transitioning from an untamed and raw land inhabited primarily by nomadic Anglo and Hispanic males and American Indians into a place more welcoming to families looking to put down roots. Mattie Morgan Power lived in New Mexico as a young girl, when it was less hospitable to white families. Her older brother Wiley Morgan had struck out on his own when he was in his teens, during the chaotic decades following the Civil War, and worked as a cowboy in the New Mexico and Arizona territories, places even more dangerous than the Hill Country at the time. Wiley Morgan convinced his parents to move the family to southwestern New Mexico in the 1870s, but their stay was brief because it was difficult to make a living raising cattle among outlaws and Apaches in the arid Southwest. Sebe and Amanda Morgan returned to Texas with the younger children, including Mattie, while their oldest remained in the territory, a place where an ambitious young man like Wiley could find advancement.[1]

In the early 1870s, Anglos like Henry Clay Hooker, who established the Sierra Bonita Ranch in the Sulphur Springs Valley near the border between Arizona and New Mexico, introduced large-scale cattle ranching to the region. Apaches remained in control of the land, despite efforts by the United States military to contain them, so there were few Anglo or Mexican settlers in the area. Hooker, as one of the sole providers of beef for the military forts, managed to prosper. Soon smaller ranchers poured in from Texas seeking new rangeland, and young cowboys like Wiley Morgan followed. These young men worked odd jobs in the winter and summer and joined the roundup in spring and fall, but because the majority of them were single, cowboys often engaged in excessive gambling, drinking, and whoring and had run-ins with the law. Henry Hooker's philosophy on hiring cowboys on his ranch reflected the prevailing attitude among stockmen: "We take a man here and ask no questions. We know when he throws his saddle on his horse whether he understands his business or not. He may be a minister backslidin,' or a banker savin' his last lung, or a train robber on his vacation—we don't care. A good many of our most useful men have made their mistakes."[2]

Wiley Morgan thrived in Arizona and New Mexico, accumulating a herd of cattle. In 1887 he returned home to Texas and married schoolteacher Amanda Sue Tomlinson, returning with her to settle in southwestern New Mexico. After the last Apache clans were removed to reservations in the 1880s, and as economic conditions in Texas deteriorated further in 1890, Wiley convinced his parents as well as his sister, Mattie Power, and her new family, to take a chance and journey west once again to southwestern New Mexico.[3] Grant County, where they settled, was an enormous expanse of land bordered by the Arizona Territory to the west and Mexico to the south. When silver was discovered there in 1870, tents quickly popped up and prospectors who had failed to find their fortunes in California or Nevada poured in, hoping to finally strike it rich. Silver City quickly became known as the "treasure vault of New Mexico" for all the ore it produced, and its wealth allowed the investment of millions of dollars in local infrastructure. Churches, schools, and even a college campus were built, and the once isolated mining and cattle towns of Grant County were increasingly connected by railroad and telephone lines. The violence associated with those towns dissipated somewhat by 1890, as territorial officials in both New Mexico and neighboring Arizona sought legislation to curb vice and rustling to protect the corporate investments in the territories and to encourage future immigration of families like the Powers and Morgans. The transformation was incomplete, however, and pockets of criminality remained in outlying areas where an increasing number of ranchers and farmers vied over scarce resources.[4]

Jeff Power joined his in-laws, the Morgans, in Gila, a community located about twenty-eight miles northwest of Silver City, far from its saloons and brothels. The area was, and continues to be, primarily a farming and ranching community of just over 350 people near the banks of the Upper Gila River neighboring the Continental Divide, an imaginary line that runs from north to south where rivers and watersheds flow in opposite directions toward the Atlantic or the Pacific oceans. The Gila River flows westward into Arizona, irrigating farmland along the way. With an average annual rainfall of about sixteen inches and an elevation of forty-five hundred feet, however, this was a drier environment than the Power family was accustomed to in the Hill Country of Texas. Low humidity and high elevations result in dramatic temperature swings from day to evening and from season to season. Temperatures climb past one hundred degrees in summer, and snow is a fixture in winter months on the nearby Piños Altos Range, where the highest peak soars above nine thousand feet. While the grasslands resembled the Hill Country of Texas, the steep mountains and box canyons were a far cry from the rolling hills of their former home.[5]

Jeff's mother, Jane, was the farmer in the Power family. Wherever she lived she made sure she had access to water and fertile, flat land to plant crops to sustain her family during hard times, but in the arid Southwest most irrigated farmland came at a premium and was beyond her financial reach. She soon found a choice parcel of 160 acres in the Upper Gila River Valley with access to a local irrigation cooperative called the Old Fort West Ditch Company. The ditch, or canal, tapped water from Duck Creek that eventually irrigated about one thousand acres of farm and pastureland in the region. Jane could continue doing what she did best, growing corn, planting a vegetable garden, and tending to her chickens and milk cow, on land she purchased for only four hundred dollars. Jeff, like his father, seemed indifferent to farming, so Jane lent him money to buy cattle and start his own ranching operation.[6]

Jane's land, as it turned out, was no bargain. The previous owners had been forced out by the tactics of their powerful neighbor, Tom Lyons, owner of the LCs Ranch, one of the largest cattle operations in southwestern New Mexico. Lyons was just beginning to launch a range war to dislodge all local "nesters," as homesteading farmers were derisively called, and small ranchers. Tom Lyons was born in England and, together with his Scottish partner, Angus Campbell, had found success in mining in Silver City during the boom of the 1870s. The two men sold their claim to a big mining company and invested in cattle, forming the Lyons and Campbell Cattle and Land Company, or the LCs. By the 1890s the cattle business had evolved and the era of the cowboy was closing, as cattle increasingly were brought to market by rail rather than herded hundreds of miles on the hoof. As the industry grew and prospered, cattlemen were often backed by outside investors who took over an industry that "had been a wild adventure" and transformed it into "a settled, stable business." Lyons's operation was financed by men with deep pockets from the East Coast and Europe. They often visited

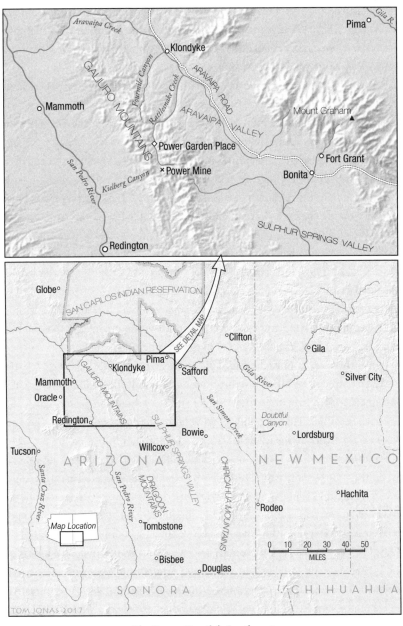

The Power Family's Southwest

25

the "Wild West" to see how their investment was performing, and Lyons was always scrambling to impress them. Perhaps to distract from the fact that there was often more money needed to run his operation than was flowing back into the pockets of investors, Lyons entertained lavishly at his home and organized elaborate hunting parties to convince them the ranch was prospering. These hunts were enormous undertakings, where money was spent freely on equipment, food, and liquor. When lit up at night, the expanse of tents set up for the financiers was so large it had the appearance of a city.[7]

Raising cattle on a frontier with limited water supplies often led to cutthroat tactics, especially when large sums of money were at risk. To succeed, men like Lyons often used intimidation to thwart competitors. The small ranchers in the vicinity viewed Lyons as a violent despot who brought trumped-up charges against them and then used his influence over local law enforcement and courts to gain convictions. During the 1890s the local courts were clogged with lawsuits, injunctions, and criminal charges brought by the cattle baron. Lyons and his employees were also charged with numerous crimes, but as the local newspaper noted, he always had "been lucky in Grant county courts," insinuating that he bribed jurors and local officials.[8] It was impossible to live in Gila without getting embroiled with the contentious Tom Lyons, even for a grandmother like Jane Power.

Just as the Powers moved to Gila, Lyons relocated the LCs Ranch headquarters less than a mile from Jane's property. Lyons had built the Old Fort West Ditch on Duck Creek to irrigate pastureland for the sixty thousand head of cattle that he ran on a million acres of public grazing land, but now local farmers, like Jane Power, were diverting the water for crops instead, siphoning off more than Lyons believed was their fair share. Lyons convinced the court to issue an injunction to cut off the water supply from Duck Creek to the Power property in the spring of 1891. Jeff later told friends that his mother had "pinned up her dress, took both a shovel and a shotgun to the head of their property where she pulled up a head gate and released water onto the Power farm." When Lyons showed up to complain, she said, "'You run a widow woman and her two kids off this place before we come here, but you ain't goin' to run us off.'" Jane took legal action, and after review by the court, the injunction was lifted and she returned to her farming.[9]

Lyons was persistent in his battle to dislodge Jane Power from her land, and soon went on the offensive once again. In the springtime when newborn calves were not yet branded, it was easy to gather up cattle that belonged to someone else, wittingly or unwittingly. The small ranchers in the region often took advantage of the large LCs operation, claiming unbranded calves, called mavericks, for their own. Lyons retaliated by running advertisements in the *Silver City Enterprise* stating he would offer a $250 reward for information leading to the conviction of anyone rustling cattle from the LCs Ranch. Neighboring ranchers fought back with articles in the local newspapers condemning his tactics, suggesting that Lyons's cowboys, not the small operators, were doing most of the rustling, and often brandished guns and threatened small operators believed to be taking his cattle. Rumors were rampant that Lyons paid deputies to arrest and sometimes even to kill folks who got in his way. In April 1893, Jane Power became a victim in Lyons's range war when she was charged with grand larceny. Unfortunately, the files related to the case have vanished, so we do not know all the details, but grand larceny at that time almost always involved theft of livestock. The same day Jane was charged, Lem Childers, the foreman of the LCs Ranch, was also charged with grand larceny—probably not a coincidence. It is likely that Jane and Childers accused each other of rustling, and charges in both cases were dropped when there was insufficient evidence to go forward.[10]

Cattle barons and rustlers were not the only nemeses of the Power family in New Mexico. From 1892 to 1894 drought left many cattle dead. The federal government demonetized silver, dealing a crushing blow to the local mining industry, and nationally the economy plunged into a devastating depression. In the Southwest small cattle operators increased their raids on cattle from their larger neighbors, resulting in numerous arrests, shootings, and charges of bribing local officials. New Mexico became a hotbed of murders in the 1890s, an outgrowth of the power grabs that were occurring during the economic hard times. In 1896 Albert Jennings Fountain, a lawyer and legislator who had prosecuted many cattle rustlers, went missing along with his young son. Left behind at the scene of their disappearance, in the desert outside of Las Cruces, were the politician's buckboard wagon, some papers and personal items, and two pools of blood, but neither his body nor his son's body was ever found, and no one was ever convicted of their murders. Cowboys who probably knew what had happened in these murder cases often refused to divulge information to authorities, fearing retribution by powerful ranchers who held tremendous political power in the region.[11]

During the 1890s a movement that had been born in the Texas Hill Country, Populism, spread through the hard-hit agricultural regions of the Midwest and the mining communities of the West, especially New Mexico. Small ranchers and farmers were frustrated with the economic downturn and bitter about what they believed were injustices in the economic system. They viewed as villains the cattle barons like Lyons who monopolized grazing land and water supplies, as well as the railroad operators who charged exorbitant fees to bring goods to market. The problem was compounded by public officials who looked away as their wealthy and powerful friends took advantage of the situation. One New Mexico sheriff complained that train robbers had "'more friends out there than the officers.'"[12]

The "silver-rich" Grant County Populist rhetoric offered a panacea for impoverished farmers and ranchers to combat monopolies and corruption. In New Mexico, many southern Democrats embraced the People's Party, the political arm of the Populist movement. It is impossible to know if Jeff Power joined the Populist movement, how he voted, or even if he voted at all, because voter records from that time were not preserved. As a woman, Jane Power, of course, did not have the right to vote, but both she and Jeff were in debt in the 1890s and neither one had much respect for local authorities, who had repeatedly failed to protect them from threats by powerful ranchers like Tom Lyons. Jeff abhorred the violence that threatened his family, and like so many of his neighbors, he idolized Billy the Kid and Jesse James, who had preyed on the powerful railroad companies and cattle barons who threatened the success of small ranchers like himself. Even if he was not registered as a member of the People's Party, he surely was a populist in spirit.[13]

The 1890s proved a pivotal decade for the Power family in New Mexico. They survived the economic downtown, probably owing much to the seventeen acres under cultivation on Jane's farm, which could provide food no matter what happened on the range around them. The family expanded during those difficult years. John Grant Power, the second son of Mattie and Jeff, was born just after their arrival in New Mexico, in September 1890. In the spring of 1893 Mattie gave birth to a third son, Thomas Jefferson Power Jr., the fourth-generation Power male to bear that name. In November of the following year the first girl in the family, Ola May, was born. By 1897 the economy was finally turning around, but Jeff, the father of four young children, was dealt a personal blow. He was completing construction of a new adobe home on his property in late February. For insulation, Jeff and neighbors were tossing dirt and hay on the roof, which was supported by a center pole. Evidently, the pitch of the roof was not steep enough, and the pole slipped out of place. The men stood by helplessly as the roof collapsed on the three women who were inside. A neighbor was unhurt, but Jane Power was badly injured and Mattie Power was killed instantly.[14]

The funeral took place the following afternoon, and Mattie was laid to rest in the shade of some oak trees on their property in Gila. When she was alive, Mattie had told her mother-in-law she did not want to be buried in the town cemetery, where the badgers dug up the graves. Now she would spend eternity under the expansive trees on Jane Power's land overlooking the canal and fields, her grave covered with large rocks to deter any scavengers. A marble headstone erected by Jeff speaks volumes about his feelings for his wife. Two engraved clasped hands, one male and one female, dominate the monument. In the nineteenth century, clasped hands held significant meaning, suggesting a farewell to the earthly existence of one marriage partner and a promise that the couple would be reunited in death someday as they were in life, their devotion intact. A bouquet of flowers carved on the side of the gravestone symbolizes condolence and grief, and stalks of wheat adorning the base and edges represent productivity, bounty, and fertility, a reference to their four children.[15]

The anguish of losing his wife in an accident that was likely his fault must have weighed on Jeff's mind. His son Tom later said that Jeff went on an "aimless odyssey" after Mattie's death, traveling and working in various locations around the West. Ola was only a little over two years old, young Tom was not yet four, John was six, and Charley had just turned eight when their mother died. Most men would have sought a new spouse to help with the chores and raise the children, but Jeff remained single, perhaps, as friends later suggested, because he "cherished the memory of his Mattie."[16]

Jane Power stepped in to help raise her four grandchildren. She was known for her toughness, garnered from decades of living on the frontier, but she could neither read nor write, signing only her "X" on legal documents. Evidently, she did not prioritize education for her grandchildren, either. The 1900 census shows that the Power children, then between the ages of four and eleven, were not attending school, while most of the neighbor children were. Furthermore, according to the census, neither Charley nor John, who were eleven and ten, respectively, could read or write. In fact, the census enumerator noted that John could not even speak English, perhaps an error on the official's part or perhaps an indication of what many have suggested: that John had a learning disability. Joe Bleak, a close friend who first met the Powers when they were living in Gila, later said that he attended class with the Power children at the old Horne schoolhouse, but like most children in rural areas of that era, they spent only a few months out of the year in the classroom, achieving low levels of literacy.[17]

The three Power brothers, like most boys their age, worked long hours helping with the cattle and the crops. By the time each reached age nine or ten, he would be out with his father fixing fence and rounding up stray cattle, while Ola helped her grandmother cook, clean, and tend the chickens and milk cow. All the Powers were exceptional with animals and adept with guns. As a neighbor of theirs in Arizona later recalled, "They lived close to nature and were familiar with the habits of the wild life they hunted and trapped. . . . To them their six-shooters and rifles represented food for their table and protection for their cattle and horses from the wild animals."[18]

As they grew, each child developed his or her own characteristics. The oldest boy, Charley, was always the tallest and strongest, with dark hair and a dark complexion; his brother Tom said he "looked more like a Cherokee Indian," referring to their grandmother's purported ancestry. The most ambitious and determined of the bunch, as a teenager Charley began to accumulate cattle bought with his wages as a cowboy. The second son, John, had sandy hair, light brown eyes, and looked like his maternal grandmother, Amanda Bybee Morgan, who was of northern European ancestry. He was the shortest of the Power boys and had a special way with animals, especially horses. John obviously struggled in school—his younger brother Tom had far superior writing skills—which perhaps explains why he was the most taciturn of the family. Tom, with light brown, curly hair and light brown eyes like his father, was good-looking, outgoing, and talkative, and the best cowpuncher in the family. Ola was a tall, pretty, dark-haired girl, who, like her older brother John, felt more at home with animals than with strangers. Of necessity, the children became, according to family friends, "hard workers, hardy and resourceful."[19]

As the Power boys grew up and assumed more responsibilities with their father's herd, they were introduced into the cutthroat world of cattle ranching on the New Mexico frontier. In August 1904 Jeff and his oldest son, Charley, who was just fifteen at the time, were charged with "unlawfully drawing a deadly weapon and handling same in a threatening manner," in another apparent attempt by Tom Lyons to drive them off their land. The Power men allegedly used a pistol to threaten Peter Turman, a young ranch hand who lived with two of Lyons's alleged hired gunmen, most likely during a disagreement over cattle. Almost a month after the incident, both Jeff and Charley were arrested by the local sheriff at their home, taken into custody without resistance, and released on a one-thousand-dollar bond. The case never went to trial, because the prosecutor withdrew charges when it became apparent he lacked the evidence for a conviction, but the steady onslaught of criminal and civil charges was taking a toll on a family with few resources to pay expensive legal fees.[20]

Drought, floods, threats, and violence were a mainstay on the southwestern frontier, as parties vied for economic control in a region where hard currency, water, and suitable grazing land were in short supply and local law enforcement often prioritized "self-aggrandizement" over upholding the law. How a man handled himself under such volatile conditions determined his fate in life. Jeff and Jane Power used the courts as best they could to protect their property and their loved ones, but it was a strategy that had only limited success at a time when more aggressive tactics were employed by others all around them.[21]

4

FRONTIER HONOR

Wild. Reckless. He was a renegade.

Wiley Morgan and his brother-in-law, Jeff Power, were both born in Texas at a time when a culture of honor was a defining concept among southern white males. As historian Patrick Q. Mason notes, "When a man's honor was impugned, it was imperative that he confront the transgressor in order to save face; turning the other cheek was not a compelling masculine value in the honor-bound South." Threats, shaming, and even killing became the methods many men employed when insulted. Historian C. L. Sonnichsen has suggested that frontier folk law in Texas "produced a habit of self-redress more deeply ingrained, perhaps, than anywhere else in the country." After the Civil War, as displaced southerners poured into the territories of the Southwest, they brought with them a propensity for excessive gambling, imbibing, and braggadocio as well as a sense that both individual and family honor should be preserved at all costs. In a place where vast distances separated homesteads, law enforcement was spread thin, and competition for grazing land was stiff, men often were required to defend their property as well as the lives of their families. By the early twentieth century the American legal system had evolved to uphold the notion that when under attack, "if otherwise without fault, a person could legally stand fast, and without retreat, kill in self-defense." In this setting and with this mindset, protecting one's property and one's honor often became indistinguishable; violence in self-defense was not only tolerated, but expected.[1]

Jeff Power's in-laws, the Morgans, were a family of risk-takers who fit the prototype of southern men of honor unwilling to turn the other cheek. Tom Power once described his maternal grandfather Sebe Morgan: "Wild. Restless. He was a renegade."[2] Wiley Morgan was the oldest of Sebe's children and the wildest of the bunch. Similar in demeanor to powerful ranchers like Tom Lyons, Wiley's ambition bordered on ruthlessness, and his explosive temper occasionally landed him in trouble with the law, but it was exactly that volatility that allowed him to survive and even thrive as a young cowboy during the dangerous decades of the 1870s and 1880s in the Arizona and New Mexico territories.

In his prime, Wiley Morgan stood just over five feet, eight inches and weighed 157 pounds, a bull of a man with jet-black hair, steel-gray eyes, and a bushy mustache that disguised the fact that he was missing a few front teeth. Despite being married with children, he always remained a rootless cowboy, moving his family from place to place seeking new opportunities. Wherever he lived, he joined the local cattlemen's associations, voluntary organizations comprising large cattle owners, and often served in a leadership capacity. These cattlemen's associations introduced mandatory brand registration and hired inspectors, detectives, and range deputies to patrol the range for rustlers. Morgan was also active in politics, often serving on the local school board or as a Democratic precinct judge. At a time when much of male social life revolved around politics, his civic activities earned him a position of trust among members of his community, even when his reckless behavior raised eyebrows among neighbors and friends.[3]

Although he had convinced his own parents, as well as Jeff and Mattie Power, to move to New Mexico in 1890, almost as soon as they arrived, Wiley Morgan struck out on his own for a plum job in the Arizona Territory as a foreman at the Mule Shoe Ranch at Hooker's Hot Spring in the Sulphur Springs Valley. He was allowed to mingle his cattle with his boss's on a share basis, enabling him to quickly increase his herd, but he discovered that easy profits came with ample risk. In 1899 Morgan learned from fellow members of the Cochise County cattlemen's association that a neighboring rancher, John Duncan, had in his possession a calf that did not belong to him. Morgan, his brother George, and cattlemen H. C. Abel and J. W. Mitchell rode up to visit Duncan's ranch and brought along what they thought to be the calf's mother to see if it would "come to its mother and suck." When it did, the men confronted Duncan, who offered to return the calf. The Morgan brothers, however, could not hold their tempers over the theft. According to witnesses, an unpleasant exchange occurred. George Morgan told Duncan, "'You see what you get for meddling with other people's business?'" Duncan responded, "'Whose business?' George Morgan replied 'my business.' Duncan retorted 'you're a — liar' and, according to Mitchell, threw his hand on the pistol." In an attempt to protect his brother's life and his family's honor, Wiley moved to shoot, but before he could do so, Duncan took off on horseback over the crest of a hill with Wiley following in pursuit. When the other men finally caught up with John Duncan and Wiley Morgan, they found Duncan shot dead.[4]

Wiley fled the scene, while his brother and J. W. Mitchell turned themselves in to authorities. Even though there was no evidence either man took part in the slaying, George Morgan and Mitchell were indicted for murder, as was the fugitive Wiley Morgan. Wiley hid in the mountains for over a month, leading local journalists to declare, in their boilerplate language for fugitive stories, "he could easily hold a pursuing force at bay" from his hideout. Eventually, Wiley surrendered peacefully to local officials in Willcox, where he told the sheriff he acted in self-defense when threatened by Duncan and stated that he would have surrendered to authorities sooner if his brother George had not been charged with murder. George Morgan was released on bail, and eventually the murder charge against him was dismissed. The case against Mitchell was dismissed as well, but only after he agreed to testify against Wiley Morgan.[5]

Wiley's murder trial, held in December 1899 in Tombstone, took place as the territory was lurching toward statehood and politicians were anxious to demonstrate that law and order, not vigilante justice, prevailed in the court system. Although historians view the 1890s as the time when the frontier closed in the United States, in pockets of the Southwest those old ways prevailed much longer, and individuals like defendant Wiley Morgan did not amend their ways overnight. When the prosecution placed Mitchell on the stand, he failed to incriminate Morgan as hoped, telling the court "he was afraid Wiley Morgan would kill him if he done otherwise." According to Mitchell, Morgan said to him: "'There are two or three other — — I will have to kill yet.'" When it was his turn to testify, Wiley Morgan denied threatening to kill Mitchell and claimed the deceased, John Duncan, had threatened to kill him prior to their deadly encounter, so Wiley felt entitled to defend himself. Although witnesses said Duncan made repeated threats to Wiley's life, the judge, who evidently was well-versed in the ruthless tactics of many leading southwestern ranchers, dismissed that testimony, telling jurors that it was a "regular and common practice" of members of the cattlemen's associations to bribe witnesses to corroborate testimony of fellow members. When testimony concluded, the judge insisted that the jury find Morgan guilty.[6]

Morgan was convicted of second-degree murder and sentenced to twenty years in the Arizona Territorial Prison at Yuma. He was thirty-nine years old, a successful rancher with a wife, three young children, and a fourth on the way. His wife, Amanda, was mortified. The couple scrambled to transfer the remainder of his cattle into her name to protect against a civil lawsuit and hired lawyers to launch an appeal. While he sat in the hellhole that was the prison at Yuma, where the cells built entirely of stone baked in summer temperatures that sometimes reached 120 degrees, Amanda rented a home in town so she and her children could be close to her husband. She brought lemonade to him in the prison yard that summer, and was so ashamed of his status that she told the census enumerator her husband was a guard as the prison, rather than admit he was an inmate. In August she gave birth to their fourth child, Wiley Jr., alone.[7]

Wiley took his conviction in stride, claiming to friends and family that life at the prison was not so bad and he was content to serve out his sentence. He took up woodworking to pass the time and became friends with the guards, demonstrating the kind of behavior that could earn him early parole and thereby avoiding the "snake" cell where troublesome inmates were kept in darkness for days, chained to the floor. While Arizona courts were quick to convict, they were also quick to forgive first-time offenders, with judges overturning cases and governors handing out pardons freely, often only after a small fraction of a sentence was served, provided the convicted had the means to hire high-priced attorneys. Amanda Morgan, left alone to raise her young family, was anxious to get her husband out immediately. She sold many of his prized cattle and even his ranch in Cochise County to raise the thousands of dollars needed to pay the lawyers' bills—transactions that Wiley would complain about for the rest of his life. His attorneys arranged for his release on a ten-thousand-dollar bond, paid for by his parents, while they successfully appealed for a new trial. Amanda made sure he had the best legal team available, which now included well-known Cochise County attorney Allen R. English.[8]

When the court reviewed Morgan's case in December 1901, newspapers reported that "many important witnesses were missing." To what extent they vanished because of Wiley's alleged threats to kill them is unclear, but the new jury could not reach a decision either. The judge refused to dismiss the case, so Morgan's attorneys appealed to the Arizona Territorial Supreme Court in the summer of 1903, convincing the court that the judge who presided over his original trial had acted improperly when he suggested witnesses were bribed and when he instructed the jury to find Morgan guilty. The high court agreed, and his conviction was overturned.[9]

Wiley Morgan's murder trial demonstrates that the Southwest's legal system was often biased toward the wealthy and powerful. He had killed a man, allegedly threatened to kill others who testified against him, and eluded authorities trying to arrest him for a month, yet Morgan walked away from prison after serving fewer than sixteen months of his twenty-year sentence. His parents helped him raise bail, and he had his own resources to launch several appeals and hire the finest lawyers, even if it meant selling off prime land and prized cattle. As the *Bisbee Daily Review* noted: "Morgan is said to have been in comfortable circumstances at the time of the killing of Duncan, but to have become well-nigh impoverished by the expense attending his attempt to secure acquittal of the charge still pending against him." Poor men, especially men of color, might languish in prison for years without access to skilled attorneys, but men like Wiley Morgan could pay for legal talent able to engineer a quick release.[10]

Morgan's trial also reveals how much of our knowledge of the West is cloaked in misinformation. As folklore scholar Arthur L. Campa has noted, we tend to believe that history and folklore are two distinct fields, and that history depends on exact science while folklore is based on old wives' tales. But as any student of history, especially the history of the Old West, will tell you, the two are much closer than people suspect, and Wiley Morgan's murder case provides insights into how factual history and folklore are often difficult to distinguish.[11] In 1951 historian C. L. Sonnichsen published *Billy King's Tombstone,* a lively series of stories about life in Cochise County in the late nineteenth century. One of King's tales focuses on Morgan's trial and makes a folk hero of his attorney, Allen English. According to King, "It was no effort at all for him to soar for hours in those lofty regions," and English's words were so well-oiled that "even the cultured and the skeptical heard him with admiration." King alleged English was inebriated when he made his closing arguments at Morgan's trial, stating that "he was a good lawyer drunk or sober, but possibly a shade better when drunk" and he made "one of the best speeches he ever made, and it cleared his man." As this bit of folklore recounts it, Allen English, an exceptionally talented but intoxicated orator, saved Morgan from injustice. The reality, of course, was that the legal system had performed the way it was designed, allowing a review of the case—albeit only if the convicted had the means to hire the proper attorneys—to ensure that individual rights were preserved. But because checks and balances do not make for exciting storytelling, to this day the Billy King version portraying Allen English as Wiley Morgan's knight errant continues to be repeated as fact, and Morgan himself has been transformed by modern-day folklorists into a "gunslinger."[12]

Even though he had lost much of his personal wealth during the legal process, Morgan borrowed money from friends and family and found work as a foreman on the Camp Stool outfit, near Mammoth, Arizona, enabling him to make a fresh start. Over the next few years he saved enough money to go into the saloon business in Klondyke and started to rebuild his cattle operation in Aravaipa Canyon in Graham County, where his brash tactics continued to send him to court. Despite his aggression, and perhaps even because of it, he earned positions of respect such as inspector for the county Livestock Sanitary Board, member of the Klondyke School Board, and local leader in the Democratic Party, where his opinion was often sought by others. Even in the 1940s, long after the frontier had closed and he had moved to Los Angeles, he continued to use threats to protect his interests and his pride. He was frail and in his eighties when he placed a down payment on a piece of property in southern California, and later changed his mind about the purchase and asked for a refund. When the real estate agent refused his request, Morgan pulled out the pistol he was carrying and slammed it on the table, convincing the startled agent to return his down payment. To the end, Wiley Morgan remained a gruff, honor-bound frontiersman.[13]

Although Wiley Morgan and his brother-in-law, Jeff Power, were both stock-men, about the same age, and born and raised in Texas, their personalities could not have been more different. Jeff was a hard worker, but he was never aggressive like Wiley, and when his honor was threatened he did not resort to violence. As his son Tom later recalled, Jeff never mistreated anyone or initiated a confrontation, and the only time he demonstrated a temper was "when people pushed him around and even then he didn't do much about it."[14] Whether this behavior that was so foreign to most southern men was a result of his nature or of circumstance is uncertain. After all, Jeff Power was never truly head of his own household while his mother was alive.

After Jane left Sam in Texas, Jeff's mother became the undisputed head of the Power household, a position she held for the rest of her life. While she conformed to nineteenth-century expectations that a woman would preside over the domestic sphere, rearing her son and grandchildren and tending to household chores, Jane also held the Power family purse strings. She made all real estate purchases for her family, and her farming pursuits put food on the table even when her son's cattle business was failing. She made important decisions about where and how they would live, probably consulting with Jeff, but also sometimes vetoing his ideas and only lending money to him for undertakings of which she approved.[15] Jane Power was no aberration: there were many female heads of households in the West. Some were widows, while others had never married or were divorced or abandoned by their husbands. And then, of course, there were women like

Jane, who left their spouses and set out on their own. Women homesteaded land, opened respectable businesses in mining towns, taught school, and even practiced law. Many western state and territorial legislators understood this phenomenon, so they often accorded women more legal rights than their counterparts in the East, especially more liberal divorce and property laws, and they even granted them the right to vote earlier than women in the rest of the country.[16]

The presence of numerous female heads of households in the West raises the question: how did they respond to threats to their home and kin? Historians have used the concept of a frontier code of honor to explain how privileged white males defended property through gunfights and vigilantism, but deny it applied to women. Stories of frontier violence often place women in the background, where they never picked up a gun and used only moral suasion to diffuse threats to their home, their children, or their person. A woman like Jane Power was "a woman in a man's story," as historian Kathleen Chamberlain has described another such woman, Susan McSween, who was embroiled in the Lincoln County War in New Mexico in the 1880s. McSween, Jane Power, and many other women tested the argument that women did not stand up to men. When threatened, they responded with a variety of tactics, including legal action, verbal threats, and in Jane's case, even threats of physical harm to aggressors.[17]

Jane Power appropriated important elements of the culture of frontier honor to stand her ground. She shamed her husband for his drunken behavior by having him arrested, humiliated Tom Lyons by suggesting he was a coward for threatening widows and their children, and repeatedly demonstrated a willingness to use a weapon to defend her property. While she never was driven to the point of killing a man, certainly those men she confronted took her and her rifle seriously, and they all backed down, earning her the moniker of "Shotgun Sal." Despite her appropriation of some aspects of male culture, her most effective tactic was reliance on the courts to resolve squabbles over land, water, or cattle. She successfully launched suits and counter charges, knowing that most juries and judges would favor her word over that of a man who had threatened her. Nor did she raise a firebrand. Jeff Power mimicked his mother, employing a balanced approach of threats and legal proceedings to check aggression by others.[18]

Jeff Power's adoption of his mother's methods was a rational decision, because he had few resources at his disposal—no siblings and few social connections or financial assets—to fend off attacks. Jeff's herd was small, so the fees for him to join the local cattlemen's association were prohibitively expensive, leaving him without the protection those organizations offered against rustling. He was never active in politics like most of his peers, and therefore lacked potential allies from those circles. Some people called Jeff Power an "unsociable old mountaineer," but without a wife to insist he attend the local church social or the July Fourth barbecue, he opted instead to retreat from society after Mattie's death. In doing so, he became increasingly disconnected from the larger local community, an outsider to all but a handful of close friends and relatives.[19] Dime novels and Western films tout the individualism of the Old West, but people who lived on the frontier did not operate in a vacuum; their social networks were indispensable to their success.

Regional drought in 1903 and 1904, followed by floods in 1905 that turned the main street of Silver City into a raging river, left almost all of Jeff Power's cattle dead. As the hard times continued in Gila, their patience and financial resources worn down, Jeff and Jane realized they had no alternative, and finally decided to move away in 1907. In February of that year Jeff filed a homestead claim on eighty acres of land in Willcox, just over the territorial line in Cochise County, Arizona, not far from where Wiley Morgan, his brother Will, and their families had established ranching operations. There was enough land on their parcel for Jane to grow food for the table, but there was not enough land to graze cattle. Public land was becoming difficult to come by, and what had been the domain of ranchers when Wiley Morgan punched cattle in the Sulphur Springs Valley from the 1870s to the 1890s had recently transitioned with an influx of homesteaders establishing farms.[20] Just east of Willcox Jeff found the solution to his problems. In April 1907 Jeff and his mother, Jane, partnered with Virgil and Pearl Harrington to purchase a mining property in Doubtful Canyon, which straddles the New Mexico-Arizona line about twelve miles west of Lordsburg. The Doubtful Mine held little potential for ore, but it had a well and a water storage tank, and was adjacent to plenty of good public grazing grassland.[21]

Steins Peak, named for a military officer who led an expedition there against the Apaches in the 1850s and negotiated an agreement with Chiricahua leader Cochise, is the dominant physical feature in Doubtful Canyon, a dry and desolate area where the Chihuahuan Desert meets the Sonoran Desert and where the wind blows endlessly. Today Interstate 10 runs through the southern portion of the canyon, and in previous times it was an important transportation corridor as well, but one fraught with danger. To the south are the Chiricahua Mountains, where Apaches launched attacks on encroaching Anglos until the 1880s. The first stage line carrying mail, the Butterfield Overland Stage, ran through Doubtful Canyon in 1857, and attacks were so frequent that the drivers warned passengers that "Doubtful Canyon was so

named 'because it's always doubtful whether we'll reach the other end alive.'" Fort
Bowie was established nearby during the Civil War by the U.S. Army to suppress
the attacks, and despite the soldiers' presence, as late as the 1880s and 1890s rustlers
and outlaws roamed the isolated canyon. By the time the Powers and Harringtons
purchased their property in Doubtful Canyon, those outlaw days were mostly
over and the region was populated by prospectors searching for gold, silver, and
copper in the Peloncillo Mountains to the east. At the town of Steins Pass miners
could enjoy the basic amenities found in most camps—a general store, a saloon, a
restaurant—but its location in the middle of the desert meant that water had to be
transported in by train, often fetching up to one dollar a barrel.[22]

While the Harringtons and Powers had vital well water for their ranching
operations, there were other problems. The Harringtons quickly lost eighteen
horses to the locoweed that grew in the area, and decided to leave. Jeff and Jane
did not have the cash to buy them out, so the Harringtons sold their half of the
mine and the ranch, as well as much of their cattle, to James W. Gould and James
A. and Mary E. Baird, prominent New Mexico ranchers. The new partners were
evidently not to Jeff and Jane's liking because a few months later, just before
Christmas 1908, they sold their shares of the mining and ranching properties
to Gould and the Bairds as well. Unlike the Harringtons, however, the Powers
wished to stay in the area, so Jane submitted a homestead application on public
land nearby and then, in partnership with her grandson Charley, submitted an
application for a new mining claim, also named Doubtful, about one and a half
miles southwest of the original claim.[23] Jane and Jeff would have ample room to
run their cattle on public land while retaining the proceeds from the sale of the
property to Gould and the Bairds to buy more cattle.

Before long, however, the Powers ran into the same problems they had experienced in Gila when they came under legal attack from their new neighbors.
On September 16, 1909, James W. Gould and James and Mary Baird charged
Jeff Power with "obtaining money under false pretenses," and he was indicted
in Grant County, New Mexico. The plaintiffs claimed that after they bought
the Doubtful Mine from Jeff Power they could not obtain possession of their
property. Jeff hired a well-known criminal defense attorney, James S. Fielder, to
defend him, and Fielder successfully convinced the jury in Silver City that Jeff
was not guilty. While they were waiting for the trial's outcome, the Power family
remained in Doubtful Canyon, although perhaps fearing trouble from Gould
and the Bairds, Jeff had his youngest son, Tom, move their cattle north into
Aravaipa Canyon, where the Morgans had relocated their ranching operations.[24]

Despite the loss in court, Gould remained determined to drive the Powers out of Doubtful Canyon, and in July 1910 resorted to force to accomplish his goal. Gould and two other armed men forcibly entered the Power home and threatened to kill the entire family, including Jane and sixteen-year-old Ola, if they did not leave the premises. No gunfire was exchanged and the Powers cooperated, gathering up their things and watching as their assailants burned their home to the ground. The two men Gould brought with him were Elmer Archer Lyall and Jesse Wayne Brazel. Lyall was a rancher in Doubtful Canyon and served as deputy to the Grant County sheriff, but he did not appear to be at the Power home in any official capacity that day because he held no warrants or eviction notice. Jane and Charley Power had filed all the proper paperwork for their Doubtful mining claim and homestead, so there was no legal ground for their removal. Gould's other accomplice, Brazel, had bought the Bairds' share of the Doubtful property and was now Gould's business partner. The Powers undoubtedly had heard of the young ranch hand, who had recently gained notoriety for killing the Southwest's best-known lawman, Patrick F. Garrett.[25]

On February 29, 1908, Jessie Wayne Brazel walked into the Doña Ana County sheriff's office and confessed to killing Pat Garrett, the sheriff who had shot and killed Billy the Kid in 1881. Garrett was unpopular because he owed many people money, drank and gambled excessively, and was quarrelsome, but he was also an effective lawman whom authorities often brought in to investigate high-profile murders in southern New Mexico. At the time of his death it was rumored that Garrett was close to bringing charges against local ranchers for rustling, and perhaps even for the murders of Albert Fountain and his son. Few people believed that the good-natured cowboy Brazel, who worked for one of the largest spreads in the region, William Webb Cox's San Augustine Springs Ranch, could be Garrett's murderer. When Cox hired prominent attorney Albert B. Fall to defend Brazel, stories quickly surfaced that Brazel was Cox's pawn, asked to take the blame in the Garrett murder for someone else. After a one-day trial in May 1909, during which Jim Baird testified that Garrett had threatened Wayne Brazel's life, a jury agreed with defense attorney Fall's argument that Brazel had shot Garrett in self-defense, even though the medical examiner determined Garrett was shot in the back of the head and almost simultaneously in the stomach while urinating by the side of the road.[26]

While it remains unclear what role Brazel played in the death of Pat Garrett, shortly after his acquittal he came into sudden wealth. In May 1910, Brazel incorporated the Long S. Land and Cattle Company in Lordsburg with forty thousand dollars in initial capital. As agent and director of the privately held firm he held half the shares in the company, which he used as collateral to make various purchases to run the operation. He spent six thousand dollars to purchase the Harrington Wells Ranch in Doubtful Canyon from Jim Baird and Jim Gould and then acquired Baird's share of the Doubtful Mine, previously held by the Harringtons and the Power family, thereby becoming an equal partner with Gould in the claim. Brazel then borrowed over five thousand dollars to stock the Long S. with cattle and submitted a homestead application for an additional 160 acres in the Animas Valley so there would be sufficient room for grazing. Evidently, the Power family's continued presence in Doubtful Canyon somehow threatened Brazel and Gould's plans. Perhaps they feared the additional cattle would jeopardize the water needed to run the Long S., so they took matters into their own hands. As historian William A. Keleher has argued, in those days, "the man who had the waterhole was the man who controlled the public range."[27]

It was never Jeff's or Jane's way to respond to threats with violence; instead, they did what they always had done and turned to the courts. Their three assailants at Doubtful Canyon were charged with forcible entry and detainer. Jane and Charley Power asked for redress for the loss of the mine, claiming the "defendants have made threats against the plaintiffs to inflict with bodily injury if plaintiffs attempt to regain possession of premises," and asked for a writ of restitution and judgment against the defendants for court costs. In the fall of 1910, Gould, Brazel, and Lyall were summoned to the Bowie justice court, where a judge found the three men guilty and awarded the Powers five hundred dollars in damages plus court costs.[28]

Despite losing twice—the criminal case against Jeff in New Mexico for obtaining money under false pretenses and the civil case launched by Jane and Charley in Arizona—Gould did not back down. He hired Cochise County's most notable attorney, Allen R. English, the same lawyer hired by Amanda Morgan to defend Wiley, and he appealed the civil case concerning ownership of the Doubtful Mine to the Cochise County district court. Both sides waived the right to a jury trial, and Judge Fletcher Doan, after reviewing new evidence introduced by the defendants, overturned the lower court's decision, ruling that Jane and Charley Power were not the rightful owners of the mine. The new evidence and the judgment have vanished from the case file, so it is impossible to determine why the seemingly legitimate Power claim was denied, but this was the first and only loss of a legal case by the Power family.[29]

Although Jeff loved to tell tall tales of his adventures to friends, neither he nor any of his family members ever relayed an account of their confrontation with

James Gould, Arch Lyall, or Wayne Brazel, surprising given his admiration of Billy the Kid. Certainly, Jeff Power would have liked to brag about staring down the man who had killed the Kid's slayer. Instead, of his stay in Doubtful Canyon Jeff later only commented that it had been "comparatively uneventful," and that a fire had destroyed their home and driven them out. Jeff and Jane wisely attempted no further court challenges, and Jane allowed her homestead application in Doubtful Canyon to lapse. They understood that dead bodies were still found out in the desert in southern New Mexico when the wrong men were crossed.[30]

The legal fees needed to litigate the Doubtful Canyon charges devastated the Powers, requiring Jane to sell her ranch in Gila, property she had held for twenty years. She and Jeff temporarily moved the family onto the property he was homesteading west of Willcox and enrolled the three youngest children in school for the year. Ola was sixteen, Tom seventeen, and John twenty. The world was changing and increasingly, good paying jobs required applicants to read and write. Perhaps Jane and Jeff agreed that it was time for the children to learn what they could in the classroom before they were too old.[31]

For Charley, who was an adult at twenty-one, it was too late for an education. He was off on his own much of the time, and as early as 1908 he visited his two uncles, Wiley and Will Morgan, near Klondyke in the Aravaipa Canyon region of Graham County, located just about fifty miles northwest of Willcox. On a subsequent visit, he purchased a mining claim from E. L. Ferguson, who was running goats on a beautiful clearing located miles from the nearest town or neighbors. The Power family would make one last move in the spring of 1911, settling on Charley's claim along Rattlesnake Creek.[32]

Once settled in his new surroundings in Aravaipa Canyon, Jeff Power proudly bragged to anyone who would listen about his abilities as a gunfighter. In one of his tales he claimed to have killed a Mexican horse thief just outside of Silver City while helping a neighbor trail two men into the Mogollon Mountains, where, Jeff boasted, he had remained cool and bided his time, and then let one of the thieves "have it." Jeff later told friends he reported the death to local authorities and went through an inquest, but no charges were filed. It is unlikely that Jeff's story was true—there is no evidence of this incidence in the Silver City newspapers or Grant County court records—but why would he lie about killing a man? Perhaps after his confrontation in Doubtful Canyon with Gould, Lyall, and Brazel and the resulting loss of his property, Jeff's tough talk was the only weapon he had left to warn people to leave him and his family alone.[33]

5

ARAVAIPA CANYON

Deadly in its isolation

It is hard to imagine a place more removed from civilization than Aravaipa Canyon. Located about fifty miles northeast of Tucson, the region, generally referred to simply as Aravaipa, contains not only the canyon itself but nine side canyons and their surrounding tablelands, situated on 540 square miles of rugged terrain. Mountain ranges, including the Santa Teresas, Pinaleños, and Galiuros, sport elevations ranging from 4,500 feet to over 10,700 feet. Above the canyons that cut through Aravaipa, barrel, prickly pear, and cholla cactus, as well as other thorny desert vegetation that torments man and beast alike, grow among the limited grasslands. Along the numerous creeks that dissect the region, heavy timber is found—cottonwood, sycamore, live oak, mesquite, and walnut. The word "aravaipa" is Apache for "laughing waters," and children who grew up there often told stories about going down to the larger of the creeks, such as Aravaipa or Copper, to catch minnows, catfish, or trout, the waters so clear under the bluffs and sycamore roots that the children could easily catch the fish with their bare hands. Hunters marveled at the abundance of deer, quail, rabbits, and turkeys in the region, but settlers also had to contend with the usual predators—coyotes, badgers, bobcats, mountain lions, and foxes—preying on their livestock.[1]

Father Eusebio Kino, an Italian Jesuit priest who established Catholic missions in the Sonoran Desert, was allegedly the first European to travel in the vicinity, and during his travels in 1697 he came into contact with the Sobaipuri, or Upper Piman, who lived in Aravaipa. When Spanish authorities tried to seize control of the region, they relocated the Native population to the San Pedro Valley, but the Pima were quickly replaced by the Aravaipa band of the Pinaleño Apaches (Tsè jinè clan). For almost two centuries the Aravaipas defied attempts by Spain, Mexico, and the United States to control their isolated canyons. It was not until the 1870s, when the United States military established a fort in the area, Camp Grant, that the indigenous population finally lost control. The Aravaipa Apaches faced an onslaught of problems that caused their population to plummet: warfare and disease from contact with Anglo and Mexican settlers, compounded by limited available water and tillable land. Many came to the fort for rations and lived peacefully near Aravaipa Creek under the protection of the army until 1871, when they were attacked by Tucson residents who blamed the Aravaipas for continued raiding. Over one hundred Aravaipas were brutally slain, and twenty-nine—mostly women and children—were taken into captivity in what we now call the Camp Grant Massacre. During the next few years, the U.S. Army rounded up and marched the Apaches through Aravaipa Canyon to their new home on the San Carlos Reservation. The location lacked sufficient water or arable land to grow crops to support inhabitants, but this action appeased Anglo settlers' insatiable appetite for new land.[2]

With the removal of the Apaches from Aravaipa, ranching, farming, and mining activities among Anglo and Mexican settlers increased, but the region's terrain prevented it from becoming an economic center of growth. Few roads could be built in the canyon land, so "everything from extracting minerals to bringing a midwife" was a difficult and dangerous undertaking. Its remoteness also protected its inhabitants, "mountain lions and moonshiners" alike, from discovery. It was, quite simply, a place where people relocated when, in the face of misdeeds or misfortune, they had nowhere else left to go. The federal government, understanding the limits to its development, established the Crook National Forest in Aravaipa in 1908, part of a national effort to preserve public lands. Prospectors could stake mining claims, ranchers could graze their herds on the limited public rangeland, and farmers could homestead, provided they filed the proper paperwork and paid the necessary fees to the U.S. Forest Service.[3]

The settlers believed to be the earliest permanent non-Indian residents of Aravaipa were Dan Ming and the Salazars, who established small ranching and farming operations in the late 1870s. Ming was born in Kentucky and arrived in Arizona Territory in 1872, supplying beef to military posts and participating in General George Crook's expeditions against the Apaches. Epimenio Salazar and his wife, Crespina, were both born south of the Gila River in a region that belonged to Mexico until the Gadsden Purchase of 1854, when ownership transferred to the United States. Like the Salazars, approximately 60 percent of the families living in Aravaipa originally came from Mexico, while the other 40 percent were, like Dan Ming, from southern states, primarily Texas, Missouri, and Kentucky. Most people in Aravaipa lived on scattered ranches raising goats or cattle, and when the Power family arrived, there were only about one thousand people in the entire region. Many families homesteaded along Aravaipa Creek, but the scarcity of fertile farmland and grassland meant it was difficult to eke out an existence. Men supplemented family incomes by hiring out as cowboys or miners while women planted gardens, and everyone hunted and trapped wild game to put food on the table. The town of Klondyke, home to approximately thirty ranching families when the Powers arrived, was established by prospectors who had failed to find their fortunes in the Yukon, hence the name. The Klondyke store served as the post office and local justice precinct where men gathered to vote. Next to the store there was a saloon owned by Wiley Morgan, and nearby was a schoolhouse for the primary grades.[4]

In Mammoth, a mining camp located ten miles west of the Galiuro (pronounced either *gal-ee-oor-o* or *gal-oor-o*) Mountains, which formed the western edge of Aravaipa, considerable gold was found in the 1890s. So to many prospectors, the neighboring Aravaipa mining districts held great promise. Large mining companies invested hundreds of thousands of dollars in improvements to the local mines and roads, and over the subsequent decades they employed local farmers and cowboys seeking outside income to work those mines. Despite the expensive effort, very little silver or copper was ever extracted from the Aravaipa region. The Copper Creek district on the western slopes of the Galiuros lay in neighboring Pinal County and produced a modest amount of copper prior to 1930. Grand Reef Mine, located three miles north of Klondyke, produced mostly zinc and lead over the years, but by 1903 the large mining company that ran it found it unprofitable and abandoned the operations, leasing the claims to locals.[5]

A secondary mining district, the Rattlesnake Mining District, was in the higher altitudes of the Galiuros, just south of the mining claim purchased by Charley Power, and consisted of only three low-grade mines. The most significant producer in the district was Gold Mountain, a small mining camp established in the late 1880s along Rattlesnake Creek, about two and a half miles from the Power claim. In 1902 the Consolidated Gold Mountain Mining Company of Tucson invested heavily in the mines, and for a short time the camp was large enough to support a saloon and brothel as well as scattered tents and cabins to house miners. Gold Mountain's boom was short-lived, so some locals speculated that the mine was salted with gold dust to attract speculators, and by the time the Power family arrived the camp was abandoned. The Rattlesnake Mining District recorded production of only 163 ounces of gold during its entire run. Even if precious ore had been found in greater abundance, the steep grades in the Galiuros made it prohibitively expensive to build and maintain roads to bring heavy mining equipment in or to transport ore out of the canyon. With so few economic opportunities, Aravaipa was the least populated and least prosperous region of Graham County.[6]

Graham County was formed by the state legislature in 1881 and was originally the size of the state of Massachusetts. The northern portion of the county was, and remains today, mostly comprised of the San Carlos Indian Reservation, under the jurisdiction of the federal government and separate from the local economy. To the east, near the border with New Mexico, Clifton was its largest and most prosperous town, with about half of the county's population in 1910. The Longfellow Mine, located just north of Clifton, provided an economic bonanza for the county after its discovery in the early 1870s. Two large mining companies—which eventually would become known as the Arizona Copper Company and the Phelps Dodge Company—invested millions of dollars in smelters, railroads, and mining operations around Clifton and Morenci. The central part of the county, the Gila Valley, is dominated by the upper Gila River, which runs from New Mexico in a northwesterly direction and contains on its banks most of the arable land in the region. This is where Mormons established farming communities in the late 1870s, and where the county seat of Solomonville was located.[7]

Until roads were built in the mid-1910s, most residents of Aravaipa, located in the mountainous southwest corner of the county, remained separated from the rest of the county by distance and culture. The canyon's ranchers and farmers preferred to take the half-day train trip to Willcox in neighboring Cochise County for provisions and to enjoy the saloons, rather than travel the poor roads down into the Gila Valley and the towns of Safford, Thatcher, or Solomonville, which remained an arduous two-day trip by wagon. Not only was the trip to Willcox more convenient for Aravaipans, but its inhabitants were also ranchers and farmers from the South and Mexico with whom they had more in common than the Mormons of the Gila Valley.[8]

The social life of Aravaipa was typical for a rural southwestern ranching and farming community. The Mexican American community, centered primarily on the east end of Aravaipa, hosted dances and fiestas to celebrate both American and Mexican holidays, often held on the Salazars' property. Although no Catholic church was erected, a priest made regular visits to say mass in private homes. Among the Anglo male population, the two saloons in Aravaipa, one near the Grand Reef Mine and Wiley Morgan's saloon in Klondyke, were important centers for entertainment. Family activities—barbecues and dances—were held at the Klondyke school. Most Anglo residents were Methodists or Baptists, but lived in such scattered locations that for many years visiting ministers held services only on the third Sunday of the month. Thus the Union Church, the first church constructed in Aravaipa, was not dedicated until the summer of 1915. The area around Turkey Creek and Table Mountain was often referred to as "Mormon country" because a handful of families belonging to the Church of Jesus Christ of Latter-day Saints (LDS) lived there. Rodeos brought together the best of the local cowboys, regardless of religion or ethnicity, to show off their skills at the end of the roundup.[9]

The heart of Aravaipa's economy was cattle, but by the time the Power family arrived, there were already signs that industry was in decline. The region shared many of the same characteristics as their previous home of Gila, New Mexico, located just one hundred miles east of Klondyke as the crow flies. Both locations reaped the benefits provided by the Upper Gila River, but the land was show-ing signs of deterioration after years of devastating droughts and overgrazing. Although ranchers were required to pay a fee to the federal government to run their cattle on federal land, few residents complied, and until 1934 Aravaipa was essentially unrestricted public range. This meant, according to the federal agency that oversaw the land, that "cattlemen followed a system of casual self-regulation." Unfortunately, that self-regulation was ineffective. Rangeland specialists cau-tioned as early as 1910 that "free or open range grazing has failed utterly wherever tried," and that the goat and cattle industries had been a "feast and famine proposition." Livestock destroyed much of the limited choice grassland, and between 1910 and 1920 the cattle population of Graham County declined from 100,000 to 51,000 head.[10] When Jeff Power and his sons first moved their straggly two hundred head of cattle into Rattlesnake Canyon, they received a rough welcome from locals who did not take kindly to newcomers bringing additional livestock to graze on land already showing signs of depletion. When the Power men stopped to water the cattle in the creek, local cowboys came riding by and "choused" the cattle, cowboy slang for frightening and scattering stock. A few days later Tom Power ran into the same men at the Klondyke store, where they stood in the doorway playing with their pistols, refusing to allow him to enter.[11]

The Power Family in Klondyke, 1914. From left to right: Jeff, Jane,
Charles (seated in car), Ola, Tom, and John.
Courtesy Howard Morgan.

Long before the Power family's arrival, all the prime homestead land was
spoken for, so they were forced to pasture their herd around Charley Power's
mining claim in Rattlesnake Canyon, located about eighteen miles south of
Klondyke. Rattlesnake Canyon is located between the Santa Teresa and Galiuro
mountains, and like so many canyon lands of the Southwest where wind, erosion, and water have worked their magic, the region features awe-inspiring
geologic formations. Originally named Sierra de San Calistro by the Spaniards,
the Galiuros were formed out of a series of volcanic eruptions that took place
over 25 million years ago. Subsequent block faulting caused layers of the ash
left behind to rise into spectacular ridges marked by formations that resemble
church spires. Scattered among the canyons are large boulders that appear as
if they were stacked by a race of giants. Rattlesnake Canyon is a treacherous
place for cattle, horses, mules, and their riders alike. Sure-footed goats had an
easier time on the rocky terrain, but as Tom Power later noted, "nobody wanted
that country. It was good cow country but it was too rough!"[12] Other ranchers
avoided settling in Rattlesnake Canyon and grazed stock on more level ground.

Rattlesnake Canyon looking north, with the clearing at Power Garden Place
in the foreground and Kielberg Canyon beyond it, denoted by the
jagged canyon walls to the right. Photo taken in 2006.
Courtesy Steve Porter.

The dangerous terrain was not the only problem the Powers faced. The region
averages only about eighteen inches of rain a year, so much of the lower part
of Rattlesnake Creek that runs through and defines the canyon dries up in
the summer and, during periods of drought, may be empty for years. Like all
ranchers in the desert Southwest, in wet years locals could cut and gather wild
Johnson grass and dry filaree to feed their livestock, but during droughts they
were forced to cut prickly pear cactus and burn off their spines for feed. Often,
impatient, starving cattle would eat the cactus growing on the range with the
spines intact, causing painful damage to their mouths and stomachs. When the
Power family first arrived, rattlesnakes caused such heavy losses among their
cattle that the men were forced to locate their den and gas them. As author
Thomas Cobb, who has written a fictional account of the Power shootout, has
noted, although Rattlesnake Canyon was "beautiful in its isolation," it was also
"deadly in its isolation."[13]

The clearing the Power family settled on—what they called Garden Place, but
is known today as Powers Garden—is located along the part of Rattlesnake Creek

where water usually runs year-round from its source at Rattlesnake Spring. The large clearing of flat land, an unusual sight in such rugged canyon lands, was likely originally created by the Aravaipa Apaches, who used fire drives to hunt and to clear for farming. When the Power family arrived on Charley's newly purchased mining claim, they found a corral for the horses, several acres that had been fenced, and a small, two-room cabin built by the previous owner. Along the creek grew sycamore, alder, wild cherry, and maple trees, providing cover and sustenance for the deer, quail, foxes, cougars, mountain lions, and black bears. There was ample water, game, and tillable land; it was a place the Powers could thrive for years.[14]

Despite all the difficulties associated with living in their new canyon home, which included cold winters, spring floods, summer heat, and long distances over rough trails to market, the Powers "found the peace and beauty of the canyon almost irresistible." Like Texas and New Mexico, Aravaipa was a place where "hot-headedness, big talk, and violence were the accepted reactions" to any slight. However, the Power family, located miles from neighbors, found respite from threats in their first few years in Rattlesnake Canyon. Unlike their tenures in Gila or Doubtful Canyon, where they were consumed with run-ins and legal battles with ranchers, there were no civil or criminal charges filed against them for over five years until 1916, when their cantankerous and often inebriated neighbor, Jeff Clayton, falsely charged them with stealing mining equipment, a matter that was quickly resolved by local law enforcement.[15]

The remoteness of Rattlesnake Canyon meant that folks wishing to avoid the law often found refuge there. There were rumors that Jeff Clayton, who had been a gambling and drinking partner of Tom Lyons back in Gila, New Mexico, was part of Francisco "Pancho" Villa's forces during the revolution against the Porfirio Diaz regime in Mexico. Elliot Lark Ferguson, who sold the mining claim at Garden Place to Charley Power, also had a past reputation for criminality. Ferguson, also known as Pete Spence, was a suspect in robberies and killings in Texas and Arizona, including the murder of Morgan Earp in 1882 in Tombstone. In 1909 he was almost sixty and was about to marry Laura Jane Clanton, widow of his longtime friend Phineas Clanton, when he found young Charley Power willing to take the property off his hands. Apaches who escaped the San Carlos Reservation often sought sanctuary in the canyon, as did cattle rustlers or smugglers moving contraband over the border into old Mexico or New Mexico. Although most canyon residents were law-abiding citizens who were simply too poor to purchase land in more desirable locations, outsiders living down in the Gila Valley often looked upon them with suspicion because they chose to live amongst outlaws in a primitive and dangerous locale.[16]

The lack of level farmland and good grazing land in Rattlesnake Canyon meant that there were few homesteading families in the vicinity, and the most immediate neighbors to the Powers were single, male prospectors working their claims. Stories continued to circulate indicating gold might be buried in the abandoned Gold Mountain claims, convincing a handful of individuals to continue prospecting. Commodore Perry Tucker, a Texan who had grown up in Gillespie County at the same time as Jeff Power, was working the Abandoned and Burro claims, located about five miles south of Power Garden Place, with partner Al Bauman, and the two men convinced several investors their mine held promise. Ed Knothe bought the Long Tom mines in the Rattlesnake mining district, located just south of the Abandoned and Burro claims. No one knew much about the reclusive Knothe, just that he was a German immigrant in his forties who lived alone and who had been in the area for a while, perhaps a holdover from when Gold Mountain was a thriving mining community.[17]

Ed Knothe lived a mile or so north of his mine along Rattlesnake Creek and about one hundred yards from a father and son team of prospectors, John Maddison Murdock and his son James Jasper, better known as "Jay." The Murdocks first met the Power family when they were on a prospecting trip in the Galiuros in 1911, but Jay and his father did not return to the area again until 1914, when they staked several claims. Knothe was a rarity—a lone miner who did nothing but work his own claims—but the Murdocks were more typical prospectors who spent most of their time working for large mining companies in towns like Clifton or Bisbee, earning enough wages to allow them to quit and work their own claims until they struck it rich or their money ran out, forcing them to return to work for the big operators.[18]

The Murdock claims in Rattlesnake Canyon never produced any ore, and the father and son had no apparent source of income. Many locals characterized John and Jay as "roustabouts," men who made a quick buck any way they could. Rumors suggested they were making whiskey at their mine instead of searching for gold, and while that may have been true, it is certain the two Murdock men also used the canyon as a refuge after run-ins with the law. They had been in a brutal street fight in Bisbee with Jay's stepfather, Nate Braley, during which guns and knives were drawn in front of the Red Light Saloon on Brewery Gulch. All three men suffered serious injuries in the melee, and initial reports by the press indicated that many in the crowd of a hundred that had gathered to watch believed

Jay Murdock would not survive the thrashing. The combatants dropped charges and Jay recovered, but the Murdock men would continue to find themselves in difficult straits.[19] A few years later Jay married a Mormon woman, Catherine Fuller, in Cochise County, and together they had a daughter. Just two months after her birth, Jay left his wife and child. Catherine successfully sued Jay for divorce for abandoning his family. The court awarded her custody of the child while Jay was ordered to pay child support, but he quickly disappeared into the Galiuros with his father, where he told everyone he was a widower with a young daughter being raised by family members.[20]

Charley Power's mining claim in Rattlesnake Canyon had been located by George and James Branson, brothers from the nearby town of Oracle who staked most of the original claims in the Rattlesnake District at the turn of the century. No gold was discovered, so the claims were quickly abandoned, but two were reclaimed shortly after by Elliot Lark Ferguson, who established a goat ranch on the Branson mines before selling them to Charley Power in the summer of 1909. For Ferguson and Charley Power the claims were valuable only because they offered access to water at Rattlesnake Creek and level ground for farming and grazing, not for their ore potential. Ranchers could buy claims for small fees—Charley paid only fifty dollars for his—and under the Forest Homestead Act of June 11, 1906, he could graze his herd on the public lands, cut timber, and divert water for the mine.[21]

Although the mining claim allowed the Powers access to public grazing land, it only allowed for a 1,500-by-6,000-foot patch of land to dwell on, not enough for his grandmother to grow crops, so Charley filed a homestead application with the U.S. Forest Service on July 7, 1911, to secure the 160 acres surrounding the claim. Many early residents of Aravaipa, perhaps as many as 20 percent, simply squatted on their land, clearing it and constructing buildings without filing a homestead patent, but the Powers wanted to stay and to prevent neighbors encroaching on Garden Place. Their plans, however, did not coincide with the policies in place with the General Land Office of the U.S. Department of the Interior, which oversaw the homestead process. When the Galiuros became part of the Crook National Forest, it was the federal government's intention to protect all precious watersheds in the desert environment, so homesteaders like the Powers could not monopolize a source. The assistant forest ranger who surveyed the land, Francis Lee Kirby, recommended granting the Powers just under nineteen acres of a long, narrow strip of the clearing located along Rattlesnake Creek, not the 160 acres Charley specified in his application. It was Kirby's opinion that it was the only arable strip of land with sufficient access to water, and the rest of the proposed homestead was better suited for grazing and therefore could not be fenced. Kirby's analysis did not take into consideration that the steep canyons surrounding Power Garden Place were hardly suitable for grazing, which was why other ranchers never used it. In his homestead application, Charley also requested exclusive access to the only water from Rattlesnake Spring, located in the rocky canyon above his cultivated land, and Kirby denied this, too, because the water ran year-round and was needed to preserve the forest cover in the bottomland.[22]

The U.S. Forest Service has acknowledged that some of its officers "were occasionally overzealous in rejecting homestead applications," and with the benefit of hindsight it can be determined that Ranger Kirby, who was in his early twenties and new to the job, may have held more authority than he had common sense. Cattlemen and goat men often viewed Forest Service officers as their enemies, because they regulated and policed the range to which ranchers wanted unfettered access. Kirby aggravated already tense relations by bickering with numerous local ranchers and prospectors. With his cursory rejection of the homestead application, the ranger irritated Charley Power, who threatened to take his case to court unless the decision was reversed. Kirby refused to acquiesce, and instructed Charley to amend his application to include only the nineteen acres of land at Garden Place, without access to the spring. But in what was undoubtedly a heated conversation held in June 1912, Charley told the forest ranger, "nothing doing." The denial of the homestead request left Charley Power with only two options: to pay for an expensive hearing to plead his case—one he could well lose—or to simply claim squatters' rights, considering that he had bought the claim prior to the land coming under Forest Service jurisdiction. Charley informed Kirby he was not budging, and the ranger in turn complained to his superiors about the situation, telling them, "the applicant is still living on the land and working on it the same as though it was his own. Please advise me what action is desired." Since the federal government did not have the legal power to act, Kirby could not evict them and the Powers lived there unmolested for years.[23]

Jeff and his three sons added two rooms on to the existing small cabin, diverted water from Rattlesnake Creek to irrigate their crops, and quickly settled into a familiar routine in their new home. Granny Jane cooked meals of salt pork, cornbread, and beans in a cast iron pot over an open fire. She and Ola planted a vegetable garden and an orchard of fruit trees, and then battled with the raccoons, skunks, and rabbits for their bounties. There were chickens to feed and a cow to milk, and Ola's cat, named Tomba, patrolled for rodents. The brothers—Charley, John, and Tom—were all hired out to neighboring ranchers to help with the spring and fall roundups or worked in the local mines to bring in extra cash. Jeff hunted for game, performed chores on the farm for his mother, and worked the herd with his sons, registering his THS brand with the Livestock Sanitary Board, the cattle regulatory agency. Although ranchers were required to pay the Forest Service for grazing permits, Jeff never bothered with that formality, and public records demonstrate that only a handful of people living in the region conformed to that law. In this dangerous terrain, all family members routinely wore knives or pistols, since there was no telling when a rattlesnake, bear, or mountain lion would threaten them. Even Jane, who was in her early sixties, continued to carry a pistol and a bowie knife.[24]

The four Power children were fully grown in the summer of 1911. Charley was twenty-two, and neighbors noted he had a passion for automobiles and motorcycles, which were all the rage. He was the most hardworking of the boys, but he had developed a stubborn, combative streak, as demonstrated in his dealings with Ranger Kirby. Many people commented that the next oldest boy, John, who was not quite twenty-one, inherited his father's quiet nature and rarely spoke to outsiders. He was the shortest of the Power men and was very adept with animals. His horse, Maud, was so well trained that she followed him around like a dog. The third son, Tom, was by age eighteen a restless young man, always on the move and looking for adventure like his Uncle Wiley Morgan. At sixteen Ola, attractive with long dark hair, drew interest from boys, but like her brother John, she remained shy. Her brothers liked to tease her, sometimes even roping and tying her while she rode a horse, but they were also protective of their little sister. As the youngest and the only daughter, even as an adult Ola always remained Jeff's "Baby," and neighbors knew her as a sweet young woman who always had a smile on her face and a kind word for everyone. She accompanied her grandmother to church services when the preacher made the trip to Klondyke and attended dances at the school with her brother Tom.[25]

In many respects, their lives remained like earlier generations of Powers who had lived in Kentucky, Arkansas, or Texas. Their home was a wooden cabin without access to electricity or indoor plumbing and, far from the entertainments offered in the Gila Valley, they amused themselves after a long day of tiring physical labor. In the evenings Ola played her fiddle and John strummed his guitar, while Tom turned backflips on a bench. The family often played pitch, a popular card game, in the candlelight, and occasionally entertained the Morgans and the few neighbors who happened to make the long trip to Garden Place. And it was not just Jeff's immediate family members who continued to live in the same

Charles Power was the oldest of Jeff and Mattie's four children.
This photo was taken in Klondyke not long before
he left his family to return to New Mexico.
Courtesy the Ryder Ridgway Collection, held by Maxine Bean.

manner as prior generations of Powers. In the early 1910s Jeff's aunt Elizabeth
Power Scott, the youngest sister of his father, Sam Power, was still living in a
log cabin with her husband, homesteading in rural western Idaho. Altercations
with neighbors may have driven Jeff and Jane's family far from civilization into
Rattlesnake Canyon, but the family also had a deep affection for a simpler way of
life that could still be found in a few remaining corners of the western frontier.[26]

Relatives and neighbors in the region shared the same rustic life. The Morgan
ranch, the I Bar I, was headquartered in Klondyke, so Wiley's sons George,

John Power on his horse, Maud, taken at Klondyke in 1914.
Courtesy the Ryder Ridgway Collection, held by Maxine Bean.

Burt, and young Wiley Jr. ran their cattle on the open range of the eastern and western slopes of the Galiuros, where their cousins the Power boys often joined them. Tom Power and George Morgan were especially close friends. Their Uncle Will Morgan, his wife, Ida, and their sons, Joe and yet another boy named Wiley, also lived nearby, in Redfield Canyon. On special occasions, like July Fourth celebrations, the families would all get together at the I Bar I for roast beef barbecue and lemonade in the shade of the trees.[27] Aravaipa pioneers the Salazars were also part of their circle of friends, and son Guadalupe (Lupe), who was just a year younger than John Power, often rode the range with the Morgan and Power men.

Tom Power (left) and his cousin George Morgan, the son of
Wiley and Amanda Morgan, often herded cattle together.
Courtesy the Ryder Ridgway Collection, held by Maxine Bean.

Beyond the immediate family, the Powers found a handful of friends with
similar backgrounds living in the canyon. The Habys ran a goat ranch about
twelve miles north of Garden Place, where the Aravaipa and Rattlesnake creeks
converge. Like the Powers, the Habys came from the Hill Country of Texas.
Though born in America, both Gregor Haby (known as Gregory) and his wife,
Mary Ann, were the offspring of German parents and spoke English with heavy
German accents. The Powers were frequent visitors to their home, because the
Haby place was on the way to Klondyke, located on the last stretch of relatively
level terrain before entering the canyon. Early automobiles could not drive up
the steep inclines in Rattlesnake Canyon without flooding a carburetor, so when
the Powers bought a Model T they left it parked at the Habys and then rode
horseback the rest of the way home. Mary Ann Haby was almost like a mother
to young Ola, teaching her things that her own mother would have taught her
if she had lived, and Ola spent weeks at a time at the Haby ranch.[28]

A few years after the Powers moved to Rattlesnake Canyon, the Bleak family
bought a goat ranch in Fourmile Canyon north of Garden Place, where they
recycled abandoned mining equipment to construct their home, even managing
to turn an old boiler into a fireplace. The Powers and Bleaks had known each other

since the early 1890s, when the Bleak children attended school with the Power children in Gila, New Mexico. Joe and Esther Bleak were part of the small local LDS community, and their son Joe Bleak later recalled that "Tom was almost like a brother to me." There were rumors of a romance between young Tom Power and Mary, the youngest of the Bleak children, but she ended up marrying a member of a more prominent local family, the Wootans.[29]

Among those who knew them well, including the Bleaks, Habys, and Salazars, the Powers were viewed as kind, honest, generous folks, but they always remained outsiders in the larger community because they rarely attended the numerous barbecues and picnics. As Merrel Haby put it, the Power brothers "were pretty good boys. They were never any hands to mix much with anyone." The Power women attended some of the gatherings held in the canyon, but the men, except for young Tom, were not as sociable as most others in Aravaipa and stayed primarily to themselves. They did not join the local cattlemen's association, even though Wiley Morgan was a founding member, and remained uninvolved in local politics. Even as Jeff's children came of age, each failed to register to vote.[30]

Perhaps because of their asocial behavior, the Power men seemed odd to locals. As one neighbor observed when the Powers first arrived, "They were mighty suspicious of any strange track or sign; regardless of what they were doing—hunting, punching cows or prospecting—they would drop everything to trail a strange horse or to check some hunter to find out who he was and where he was from." Given their past problems with men like Tom Lyons, Jim Gould, and Wayne Brazel, their caution was understandable, but those were episodes the Powers discussed with no one. Most locals who were outside of their close-knit social circle were wary of the Powers, believing they were different, somehow more rough around the edges, and some folks even speculated that they were fleeing the law or rustling cattle. "They pretty soon give out the notion that they wasn't to be fooled with," according to a rancher from Bonita. "Now, that didn't sit too well with some folks hereabouts. . . . The Powers wasn't sociable; they wanted to stay to themselves, and right away people said there must be something wrong with them. So they made up stories about what kind a people the Powers was," and as events would unfold, those stories often were unkind.[31]

The Power family also encountered the Wootans, arguably the largest and most powerful family in Aravaipa at the time. One local resident recalled, "all you had to do was shake a tree and a Wootan would fall out." William E. Wootan Jr., more commonly known as "Black Bill," moved to Arizona in 1887, pushed out by hard times in Llano County, Texas. He was just a few years older than

Jeff Power, and both men had been born and raised in the Hill Country during the same turbulent years, but came away with very different views of military service. Unlike Jeff Power's father, who had avoided conscription, Wootan's father had served in a frontier regiment during the Civil War, tasked with policing outlaw and Indian depredations. Wootan was one of eight children, and after his marriage to Sarah Chapman he would become the father of eleven children of his own, many of whom would marry into the local families in Aravaipa. By the time the Power family arrived in the canyon, it certainly would have appeared to an outsider that a Wootan, or a member of the extended family, was everywhere in the small community.[32]

Upon his arrival in Aravaipa, Black Bill Wootan initially went to work for Dan Ming and other pioneer ranchers, and quickly began to build his own herd. As an early settler, he homesteaded choice pieces of land and became a respected member of the canyon community. His oldest son, Joseph Frank (who went by "J. Frank"), was born in Llano County in 1876 and arguably became the most influential of the Wootan clan as he grew into manhood. An imposing figure at six feet, three inches, J. Frank served in numerous local political capacities in addition to running his cattle ranch—election judge, deputy assessor, deputy recorder, justice of the peace, and deputy sheriff. As the Powers were settling into Aravaipa, he won the Democratic primary for representative to the county board of supervisors. Despite losing in the general election, he continued to participate in local politics, serving on the Democratic Central Committee for Graham County, as well as reporting the Aravaipa news for the local newspaper, the *Graham Guardian*. When J. Frank and his wife, Millie, celebrated their silver wedding anniversary at their home in the summer of 1912, almost all the leading ranchers in the community were invited, including Wiley Morgan. The unsociable Powers, however, were not among the attendees.[33]

Although the Wootans were socially, politically, and economically prominent, they also had their fair share of differences with neighbors and other family members. In 1908 Black Bill Wootan sued his wife, Sarah, for divorce, claiming she had deserted him, and in 1913, just after he was appointed deputy U.S. marshal, he was shot in the face during an angry exchange with a neighbor. Black Bill's son, J. Frank Wootan, was involved in protracted litigation with a neighbor over water rights on their property, and there was even a legal battle with other Klondyke residents over where the Klondyke school would be built. Another son, William Lee "Braz," was known as a "veritable slave driver" among his hired hands, a man who would not even grant them a day off when they married. While they wielded considerable influence in the region, the Wootans, like most families in cattle country, occasionally had contentious relations with their neighbors and even with other members of their family.[34]

Thomas Kane Wootan was born in 1882 in Llano County, Texas, the fourth child born to Black Bill and Sarah Wootan. Kane was an expert cowboy who loved to perform in rodeos and often won prizes, but seemed to spend more money than he made in the cattle business. By all accounts, Kane was a loving husband to his wife, Laura, and to his four daughters, but perhaps too indulgent. According to family members he was a pushover and doted on his girls, buying toys, clothing, and candy for them, and as his family grew and cattle prices dropped, debts to local merchants piled up.[35] By the early 1910s Kane Wootan increasingly used his herd for collateral for loans from local banks and family members to pay his bills. He was forced to sell or mortgage much of the land he owned and took salaried positions to supplement his meager income as a rancher. He served as a livestock inspector and as ranger deputy sheriff for Aravaipa from 1913 to 1915, and although those low paying jobs did little to staunch the flow of red ink in his personal accounts, they gave Wootan entree to the field of law enforcement and allowed him the opportunity to work with another lawman patrolling Aravaipa: a man with a very different background, Robert Franklin McBride, who was part of the community of Latter-day Saints living in the Gila Valley of Graham County.[36]

6

THE GILA VALLEY

One of Graham County's boys

The Gila Valley, where Deputy Frank McBride lived with his wife and seven children, was a far different place from Aravaipa Canyon, where he and Kane Wootan patrolled for outlaws. While the ranchers and miners in the mountains lived in rudimentary cabins, the folks living in settlements along the Gila River were far more likely to be farmers who had access to modern conveniences like telephone lines and indoor plumbing. In February 1914 electric lights illuminated Safford, the largest town in the valley, for the first time. In the towns along the riverbank there were banks and stores, and residents could enjoy the new motion picture theater and roller rink as well as vaudeville shows and circuses when they came to Safford.[1]

Much had changed since the late 1870s when Frank McBride first arrived in the Gila Valley as an infant with his parents, Peter and Ruth Burns McBride. Then the region was just an outpost occupied by a mixture of farming families and merchants, mostly from southern states or Mexico, with a sprinkling of outlaws. The early small villages of the valley, like Safford and Solomonville, consisted of a handful of adobe homes, a grist mill, a few stores, and stockyards for the protection of livestock against Apaches, as well as those staples of frontier towns, saloons and brothels. Brigham Young, the leader of the Latter-day Saints, had instructed William Flake to find new land where Mormons could take up a mission on the Arizona frontier, part of a larger effort by the church to establish a string of LDS communities from Idaho to Mexico. Families like the McBrides made the difficult journey from Salt Lake City into Arizona, settling originally either along the Salt River in Maricopa County in central Arizona or, as in the McBrides' case, along the Little Colorado River in Apache County in eastern Arizona. Many of the early Mormon communities did not last long, however, because the Little Colorado flooded and washed away fields in some years, while in others it lacked sufficient water for cultivation. After a few unsuccessful harvests, the McBrides joined other LDS settlers further south in a new community, Smithville, in the Gila Valley of Graham County.[2]

In 1879, an expedition of Saints had scouted the Gila Valley for Mormon settlement, deeming it a more promising location, considering that the Gila River was larger and had a more regular flow than the Little Colorado. Smithville, later renamed Pima, grew slowly, and one settler recalled it was just a "mesquite wilderness with a few houses built of cottonwood logs" in the early years when the McBrides first arrived. Settlers lived in tents or wagons until their homes were built and worked together as a community to construct irrigation canals, which required clearing away the masses of mesquite thickets from the banks of the Gila—a task at which Frank McBride spent many hours as a child. Food was scarce in those early years and disease, especially malaria, was common. Because the colony was located in Apacheria, LDS minutemen were constantly on guard for attacks.[3]

Two practices brought by Mormon settlers to Arizona, communalism and plural marriage, caused tensions with non-Mormons. Some Mormon families voluntarily embraced the United Order of Enoch, envisioned by Latter-day Saint church founder Joseph Smith Jr. as a way to unify "a people fragmented by their individualistic search for economic well-being." Members believed all possessions, both personal and real property, belonged to the Lord, and voluntarily deeded them over to a bishop of the LDS church. Mormon leaders justified plural marriage, an even more controversial tenet of the church than communalism, because it was practiced in the Old Testament, but many Gentiles considered it, along with slavery, to be one of the twin relics of barbarism.[4]

In Utah and eastern Arizona the Saints had experienced hostility from non-Mormons over polygamy and the United Order communities, which, along with frequent criticism of federal authority by church leaders, placed them outside of mainstream American politics and religion. Resistance to Mormon settlers and their unusual practices in the Gila Valley, however, was initially less evident. Local Gentiles praised the Mormon newcomers for their work ethic and willingness to uphold the laws, noting their communities acted as buffers against outlaws and Indian attacks. Perhaps there was less opposition because the Latter-day Saints who joined the Protestants, Catholics, and Jews already living along the Gila River were a small minority of the county's total population, constituting only 11 percent of Graham County voters.[5]

Another reason Mormons were welcomed by non-Mormons in the Gila Valley was that only a few remained isolated in United Order communities, while a majority were forced by circumstances to integrate themselves into the larger economy of the county. In the 1870s and 1880s Arizona's main industry was mining, but ranchers and freighters were also needed to feed the territory's miners and soldiers and to transport food and supplies. LDS church leaders discouraged their followers from engaging in those three industries and instead encouraged them to pursue agriculture. But it was difficult to find good farmland in Arizona's arid climate, so to survive, Saints in Graham County often took jobs as cowboys or freighters, and even occasionally found employment in the mines around Clifton or Globe in neighboring Gila County.[6]

Graham County's non-Mormon residents may have been tolerant of the practices of plural marriage among Mormons, but the federal government was not. Although officials in Washington, D.C., attempted to halt polygamy as early as the Civil War, it was not until 1882 that members of Congress passed the Edmunds Act, which declared polygamy a felony, and federal efforts to enforce the law began in earnest. Initially, LDS leaders in Utah defied the federal government's efforts to ban plural marriage, invoking their constitutionally protected right to religious freedom. LDS president John Taylor refused to back down from his proclamation that "polygamy is a divine institution. It has been handed down direct from God. The United States cannot abolish it. No nation on earth can prevent it, nor all the nations of the earth." Their defiance exacerbated relations with the federal government, and Taylor assumed more control of Mormon communities in outlying areas so the church could offer protection to Saints fleeing prosecution in Utah.[7]

In February 1883, Christopher Layton was sent by the church to the Gila Valley to establish the St. Joseph Stake, with its boundary extending south into Mexico to allow its members to flee over the border if necessary while remaining within the purview of the church. Layton, chosen stake president, acknowledged that the Gila Valley's location close to the border with Mexico would provide a haven for polygamists like himself fleeing Utah, noting, "my wives and children agreed that, although they disliked very much to be without my presence, they would rather know that I was at liberty" in southern Arizona "than have me dodging the hands of the law." Until then Pima and other LDS communities in the Gila Valley like Thatcher, Smithville, and Matthewsville had received minimal attention from church leaders in Salt Lake City, but all that changed quickly as the remote outpost became a sanctuary for polygamists.[8]

As increasing numbers of polygamists entered Arizona, Gentile residents raised a storm of protest. In Tucson, the territory's largest city, newspaper publishers Louis C. and Josephine Brawley Hughes launched a vicious campaign against Mormons, and in 1885, under public pressure, the territorial legislature instituted a test oath, which stripped citizens of their voting rights if they belonged to an order or sect that taught plural marriage. Arizona Governor Lewis Wolfley reported to Congress that the Mormons were an "unwelcome and dangerous element" in Arizona society, while a newspaper in eastern Arizona editorialized: "the Mormon disease is a desperate one and the rope and gun is the only cure. . . . Don't let them settle on any more of our land. . . . Down with them. Grind out their very existence." Many prominent polygamist leaders were imprisoned, forced into hiding, or opted to move to Mexico.[9]

In 1882, just as the federal government began escalating its war on polygamy, Frank McBride's father, Peter, took a second wife, Laura Lewis. As anti-Mormon sentiment hit fever pitch in Arizona in 1884, LDS President Taylor instructed Layton to move the polygamist inhabitants of the St. Joseph stake, like Peter McBride, into Mexico. It was at this time that young Frank McBride, age nine, began to keep a diary of the tumult experienced by his family. His father left for the Carrolitos Valley, in the state of Chihuahua, Mexico, with his new wife, whom Frank called "Aunt Laura," and their infant daughter, but because there was disharmony between Peter's two wives, Frank's mother, Ruth, stayed behind in Pima to care for their four children. The anguish caused by the separation from his father is evident in Frank's diary entries, but he found some comfort in what he heard from church leaders: that the disruption to his family was necessary to keep his father "safe from the power of his enemies," the federal government. In 1885 the McBride wives switched places, with Laura and her daughter returning to Arizona and Ruth and her children traveling to join Peter McBride in Mexico. Frank was overjoyed by the reunion with his father. When anti-Mormon feelings dissipated somewhat after the 1894 election of Democratic President Grover Cleveland, who backed away from the strident anti-Mormon rhetoric of the previous Republican administration, the McBrides and other polygamist families hiding in Mexico returned to the Gila Valley, but Frank would never forget that dark period of his life when his family was separated.[10]

Although tensions were reduced, the polygamy battle had driven a wedge of distrust between Mormons and non-Mormons in Graham County, as the LDS church in Utah now became more involved with the direction of local church activities. Harmony was further eroded when a brazen robbery took place in the Gila Valley in 1889. Highwaymen ambushed a United States Army wagon train carrying over $28,000 in payroll as it traveled outside of Frank McBride's hometown of Pima, at a pass called Bloody Run. Eight soldiers were injured defending the wagon, and the bandits made off with the payroll. Named for the paymaster in charge, the Wham payroll robbery stunned and divided the Gila Valley where Frank McBride lived. The federal marshal arrested seven men, six of whom were either Latter-day Saints or belonged to families who were prominent church members. Among them was Gilbert Webb, believed to be the ringleader who orchestrated and carried out the theft, and his son Wilfred, who was Frank McBride's uncle.[11]

While St. Joseph Stake president Christopher Layton admonished the Saints to cooperate with the federal investigation into the robbery, many church members defied officials and refused, silently rejoicing at the attack on the federal government that had persecuted them for their religious practices. They had been forced to "lie for the Lord" so often over the years to protect themselves from prosecution for plural marriage that federal authorities found few witnesses among the LDS population who would come forward to testify for the government's case. The primary non-Mormon witnesses were the soldiers who came under attack during the robbery, most of whom were African American. Although they provided credible testimony against the defendants, racist attitudes prevailed and their evidence was not believed. A jury found the seven defendants not guilty.[12]

The Wham payroll was never recovered. For years it was rumored to be buried in a chicken coop owned by one of the defendants, used to pay defense attorneys and to finance a few ranching operations in Graham County, including Wilfred Webb's 76 Ranch. Even after the trial's conclusion, bold stagecoach robberies continued in the Gila Valley. Federal authorities once again investigated Wilfred Webb, as well as his brother-in-law, Jacob Burns, who was also Frank McBride's uncle. Webb and Burns, both employees of the U.S. Postal Service, were suspected of passing on information they gleaned in the mail to the thieves. One resident of the Gila Valley recalled that "businessmen between Globe and Willcox were so fearful of the Webb gang that they refused to ship money on the regular stage coach runs" during the early 1890s. Although United States Marshal W. K. Meade was convinced that Webb and Burns had organized the mail theft in 1894, he could not find witnesses willing to testify against them or sufficient evidence to charge them.[13]

Frank McBride was raised in a family that rebelled against the laws of the federal government, and in a community that not only tolerated such behavior, but also applauded it. His father continued to live openly and without repercussions with his two wives, who bore him children long after the federal government outlawed polygamy and the LDS church denounced its practice. Because of his connection to the Wham and stage robberies, McBride's Uncle Wilfred Webb became something of a folk hero among the Mormons of the Gila Valley. As one resident put it, "anyone who could rob the U.S. Government and get away with it deserved some recognition." Webb himself always remained evasive about his participation in the robberies, only replying when asked: "'I neither affirm nor deny, but the United States Courts acquitted me." Yet voters elected him to the territorial house as a Graham County representative in 1903, and reelected him in 1905, when he was chosen house speaker by his peers. Webb was selected by his constituents as a delegate to the state constitutional convention in 1910, and remained a powerful force in politics in the Gila Valley as his nephew Frank McBride launched his own political career.[14]

Given his family history, it is tempting to assume that Frank McBride was a foe of the federal government that had persecuted his relatives, but that could not be further from the truth, as he would pursue a career in politics and law enforcement. It could also be argued that McBride chose that path to cleanse his family's reputation, but it is also likely those experiences convinced him that opposing the federal government was wrongheaded, especially considering that he came of age at a time when his church was seeking ways to prove its loyalty to the nation. The transition began in 1890, when LDS church president Wilford Woodruff, seeking statehood for Utah, dismantled church policies that had caused so much friction with the federal government. He issued an official church manifesto, which outlawed the practice of plural marriage within the church, and what few United Order colonies remained were disbanded as well. State and federal prohibitions on voting and office holding by polygamists were lifted and Mormons filled the registration rolls of the Democratic Party, which had been more tolerant of Mormon practices than the Republicans. When Utah finally attained statehood in 1896, church leaders realized they had entered a grand bargain with the United States, promising to uphold its laws. In many ways the hierarchical LDS church had "contradicted individualistic and independent strains in other Americans," most notably the dominant Protestants. To combat negative criticism, church leaders began to instruct rank-and-file members to be patriotic citizens. Historian Thomas W. Simpson argues that as Mormon life increasingly intersected with non-Mormon life, Latter-day Saints "would undergo a radical transformation of consciousness and identity. They would fall in love with America again. Outsiders became insiders; those on the margins entered the mainstream." As he reached adulthood, Frank McBride clearly embraced the new Mormon identity, demonstrating a profound loyalty to his country and respect for law and order.[15]

McBride did not initially choose law enforcement as a career, because it was an occupation field long dominated by non-Mormons in Arizona. Most Mormons were raised to be farmers, while sheriffs and their deputies were usually chosen from the ranks of ranchers and military veterans, men who had many years of experience in the saddle tracking outlaws. Rather, McBride ended up in law enforcement only after trying many other, more traditional career paths occupied by members of his church. Along the way he benefited from his community's emphasis on education, which, in turn, allowed him to excel in future endeavors. He attended the local grade school in Pima, and even received a year of secondary education at the St. Joseph Stake Academy, an unusually good education for a boy on the frontier. His father, a Scottish immigrant, was an educated man who taught music and was involved in Sunday school and, as an adult, Frank too devoted much of his time to his religious duties and music, becoming an adept public speaker and singer. His education, the ease he demonstrated in public settings, and his piety would all provide him advantages in the Gila Valley.[16]

Although Frank McBride was raised in a family of farmers, he preferred riding horses to raising alfalfa. After his 1899 marriage to Clara Sims, a lavish affair with over two hundred guests, he and his brother Howard borrowed money and invested in a small ranch, running about seventy-five head of cattle. But like many small operations his ranch failed, and in 1901 most of his cattle were sold by the county to pay back taxes. He spent the next two and a half years in San Antonio, Texas, fulfilling his missionary requirement for the church, and when he returned to the Gila Valley he took a variety of odd jobs, including working as a cowboy and a carpenter, as well as freighting in Globe, where the Roosevelt Dam was under construction. When he returned to Pima in 1904, he got his first taste of law enforcement by serving as a town constable. Around 1908 or 1909 McBride took a job as a foreman for a cattle company in Fairview in the Gila Valley, a position he initially coveted, but his perception of cattle ranching was quickly shattered. McBride was uncomfortable with the "chicanery going on in most cattle companies in those days," according to his son Darvil, because he "was always interested in upholding the law," and he quit after only a short time in the job.[17]

His Uncle Wilfred Webb likely helped Frank obtain his next position and first political appointment: a clerkship in the territorial legislature during the 1907 and 1909 sessions. McBride arrived at the capitol at a critical period, when local politicians were focused on obtaining statehood. Arizona's overtures to Congress had been turned down repeatedly under the advice of Senator Albert J. Beveridge of Indiana, chairman of the Committee on Territories. After a visit to Arizona in 1902 Beveridge and fellow committee members rejected the possibility of the territory joining the Union, because in their estimation there were too many inhabitants who spoke only Spanish, could neither read nor write, and spent day and night in the saloons, brothels, and gaming halls of mining towns. To counteract Arizona's negative image in Congress, progressives began agitating for a wide range of reform legislation, which included bills that outlawed vice, hoping to change the committee's opinion of Arizona's population.[18]

Progressives were comprised mostly of middle class, Protestant, educated reformers who believed a stronger central government was needed to guide human progress and was preferable to individualism, which was prone to be "'unsafe in politics and unsound in morals.'" Although an earlier generation of progressives, like newspaper publishers Louis C. and Josephine Brawley Hughes, had campaigned against Mormons, a new generation was coming of age that realized the efficacy of working with the Latter-day Saints on issues they had in common. Many of the goals of progressives—including granting women the vote, as well as outlawing liquor consumption, prostitution, and gambling—dovetailed with goals of the Mormon Church. The popularity of these reforms among the general population allowed Mormons to assert newfound authority and leadership in state and local politics that was previously beyond their grasp.[19]

The political reform issue that intrigued Frank McBride the most was prohibition of liquor. The temperance movement was the greatest social movement of the second half of the nineteenth century in the United States, as unbridled alcohol consumption adversely impacted not only families, but also hurt businesses when employees had accidents on the job or missed work. In 1901 the first local option law, which gave voters a tool to close saloons in their own communities, was passed by Arizona legislators, largely through the influence of the Mormon church. Over the following few years, many local option law elections were held, with mixed results. In urban areas and mining towns saloons remained opened, but in the small towns dominated by Mormons the "drys" prevailed.[20]

In the Gila Valley, the Mormon communities of Thatcher, Pima, Central, Layton, Hubbard, and Matthewsville all outlawed liquor by 1905. Only Eden and

Safford, two towns with somewhat larger non-Mormon populations, remained wet, because the law required the support of two-thirds of the voters. With the assistance of clerk Frank McBride, Representative W. W. Pace of Graham County, a Democrat and a member of the LDS church, ushered a bill through the legislature in 1909 allowing municipalities and local districts to go dry by a simple majority vote. After the Pace Bill went into effect in 1910, all of the communities in the Gila Valley voted to end alcohol consumption. The sole surviving saloon in the county was Wiley Morgan's in Klondyke, and even he came under pressure from prohibition forces. During the July Fourth barbecue celebration that year, normally a day of riotous drinking in Klondyke, Morgan's saloon was closed, and as the *Graham Guardian* correspondent reported, "we had no liquor or drunkards on the grounds and everything went smoothly."[21]

Taking advantage of the popularity of prohibition among Gila Valley voters and his role in passing the Pace bill, in September 1911 McBride announced his candidacy for sheriff of Graham County on the Democratic ticket. His choice of office was surprising, since his only prior experience in law enforcement was limited to a short stint as town constable, not the usual credentials for the office of sheriff, which, as historian Larry Ball has noted, "constituted a great prize on the southwestern frontier." McBride's own campaign notice underscored the fact that he had little experience: "Everybody in Graham county knows Frank well; knows his ability and integrity; they also know the kind of officer he would be. He is one of Graham county's boys . . . one upon whom the party could always rely to fight for its principles, and a man who has demonstrated that he is capable of becoming a good officer." Under normal circumstances candidate William T. Johnson, a rancher who had served as a lawman for years in Graham County and volunteered during the Spanish-American War, would have been considered the best-qualified candidate for sheriff, but 1911 was not a normal election year in Graham County.[22]

That year the electorate in Graham County was transformed almost overnight when the legislature created Greenlee County, carved out of the eastern portion of the county. Graham County lost its most populous city, Clifton, where approximately 50 percent of voters resided. With the mining population removed from the electorate, the Mormons of the Gila Valley became the largest bloc of voters in what remained of Graham County, and all assumptions about who was best qualified to be sheriff were renegotiated. John Birdno, the LDS publisher of the *Graham Guardian* and the chair of the Graham County Democratic Committee, was anxious to see a Mormon sheriff elected. In prior election years, rancher William Johnson would have been the favorite among the miners of Clifton, but he was a former saloon owner, and with the Mormon electorate ascendant in 1911, he finished last in the three-man primary race. The contest was much closer between the two Mormon candidates, who had both pledged to uphold the prohibition law: Frank McBride and Thomas Alger. Alger had held no prior elective office and never served in law enforcement or the military, but his grandparents and father were among the first baptisms conducted in the Church of Jesus Christ of Latter-day Saints in 1830, and his parents were married by LDS church founder Joseph Smith Jr. himself. It was these qualities that appealed to a majority of Democratic voters, and Alger narrowly beat out Frank McBride in the primary and went on to win office in the general election.[23]

The defeat did not deter McBride and, in fact, likely inspired him to enhance his law enforcement credentials for a future run for the sheriff's office. In 1912 he was named an inspector by the Livestock Sanitary Board, a commission that registered brands and enforced livestock laws, and McBride joined fellow inspector Wiley Morgan on patrol in Aravaipa. In January 1913 the county board of supervisors appointed McBride as ranger deputy, a newly created position established at the request of the local cattlemen's association to patrol for cattle rustlers in Aravaipa. Traditionally, sheriffs appointed deputies who reflected the make-up of the local population, and in Aravaipa that would have meant a rancher from a southern state or Mexico. However, an emboldened LDS-dominated board of supervisors and the new Mormon sheriff, Tom Alger, saw fit to appoint a man whose culture and religion were alien to most canyon inhabitants. For the first time, a Mormon deputy was on duty in Aravaipa.[24]

Distance and poor roads had left the two regions disconnected, but cultural values also separated the miners and ranchers of Aravaipa from the Mormons of the Gila Valley. When Deputy McBride first traveled to Aravaipa, no church had yet been dedicated, which shocked Mormons in the Gila Valley. LDS newspaper editor John Birdno proclaimed, "Just think! Here in the United States, in the State of Arizona, in the county of Graham, was a community where marriages were performed, children born and grew to manhood and womanhood who never attended a church service or Sunday school. There are few places among the so-called heathen lands, where the foreign missionary has not reached them." Of course, priests and ministers had visited Aravaipa for years, baptizing babies, marrying couples, and holding worship services, yet because no permanent church was established until 1915, canyon residents were viewed as heathens by many Mormons in the valley.[25]

More important to Deputy McBride, Aravaipa, with three wet-voting precincts, remained the last holdout in the prohibition campaign in Graham County.
In the fall of 1913 McBride made his first trip into Aravaipa, where he worked
ostensibly with the new livestock inspector who had replaced Wiley Morgan,
local resident Kane Wootan, to locate a horse thief, but it soon became clear
McBride's real agenda was to investigate Wiley Morgan's saloon in Klondyke.
According to one of McBride's offspring, "Dad hated the use of alcohol and
the destructive effects it had upon marriages, family and individuals," and he
took "personal satisfaction" in arresting those who violated the law. The newly
appointed deputy soon discovered, probably from his colleague Wootan, that
Morgan was serving liquor to minors under the age of twenty-one. Wootan's
younger brother Richard, age seventeen, had been drinking at Morgan's saloon the
prior New Year's Eve with his friend, who was nineteen. McBride also ascertained
Morgan's thirteen-year-old son, Wiley Jr., had been in the saloon that night.
McBride arrested Morgan for allowing underage drinking and for permitting a
minor under the age of sixteen into his establishment. McBride escorted Morgan
to the county courthouse in the Gila Valley, where the saloon owner pled guilty
to the misdemeanor offenses and paid his fines.[26]

Wiley Morgan's arrest by McBride had a profound impact on local politics.
In the fall of 1913 a local option election was held in the remaining wet precincts
in Aravaipa: Klondyke, Bonita, and Stanley Butte. In the 1912 general election,
Arizona's male voters had granted the right to vote to women, so the local prohibition measure on the ballot the following year generated tremendous interest
among newly enfranchised women. Jane Power, Wiley Morgan's wife, Amanda,
and many other women in Aravaipa made the long trip down into the Gila
Valley to register to vote and then cast their ballots in the fall election. Even Jeff
Power, a man usually indifferent to politics, registered to vote in the prohibition
election.[27] In the Bonita and Stanley Butte precincts, voters split over the issue,
but in Klondyke prohibition forces scored a decisive victory, 37 votes to 5. The
local newspaper noted, "the prohibitionists were helped considerable in securing
signers to the petition for a prohibition election in those three precincts by the
arrest and conviction of a saloonkeeper [Wiley Morgan] in Klondyke for selling
liquor to minors." Only eight years earlier a local newspaper had adopted quite
a different tone, suggesting the whizzing bullets and yelling emanating from
Morgan's Klondyke saloon were evidence of a vibrant local economy. Because
of the prohibition campaign launched by Mormons in the intervening years, his
business had become a disgrace to the community.[28]

Graham County was the first county in Arizona to go completely dry, a result that, according to the *Graham Guardian,* "was largely secured by the stand taken by the Mormon church in favor of prohibition and backed by the other denominations in the Valley." Although the inclusion of female voters for the first time was the more likely reason the Klondyke precinct voted to go dry, Frank McBride could point to his arrest of Wiley Morgan with pride and portray himself to voters as a crusading prohibitionist. The Mormon newspaper boasted, "Graham county not only leads as a prohibition county, but also as the cleanest and most moral county in the state, and should be an example in this respect of the other counties in the state."[29]

Deputy McBride continued to make frequent trips to Aravaipa over the next few years to bedevil bootleggers and arrest thieves, and although his primary function was to apprehend cattle rustlers, he also focused on the enforcement of the numerous game laws recently passed by the state legislature. Hunting seasons were imposed, licenses were required, and strict guidelines stipulated how game could be killed and butchered. McBride made "a special investigation of the conditions regarding hunters" and discovered that residents of Aravaipa were not complying. Most were descended from generations of hunters and continued to rely on game as a vital source of food for their tables, so unsurprisingly, they resisted the new regulations.[30]

McBride warned locals that he would "thoroughly enforce the state game laws in its entirety," but quickly wore out his welcome in Aravaipa, as residents began to question his bona fides as game warden and ranger deputy. After he spent Thanksgiving Day 1913 at his Uncle Wilfred Webb's 76 Ranch, McBride killed "a fine buck" on the way back home to Pima, "but only," the press chided, "after he had fired seventeen shots at it, which is some shooting for only one deer."[31] With so much of his time spent on hunting regulations and rooting out liquor law violators, evidently McBride had little time to tackle his primary duty of apprehending cattle rustlers. In the spring of 1914 members of the local cattlemen's association petitioned the board of supervisors to appoint an additional ranger deputy and, when they approved the position, Sheriff Alger appointed livestock inspector Kane Wootan.

McBride and Wootan worked together as ranger deputies over the next four years, but residents of Aravaipa clearly felt more comfortable with Wootan than with McBride. As one local reported in early 1915: "Kane is always on the go and . . . we all try to be good as we might be taken unawares." But when Frank McBride arrived in Klondyke searching for thieves, there were complaints about the lawman, whom canyon residents considered an outsider: "We wondered why

he came so far to look [for thieves], as we know of none in these parts." Perhaps
Aravaipa residents preferred Kane Wootan over Frank McBride because he was one
of their own and understood the mentality of ranching and mining people, while
McBride focused his energies on enforcing the escalating number of regulations
that most Aravaipa residents abhorred, leaving the impression he was trying to
turn their canyons into the stable, orderly communities found in the Gila Valley.[32]

Sheriff Tom Alger, likely sensing the discord, increasingly assigned McBride to
duties in the Gila Valley, where the energetic deputy would "let out a war whoop"
whenever he learned an arrest warrant was issued for a fugitive, and then gallop
off to capture the culprit. More time in the valley meant more time to spend
on politics. In 1914 McBride was appointed secretary-treasurer of the Graham
County Democratic Committee and campaigned for other Mormons seeking
office, pivotal steps in his pursuit of the sheriff's office. He then became involved
in a political campaign to relocate the county seat to Mormon-dominated Pima,
where he lived with his wife and growing family.[33]

The creation of Greenlee County and the resulting realignment in Graham
County politics raised awareness that the residents of Aravaipa Canyon and
the Gila Valley were out of step with one another. In 1914 James Quinn, the
superintendent of the Grand Reef Mine near Klondyke, won a seat on the county
board of supervisors campaigning on the notion that his portion of the county was
unrepresented in county government. He then spurred construction of a new road
that would connect the Gila Valley to Klondyke, and when completed, it reduced
the thirty-two-mile trip that once took two days by horse-drawn wagon to a few
hours in an automobile. The Aravaipa Road played a major role in linking isolated
Aravaipa to the Gila Valley and the outside world for the first time, allowing
canyon and valley residents to interact on a more regular basis. In March 1915, to
celebrate the road's completion, the Safford Chamber of Commerce proposed a
road race up into Klondyke from the Gila Valley. Billed the Sociability Run, the two
days of festivities were held ostensibly for Gila Valley residents to get "acquainted
with the people of the west side of the county," but were also designed to lobby
Aravaipa voters who would participate in an election to pick which city, Safford
or Pima, would become the new county seat. Mormons from Pima, including the
Frank McBride family, made the journey into Aravaipa to solicit votes.[34]

Sixteen cars filled with fifty-six people were, according to the local Mormon
press, welcomed "with open arms" by the people of Klondyke, who arrived from
their ranches on horseback and in wagons, buggies, and jalopies. Beef and goat
were barbecued by the men and "good things prepared by the ladies," including

cakes, pies, and ice cream. There were barrel races, goat and calf roping competitions, and Ranger Deputy Kane Wootan was a standout competitor, winning many of the prizes. A Latter-day Saints elder spoke to the crowd, explaining the doctrines of his church, followed by a supper at the Grand Reef Mine, with music and dancing until dawn.[35]

Deputy McBride's oldest child, Gladys, was about fourteen when she joined her family and other Mormons from Pima for the festivities, and it was clear from her perspective that the farmers from the Gila Valley and the ranchers and miners from Klondyke were different from one another. "I remember thinking that these country people all looked a little strange to me. They were people from the open cattle ranges and I recall one girl in particular. She stood off by herself leaning against a wagon wheel. Most of us farm community girls were dressed in outdoor clothes; gingham dresses. . . . This one girl stood there and she was all dressed up in a lace party-like dress. She had white shoes and stockings and a broad rimmed floppy hat with flowers on it. I kept looking at her and wondering what she was doing all dressed up like that. I noticed, too, that she didn't associate with anyone else." That girl was Ola May Power, who was twenty years old and likely wearing her mother's clothes from another century. Later in the day, while Gladys McBride was scooping ice cream cones for folks from Aravaipa, a "little old withered-up lady" kept returning for one cone after another. The woman was Ola's grandmother, Jane, who was unfamiliar with such delicacies and kept repeating, "'My this is good. We don't have anything like this in the canyon.'"[36]

Despite the success of the Sociability Run, the Mormons of Pima were unable to impress the residents of Aravaipa enough to win over their vote. The county seat was moved to Safford rather than Frank McBride's hometown of Pima, but that did not deter him in his pursuit of the sheriff's position. The following month McBride declared himself a challenger to incumbent sheriff Tom Alger. While he could point with pride to his record of bringing bootleggers, murderers, and cattle rustlers to justice, entering the race was a risky move and an affront to his boss. In his announcement McBride asserted: "During his term of office, Mr. McBride has worked in perfect harmony with his superior officer and has done his duty at all times to the best of his ability." Of course it was clear that period of "perfect harmony" was at an end. State law prohibited ranger deputies from being "perniciously active in politics," so Alger immediately requested the county board of supervisors to terminate McBride from his post, and his request was granted retroactively. Unfazed, McBride plunged headlong into his well-orchestrated campaign for sheriff.[37]

McBride's campaign material included a photo postcard of himself standing next to his horse, Big Boy, and emphasized his "good character and clean habits," his work in Aravaipa, where he was "called to duty at all times, day and night," and his life-long loyalty to the Democratic Party. Arizona voters had passed a statewide ban on alcohol consumption in 1914, and McBride reminded voters of his commitment to uphold that law, but he also darkly suggested that the "the lawless element" living in the county opposed his election. Mormons in his hometown of Pima turned out in force, and he was chosen the Democratic nominee over Alger. But the election demonstrated he was not well liked in Aravaipa: he received only one vote in the Klondyke precinct.[38]

In the general election in a Democratic-leaning county, McBride had no trouble defeating Republican Mormon candidate Brigham (Briggs) F. Stewart, but in the Klondyke precinct he only narrowly beat Stewart, 33 to 31 votes, far underperforming other Democratic candidates who won by much larger margins and further underscoring that McBride was not popular with Klondyke voters. After his election, McBride named fellow Latter-day Saint Martin Kempton his undersheriff. Kempton was an alfalfa farmer with no prior law enforcement experience, but local Mormon leaders asked McBride to appoint him because he had recently injured his foot when he accidentally discharged his rifle while hunting. Martin and his wife, Sena, had six children, and as he was unable to farm, he was in need of a steady income. Undersheriffs performed the bulk of the office work in the sheriff's department, something the invalid Kempton could tend to until he fully recovered from his injury and returned to farming.[39]

The sheriff-elect soon discovered that his ability to effectively police Graham County, especially in the remote canyons, was in jeopardy due to cost-cutting efforts. In 1916 the salaries for county officers were increased by the state legislature, so the county board of supervisors, under pressure from the Graham County Taxpayers Association to cut expenses elsewhere, refused to appoint anyone to the two deputy ranger positions in Aravaipa. The county budget cuts left Kane Wootan without his deputy job and A. G. Walker, the constable elected in the Klondyke precinct, as McBride's only officer in the Aravaipa region. McBride valued Wootan's abilities, so in the spring of 1917 he made him one of his honorary deputies, allowing Wootan to assist in select situations when McBride had room in his budget to hire extra men.[40]

The previous fall the livestock board had called for Wootan's resignation as inspector, so he no longer drew a salary from the county, and since he had sold all his property holdings in Aravaipa he had nothing to tie him to the canyon. Kane Wootan, his wife, Laura, and their four daughters pulled up stakes and moved to

Safford. Wootan had never enjoyed the cattle business or prospered at it in Aravaipa. His children could attend better schools in the Gila Valley and Laura was likely happy to trade the arduous chores required of a ranch wife for the modern conveniences of town living.[41] By forsaking his canyon roots for the valley, Kane placed distance between himself and former friends, and as events unfolded, it appears his move may have adversely affected his reputation among the folks in Aravaipa who were suspicious of his cooperation with the Mormon sheriff, Frank McBride.

When he assumed office in January 1917, McBride immediately made good on his promise to voters to enforce prohibition, using a large portion of his budget to hire private detectives to track down bootleggers. The Graham County sheriff had pledged vigilance in "ferreting out the violators of the prohibition law," so local newspapers were full of stories about the exploits of McBride and his undersheriff, Martin Kempton, as they made "it extremely unhealthy for bootleggers in this county." He worked closely with county attorney William R. Chambers and Justice of the Peace Ulysses I. Paxton, who both shared his eagerness to prosecute violators. In March 1917 McBride spent time working with Constable Walker in Klondyke, apprehending bootleggers and investigating on a murder case involving men who were bringing wet goods in from Lordsburg. According to the *Graham Guardian*, the rash of arrests made by McBride put the residents of the canyon on notice "that these law-breakers are not heroes."[42]

Although improved roads allowed Sheriff McBride to get around his far-flung jurisdiction quickly in an automobile, they also allowed bootleggers and thieves to make getaways across county lines. One day McBride saw three men driving a car that seemed to him to be too heavily loaded. He commandeered a passing vehicle and followed the suspects toward Globe, and when they tried to elude him, he shot under the car. After the suspects fled on foot, McBride found guns and twenty cases of whiskey stashed in their abandoned automobile. Bootlegging was not the only problem that increased with the availability of automobiles. A rash of burglaries occurred in which safecrackers, or "yeggmen," as they were called, used nitroglycerine to blow up the safes of merchants in the Gila Valley and made off with thousands of dollars' worth of cash and merchandise in their vehicles. McBride and his deputy, Martin Kempton, were kept busy the winter and spring of 1917 with all the criminal activity, and the sheriff had to ask the county board of supervisors to dramatically increase his budget to hire more part-time deputies like Kane Wootan to assist with the workload.[43]

Just after he took office, the new sheriff was forced to travel to the canyon to arrest a mother and son team of cattle rustlers, and to investigate the murder of a bootlegger just west of where the Power family lived. While there, McBride helped John Power recover some equipment from neighbor Jeff Clayton, who had failed to make good on his promise to pay for the items. From his work as both livestock inspector and deputy, McBride knew the Power family living in Rattlesnake Canyon, and he had not formed a positive impression of the men, calling the brothers "rough-neck cowboys" and their father, Jeff, "rabble." But the sheriff told his family that he felt sorry for Ola Power, who lived "up there, way in the top of the mountains" with her grandmother as her only female companion. McBride knew Ola led a difficult life far from civilization and understood how fortunate his own children were to live in the Gila Valley close to schools and church services, but during that visit in January 1917 he must have realized just how difficult the young woman's situation had become in recent years.[44]

7

THE ABANDONED MINES

A mine is a hole in the ground with a liar at the top.

Jeff Power's obsession with gold began in the summer of 1911 as the Powers were just settling into their new accommodations at Garden Place. His closest neighbors in Rattlesnake Canyon, the Murdocks and Ed Knothe, were prospectors who believed in the promise of the local mining district, and an article published in the *Bisbee Daily Review* confirmed their suspicions. A mineral expert had ventured into Rattlesnake Canyon and traveled extensively with forest ranger Lee Kirby, noting the region "had been but slightly prospected. . . . It might be well for prospectors to look it over again." The suggestion that Gold Mountain and the Abandoned Mine Basin, located just a few miles to the south of the Power property, had unrealized potential clearly intrigued Jeff Power, who was still struggling to make a living raising cattle.[1]

Not long after the article appeared, Commodore Perry Tucker, who held claims in the Abandoned Mine Basin of which the mining expert had spoken so highly, approached Jeff Power while he was working with his sons on Jane's garden. Tucker told Power he had been quarreling with his partner, Al Bauman, and wanted out of the mine, and he offered to sell Jeff his half of the Abandoned and Burro claims for twenty-five hundred dollars. Jeff did not have the money and turned down the deal, but his interest was piqued. The gold bug had bitten both Jeff and his middle son, John, and they started prospecting around Gold Mountain, filing new claims and purchasing less expensive established claims adjacent to the mines owned by Tucker and Bauman.[2]

The Abandoned Mine Basin claims were all located at the headwaters of a yet unnamed canyon that intersected with Rattlesnake Canyon just over two miles south of Gold Mountain. Danish rancher Emil Kielberg and his wife, Ida, had explored the canyon in the early 1900s and staked a few claims, but it was not until the 1930s that the canyon was officially named Kielberg Canyon.[3] The mines owned by Tucker and Bauman were originally claimed and then abandoned by George and James Branson around the turn of the century—the same men who staked the claim Charley Power bought at Garden Place in 1911. In December 1905, Al Bauman and Tom Casias reclaimed the several Branson mines they believed to have the most potential: the four Gold Reef claims, which were aptly renamed the Abandoned mines, and the Dead Horse Mine, which they called the Burro Mine.[4]

Bauman and his partners built a small cabin about one hundred yards from the mine opening and constructed an *arrastra* at the site, a rudimentary mill that allowed miners to hitch a mule, horse, or even a man, to a center post and walk around in a circle, dragging heavy stones to crush the ore. This slow, laborious method had been used for centuries to separate ore from rock, but in modern copper mining camps it was replaced by a stamp mill with an engine run by a boiler or electric power. There was no electricity or consistent water sources in the canyon, and the mines were over twenty miles from the nearest mechanized stamp mill, located at the Grand Reef Mine, and sixty-five miles from the nearest railroad station, in Willcox, so the arrastra had to suffice. Improving a gold mine requires capital, so Bauman turned to several investors, including Commodore Perry Tucker and Richard C. Elwood, for loans, and issued both men shares in the mine as collateral. Tucker promised Elwood, whose quarter share was valued at five hundred dollars, that he would try to find a buyer willing to purchase his share for twenty-five hundred dollars within the next two years. It was then, in 1911, that Tucker first tried to interest Jeff Power in the mine.[5]

According to an Old West adage often attributed to Mark Twain, "A gold mine is a hole in the ground with a liar standing on top of it." Prospectors often told exaggerated stories about a mine's potential, and occasionally even "salted" a mine with gold dust collected elsewhere to lure unsuspecting buyers. Some even planted stories in the local newspapers extolling the potential of a given mine, like the article that appeared in the *Bisbee Daily Review*. As later court testimony would suggest, Tucker was such a man, and Aravaipa newcomer Jeff Power was his primary target. Tucker was also contentious: Rattlesnake Canyon prospector Jay Murdock referred to him as "a Napoleon-type man, small, commanding."

Soon Tucker started arguing with the local forest ranger Lee Kirby, the same man who had a run-in with Charley Power regarding his homestead application, over the virtue of two women living in Klondyke. Neither Tucker nor Kirby seemed willing to end the debate, so hard feelings festered between them.[6]

One afternoon in mid-January 1912 Bauman and Tucker were working the mine when they heard a noise outside the mouth of the tunnel. "As a rule," Bauman later testified, "anybody coming there would be Powers," but this time it was the forest ranger. Tucker said to Ranger Kirby, "'thought I told you not to come here anymore'" and, after a short exchange, Kirby left the tunnel with Tucker following him. Bauman remained in the tunnel until he heard gunfire. When he ran outside, he found the forest ranger uninjured and Tucker riddled with bullets, shot in the eye, heart, lower body, calf, and left hand. Bauman later testified at the inquest that a gun was in Tucker's right hand when he died, cocked with his thumb on the handle and finger on the trigger, suggesting he was attempting to shoot Kirby when he was hit. Members of the coroner's jury were initially skeptical of Kirby's claim of self-defense. It was general knowledge that Tucker was left-handed, but because he had been shot by a federal official, whose position granted him law enforcement powers, the jury reconsidered and eventually determined the deceased had shifted the gun to his right hand after his injury to the left. The coroner's jury exonerated the forest ranger of all wrongdoing.[7]

With his troublesome partner conveniently dead, Bauman was now assigned a new partner, Klondyke storekeeper and executor of Tucker's estate, John F. Greenwood. In 1912 the two men sought additional investors, attracting Ed Lyman and Harry Neil of Bisbee to make improvements to the mine. After considerable expense a small amount of ore was allegedly produced, and Jeff Power and his sons were hired to pack the ore out of the canyon in the fall of 1913. It was at this point that Jeff Power, who was by then "possessed by the lure of gold," mortgaged his cattle to buy a quarter share of the Abandoned and Burro claims from the estate of the deceased Tucker for one thousand dollars.[8] The purchase made Jeff a partner with Al Bauman and Richard C. Elwood, who each owned a quarter share, as well as Ed Lyman and Harry Neil, who jointly held the fourth quarter, and the five partners continued assessment work together. Jeff Power was convinced "his wildest dreams were about to come true."[9]

Over the course of the following year, European nations entered the Great War and German submarines began sinking cargo ships in the Atlantic Ocean, cutting off goods from American markets. Embargoes drove up the price of ore, and mining production increased accordingly in Arizona. Low-grade ore mines in remote locations like Aravaipa that were unprofitable to operate in peacetime were now reopened. The shuttered Grand Reef Mine was made operational, and its owners began construction on a road from the mine to connect with the new road the county was building from the Gila Valley to Klondyke. Additional stamp mills were brought in to process ore taken from Grand Reef, and residents of Klondyke and Bonita put together a proposal to construct a telephone line from the Gila Valley to their section for the mining operations. Locals started to dream of the economic boom that might follow.[10]

With ore prices high, marginal operations like Jeff Power's mine attracted potential investors, and over the next few years there were several more articles in local newspapers suggesting a mining boom was imminent in Klondyke. In February 1915 the *Graham Guardian* relayed that "a mine promoter has arrived to take over the T. J. Power gold property on Rattlesnake, and if nothing happens, we will soon having something doing." That potential buyer backed off, but others would continue to call on Jeff Power and his partners, continually raising their hopes that they would become wealthy men.[11]

Not everyone in the Power family was convinced investing in a mine was the right decision. Jeff could have approached his mother, Jane, for the cash for the purchase, considering that she had lent him money to buy cattle in the past and still held much of the proceeds from the sale of her property in New Mexico. Instead he took out a loan from the Sulphur Springs Valley Bank, an indication that Jane was skeptical about the mine's prospects. His oldest son, Charley, evidently also believed investing in the mine was a mistake. He left the family sometime in 1915 because he had enough of the "rough, primitive and uncertain life" in Rattlesnake Canyon, returning to southwestern New Mexico where he joined his Uncle Will and Aunt Ida Morgan, who had given up on ranching in Aravaipa.[12]

With Charley gone and Jeff and John busy prospecting, it fell to the youngest son, Tom, now twenty-two, to bring in an income to support the family and pay for mining equipment needed for their operation. In the copper camps workers were in high demand to keep the mines running twenty-four hours a day during the war, so Tom left for Globe, where he worked as a mechanic for the Superior and Boston Mine at Copper Hill. Tom was an energetic and resourceful man, and soon found an additional way to earn cash. When a statewide prohibition law went into effect on January 1, 1915, there was good money to be made by folks willing to break the new law, especially in mining communities where whiskey sold for up to eight dollars a quart. Bootlegging was a misdemeanor, punishable with a fine—usually no more than one hundred dollars—and imprisonment, or both, but many who were convicted went back into business as soon as they paid their debt to society. Tom Power partnered in the bootleg business with Tilden and Tom Scarborough, who were old friends from Lordsburg, New Mexico, and now worked with Tom at the Copper Hill Mine. The three men fixed up an old car and made a few runs from Lordsburg, where liquor was still legal, to Globe. But before long, professional bootleggers moved into Arizona from all over the country to take advantage of the situation, and their profit margins dropped, so the trio gave up their illegal business.[13]

In the spring of 1915 Tom was summoned home from the mines of Globe to Rattlesnake Canyon to help his father with an enormous project. Taking a cue from the larger local mine operators who were building roads to connect with the new county road under construction, Jeff began work on what would become known as Power Road. It was little more than a trail that ran from his claims to the Aravaipa Road, a distance of twenty-one miles. Because of the steep grades and rugged terrain, heavy equipment and trucks were of little use, so the trail had to be cut by hand and materials hauled in by pack animals, requiring hundreds of hours of labor. Fallen trees and boulders had to be moved, hampering progress, so construction lasted most of 1915 and 1916. With Charley gone, Jeff needed additional help, and he found it in a former soldier who was down on his luck, Tom Sisson.[14]

Thomas Joseph Sisson, born in 1869 in Livonia, Minnesota, was the youngest son of a Union Army veteran, and he himself enlisted as a private in the army in 1892 at age twenty-two. He was assigned to the First Cavalry, E Company, which was transferred to Fort Grant in Graham County in December 1892. By the time Sisson's unit reached Arizona, the Indian wars were over and the First Cavalry was assigned to mop-up operations, patrolling for escapees from the San Carlos Indian Reservation like the Apache Kid, who continued to use Aravaipa Canyon as a hideout. Over the next few years, the unit successfully contained all breaks from the reservation, so in October 1895 the First Cavalry was transferred out of Fort Grant to Fort Sill, Oklahoma Territory. Soldiers were given the option to leave the service, so Sisson, with his exceptional service record, decided to muster out, choosing to remain in Arizona rather than return to Minnesota.[15]

Sisson herded stock and worked as a blacksmith for a while in Willcox before moving to Klondyke around 1908 to homestead just north of town. There he briefly served as a constable, but because he could neither read nor write, he had difficulty delivering subpoenas for jury duty, an integral part of his job. At some point after they moved to Rattlesnake Canyon he became good friends with

Tom Sisson was a private in the United States Cavalry before he
settled in Klondyke, where he homesteaded, worked as
a blacksmith, and befriended the Power family.
Courtesy Howard Morgan.

the Power family, and told them many tall tales of how he served as an Indian
scout while in the military. In fact, Sisson was just a private, not a scout as he
contended, as that position was reserved for non-military professional trackers
or members of local tribes who enlisted in the army.[16]

Shortly after selling his homestead in 1913, Sisson was charged with grand
larceny for the theft of a horse. A juror for the trial many years later recalled, "'I
can't remember the details of the case too well, but the way I recall it Sisson was
obviously guilty; I know we weren't out on the case very long.'" Others saw it
differently. Sisson never denied taking the horse, but argued that it was simply
a case of mistaken identity and not felonious intent. Graham County historian
William Ryder Ridgway noted, "in all fairness to Sisson it must be stated that he
hardly acted in the manner of a guilty person—making no effort to conceal the
horse, riding him everywhere, nor attempting to alter its brand." Nevertheless,
Sisson was convicted and sentenced to one to ten years at the state prison, which
had been moved from Yuma to Florence, in Pinal County.[17]

When Tom Sisson entered prison on August 22, 1914, he was unmarried, forty-five years old, and a veteran with an unblemished record who had never been in serious trouble before in his life. He had been out of contact with his family in Minnesota for so long that he listed Charley Power as his closest acquaintance with prison officials. Eleven weeks after entering the state penitentiary, he walked out a free man, officially paroled by Governor George W. P. Hunt, a progressive politician who championed the cause of prison reform and freely handed out pardons and paroles to first-time offenders he thought worthy of a second chance. Sisson returned to Klondyke, but after paying legal fees for his trial and a failed appeal, he was broke. He went to live with the Powers in 1915 to work on the road and in the mine in exchange for room, board, tobacco, and a promised cut of the profits should the mine ever produce. Jeff Power never believed that Sisson had been guilty of horse theft, and he quickly became one of the Power family.[18]

By the summer of 1915 Sisson and the Power men had made good progress on Power Road, with seven miles of trail completed from the Habys' home into Rattlesnake Canyon. One day Ola May and her grandmother Jane rode down in a buggy from Garden Place to bring the road crew a nice lunch. As the two women headed back, just before they reached home, the horse driving the buggy spooked and, according to Ola, "'he seemed to go wild—he just started running and kicking something awful.'" Despite Ola's efforts to control the horse, the buggy overturned and both women were thrown out. "Dazed and shaken," Ola ran for help to the closest neighbor's house. Jane had broken her hip and sustained a serious head injury. The family and the local doctor tended to Jane for two days until she finally succumbed to her injuries. Jeff broke down and "cried like a baby" when he lost his mother.[19]

Jane was seventy-one when she died, a long life for a frontierswoman. She had raised Jeff and his four children after Mattie's death and instilled them with common sense and toughness. She repeatedly stood up to men, including her husband, Sam, and any neighbors who threatened her, and for the twenty-five years after she left Sam, she controlled the family's finances. She attended church, socialized with neighbors, and took her granddaughter to social gatherings, like the Sociability Run. Jane's death was a watershed moment for the Power family, because Jeff lost her levelheaded counsel and his last slim connection to the outside world. From then on, he turned more and more inward, focusing solely on the mine and abandoning her farm, which had sustained the family through lean times. He even gave up on his own cattle business.

Jeff sold Jane's real estate holdings and farm equipment at Garden Place as well as his herd, which brought top dollar because of the wartime beef embargo. He then used the proceeds of the sales plus his inheritance from his mother to buy another quarter share of the Abandoned claims for one thousand dollars, and spent hundreds more purchasing additional claims and mining equipment. During tough times in the past he could sell land or cattle for cash and move on to the next place, but now his family's future was inextricably tied to his mines in the Galiuro Mountains. While Jane was alive, she and Ola had canned fruit and vegetables from their garden and orchard, and those remaining canned goods would sustain them for a while at Gold Mountain. But Jeff had no savings left, so if the mine did not produce gold or if he could not find a buyer for it quickly, he would not be able to put food on the table for his family.[20]

Jeff Power now owned half of the Abandoned and Burro mines, and if he had any qualms about the risk he had taken, he must have been buoyed by an article on the front page of the local newspaper that ran in October 1915, headlined: "Big Gold Strike near Klondyke." The newspaper quoted Charley Jones and James Mulheim, mining speculators from Bisbee who had just inspected Jeff's property and deemed it "very much more than the average prospect." The Power men and Sisson had built a crosscut from the tunnel 180 feet in length under a steep hill, and in that crosscut Jones and Mulheim "measured the ore and found a width of forty feet," which indicated the Powers had located a good pocket of gold. The mining speculators also sent a sample to an engineering and assay office, and even before the results were returned, they told the press they expected the ore would "run remarkably well for so large a body."[21]

Al Bauman offered to sell his quarter share to Jeff Power at a discount rather than hold out for the anticipated payoff, which raises questions about his confidence in the legitimacy of the assessment provided by the speculators from Bisbee. Jeff already had spent every penny he had, so he could not take advantage of Bauman's offer, but John Power jumped at the chance. He scraped together five hundred dollars in savings and in January 1916, in a blinding snowstorm, took off for Safford with his brother Tom to record the purchase. Now John and Jeff Power together owned three-quarters of the mine, with the other quarter share held between Harry Neil and Ed Lyman. Allegedly, the partners continued to receive offers. Tom Power later claimed that an engineer with the Inspiration Mining Company at Miami promised that his company would pay one hundred thousand dollars for it, but Harry Neil demanded 20 percent down, which prompted management at Inspiration to refuse and walk away from the deal. It is impossible to verify whether those negotiations took place or this was just a story told to drum up interest in the mine, but regardless, the Power Mine, as it was now called, generated quite a bit of enthusiasm among locals.[22]

When he sold his interest in Garden Place after Jane's death, Jeff moved his remaining family in Rattlesnake Canyon—Ola, Tom, John, and hired hand Tom Sisson—a short distance south to the ghost town of Gold Mountain to be closer to the mine. The men went to work each day at the claim, about a two-and-a-half-mile hike over a steep ridge in an adjacent canyon, and then returned at night to sleep in a dilapidated building that was formerly the camp's saloon. They kept busy installing a stamp mill Jeff had purchased from a mining company that had closed in Fourmile Canyon. It was arduous work hauling the heavy equipment by mule over the steepest part of their road, an incline of about thirty-five degrees called Power Hill. Since there was no electricity in the canyon to run the mill, Jeff was in the market for a boiler to haul up to Gold Mountain, where there was a good supply of water from Rattlesnake Spring. His sons would have to cut trees to feed the boiler's furnace to run the mill, so he would be more dependent upon them than ever. With so much work to do, Jeff seemed oblivious to all else going on around him. Since his mother's death he had retreated even more into his own world, failing even to register to vote in the important 1916 presidential election that saw Woodrow Wilson reelected on the promise to keep America out of the war raging in Europe.[23]

Ola stayed behind alone at Gold Mountain while the men went to work each day, tending to the cooking and laundry as well as the cow, chickens, and other animals. She lived in her own cabin about one hundred yards away from the men, and with her grandmother gone, her only company for much of the day was her cat, Tomba. Some of the neighbors began to worry about her wellbeing, because they knew she was "horrible lonesome" in the canyon. When Sheriff Frank McBride visited the Powers in the winter of 1917, he took note of her situation and brought back the information to the Gila Valley, where uncharitable folks spread ugly rumors about the young, single woman who was living with four men, one of whom was unrelated and an ex-convict, in the ruins of an abandoned mining camp.[24]

8

THE GREAT WAR

In wartime, truth is the first casualty.

Kane Wootan was at the Union Church in Klondyke at seven o'clock on the morning of June 5, 1917, to serve as a volunteer registrar for the first draft registration of the Great War. Governor Thomas Campbell had declared the day a state holiday, so businesses were closed to allow all male citizens and resident aliens between the ages of twenty-one and thirty to report to their polling station and sign up for the draft. The instructions for the registration process, devised by Enoch Crowder, the head of the Selective Service Agency in Washington, D.C., had appeared in multiple issues of every newspaper in the nation. Town hall meetings were held to explain the draft, and clergymen had been instructed to use their Sunday sermons to encourage men to comply with the new law. Due to this extensive campaign to inform the public, even in Aravaipa Canyon everyone was talking about the draft, which would be the largest and most comprehensive in the nation's history to date. Kane Wootan signed up thirty-two men from the Klondyke precinct that day at the church. Among them were two of the Bleak brothers, Lupe Salazar, Kane's younger brother Richard, and several other Wootan relatives. Wiley and Amanda Morgan's son George also filled out the required paperwork for Wootan, and several of his cousins on the Morgan side registered in neighboring Bonita precinct. Noticeably absent from Klondyke's Union Church on June 5, however, were George's cousins on the Power side, Tom and John.[1]

Nationally, approximately 10 million men turned out on that first draft registration day, and newspaper editors universally declared it a tremendous success. In cities across the nation, local Councils of Defense—volunteer organizations comprising prominent local businessmen and women enlisted to generate support for the war effort—ordered church and fire bells rung and whistles blown to "impress upon all citizens their duty." In Safford, a big rally was held the evening prior in a hall decked with flags. The local band played patriotic music and county officials were in attendance, including the head of the local draft board, Sheriff Frank McBride, who made a stirring address on a soldier's duty and, according to the local paper, "evoked much enthusiasm and hearty encores." As the editor of the *Graham Guardian* gushed, "The manhood of the nation obeyed the president's call and volunteered en masse, setting at aught all the schemes and plottings of German sympathizers and the few cranks who have agitated against registrations." Similar reports came in from all over the country, but while on the surface the draft appeared a success, as newspapers printed the names of men who had complied with directives, local authorities soon realized that a significant proportion of the male population had failed to register for the draft.[2]

Many young men resisted registering because a large number of Americans initially did not agree with the federal government's decision to go to war or implement a draft. When war first broke out in Europe in the summer of 1914, the United States remained isolationist. There were some Americans, most notably former President Theodore Roosevelt, who argued that the nation should be prepared to enter the conflict, but a majority of citizens were reluctant to take sides in a war waged by Old World autocracies. Secretary of State William Jennings Bryan advocated staying out of the European conflict, as did many prominent members of Congress, especially those from the South. In 1915 the most popular song in the country was "I Didn't Raise My Boy to Be a Soldier," and when President Woodrow Wilson ran for reelection in the fall of 1916, his winning campaign slogan was, "He kept us out of the war."[3]

In early 1917 representatives of the German government tipped the scales toward the pro-war advocates like Teddy Roosevelt. The German ambassador to the United States made the shocking declaration that neutral ships on the Atlantic Ocean would be subject to attack by German submarines. As losses to American cargo and lives escalated, German Foreign Secretary Arthur Zimmerman further aggravated tensions when he sent a coded telegram to his ambassador in Mexico proposing an alliance between Germany and Mexico to enter the war together, with "an understanding on our part that Mexico is to reconquer the lost territory in Texas, New Mexico, and Arizona." Between the heavy losses in the Atlantic and the outcry over the Zimmerman telegram when it was made public, opinion in the United States shifted sharply toward support for Great Britain and her allies. President Wilson felt there was no alternative, and asked Congress to declare war on Germany and her Axis allies; the Senate and House obliged on April 4 and 6, 1917.[4]

Federal officials were left with the difficult task of convincing citizens to support the war. Many Americans were reluctant, as they had read for years about the carnage in the trenches of France and Belgium. Furthermore, the population was fairly divided in its allegiance to both sides. There were German immigrants living in the United States who did not want to fight against their homeland, and Irish immigrants were reluctant to support the British in any cause. Numerous immigrants of all nationalities had fled Europe to escape military conscription at home and did not want to fight for their new country, either. Conscientious objectors, radical labor union leaders, Socialists, progressive reformers, and even poor, rural farmers opposed America's entrance into the war for various religious, political, and economic reasons.[5]

The federal government liberally used propaganda to diffuse the initial opposition to war. The Committee on Public Information (CPI), a new federal agency, produced material to whip up enthusiasm. Sometimes the message was patriotic and intended to motivate: "From press and pulpit, and in the school room, every effort should be exerted to impress upon all citizens their duty at this vital crisis in the history of *Our Country*. Let the words ring forth, 'The world must be made safe for Democracy.'" Other times it was vitriolic, designed to incite: "Germany has habitually and as a matter of policy practiced the torture of men, the rape of women, and the killing of children." The CPI had its own radio broadcast network, as well as seventy-five thousand Four-Minute Men, amateur orators who gave pro-war speeches at schools, theaters, churches, clubs, and even on trains and streetcars in urban centers. Much of the propaganda encouraged citizens to believe there was a spy hiding under everyone's bed, stealing secrets and sabotaging munitions plants. German and Austrian citizens were required to register as enemy aliens with the federal government, and anyone who spoke with a German accent was viewed with suspicion. Sales of sauerkraut plummeted, simply because it was stigmatized as pro-German, forcing American cabbage growers to rebrand the canned good as "Liberty cabbage." The barrage of propaganda made it difficult to distinguish between fact and fiction, inspiring California Governor Hiram Johnson to comment, "'in wartime, truth is the first casualty.'"[6]

While government officials and volunteers made progress early on in convincing the public of the rectitude of the war, they found it more difficult to induce
citizens to send their loved ones to the front lines. Since the nation's founding,
Americans had preferred a volunteer army to mandatory military service, and
rejected a standing army. As a newspaper editor in Louisville, Kentucky, put
it in 1917, "The volunteer system [is] the very life of American democracy. The
conscript system means the subjugation of America to military oligarchy such
as that which has cursed Germany." Until the Great War many people viewed
military service as a burden, not as a prerequisite of citizenship, and American
culture favored the rights of individuals over the obligation to defend the nation.
The nation's first draft, during the Civil War, led to violent protests in the North
and widespread evasion in the South. With those failures in mind, President
Wilson appointed the judge advocate general for the army, Enoch Crowder, to
orchestrate the draft during World War I, and under his careful supervision
over 72 percent of the military was conscripted, a dramatic increase from the
paltry 8 percent of the Union Army that was drafted during the Civil War.
However, the change to long-standing United States military policy was deemed
"revolutionary" by most observers, and the Wilson administration was able to
sell the Selective Service Act to Congress "only as a matter of national defense
in an emergency."[7]

The draft was to be "universal and absolute," eliminating the fraud and favor-
itism that led to riots and evasion during the Civil War, and the government
moved quickly. On May 18, 1917, Congress passed the Selective Service Act, and
the first draft registration day was scheduled just weeks later on June 5, allowing
little time for protestors to organize. Federal authorities made certain that the
process was tightly choreographed, with authority originating in Washington and
flowing down to each governor, who in turn passed instructions to draft boards
comprising local businessmen and politicians. By placing responsibility in the
hands of local officials, the federal government deflected much of the criticism
regarding the draft and allowed those officials, like volunteer registrar Kane
Wootan for the Klondyke precinct, to easily identify men in their jurisdictions
who failed to register.[8]

Despite the exceptional planning and execution by the Selective Service,
military officials estimated that between 2.4 and 3.6 million men, or roughly the
same number of men who eventually served in the United States Army during the
war, failed to register. Many were conscientious objectors and pacifists, but at the
time federal policy was inflexible toward them and only allowed exemptions to

a handful of religious denominations. Even if exempted, conscientious objectors were forced to work as noncombatants to support the war. Members of religious groups who had immigrated to the United States to avoid conscription, like the Molokans from Russia, whose beliefs forbade military service in any form, refused to cooperate. On June 5, 1917, dozens of members of the Molokan colony living in Glendale, Arizona, showed up at their polling precinct in traditional garb and staged a protest, refusing to register, even though most were not United States citizens and therefore not required to serve. Nevertheless, thirty-seven men were arrested by United States Marshal Joseph P. Dillon and sent to county jail for obstructing the draft. A handful of Americans championed the plight of conscientious objectors in the United States, most notably Socialists or civil libertarians like Roger Nash Baldwin and Norman Thomas, but their voices were largely drowned out by denunciations of evaders in newspapers, sermons, and speeches, and thousands of conscientious objectors were sentenced to long terms in federal prison for refusing to cooperate.[9]

While most outspoken draft protesters were pacifists and conscientious objectors, the vast majority of draft evaders were marginalized farmers or laborers who kept their views private and quietly avoided registration. Few exemptions were allowed for men with dependents, so poor men understood that if they left for the battlefields, there would be no one left behind to bring in the crops, and their wives, children, or aging parents could become destitute. One young man from Arizona wrote to the governor asking to be exempt because both his parents had contracted tuberculosis and lived sixteen miles from the nearest town. Without him home to care for them, he wrote that he feared they would starve to death. Taking young men out of the work force hurt the local economy and worried business leaders as well. The secretary of the Arizona Cattle Growers' Association complained to federal officials that the draft had seriously affected his industry, explaining, "in many instances every man on the outfit has been taken away, and it is impossible to secure experienced cowboys to take their places. It is a physical impossibility for old men to do this work." Small mine owners like the Powers were exempted from the annual requirement to make improvements to their claims during the war, but again, if the young men who performed most of the physical labor were away fighting, gold production would stall, leaving men like Jeff Power without hope for an income.[10]

Failure to register was a federal misdemeanor, punishable by up to one year in prison. Officially, anyone who failed to register for the draft, registered late, or provided false information on forms (such as an incorrect date of birth) was identified as a "delinquent" by the military, but the general public referred to these men as "slackers." The term would eventually extend to anyone who hindered the war effort, including people who failed to buy war bonds (called Liberty bonds) or support the American Red Cross, labor unions members who went on strike demanding higher wages, or even housewives who refused to conserve food for the war effort. In the summer of 1917, policemen began stopping men on the streets, in movie theaters, or other public places and asking them for proof of their support of the war effort—a draft card or their receipt for the purchase of a war bond. If they failed to provide documentation, they could be arrested. All law enforcement officers were required to inform the local United States commissioner—a federal attorney—of any known delinquents, who would then be sent official notification by mail, telegraph, or personal messenger to report to his local draft board. If the delinquent refused to respond within ten days, he was reclassified as a deserter.[11]

Delinquents faced only misdemeanor charges, but deserters were deemed felons subject to court martial and federal prison sentences. Men who registered for the draft but failed to appear for examination or for active duty were also declared "deserters," as were delinquents who were caught and refused to cooperate. Among the thirty-seven Molokan resisters arrested in Arizona were six American citizens of draft age who refused to register and were forcibly inducted into the army and sent to Fort Huachuca, outside Tucson. When they refused to engage in basic training and participated in hunger strikes, they were sentenced to long prison terms—between fifteen and twenty-five years—for desertion and obstruction of the draft. Before long, military prisons like Leavenworth were overflowing with thousands of conscientious objectors, including Quakers, Jehovah's Witnesses, Mennonites, Seventh-Day Adventists, and Molokans.[12]

It was easy for lawmen to locate vocal war protesters and arrest them, but tracking down the estimated three million men who went into hiding because they were unwilling to fight in a war they did not believe in was an almost impossible task. Some men of draft age took drastic measures to avoid service by inflicting injury on themselves, shooting off fingers or toes or even becoming addicted to drugs. At the beginning of the war many men incorrectly believed they would be exempted if they were married, precipitating a rush to the altar. But most slackers simply relocated to new towns where no one knew them, moved over the border into Mexico or Canada, or lied about their age. At a time when few people had birth certificates, drivers' licenses, or other forms of identification, many men simply provided an incorrect date of birth that made them too young or too old for service.[13]

In large cities draft evaders often escaped detection, but in small communities where everyone knew each other it was difficult for men to avoid the authorities. With only about three hundred people living in the Klondyke precinct, Kane Wootan would have realized immediately that first draft registration day in June 1917 that the Power brothers, among others, failed to report. Sheriff Frank McBride knew the Powers from his prior work in Aravaipa, so he too would have recognized that the brothers were derelict in their duty. The Selective Service Act required "all officers to apprehend" slackers, so McBride took an inventory of draft evaders in Graham County just days after the June 5 draft date and quickly reported his findings to the top federal law enforcement officer in Arizona, Marshal Joseph P. Dillon, who was headquartered at the state capital in Phoenix. McBride estimated the total number of slackers in his jurisdiction to be about twelve, and there were men hiding out in the hills who "positively refused to register from the first." Subsequent correspondence revealed he was referring to the Power brothers living in Rattlesnake Canyon.[14]

Marshal Dillon had served for years as a sheriff's deputy in Yavapai County and held important positions, including chairman of the Democratic territorial central committee and clerk of the Arizona Supreme Court, before his appointment as federal marshal in 1914 by President Woodrow Wilson. He worked closely with the Justice Department's top official in Arizona, U.S. attorney Thomas Flynn, to advise local lawmen how to navigate the complex new rules governing the Selective Service Act. Draft resistance was a federal crime, but state officers were granted permission and even encouraged to issue warrants and execute arrests because there were insufficient federal officers to cope with the slacker problem.[15]

The Bureau of Investigation, later renamed the Federal Bureau of Investigation, was created in 1908 within the Department of Justice, but during World War I it was a fledgling operation and not yet the premiere surveillance agency that Americans today associate with J. Edgar Hoover's ascendancy in the 1920s. Many agents who worked undercover to infiltrate subversive organizations had limited or no training, and there were rampant complaints from veteran lawmen that the "government men," as they were called, often conducted investigations improperly, even failing to conceal their identities when they worked undercover. During World War I, BI Chief Alexander Bruce Bielaski oversaw the direction of three hundred agents who were overwhelmed investigating 220,000 cases concerning pacifists, labor union radicals, saboteurs, foreign agents, conscientious objectors, delinquents, and deserters. Given its limited manpower and small budget, the bureau placed priority on investigating outspoken antiwar agitators, spies, and striking workers who threatened to disrupt the Selective Service and the war effort, while only minimal effort was made to apprehend men who hid from the draft.[16]

During the summer of 1917 local jails around the country filled up with slackers reported by friends and neighbors to county sheriffs, but often when those cases were investigated by BI agents it was discovered the men were not of draft age or had registered elsewhere. Sheriffs were forced to cover the costs of those mistaken incarcerations, which played havoc on their budgets. Not only were slacker arrests time-consuming and expensive, they could be dangerous. Numerous officers who arrived at the home of a delinquent or deserter were greeted with the barrel of a rifle. In Arizona, a federal agent became furious with Gila County sheriff Tom Armer when he did "not appear to be enthusiastic over the job" of arresting a slacker in his jurisdiction, but as one of his deputies explained, it was a "job which meant either killing these fellows or getting killed."[17] During the early part of the war most sheriffs were cautious in their approach to evaders, more eager to arrest dangerous criminals than political dissidents.

Sheriff McBride was an exception, a lawman who pursued slackers from the start of the war with the same energy he pursued bootleggers. Just after the Selective Service Act was announced in May 1917, McBride put a notice on the front page of the local newspaper, stating that registration was "not a matter of choice. . . . We are very desirous that the citizens of Arizona, and especially of Graham county, will make a record in this matter that will be, or could be, envied by all. We hope there will be not one person in all our broad land who will earn for himself that unenviable reputation of being a 'slacker.'" Some of McBride's determination to uphold the draft laws was derived from his faith. Although from 1914 until 1917 the Mormon Church was, like the rest of America, isolationist, LDS leaders fully committed to the effort once the United States declared war. The church-owned *Deseret News* declared that each American must be "ready to give it every ounce of efficient support he can command." Mormons belonged to a conservative hierarchical religion and had banded together in tight-knit communities on the frontier, and now they readily embraced the government's edicts to band together for the nation's security. During the war, one observer noted that Salt Lake City was "the most patriotic place I have visited," and for "all intents and purposes the organization of the Mormon Church converted into a war machine."[18]

Sheriff Frank McBride and his undersheriff Martin Kempton spent the early months of the war rounding up the known delinquents in the communities of the Gila Valley with great success, but McBride was troubled by federal policies that hampered his efforts. According to the Selective Service Act, foreign-born men were required to register, but could not be drafted because they were not citizens. Unfortunately, the quotas local draft boards were required to fill were based on total male population and did not take into consideration the large percentage of foreign nationals residing in the Southwest. In Graham County, officials estimated 40 percent of the adult male population was not United States citizens, meaning an unduly heavy burden fell on the remaining male population of draft age to fill military quotas. Many male Mexican American citizens and Mexican noncitizens failed to register because they did not have a strong command of English and did not fully understand the draft requirements, so federal authorities encouraged local authorities to simply register these men as soon as possible without repercussions. But McBride was clearly agitated by the reluctance of the Hispanic population to cooperate, and he and Undersheriff Kempton rigorously rounded up dozens they believed to be draft evaders, even though judges quickly released most of them when they discovered the men were not United States citizens.[19]

McBride was also frustrated by his inability to arrest slackers, including the Power brothers, he believed were hiding out in the hills outside of the Gila Valley. The sheriff was already suspicious of what he called the "rabble" that dwelled in Rattlesnake Canyon and understood that locals were hostile to a Mormon sheriff and unwilling help him. McBride also knew his budget-conscious board of supervisors would not approve a posse into the mountains—they already had turned him down for less expensive expeditions—and they had stripped his budget for a deputy in the canyon, so a federally funded posse was his best option. McBride told Marshal Dillon in June 1917 that if the Power brothers showed up in town, he would "not neglect to get them," but "if it is that necessary to make a special effort to get these parties at once I would suggest that you send a Government man, and I will be glad to do all I can to assist." Unless the Power brothers committed a more egregious crime, the United States attorney for Arizona could not respond to the sheriff's request, and as long as Tom and John continued to hide out in the Galiuro Mountains, they remained beyond McBride's grasp.[20]

Beyond the expense, there was the question of the legality of a posse in such a situation. Federal law stipulated that sheriffs could only form a posse to arrest dangerous criminals, not for nonviolent offenders, and during World War I the Department of Justice did not authorize any posses in Arizona to apprehend men solely for the misdemeanor charge of refusing to register. In a case similar to that of the Power brothers, two men were reported delinquent by Gila County sheriff Tom Armer, who asserted the slackers had "openly announced that they will resist arrest." A posse was authorized by the U.S. Attorney's Office because of that threat, which many deemed a felony, but the operation was cancelled at the last minute when it was determined that neither suspect was of draft age.[21] Although federal agents cheered McBride's resolve to uphold the Selective Service Act, they were unable to assist him with the Power brothers because there were no substantiated reports that they intended to resist arrest.

Although many years later the Power brothers would insist that a recruiting officer gave them incorrect information about how to sign up, official federal correspondence confirms that Tom and John "positively refused to register from the first." Jeff Power first heard about the draft in the spring of 1917, when he traveled to the Gila Valley to get supplies and take Ola to the doctor. He brought a newspaper back to Rattlesnake Canyon to share the news with Tom, who had just turned twenty-four, and twenty-six-year-old John. The brothers were well known around Klondyke and could not avoid detection, so they borrowed a tactic likely used by their grandfather Sam Power during the Civil War and simply hid out in the hills. Although others would later assert that they were under the influence of their father, who forbade them from entering the military, their twenty-eight-year-old brother, Charley, who was living beyond his father's reach in New Mexico, also failed to register.[22]

While Charley, John, and Tom Power gave no conclusive reason for refusing to submit to the draft, Power family history provides us with some clues. The Power men were not religious, so they were not conscientious objectors, nor were they overtly political, but they were poor and had southern roots, and draft resisters were found disproportionately among that population. Although the South has a rich history of militarism, many rural farmers were members of agrarian organizations suspicious of corporate power. They drew their beliefs from Jeffersonian democracy and populist rhetoric and condemned the inequalities they saw in the capitalist system. Many southerners still remembered the unequal burden placed on the poor during the Civil War, and they even revived the old slogan, "rich man's war, poor man's fight" during World War I to describe how northern industrialists and Wall Street bankers were profiting from the war, while poor laborers and farmers were sent to fight and die on the Western Front. A handful staged protests, but most simply ignored the government's requirement to register, and about 28 percent of the nation's deserters during World War I came from the former confederate states, a far higher proportion than from other regions. During the Civil War, Jeff Power's father, Sam, and father-in-law, Sebe Morgan, had avoided service and his uncle Thomas Power had deserted the Union Army, and none of his grandsons registered during World War I. No doubt those three men shaped Jeff's opinion of conscription, which he in turn passed on to his own sons. According to neighbor Jay Murdock, Jeff told Tom and John not to register: "'If you sign the register,' he would say to his boys, 'you become a soldier and will have to obey, but there is not a law in the world to make a man put his name to something he doesn't want to.'"[23]

The Powers did not just oppose the draft, but they also failed to support the war in any way. Newspaper articles, newsreels in the movie houses, Sunday sermons, and Four-Minute Men talks all emphasized the importance of a united nationwide effort and bombarded Americans with the need to purchase Liberty bonds and join the American Red Cross. Wiley Morgan was awarded a citation for selling war bonds, but evidently he never convinced his brother-in-law, Jeff Power, or his nephews John and Tom to buy one, as their names were absent from the lists of subscribers printed in the local newspapers. Despite being a military veteran, Tom Sisson also failed to purchase a war bond or join the Red Cross.[24] Beyond their unwillingness to help finance the war effort, there were rumors that Jeff Power made angry statements against the war. According to a Pima butcher shop owner, John "Sandy" Mangum, when Jeff Power visited his store in the spring of 1917 he said, "'This is your war. That country over there (meaning the Galiuro country) is ours; we don't want nothing to do with your war. If Uncle Sam takes my boys they'll do it over my dead body.'" At that early point in the war Power was not alone in his sentiments, as many people across the country agreed that the government had no business sending "our boys to fight and die for something that ain't no concern of ours."[25]

Fearful antiwar talk would hurt the effort to raise an army, federal officials acted quickly to criminalize comments against the draft or the war, cloaking the action in laws designed to prosecute spies. Prior to United States entrance in the war there were instances of German sabotage on American soil, and although the attacks ceased after federal agents' crackdowns on suspicious aliens, newspapers continued to report that citizens should be on alert for enemy agents and saboteurs. In the Southwest, where the press printed reports that an invasion from Mexico was imminent, and where revolutionary leader Pancho Villa and his followers had clashed with U.S. troops on the border in 1916 and 1917, residents were especially on edge. The Wilson administration did little to calm the public's nerves, actually conflating fears in public messages and newspapers by erroneously claiming spies were "everywhere." Given the tense environment, Congress easily passed the Espionage Act in June 1917 to punish foreign spies, but the law reached much deeper, criminalizing any form of obstructing the draft by words or deeds.[26]

The Espionage Act gave the United States Post Office the authority to seize publications critical of the war and gave federal authorities permission to investigate
anyone speaking out, even for something as trivial as criticizing the American
Red Cross. Americans were asked to turn in friends or family members who made
antiwar or anti-draft comments, either publicly or in private conversation. Failure
to comply invited trouble. Individuals who condemned the Red Cross as a graft or
discouraged others from donating were placed under surveillance and interrogated
by the Bureau of Investigation. In Graham County, Sheriff McBride worked with
federal agents investigating suspicious Germans and others who made "treasonable
utterances." During the eighteen months of America's involvement in the war,
thousands of people were prosecuted under the act, which carried a maximum
penalty of twenty years in federal prison and a ten-thousand-dollar fine. One of
the best-known cases was that of Socialist presidential candidate Eugene Debs,
who was sentenced to ten years of hard labor in a federal penitentiary and stripped
of his citizenship for inciting resistance to the war in a speech. The author of the
Espionage bill, United States Attorney General Thomas Gregory, himself noted
"that never in its history has this country been so thoroughly policed." Numerous
historians have concurred with Gregory's assessment, including Jeanette Keith,
who suggests World War I was the "nadir, to date, of American civil liberties."
By 1918 people understood "that, unless they offered at least public support for
the war, they risked a visit from the BI at the least and time in a federal prison or
death at the hands of a mob of vigilantes at the worst."[27]

In the Southwest, the Espionage Act was used not only to silence individuals,
but also to quell the rising power of labor unions. Copper from Arizona mines
was needed for the war effort to manufacture shell jackets, cable, and wire, so
production rose dramatically from $40 million in 1910 to $200 million in 1917.
Profits were enormous—Phelps Dodge made over $24 million in 1916—but when
workers demanded increased wages, management refused. Twenty strikes erupted
in 1917 in Arizona alone and copper company managers used the Espionage
Act to end the work stoppages, claiming that German agents had infiltrated the
labor unions and their influence was used to direct the strikes. Although the
International Union of Mine, Miller, and Smelter Workers (IUMMSW), commonly known as the International Union, led most of the strikes, mining company
executives asserted that the more violent and radical Industrial Workers of the
World (IWW), derisively labeled the Wobblies, was controlling union activity
in the state. Leaders of the IWW, which had only a small following compared
to the more moderate labor unions like the International Union, condemned

capitalism and often used extreme tactics, including sabotage of industry, to make their point, creating contentious relations with corporate management.[28]

In July 1917, when the unions ordered a strike for higher wages that shut down the mines in Globe, Morenci, Bisbee, and Jerome, Walter Douglas, who managed Phelps Dodge's mining operations in Arizona, told union members in Globe, "There will be no compromise because you cannot compromise with a rattle-snake . . . that goes for both the International Union and the IWW. . . . I believe the government will be able to show that there is German influence behind the movement. . . . It is up to the individual communities to drive these agitators out as has been done in other communities in the past." Arizona Senator Henry Ashurst asserted that German agents were behind the strike, saying IWW stood for "'Imperial Wilhelm's Warriors,'" referring to Germany's leader, Kaiser Wilhelm II. Phelps Dodge had bought control over most of the newspapers in the copper towns of southeastern Arizona in the years running up to the war, and while the financial support of the state's largest employer benefited small publishers, it also became "the string that eventually became a noose" as editorial control was ceded to the copper giant. Additionally, wartime rules stipulated that editors could not publish antiwar sentiments, so Arizona newspapers were filled with articles denouncing the striking workers for being pro-German and harming the war effort. The majority of the state's electorate, which had been pro-union and progressive prior to the war, began to view the labor movement with suspicion.[29]

In the spring and early summer, as the Bureau of Investigation began receiving reports from copper company managers that the unions were infested with enemy agents—reports that were later debunked—federal deputy marshals and BI agents infiltrated the IWW and IUMMSW. In July 1917, just a month after the first draft registration day, soldiers and local law enforcement officers were sent by Arizona Governor Tom Campbell to Globe, Bisbee, Jerome, and other mining camps to avert violence among striking workers. Graham County sheriff Frank McBride brought "carloads of deputies" to Globe on July 4 when miners went on strike, and Marshal Dillon's deputy marshal in Globe, Frank Haynes, worked undercover with BI agents to investigate and arrest numerous strike agitators. Former governor George Hunt, a friend of labor unions, was sent to Globe as a personal representative of President Wilson to negotiate between the two sides. He kept the peace there, but in Bisbee and Jerome, no agreement was made and relations quickly deteriorated.[30]

With the backing of Phelps Dodge management, Cochise County sheriff Harry Wheeler appointed 2,200 temporary deputies who rounded up over 2,000 striking workers from their homes in Bisbee at gun point and detained them at the local baseball field. In the process two men were killed and dozens injured, as deputies broke down the doors of homes to make arrests. Some striking miners promised to go back to work and were released, but almost twelve hundred—about 90 percent of whom were foreign born, mostly from Mexico and Italy—were crammed onto boxcars and sent to Columbus, New Mexico, where they were left without food or water in the middle of the desert. At the time, Walter Douglas, Harry Wheeler, and others justified the deportation as an "action against 'alien enemies' engaged in a nationwide conspiracy," asserting striking miners "were a part of a revolution to defeat and overthrow the Government."[31]

As historian Katherine Benton-Cohen argues, "even by the standards of World War I, a time of grave assaults on civil liberties, the Bisbee Deportation stands out." When President Wilson originally asked for the passage of the wartime acts in May 1917 to secure the nation's defenses, he hoped they would encourage Americans to be vigilant against invasion, but he also worried that some Americans might cross over the fine line from vigilance to vigilantism. In Arizona, where concerns were heightened by close proximity to the border and labor unrest, that line was crossed. Wilson was shocked by the overt use of force in Bisbee and sent a federal investigator, Felix Frankfurter, upon whose recommendation Wheeler and Douglas as well as hundreds of others were indicted for kidnapping. However, there were no convictions for those involved in the Bisbee Deportation, because the copper press had convinced the locals who comprised the juries that the action against the striking unions was justified.[32]

While radical union activities remained the focus of antiwar investigations by the Bureau of Investigation in the Southwest, an incident in Oklahoma in August 1917 made draft resisters like the Power brothers a new priority for the federal government. Approximately five hundred (some estimates suggest as many as one thousand) farmers in eastern Oklahoma planned a march to Washington to protest the draft. The protestors were mostly poor sharecroppers—black, white, and American Indian—who said they planned to eat the green corn growing in the fields to sustain themselves along the way to the nation's capital, hence the name attached to their movement: the Green Corn Rebellion. They told officials they could not afford to leave their farms unattended if sent to war, because their families would lose their land. Many also claimed allegiance to radical antiwar groups like the Working Class Union and the IWW, but the real source of their anger was derived from their affiliation with the Populist movement, long suspicious of corporate power. Their denunciations of the inequalities found in the

American economic system sent jitters through the law enforcement community in Oklahoma. Fear of an uprising by radical draft resisters mobilized over seventy local lawmen who, over the course of several weeks, brought 450 men into custody. The Green Corn Rebellion also left three men dead and made headlines around the country, drawing the ire of politicians and newspaper editors alike, who cavalierly suggested resisters should be loaded onto ships to be sunk by German submarines in the Atlantic or lined up and shot by firing squads.[33]

Federal agents thwarted a similar anti-draft uprising that same week in Emory, Texas, forcing federal agencies to consider all known slackers as serious threats who required investigation. Just days after the Green Corn Rebellion, the Power brothers were placed under surveillance by the Bureau of Investigation. They remained in hiding in the Galiuro Mountains and had done nothing specific to elicit attention, but rather were caught up in a larger dragnet designed by the Department of Justice to prevent further antiwar demonstrations. Special Agent-in-Charge Charles Breniman of the San Antonio bureau, who was investigating the Green Corn Rebellion defendants, assigned an agent from the Tucson office to their case on August 14, 1917, asking him to investigate John and Tom Power "as having refused to register. . . . They are said to be hiding in their endeavor to evade the law." Agents were dispatched to determine whether Tom Power had been a member of a labor union when he worked at the Copper Hill Mine in Globe. Undoubtedly, he had been exposed to plenty of antiwar commentary in the mining camp—his close friend and bootlegging accomplice, Tilden Scarborough, declared on his draft registration form that he believed the Selective Service Act was unconstitutional—but federal agents found no evidence that Tom or his brother John were radicals or planning an uprising, so their case languished for months.[34]

At the beginning of the war, government officials and most local law enforcement had shown some restraint in going after slackers, but by the fall of 1917, violent labor unrest, the Bisbee deportation, the Green Corn Rebellion, increased military quotas, and a relentless barrage of propaganda changed the popular mood. Draft evaders were increasingly considered dangerous enemies of the state capable of all manner of other crimes. "There must be a kink in the brain of a draft evader the first place," wrote one newspaper editor. "Something is wrong with the brains, no doubt—dangerously wrong." Furthermore, as conscripts were called up for duty, the draft was no longer an abstract concept to be debated, but rather a reality that weighed heavily on the minds of Americans. In September 1917, the town of Safford honored the first contingent of Graham County's military inductees with a parade down Main Street. The six soldiers started from the courthouse, led by Sheriff McBride mounted on a horse and carrying an American flag, while several local bands played and members of the junior Red Cross followed. The *Graham Guardian* reported: "Patriotism was rampant and the Stars and Stripes swung to the breeze from all the business houses on the line of march." McBride then spent time with each family gathered at the train depot to see their sons, husbands, and brothers off to war with the realization they perhaps were saying goodbye for the last time.[35]

The slackers residing in his jurisdiction clearly angered the Graham County sheriff. In correspondence and phone calls to Department of Justice officials McBride vented his frustration and requested action. When none was forthcoming because agents lacked the manpower to fulfill their mandates, McBride took matters into his own hands and initiated an investigation against the Power brothers, sending someone to Willcox to investigate their school records and verify that they were of draft age. On November 22, the sheriff wired BI special agent Claude McCaleb at Deming, New Mexico: "Two slackers here. Think evidence is positive. School census tells the tale. May leave any time wire instructions at once." Agent McCaleb instructed McBride to file the case and notify the United States attorney in Phoenix, but once again ignored the sheriff's request for a posse to apprehend the pair.[36]

Far from the wartime activities in the Gila Valley, the Power family continued to work their mine in the Galiuros. At the end of November 1917, Ola Power turned twenty-three. There was no celebration. It was just another day alone at her cabin at Gold Mountain, tending to chores and worrying about her brothers, who were hiding out from the law. She had been feeling poorly since the spring, and the doctor in Pima was treating her for tonsillitis, but it was not just physical pain she was feeling. She was lonely and depressed since her grandmother's death, according to Henry Allen, a young Mormon ranch hand who was working with Jay Murdock, building fence for a large cattle operator. One day at the end of November, a horse belonging to the Powers wandered over to the Murdock camp. When Allen and Jay and John Murdock returned the horse, Allen recalled, "We visited with Ola and she was all right that morning even though she seemed down and out of sorts. We planned to come back the next day but couldn't make it and it wasn't until a week or so later that we heard Ola had died."[37]

9

SHOOTOUT AT DAWN

Throw up your hands!

Sheriff McBride first heard about Ola's death when Tom Sisson drove the Power car from the Haby place into Safford to purchase a coffin. McBride's daughter Gladys later recalled her father asking her, "'Do you remember the girl that we saw at the Klondyke picnic? . . . She has been found dead. Way out there in the mountains in the cabin where she lived. This poor girl. She never knew any life except mountain life. I have to go to Klondyke to investigate the circumstances surrounding her death." The sheriff left for Klondyke early on Friday morning, December 7, 1917, taking the county medical examiner, Dr. William E. Platt, a fellow Mormon, with him. Kane Wootan joined them at the Haby home, where Ola's body had been conveyed on horseback.[1] The investigation into her death would bring McBride and Jeff Power, with their opposing views of conscription, face-to-face for the first time since America's entrance into the war.

The next day Klondyke precinct coroner Joe Bleak and a jury of six men assembled to determined what had caused Ola's death. They heard the testimony of four people: her father, Jeff Power, Tom Sisson, Rattlesnake Canyon resident Joe Boscoe, and Dr. William Platt. Power stated that on December 6, he and Sisson were working at their blacksmith shop, and "Ola May Power made 1 or 2 stops there after saurkraut [*sic*] and other eatibles and telling them supper was ready." Jeff continued, informing the jurors that when he arrived at her cabin, "I found my daughter in convulsions laying across the bed. I ran out & called out to Tom Sisson to come quick that Ola was dying. I sent Tom after Mr. & Mrs. Bosco [*sic*].

Ola May Power's mysterious death on December 6, 1917,
would initiate a confrontation between her father, Jeff Power,
and Graham County sheriff Frank McBride.
Courtesy the Ryder Ridgway Collection, held by Maxine Bean.

My daughter died before they arrived." When it was Tom Sisson's turn to testify, he corroborated all of Power's statements.[2]

On the frontier, female family members usually tended to the sick and dying, but because Ola was the only woman left in the immediate family and Wiley Morgan's wife, Amanda, had died the year before, when Jeff found his daughter writhing in pain at her cabin, he sent Tom Sisson to fetch an outsider, the closest woman in the vicinity, Mellie Boscoe. Mellie and her husband, Joe, lived about ten miles from where the Powers were residing at Gold Mountain and were newcomers to Rattlesnake Canyon. She did not know the Power men, but she had heard rumors about how unsociable they were. She met Ola only once prior to her death, when the young woman had visited her place to sell chickens, and Mellie had formed the opinion that the young woman was frightened of her father. When the Boscoes arrived at the Power home in Gold Mountain on the afternoon of December 6, expecting to care for an ailing Ola, they instead were greeted with an awful stench and her corpse.[3]

When the coroner called Joe Boscoe to testify about Ola's death two days later, he stated that he and Mellie "arrived at the Ranch of Mr. Power and found his daughter dead, she was cold and ridgid [sic]. Mr. Power asked Mrs. Bosco if she wouldn't wash & dress his daughter. Mrs. Bosco was unable to manage her by herself so I helped wash & dress the deceased. I didn't see any marks of violence on her person." Ola's body was so rigid that Mellie and Joe struggled to get Ola dressed in the blue silk dress with a white collar that Jeff picked out, leading Mellie, who had never prepared a body for burial, to question Jeff Power's and Tom Sisson's assertions that Ola had been dead only for several hours. In fact, rigor mortis occurs roughly three to four hours after death and dissipates within twenty-four hours, so the time frame for Ola's demise that Jeff Power and Tom Sisson offered to the coroner's jury squared with the available medical evidence. Evidently, the Power men had folded Ola's hands across her chest when she died and, according to Mellie, her husband "Joe had to literally pry her hands away from her body so that we could get them in the sleeves of her dress." The Boscoes watched over Ola's remains that night as her cat, Tomba, scratched at the shingles of the roof "making mournful, unearthly sounds," and while her brothers Tom and John stood watch outside the door.[4]

The next day, when Ola's body was transported to the Haby place for an autopsy, Tom and John disappeared. They had eluded McBride for six months, and now that their sister's death brought the sheriff to their doorstep, they were forced to go into hiding to avoid arrest, leaving their father to address the questions posed by authorities. As Dr. Platt prepared to examine Ola's body, Gregor Haby convinced Jeff Power to accompany him to the pasture to look at some animals so he would not have to endure the heart-wrenching spectacle. Mary Ann Haby later recalled that when McBride and Dr. Platt first arrived at her home:

> Right away they became suspicious that something [was] wrong. For one thing her body was black from breast up; then Dr. Platt suspicioned a broken neck and he seemed to have an idea she might have died from an abortion. I tried to tell him that I knew Ola well and was certain nothing of that sort

was wrong. We had quite a quarrel about this and for that reason I wanted to watch while he performed the autopsy; he had asked me to as he wanted a woman in the room. We laid Ola on a table in that bedroom and Dr. Platt performed the autopsy there. He hadn't brought along his instruments—I suppose he didn't think he would need them—so he borrowed Kane Wootan's pocket knife and used it. He took out her stomach, heart and most of her insides. Her stomach showed a few little white spots. Then he took out part of her spinal column and laid it on a newspaper; the second joint at the base of her skull was dislocated so badly that I could lay my little finger between the joints—but her neck wasn't broken. Then he examined her sexually and she was a pure virgin as her seal had never broken.[5]

None of the more salacious details of the autopsy made it into Joe Bleak's report, perhaps because he was a close friend of the Power family. He was a local goat rancher who had been elected as coroner for the Klondyke precinct, and like most coroners at that time Bleak had no medical training. Only Dr. Platt could provide a scientific assessment of the cause of death, and while he may have had his suspicions, he provided no definitive answers under oath. He testified he "could not find the cause of the death of Ola May Power," so the coroner's jury concluded, "Ola May Power came to her death from an unknown cause."[6]

After Ola's inquest, McBride's suggestion that a member of the Power household was responsible for her death prompted an argument with Jeff Power, and the two men nearly came to blows. Jeff was apoplectic over McBride's assertion that he, Sisson, or Ola's brothers had harmed her. Jeff insisted the last word spoken by Ola was "poison," so McBride had Dr. Platt remove Ola's stomach and send it to the state laboratory for testing.[7] Insensitive to Jeff's loss, McBride continued to badger him, demanding that Tom and John come into Safford to register for the draft. According to Joe Bleak the sheriff, alluding to newspaper stories falsely asserting that all slackers would be executed, told Jeff, "'If you got an idea your boys are going to be stood against a wall and shot—why get that idea out of your head.'" Before he left, McBride managed to get Jeff to agree to send his sons into Safford to register, but fearing arrest, Tom and John Power were absent from their sister's funeral. Reportedly the brothers took a "position on a high mesa, just south of the Haby place, and viewed the funeral procession as it wended its way down the valley to the Klondyke cemetery," where Ola was buried next to her grandmother. Tom later recalled that his father told them "there was nothing more we could do, and to go back home and feed the livestock."[8]

While many people were already talking about the slackers hiding out in Rattlesnake Canyon, now Ola's death led to gossip that the Power men were guilty of more heinous crimes as well. While waiting results from the lab, residents of the Gila Valley, hearing that Ola may have died of a broken neck, spread rumors that Ola had been sleeping with her brothers, her father, Sisson, or possibly all four, and when they discovered she was pregnant, they murdered her. These toxic stories, a result of the unrelenting propaganda that asserted slackers were dangerous men, combined with prevailing cultural beliefs that it was improper for a young, unmarried woman to live unchaperoned among men, made it into a Gila Valley newspaper. Klondyke residents who knew the Powers were outraged, and insisted that Ola was an exemplary young woman and that the men of her family loved her and would never harm her. Mary Ann and Gregor Haby's son Merrel believed the Power boys were blamed for her death "not from within but from without. Long time neighbors knew the boys and knew that that would not be the case because those boys thought the world and all of the girl and always treated her that way." Even though Mary Ann Haby, Mellie Boscoe, and even the sheriff's daughter Gladys McBride all later concurred that the autopsy revealed Ola "had not been sexually molested or anything like that," the rumors of a pregnancy, abortion, and murder persisted.[9]

The stories that circulated in Aravaipa about her death were less vicious, but damaging nonetheless. Many believed that Ola was in love and wanted to marry, and some folks suggested her lover was a young soldier stationed at one of the nearby forts, while others claimed he was a cowboy named Red from Willcox. When her father forbade her from marrying him, some people speculated that Jeff himself, or perhaps his sons or Sisson, had killed Ola and her lover as they tried to elope. Others theorized that her death was accidental, that John or Tom, who often roped and tied up each other and Ola for sport, might have caught her around the neck and killed her by accident. Henry Allen, the young Mormon ranch hand who had visited her just before she died, was convinced Ola was depressed from living alone in the canyon and committed suicide by ingesting strychnine or cyanide, poisons commonly found at ranching and mining operations.[10]

Those who knew the Powers best believed that illness took Ola's life. Some thought she finally succumbed to the throat ailment doctors had been treating, while others suggested that food poisoning was to blame. Botulism was common at the time, a result of improper canning techniques. When her grandmother Jane was still alive, she and Ola harvested fruits and vegetables from their garden and canned them for use in the winter. People theorized perhaps one of the jars of sauerkraut she was preparing for supper when she died was not sealed properly or had been jostled when they moved from Garden Place to Gold Mountain, allowing bacteria to contaminate the contents. Tom Power later noted that his sister often ate cold food, and he too worried that she might have died of food poisoning. His father, Jeff, and brother, John, however, suggested treachery instead, perhaps to combat the many scurrilous rumors aimed at them. They claimed that some outsider poisoned their food supply, trying to kill the Power men for their mine, and the culprit accidentally killed Ola instead. They were so convinced the food supply was tainted that they destroyed all the canned goods stored at Gold Mountain.[11]

When the report from the state laboratory came back a few weeks after the autopsy, it ruled out poison, convincing Sheriff McBride that Jeff Power and Tom Sisson had lied to him under oath about Ola's death. Although many people living in the Gila Valley would later insist that Dr. Platt determined she died of a broken neck, if true, he never officially reported it. In fact, when her death certificate was finally filed with the Arizona State Board of Health on February 8, over two months after her death, the official cause remained unchanged from the autopsy report: "Do not know. Supposed to be accidental." Although Joe Boscoe testified at the inquest that there were no signs of violence on her body, nevertheless Bureau of Investigation special agent Claude McCaleb in Globe received a phone call about Ola's death from Sheriff McBride on December 18, 1917, which he reported to his superiors: "Sheriff McBride, of Safford, Arizona, phoned me yesterday and stated that there were two slackers out in the hills near Safford and their being at large was having a bad effect upon the situation down there. He further stated that their sister had been brought from the camp, with the statement that she had taken poison but that an autopsy developed that her neck had been broken. He asked that a government man be sent there as soon as possible in order to work on the case and if possible bring these men to justice."[12]

Up to this point, the Bureau of Investigation's months-long probe into the Power brothers had led nowhere, but now Sheriff McBride's suggestion that Ola died violently finally forced the Department of Justice into action. Agent McCaleb sent a message to his boss in El Paso that McBride needed "help with two defiant slackers," and received authorization to proceed. He arranged to meet with McBride during a stopover at the Safford railroad station on January 3, 1918, but his interview seemed more designed to assess the character of the Graham County sheriff rather than to gather information about the Power brothers. After their conversation, McCaleb told his superiors that his impression of McBride was that he was "very patriotic and reliable. . . . I have always found Mr. McBride to be willing to assist the government in every way possible. He is conservative, and his statements can be relied upon."[13]

With McBride's integrity established, the Department of Justice authorized warrants for the Power brothers under the Selective Service Act. Although many people would later question the legality of those warrants, Sheriff McBride worked closely with both state and federal officials to assure they were executed properly. He first approached Graham County justice of the peace Ulysses I. Paxton on December 28, who initially refused to cooperate, incorrectly assuming he did not have the authority as a state officer to authorize federal warrants for draft evasion. McBride next consulted with the United States attorney Thomas Flynn in Phoenix, while Paxton spoke with Graham County attorney William Chambers, and both confirmed that a state officer was indeed empowered to issue warrants for that federal crime. In the meantime, the United States Supreme Court ruled that the Selective Service Act was constitutional, eliminating the last legal barrier to prosecuting slackers.[14]

Paxton swore out the complaints against the Power brothers on January 21, 1918, and McBride then forwarded them to the U.S. Attorney's Office for authorization. They were approved, and U.S. Marshal Joseph Dillon was contacted to execute the warrants. Dillon sent a letter to his deputy marshal in Globe, Frank Haynes, on January 25, 1918, instructing him to arrest the Power brothers: "Dear Sir: Enclosed find two warrants for John and Thomas Powers. The warrants are not complete, and the United States Attorney has attached a slip of paper to each warrant showing what should be added and requests that you have the Justice of the Peace who issued the warrants attend to it before the warrants are executed. I understand that you have been fully advised with regard to these two men. I have written the Department [of Justice] asking for authority to incur the necessary expense in apprehending them, and you will not make any effort towards serving these warrants until you hear further from me."[15]

The deputy he assigned to arrest the Power brothers was a veteran lawman with nine years of experience in Gila County. Born in Tennessee and forty-four years old, W. Frank Haynes had grown up in Texas before arriving in Globe around 1900, where he found work as a conductor for the local railroad. Haynes was active in politics and in 1908 was selected as a delegate from Gila County to the state Democratic convention. In 1909 he became Gila County sheriff John Henry Thompson's deputy and was appointed deputy U.S. marshal for the Globe District.[16]

Frank Haynes became sheriff of Gila County in January 1912, when Sheriff Thompson was indicted for murder (he was later exonerated). Haynes was elected to the post in 1914 and served until he lost his bid for reelection in 1916, after which he continued to serve as deputy under the new sheriff, Tom Armer, and to simultaneously hold his position as deputy U.S. marshal. Haynes was an accomplished lawman who earned praise from local as well as federal officials. As the *Daily Arizona Silver Belt* opined when he became deputy marshal, "Frank Haynes . . . is thoroughly competent to fill the position and the selection is a popular one." Over his years in law enforcement, Haynes spent countless days and nights on the trail of burglars, horse thieves, and murderers in a combustible region, tending to saloon brawls in the mining camps, infiltrating labor unions with federal agents, and defusing riots. Gamblers who continued to operate in his jurisdiction after wagering was outlawed were a special target of the Gila County sheriff, but Haynes also managed to make inroads against the illegal trafficking of liquor and opium during his tenure.[17]

On January 28, 1918, Marshal Dillon sent his deputy, Frank Haynes, a second letter containing the warrants for Tom and John Power approved by the U.S. attorney. Dillon instructed Haynes: "Go at once to Safford and consult with Sheriff McBride, who will accompany you as one of your possemen. You are also instructed to select another posseman to accompany you, and I would suggest that this be one after consultation with Sheriff McBride. The Powers brothers are believed to be at Klondyke, and if you are successful in arresting them, they should at once be removed to Globe and given a hearing before the U.S. commissioner. I consider this necessary on account of the character of the defendants and the lack of proper jails at other places."[18] It is worth noting that in 1918, as he prepared to leave for Safford to join Sheriff McBride to arrest the Power brothers, Haynes was serving as a deputy for Sheriff Tom Armer, the same man who had irritated federal agents with his cautious approach to arresting draft evaders. We have no way to know if Haynes was the deputy who explained to the BI agent the inherent dangers of the task of apprehending slackers with the simple summation that it "meant either killing these fellows or getting killed," but we do know he was member of that experienced team of law enforcement officers who were unenthusiastic about the job.[19]

The same week that the warrants were authorized for the arrest of the Power brothers, their neighbors Jay Murdock and Henry Allen were both in Safford when Sheriff McBride called them into his office and gave them a letter to deliver to Jeff Power. It read:

Dear Mr. Powers: You must know there is much talk about John and Tom refusing to appear before the draft board and submitting to authorities to comply with the federal regulations. I am merely a County officer and have no authority to actively attempt to locate these boys, but I feel you know their whereabouts and I wonder if you wouldn't persuade them to come in and give themselves up? I feel sure it won't be long until the Government will be compelled to take this matter up and then it will be too late to do anything. If they will come in now and come to me I'll do everything in my power to prevent their being prosecuted. They can register, and when called, do their duty as good American citizens. Let's try and save your boys. McBride.[20]

Jeff Power's response to McBride's letter was: "'Well, McBride says he ain't comin' up.'" When Jeff was growing up in Texas and living in New Mexico as an adult, state and federal government struggled to protect settlers and enforce the rule of law. In Aravaipa Canyon many settlers squatted on Forest Service land and grazed their cattle on public land for years without paying for a permit. To a man like Jeff Power, who had only known a weak federal government in his lifetime, it must have seemed improbable that someone in Washington, D.C. would order officers into the back woods of the Galiuro Mountains to arrest his boys on a misdemeanor charge of draft evasion. Instead, his only concern was the local lawman, Frank McBride.[21]

On the surface, it appeared the sheriff was offering an olive branch to the Powers, encouraging them to cooperate rather than to resist, but McBride's offer was disingenuous. When he sent the letter, he knew the federal posse had been authorized and it would be only a matter of days before he and a federal marshal would leave for the Galiuros. As later events would confirm, McBride's letter was a ruse to lull the brothers into believing they faced no immediate threat, so they would come out of hiding and be present at their father's cabin when authorities arrived. With the trap set, McBride's only task was to pick the most propitious moment to capture the men unawares.[22]

As warrants were issued and preparations made for a posse to arrest the Power brothers, Bureau of Investigation special agent David Ross stepped off his Pullman car at the station in Tucson on January 19, 1918, to begin his investigation of their case. He had performed some contract work for the bureau in Butte, Montana, investigating radical labor union leaders, and he had just become a special agent, so new that he had not yet received his badge or codebook from headquarters. Senior agents were tied up with other, more pressing investigations, and Ross was completely unfamiliar with the region, with no reliable informants at his disposal. Thus, it is not surprising that in his first report on the Power brothers, made eleven days after his arrival in Arizona, he misidentified them as

> two brothers by the name of Powell, sons of Thomas Powell, living at Klondike Arizona and are of Draft age but who have failed to register, I am told they are openly defying the Government to disturb them, that they have armed themselves, sleep out in the brush and come daily to their father's house where they are fed. I am unable to ascertain the names of these two slackers nor their ages at this time, as I find that Klondike is in Graham County, Arizona, my informants not knowing either their names nor their exact ages but it is a matter of common repute they are within draft age and are defying the Officers and it is said their actions is making a bad impression upon others.[23]

Ross's comment that the men were making a "bad impression" was clearly borrowed from McBride, who had previously used similar language to describe the Power brothers' refusal to register. Ross's observation that the Power brothers were "openly defying the Government to disturb them, that they have armed themselves," was the only mention in any official report made prior to the shootout that the men intended to resist arrest. By his own admission, Ross's intelligence was unreliable, especially because he collected information in Tucson, over seventy miles away from the canyon the Powers called home. Even in Rattlesnake Canyon no one aside from the Powers and Sisson really knew their intentions, because they were in hiding. In his subsequent report filed on February 8, after he had gathered intelligence in Graham County, Ross corrected many, but not all, of the errors in his initial filing, and backed away from the suggestion that the Powers were armed and threatened to resist arrest. Instead, he stated that both Tom and John Power were of draft age, and "their father T. J. Powers and one Sisson his partner in some mining claims near Klondyke, feed these two men they [are] sleeping out in the hills." Ross also mistakenly identified their brother Charley as a deserter, rather than a delinquent, saying he "registered for the draft, was called but failed to answer, his whereabouts are unknown but is supposed to be in New Mexico."[24]

On February 8, 1918, the same day Special Agent David Ross filed his second report on the Powers, Deputy U.S. Marshal Frank Haynes arrived in Safford by train from Globe with federal warrants and authorization for a posse to arrest Tom and John Power. Before leaving for the Galiuro Mountains, Haynes waited almost two days for McBride to finish up his caseload at the county courthouse. During this time he visited Graham County justice of the peace Ulysses I. Paxton and asked him to fix the warrants for Tom and John Power, as ordered by Marshal Dillon and U.S. attorney Flynn. The misdemeanor warrants stated that both Tom and John Power had failed "to register in violation of Sec. 5 Act of May 18, 1917," the provision of the Selective Service Act requiring all men between the ages of twenty-one and thirty to register for the draft.[25] It is important to note that there were no felony warrants issued under the Espionage Act charging them with threatening the lives of officers or making statements against the war, although the men would later be accused of those offenses. Meanwhile, Sheriff McBride also went to Justice of the Peace Paxton and asked for two additional warrants to be issued by the state, one for Jeff Power and the other for Tom Sisson, for perjury, a felony. McBride told Haynes he was eager to question the two older men about the death of Ola Power, but did not indicate to the deputy marshal that he thought they were responsible for her death.[26]

Marshal Dillon placed Haynes in charge of the posse, but the additional perjury warrants issued by McBride suddenly muddied the chain of command, as they were now arresting men for both federal and state charges. Although sheriffs usually followed the commands of federal marshals in such situations, in this case the local officers knew the terrain and were acquainted with residents who might provide them with information, and therefore were given greater latitude in directing the operation. Dillon had instructed Haynes to defer to McBride's choice for the third member of the posse, and the sheriff chose Kane Wootan, who was deputized as a special federal marshal for the assignment. Wootan was from Klondyke and knew the area and the people well, and he could arrange accommodations during their stay and horses for the journey into Rattlesnake Canyon.[27]

Kane Wootan, of course, had worked alongside McBride when they were deputies together in Aravaipa, and he was a trusted member of the sheriff's team, even if budget constraints kept him off the permanent payroll. His daughter Opal had a birthday the following day that he did not want to miss, but Wootan needed any posse salary that might come his way. His wife, Laura, was expecting their fifth child and, although the family had a roof over their heads in Safford, their home was heavily mortgaged. During the previous year, he had fallen on hard times as drought struck the region. By the time Kane Wootan left for Klondyke with the posse on February 9, 1918, his debts were almost double his assets, and he was facing foreclosure proceedings on property he held in Pima County.[28]

The state warrants issued for Jeff Power and Tom Sisson for perjury allowed McBride to expand the posse, and the sheriff chose Undersheriff Martin Kempton, who, according to Haynes, "wanted to go awful bad." Kempton had done an

Sheriff Frank McBride of Graham County, 1916.
Courtesy the McBride family.

admirable job as McBride's right-hand man over the past year. Martin and his
wife, Sena, had seven children, the oldest of whom was fifteen, and they owned
their home and forty acres of farmland free and clear. Before leaving for Klondyke
Kempton paid off his outstanding bills with local merchants, leaving some people
to later speculate that he knew the trip would be dangerous, but family members
countered that this was just the way he always conducted business. McBride too
prepared for his absence, which he expected to last a few days. His wife, Clara,
was expecting their eighth child (a ninth had died in infancy) and he admonished
his oldest daughter, Gladys, to stay close to home to help her out, telling her, "'If I
could put this trip off, I would, until she gets to feeling better.'" McBride did not
indicate to his daughter or wife that he was expecting resistance from the suspects.[29]

The four lawmen—Haynes, McBride, Kempton, and Wootan—finally left
Safford for Klondyke around three o'clock on Saturday afternoon in McBride's
Model T. The forecast called for snow later that evening in the higher elevations,

Undersheriff Martin Kempton with his bride, Sena, in what is probably their wedding portrait, taken in 1902. After his death in the gunfight, she launched civil litigation against the Power brothers to win ownership of their mines.
Courtesy Martin Kempton.

a seemingly inauspicious moment to begin a long journey over treacherous mountain terrain, but one which would offer the lawmen the element of surprise. In the next several months McBride planned to announce his intention to run for reelection as sheriff, and he no doubt believed that bringing two defiant slackers to justice and solving the riddle of Ola Power's death would benefit his campaign. Of late he was coming under increasing attack in the local papers. The wave of robberies that had plagued merchants in the Gila Valley through much of 1917 continued into the new year, and some locals were convinced the burglaries were "perpetuated by thieves who have resident acquaintances with Safford's business firms," a subtle reminder of a similar series of stagecoach robberies that had taken place in the 1890s, allegedly involving McBride's uncles, Wilfred Webb and Jacob Burns. John F. Weber had assumed control of the *Graham Guardian* from John Birdno, and unlike his predecessor, the new editor was not a member of the LDS church and therefore more critical of McBride's

Special Deputy Thomas Kane Wootan, photographed
circa 1908, was a champion rodeo rider.
Courtesy Millie Wootan Barnes.

performance in office. When a man was robbed at gunpoint on the streets of
Safford in February 1918, Weber lashed out against the sheriff's failure to halt
the yearlong crime spree in the Gila Valley and chided the sheriff for his zeal in
arresting liquor traffickers. In an article that appeared on the day McBride left
with the posse for the Galiuro Mountains, Weber suggested the robberies were
likely the "work of local thieves. We don't seem to be able to ever land a robber
who breaks into stores . . . but we are hell on catching bootleggers."[30]

McBride was focused on slackers in Rattlesnake Canyon that Saturday, not
thieves in the Gila Valley. He had asked Kane Wootan to arrange for someplace for
the posse to stay that night in Klondyke, and his deputy contacted a brother-in-law,
Al Upchurch, who provided the men with supper around six o'clock at his ranch.
When the four lawmen arrived in the early evening, "'They made themselves right

at home," according to Upchurch. "They sat and talked about different things and about their plans for capturing the Powers and old Sisson. . . . About midnight they got ready to go." Upchurch provided all the men with mounts—three horses and a mule—for the long ride into the mountains, as well as rifles for Wootan and Haynes, who had not brought their own.[31]

Haynes later testified he was not sure what time it was when they left the Upchurch place, "but it was good and dark." The men first stopped at Power Garden Place, which Jeff had sold in 1915. They discovered, according to Haynes, that "there wasn't anybody home there, and we went up on above there a short ways and built a fire. I don't remember what time of night we stopped but we left there between four and four thirty in the morning." Wootan, who was leading the way, told the rest of the men he had not been up that way for five or six years, but he thought they were close to Gold Mountain, where the Powers were purported to live. McBride had visited the Powers there the year before to return mining equipment during their dispute with Jeff Clayton, so he knew the trail. At some point the sheriff commented, "we had better be a little late than too early," suggesting he wanted to wait until first light to confront the Powers, likely because state law required lawmen to make misdemeanor arrests during daylight hours. It was still dark when they arrived at Gold Mountain, and they found no one home at the old saloon or the other buildings. Wootan led them further south, where he found a freshly cut trail that took them to the top of a steep ridge. They rode down into the canyon a bit before sighting a camp just under a quarter of a mile away. They dismounted, left their mounts along the ridge, and removed their heavy overcoats and leather leggings, hoping to advance undetected on the cabin below.[32]

First light was a little after seven o'clock that time of year, but the cabin's location deep in the canyon combined with the overcast from the coming storm meant it remained dim outside later that frigid Sunday morning. Inside the cabin Jeff Power was up and getting a fire started. When Jeff and John purchased the Abandoned and Burro mining claims, they inherited the simple, one-room structure that measured about nineteen feet by seventeen feet and was constructed of heavy logs chinked with mud. The roof was shingled, and a large, stone fireplace stood on the south side, providing heat in the winter. The members of the posse had spotted the chimney smoke from up on the ridge, so they knew the inhabitants were awake, but not one of them had visited there before and they were unsure of the layout of the building. They had agreed to surround the cabin so that the men inside could not escape, but in the dark it was difficult to know where doors and windows were located, and in the stillness of the dawn it would be unlikely they

The Power cabin, the site of the gunfight, showing the east-facing door
and window, the shed and windbreak on the north side, and the trail
behind the cabin used by the lawmen. Photo taken by Harry DuBois
for Graham County attorney William Chambers in March 1918.
Courtesy the Ryder Ridgway Collection, held by Maxine Bean.

could approach without alerting the Power horses and dogs. The lawmen were at a
distinct disadvantage if they hoped to surprise the occupants of the mining cabin.[33]

The Powers had made several improvements to the cabin over the years,
installing glass, wire screens, and heavy canvas drapes on the windows, located
on the east, west, and south sides. Also added was a shed that covered the entire
north side of the cabin and could be accessed through a door from within, as
well as an exterior door on the east side. Additionally, outside along the north
wall of the shed the Powers and Sisson had installed a windbreak, constructed
of boards nailed on posts to keep the howling winter gusts off the cabin. The
rear of the structure—the west side—faced the steep canyon ridge where the
trail into the canyon, the approach used by the posse members, was located.
A wood-framed canvas door facing east was the only entrance to the main
cabin. According to the Powers, at about 7:30 A.M., as Jeff lit the fire inside and
Tom, John, and Sisson lingered in bed, there was a noise outside that startled
the dogs. Jeff, who had lived much of his life in the wilderness where mountain

lions, bears, and cattle rustlers were present, walked out the door with his rifle raised, prepared for whatever faced him.[34]

When Jeff stepped outside, the lawmen were taking up the positions they had agreed upon prior to walking down into the canyon. McBride and Haynes had not yet stationed themselves on the northeast corner of the cabin, but the two deputies, Wootan and Kempton, who had a shorter distance to travel, had already staked their positions on the southeast corner and had their guns pointed at the cabin door. Because the deputies had reached their positions ahead of Haynes and McBride, Haynes was still behind the shed and could see nothing of what happened next, and only heard Kane Wootan call out, "Throw up your hands!'" As Haynes finally moved around the northeast corner into view of the front of the cabin, he noticed a man standing in the doorway with a Winchester across his chest. Even though he was only a short distance away, it was so dark that Haynes could not make out this man's features. Haynes and McBride moved into the open, four or five feet past the corner of the structure on the northeast side. Haynes could now see that Wootan and Kempton were also about four to five feet away from the southeast corner of the cabin. All four lawmen were exposed, as was the man standing with a Winchester in front of the cabin door.[35]

Wootan called out again, "Throw up your hands!" The man in front of the cabin, who was later identified as Jeff Power, shifted his rifle to the right side. At this point McBride said, "Boys, boys, boys," seemingly addressing his two deputies, as he could only see the outline of a solitary man in the doorway. At that moment the door swung open behind Jeff Power, and another man appeared in the doorway behind him. Shots were fired and Jeff fell to the ground a few feet in front of the cabin. Neither Haynes nor McBride got off a shot during the first volley, but now both fired at the second man, later identified as John Power, who had appeared behind his father in the doorway. Haynes "could see the gun and his two hands. The barrel of the gun was fast to the door shutter. . . . This man fired at us. The first shot went down low and struck in the ground. The next shot hit something above us, I don't know what. We fired again, and this man in the door—It looked to me like he had turned his gun right over this way," towards Kempton and Wootan, and then fired two shots. "I didn't think either one of those shots took effect." After the initial exchange, only Jeff Power had been hit, so the lawmen on either end of the house retreated away from the doorway: McBride and Haynes to the north side, Kempton and Wootan to the south side. For a moment, Haynes reflected, "Everything was as quiet as could be."[36]

Prior to the confrontation, McBride and Haynes had decided that if shooting began, the four lawmen would all take positions on the four corners of the cabin, so McBride remained in the northeast corner while Haynes moved to the northwest, assuming that Kempton and Wootan were taking their respective positions on the southwest and southeast corners. Haynes was now at the back of the house, with the cabin blocking his view of his fellow officers and a darkened window on the west side preventing him from seeing inside. He did not witness what happened next, but could only hear the commotion from his vantage point. "'By this time, shooting became general," Haynes testified, "I went further up the side of the mountain, on the north end of cabin and I heard shots from within the shed room." Haynes returned to the northeast corner, where he saw McBride's "body lying at the corner near where he stood, partly north of the cabin with his feet and limbs beyond the corner. I was protected during the firing by the shed at the north of the house. . . . After seeing McBride down I went up the hills and tried to approach the cabin from another direction, but finding I could not do so." The four officers had agreed to circle around the ridge at the back of the cabin and counterattack if there was trouble, but when he arrived there, Haynes met none of the others. Because he could not see or hear anything, he decided, "the best thing I could do was to get back to the settlement and get more help." When he left the canyon, he knew Sheriff McBride was dead, but was unsure who else was alive.[37]

10

ON THE RUN

Reports were distorted to an unbelievable extent.

When the shooting finally ended, the stories began, and the storytellers—whether they were journalists, lawmen, family members of the participants, or even the survivors of the gunfight—rarely agreed on anything. If there was a consensus about the shootout, it was that no two accounts were alike. Not only was the gun battle hotly debated, but the actions of the Power family and Tom Sisson prior to the shootout became contested. Suddenly, everyone seemed to know all about this reclusive family. Except, of course, much of what was reported in the press or whispered in town or in the canyon was incorrect. Just as rumors had fueled the shootout, they now formed its legacy.

Deputy United States Marshal Frank Haynes rode relentlessly to get help after his confrontation with the Power men and Sisson. According to legend, his exhausted horse died after arriving at Klondyke, where the first person Haynes ran into was local rancher Johnny Sanford. Haynes told him that McBride was shot, but he was uncertain what had happened to Wootan and Kempton. Haynes made his way to the Upchurch Ranch, where McBride's car was still parked, in hopes of driving to Safford to send word to his superiors. But Haynes was stuck—the key was in the slain sheriff's pocket. James Quinn, a local rancher and member of the county board of supervisors, came to his aid, finding a man who knew how to start the car without a key. By that time Henry Allen, who had encountered the Power brothers and Sisson after the gunfight at the Murdocks's camp, also arrived in Klondyke and told Haynes that both Kempton and Wootan were dead and Jeff Power was fatally wounded.[1]

Haynes drove down into Safford, arriving around noon, and sent his boss, U.S.
Marshal Joseph Dillon, the following breathless telegram: "run on to powers gang
at abandoned mine seven thirty this morning sheriff mcbride deputy kempton
special deputy marshal kane witton were killed endeavoring to arrest john powers
tom powers and tom sisson slackers these men escaped on horseback father of
powers brothers fatally wounded."[2] Dillon, who happened to be in Prescott in
northern Arizona, responded immediately, notifying his deputies, as well as all
county sheriffs located in the southeast corner of the state, and warning them that
"All the fugitives are well armed and will fight." Dillon also forwarded Haynes's
telegram to his superiors at the U.S. Attorney General's Office in Washington,
D.C., adding a request for federal reward money for the capture of the three men.[3]

It was Sunday afternoon in Washington when Marshal Dillon's telegram
arrived at the Department of Justice, and no one responded to it. On Monday
and Tuesday Dillon sent two follow-up telegrams to his superiors and to Bureau
of Investigation agent Charles Breniman in San Antonio before an official finally
replied, noting that the original telegram sent by Dillon "was erroneous buried in
somebody's office for 2 days." While he waited for a response from disinterested
Washington officials, Dillon returned to Phoenix on Monday morning to direct
the posse closing in on the murderers near Redington and, should they escape,
to supervise the formation of new posses composed of lawmen and civilians
from Gila, Graham, Greenlee, Pima, and Cochise counties.[4]

The story of the gun battle went out Sunday night over the wires to all regional
newspapers, and reporters flocked to the Gila Valley and Globe to cover the
sensational story of what was being called "the first armed resistance in Arizona
to the military draft." Dillon met with reporters on Monday, telling them that
his deputy, Frank Haynes, had "escaped with his life, after he had been slightly
injured." Dillon then proceeded to explain why he believed there had been such
a tragic loss of life at the Power cabin, relaying that he and Haynes had spoken
extensively about the Power brothers and his deputy was aware of the "desperate
character" of the men before he led the posse into the Galiuros: "'Deputy Marshal
Haynes knew the Powers boys and knew that they would probably resent being
taken into custody,' said Mr. Dillon. 'It was for that reason that he took the other
officers with him. Haynes, in fact, has been waiting for several weeks to make
the arrest, but because of feared gun play, it was decided to wait until the two
men returned to their father's cabin from the hills before attempting to serve
the warrants. It was thought that in going into the hills after the men that the
Powers boys would ambush officers and slay them without a chance for their

lives.'"[5] Dillon's comment that Haynes had been waiting for several weeks until Tom and John "returned to their father's cabin from the hills" suggests that federal officials knew about McBride's letter to Jeff Power, and that it was sent as a ploy to convince Tom and John Power it was safe to come out of hiding. Dillon did not explain to the press why, if gunplay had been anticipated, he authorized only three men for the posse.[6]

The next day Dillon's deputy, Frank Haynes, failed to corroborate many of his boss's statements to the press when he testified at the coroner's inquest held at the Graham County Courthouse in Safford, never mentioning that he was expecting trouble from the suspects prior to the shootout. Under examination by Graham County attorney William Chambers, Haynes confirmed that he held two federal warrants for Tom and John Power for draft evasion, while Sheriff McBride held two state warrants for Tom Sisson and Jeff Power, but he also revealed that the lawmen had not identified themselves to the occupants of the cabin and never stated they had warrants for their arrest, as required by state law. He then described the late-night journey into Rattlesnake Canyon, and how he and his fellow officers surrounded the cabin. When a man stepped out in the doorway of the cabin with a rifle, "there was four or five shots all come in a bunch. The first shots come from the house. This old man [Jeff Power] fell." Haynes stated that after a brief pause "between the shots from the door, two close together, then two more, then the firing became more rapid, both from within and without the cabin. Jeff Powers never fired a shot."[7]

John and Jay Murdock, Henry Allen, and Ed Knothe were all about a mile away from the Power cabin when the gunfight began. Allen was staying with the Murdocks while he was helping Jay build fence for a local cattle company, so he, Knothe, and Jay Murdock were called to testify about what they witnessed that Sunday morning. All three said they first heard shots around 7:30 A.M., just after first light, but no one among them had a watch, so they could not be certain of the time. Henry Allen estimated he heard twenty shots fired and Jay Murdock believed it was between twenty and twenty-five, but both agreed they came in two bursts, with a minute or so of silence in between, corroborating Haynes's description of the battle. The entire gunfight lasted between three and five minutes, with rifle fire that went "bang" mixed with the "pop, pop, pop," of automatic six-shooters. When German prospector Ed Knothe first heard the gunfire, he ran to the Murdock camp, located about one hundred yards from where he lived, and the four men all speculated about whether the Powers were taking target practice at that early morning hour.[8]

Before long they found out what had happened, as Tom and John Power and Tom Sisson rode up to the Murdock camp heavily armed with rifles and six-shooters. They were not on their customary mounts when they arrived, but rather were riding two of the horses and the mule the lawmen had borrowed from Al Upchurch. John's face was covered in blood, and all three riders were clearly agitated. Everyone began to talk at once, making it difficult to know what was said, so there was little agreement between the testimonies of the three witnesses. However, a few facts were quickly established. John and Tom said that their father was shot but still alive and asked that someone go tend to him. The brothers stated that there were three men dead at the cabin: Sheriff McBride, Kane Wootan, and another man they did not recognize, but whom they believed was McBride's brother. No mention was made of Frank Haynes, the fourth lawman who had escaped without detection.[9]

When county attorney Chambers asked each witness what exactly the Power brothers and Tom Sisson had said to them after the gunfight, Knothe, Allen, and Murdock each told a slightly different version, but all implied the same thing: the gunfight had been anticipated by the Powers. When Henry Allen asked them what was the matter, John Power replied, "'The matter is laying over there in the yard. . . . The little thing tightened up over there. . . . Frank McBride and his brother and Kane Wooten is laying over there in the yard. . . . They killed father." Ed Knothe, who said very little under oath, recalled that he only heard John Power say, "Well, we killed them," while Jay Murdock told the coroner's jury he said to them: "'It has happened,'" to which the Power brothers responded, "'You're damned right it has happened.'"[10]

Henry Allen and Ed Knothe both testified that Tom and John Power said very little during the exchange that followed the shootout and Sisson said nothing at all, but Jay Murdock provided the coroner's jury with lengthy quotations from the Power brothers. According to Jay, Tom Power said his father had "stepped out in the yard and they told him to throw up his hands," then Jeff "dropped his gun and threw up his hands and Kane Wootan shot him." An angry Tom shot through the window, which filled his eye with glass, and then took his "rifle and punched the window out and killed Kane Wootan." Jay told the jury that John Power admitted to killing Sheriff McBride. When Chambers pressed Jay Murdock to reveal if Sisson admitted to killing Martin Kempton, Jay responded, "I didn't hear that part. I didn't hear anyone say Tom Sisson killed the other man." Jay's testimony was problematic because Henry Allen swore under oath that he was standing within a few feet from Murdock during the entire encounter with the

Power boys and Sisson, yet he had not heard any of those statements concerning who shot whom.[11]

When pressed by county attorney Chambers to elaborate why he stated, "'It has happened,'" Jay Murdock shared a conversation he had with Tom Power when he visited the family just days after Ola's death the previous December. Everyone in the canyon knew that the brothers were hiding out from the law to avoid arrest for draft evasion, so Jay asked them, "'Suppose McBride and his posse would walk in here,'" to which Tom allegedly responded, "'Let him come; I'd just as soon die now as any time and while they're getting me, I'll get some of them, maybe more than they get of us.'" He spoke of the letter sent by Sheriff McBride to Jeff Power that explained "to the boys really what it meant to be a slacker, to be a traitor to their country," and Jay swore he had warned both Sheriff McBride and Undersheriff Kempton that the brothers had threatened to kill anyone trying to arrest them.[12]

Murdock's allegation that the Power brothers threatened to kill anyone who rode the trail up Rattlesnake Canyon toward the mine was a surprising claim, given they were expecting visits from mining speculator Charlie Jones of Bisbee and other prospective investors. They were also waiting to take delivery of a boiler to power their stamp mill, and they had partners in the mine—Ed Lyman and Harry Neil—who visited their investment often. While Tom and John assiduously hid from officials like Sheriff Frank McBride to avoid arrest, Jay Murdock's statements suggesting they were willing to jeopardize the mining operation by threatening to kill anyone in the vicinity seemed out of character for the Power men, who had staked everything to its success.[13]

Jay Murdock's testimony that day not only contradicted many of the sworn statements of Ed Knothe and Henry Allen at the inquest, but reports by federal officials as well. In the exchange of letters and telephone calls between McBride and federal authorities throughout 1917 and early 1918 right up to the shootout, the sheriff made no mention that Jay Murdock had told him of threats made by the Powers to kill lawmen. While Special Agent David Ross heard rumors Tom and John were "openly defying the Government to disturb them," he was unable to substantiate those claims. McBride had tried for months to get a federal posse to arrest the Power brothers, and if he had presented evidence that they had threatened officers, permission would have been granted immediately, as it was in similar cases. It seems remarkable that the sheriff did not notify the United States marshal or the United States attorney, unless, of course, he never knew about threats made by the Powers. It was a well established fact in the community that the Power brothers were avoiding the draft, but the other people who lived nearest to the Powers—the Habys, the Bleaks, the Morgans, Henry Allen, and Ed Knothe—all failed to suggest John or Tom threatened anyone before the shootout. Only Jay Murdock made that charge.[14]

As the Powers and Sisson prepared to ride off from the Murdock camp after the shootout, they refused to say where they were going, although John Power told those gathered, "I'll see you in two or three days." The decision to run was later cited by attorneys and newspaper editors as an admission of guilt, but it might have been simply preservation instinct. Their choice to lay low for a few days recalled the time almost twenty years before when their Uncle Wiley Morgan killed a cattle thief and took to the hills, only turning himself in when tempers had cooled. The Powers later stated that once they saw the dead sheriff, they feared a lynch mob. They reasoned that if they waited a few days, they might be able to surrender to authorities in another county, whom they trusted not to kill them before they had the opportunity to tell their side of the story. They never saw Frank Haynes during the shootout, so they were unaware the deputy marshal was at the cabin and had gone into town to alert authorities. The Powers and Sisson easily could have escaped, believing no one would know what happened for hours or even days, allowing them a good start ahead of any posse. Instead they rode straight to the Murdock camp and reported the killings, asking for help for their father. When Henry Allen offered to go into town to notify officials and fetch a doctor for Jeff, Tom Power's reply was, "All right, go on," not the response expected from someone who intended to evade justice.[15]

After the confrontation at the Murdock camp, John, Tom, and Sisson headed down the trail toward the nearby town of Redington, while Allen, Knothe, and John and Jay Murdock made their way up to the site of the gunfight, where they found the body of Sheriff McBride near the northeast corner of the cabin and Kane Wootan and Martin Kempton lying near the southeast corner. They found Jeff Power alive but unconscious in a bush by the old arrastra, where his sons hid him from other assailants they believed might be lurking about. The snowfall had been light until this point, but as it came down harder, according to Jay Murdock, Power regained consciousness after swallowing some water and complained he was cold. Jay Murdock and Henry Allen dragged him back to the mine tunnel to keep him protected and warm. Allen then left to notify authorities and to get a doctor for Jeff, while Ed Knothe returned to the Murdocks' camp to fetch overcoats and tobacco for the long day and night that lay ahead of them until help could arrive from the Gila Valley.[16]

While John and Jay Murdock were alone with Jeff Power, they began to assess the gunshot wound to his chest. The bullet had gone straight through and punctured a lung, leaving a larger hole in the back than in the front, indicating he had been shot in the chest by one of the deputies. Jay Murdock said Jeff "breathed through this bullet hole. . . . I raised him up [to try to talk] and the wind just fairly whistled through there and I took my fingers and held my fingers over the bullet hole, and he could rest easier that way and breathe better." Although Allen and Knothe testified they never heard Power say a word while they were present, Jay provided the coroner's jury with lengthy verbatim quotations from the dying man. Jeff allegedly told him: "I stepped out in the yard, they hailed me and hollered 'throw up your hands' and [I] says 'We give up' and then Kane shot me. . . . I don't know what they wanted to shoot me for. I had up my hands begging them for peace." Jeff kept repeating, "Jay, I am going to die, I can't stand it." John and Jay Murdock tried to keep his spirits up, but it was evident his injuries were fatal. Jeff died at four o'clock that afternoon, and the Murdocks and Ed Knothe, who had returned by then, remained with his body all night inside the tunnel.[17]

The next morning a posse from the Gila Valley, comprised mostly of close friends or relatives of Sheriff McBride and Undersheriff Kempton, arrived at the cabin to retrieve the bodies of the slain officers. It was an emotional scene when McBride's brother Howard threw himself across Frank's body, "sobbing in great gasps." With the sheriff and his undersheriff dead, there were no county lawmen to investigate the crime scene, so members of the posse chose Joseph A. Phillips, a Latter-day Saint and an agent for the Arizona Eastern Railroad who was the current chair of the county Democratic central committee, to oversee an informal inquest. Phillips and the others present noted the positions of the bodies, collected evidence, and then packed the three lawmen on horses and brought them to Klondyke, where they were piled in a truck and transported to Safford. It is unclear whether anyone examined Jeff Power's body, as it was not retrieved, but rather left in the mine tunnel because the posse members refused to bring him into town. As one angry man allegedly said, "'let the varmints have the old son-of-a-bitch.'" In the days and weeks to follow, many other people would travel to the cabin, taking items belonging to the Powers, including personal photographs, letters, and documents, as well as spent cartridge shells and bullets. Local officials later urged the looters to return the evidence and the personal effects of the Power family, but only a handful of items were recovered.[18]

Dr. William E. Platt, the county medical examiner, never made the trip to the Power cabin to examine Jeff Power's body, and he did not have the opportunity to view the bodies of the three slain lawmen until after they had made the long journey on horseback and by car into the Gila Valley. When he took the stand at the inquest, Platt reported that Frank McBride was shot once in the right knee, twice in the stomach, and all three bullets entered his body at an angle that indicated he was shot by someone lying on the ground. A fourth and final bullet entered the right side of his head near his ear and exited in the almost identical spot on the left side of his head. Platt speculated that McBride was "probably living until he received this shot in the head."[19]

Platt testified that Martin Kempton and Kane Wootan both were shot from behind, and each was felled by a single gunshot. Kempton's facial injuries were so horrific that many people did not recognize him at first. According to Platt, the bullet entered "exactly in the center of Martin Kempton's neck and carried away the first, second and third vertebra . . . and came out at the side of the jaw and just tore the whole side of the jaw out," as well as his ear. Platt estimated the undersheriff bled to death within several minutes. Deputy Kane Wootan was killed by a bullet that entered around the third vertebra and exited through the center of his chest, leaving a "hole as big as three silver dollars." Platt surmised Wootan died almost instantly, and he had a "bruise on his face that looked like the heel of a boot. . . . It was undoubtedly produced before he died. It showed marks of injury before death," implying when he was shot, he had fallen on Kempton's boot.[20]

As the inquiry concluded, it was clear the findings of the official coroner's inquest were damaging for the Power brothers and Sisson. A federal marshal swore that the first shots were fired from within the cabin, and the lawmen were not up there under false pretenses—they had four legitimate warrants issued for the occupants. Three witnesses suggested that the men in the cabin had anticipated the gunfight and one of them, Jay Murdock, heard Tom Power suggest prior to the shootout he would not surrender without a fight. But Haynes also testified that the lawmen had not identified themselves when they arrived at the cabin, and Jay Murdock revealed that Kane Wootan had shot Jeff Power as he was trying to surrender. The inquest also highlighted the fact that the bodies of the lawmen were not inspected by officials until after they were transported dozens of miles over rough roads, that Jeff Power's body was never autopsied, and that the crime scene was immediately tainted by family and friends of the officers. The local officials' lackluster approach to the investigation may have resulted from the pervasive belief that the fugitives would never be taken alive, so evidence would not be needed for a trial. After the inquest that afternoon the county attorney determined there was sufficient cause to issue three murder warrants for the arrests of Tom Sisson, John Power, and Tom Power.[21]

That same day Clifford C. Faires of the Military Intelligence Division, who was stationed in Globe, issued the federal government's official report on the shootout. Much of the routine information in his report was clearly pulled from Frank Haynes's statements confirming the four lawmen were there to arrest the Power brothers, "charged with being slackers." But the federal account also contradicted several key points made by witnesses Frank Haynes, Henry Allen, Ed Knothe, and Jay Murdock. It read in part: "Jeff Powers came to the door and was ordered to throw up his hands and did so but that then immediately firing commenced from the inside of the house killing the two deputies and then McBride was killed on the other side of the house. Haynes who was in advance of Sheriff, coming to house from another path, then circled [the] house, saw the two dead deputies and miraculously escaped death. . . . A short time after the shooting the fugitives informed one Allen that they had killed three officers and wished more would be sent so that they could kill the G—D—S—of B—."[22]

The last statement, that they wished to kill more officers, drew the most attention from the press and from Graham County attorney William Chambers, but Henry Allen never made that statement under oath. At the inquest, he testified that John Power said only, "I'll see you in two or three days," yet this alleged threat to kill again would later be contorted to claim the Power brothers and Sisson were guilty of premeditated murder. The rest of Faires's report, based on BI special agent David Ross's investigation of the Power family, bordered on the farcical, rehashing much of the local gossip in the Gila Valley, yet it was repeated as fact by the leading newspapers in the Southwest. Faires wrote:

Jeff Powers father, was agitator threatened to shoot anyone trying to arrest his sons for being slackers. Some here claim he was a German Sympathizer. His wife left him and is living with one son Ben Tom Powers. *Ben Tom Powers,* son, aged 21, married living at Winkleman, this County, has one child. Registered [for the draft] and exempted. . . . Is quite well spoken of. For a time acted as Acting Town Marshal. John & Tom aged 25 and 28 respectively. One for a time in fall worked as miner in Copper Hill. Have not direct proof as to this. *Mrs. John McMurren,* daughter married, McMurren, formerly of San Carlos, Cattleman and Rancher now living in Tucson, AZ. Another daughter married a Doctor. *Maricopa Slim,* another son was killed in Maricopa by a circus man with Al G. Barnes Circus. *Mary* another daughter supposed to have met with foul play at ranch or mine near Klondyke.[23]

Although Ben T. Powers and J. A. McMurren quickly refuted they were in any way connected to the Power family involved in the gun battle, only one newspaper printed the correction, while numerous others repeated and embellished on the falsehood. The incorrect association with Maricopa Slim, a well-known former special agent for the Southern Pacific Railroad and deputy sheriff, led to more misinformation, with newspaper editors claiming Maricopa Slim was Jeff's son with a first wife, but he "was reported to have married an Indian woman about 35 years ago and the two younger boys were half breeds." The *Daily Silver Belt* claimed, "They are typified as ignorant and as having given officers trouble before. . . . It has been common talk among officers of the law that sooner or later this spot would be a scene of trouble." The *Arizona Republican* concurred and stated emphatically that no member of the family could read or write. The article's author went on to remark, without providing specifics, that after reviewing photographs of the three fugitives he was convinced, based solely on their appearances, that "all three men are far below average in reasoning power."[24]

People living in the Southwest who had heard so much talk about the slackers living in the mountains and organizing for a rebellion were gripped by this story of armed resistance to the federal government. Newspaper editors, noticing that hundreds of people gathered to read the bulletins posted about the shootout on the boards outside their offices, scoured the countryside for stories and often printed whatever rumors they heard about the Power family, rarely pausing to check the credibility of the informant. Threats made by the slackers—real or imagined—solidified them in public opinion as subversives capable of all kinds of other crimes. The press and government officials quickly declared, with little evidence, that the Power brothers and Sisson were agitators, German sympathizers, anti-government, and above all else, dangerous and willing to murder again. It was revealed that authorities had opened their mail at the Redington post office and discovered Jeff Power, who had recently visited to buy supplies, had written to a company asking for prices on several calibers of rifle cartridges. From this the press assumed that they were stockpiling ammunition in anticipation of ambushing lawmen.[25]

The Power brothers were four generations removed from their German ancestors, who had first arrived in Pennsylvania just after the American Revolution, but their friends and neighbors, like Ed Knothe and the Habys, spoke with heavy German accents; their parents had lived in the Hill Country of Texas, which was dominated by Germans; and Ola was cooking sauerkraut when she died. To whatever extent their father had failed to demonstrate appropriate patriotic zeal for the war—his unwillingness to purchase war bonds or his antiwar comments—based on the flimsiest of circumstances, the public quickly assumed the worst: that the Powers were pro-German traitors willing to kill patriotic citizens.

A story went over the Associated Press wire service speculating about what had caused Jeff Power to rebel against his own government, suggesting he was an anarchist opposed to the rule of law:

> All information obtainable about the Powers-Sisson gang indicates that they were outlaws in spirit and half-way outlaws in fact outside of the consideration of military draft law. Their defiance is therefore not that of a particular law, but rather of the will of law. Jeff Powers, father of the boys, *The Citizen* has information, had been engaged in litigation for years and had been so soured by his defeats that he counseled his sons to regard the government as a government of the rich for the rich and that justice was unobtainable for such as them. It is said that for years he had planned this rebellion in case the law should come for him or any of his sons with a warrant.[26]

Like many other poor southerners, and after years of legal struggles that impoverished him, Jeff certainly may have decried the "government of the rich for the rich." But it was unlikely Jeff was so "soured" by their solitary legal defeat when Charley and Jane lost control over the Doubtful Canyon Mine in 1910—a legal battle Jeff never spoke of—that he planned a rebellion against the government. He and his mother never resorted to violence when challenged over the years, but instead used the courts to defend themselves and their property. Regardless, the image of Jeff Power as a dangerous anti-government agitator would prevail in the press, casting a shadow over his sons Tom and John and Tom Sisson, who continued to evade the posses.

Over the days and weeks that followed as the hunt to locate the fugitives continued, accounts of the shootout became more and more outlandish. It was reported that Martin Kempton was shot dead when he kicked in the back door of the cabin, even though no such door existed. Likewise, the press ran stories that Tom Sisson was badly injured and the Power brothers were carrying him around on a stretcher in the Chiricahua Mountains, when in fact Sisson was the only one of the three fugitives unharmed. The men were all good hunters, but now in the press they became expert shots: "The Powers boys have a reputation for shooting that is second to none in that region. It is said that the eldest, John Powers, riding a horse at full speed in a revolver match, planted six bullets in a small tin can from an automatic."[27]

Tom Sisson was an easy target for the press, with his past conviction for horse theft and short stint in prison. Political opponents of George Hunt, the man who had paroled Sisson, pounced on his decision to allow such a dangerous man back into society, using it to tarnish Hunt's image. Wiley Morgan, attempting to deflect criticism away from his nephews, heaped blame on Tom Sisson as well, telling reporters the blacksmith was "pro German and had caused the Powers boys to evade the draft." His accusations were astonishing, given that Sisson was a military veteran with an excellent service record. His former rank in the army was that of private, but now the press claimed he was a sergeant with superhuman skills that would allow him to stave off the thousands of men trailing him. The newspapers, as well as military officials in Washington, D.C., accused Sisson of being a slacker, even though at age forty-nine he was not even eligible for the draft.[28]

It was harder for the press to make a case against the Power brothers, who had never been convicted of any crime. Nevertheless, a Lordsburg, New Mexico, newspaper invented a past for Tom and John, reporting, "The family is not favorably known, as when they were in Grant county they were into trouble most of the time."[29] Even their mine was given a new, unsavory history by the press. The summer after the shootout, an article in the *Arizona Star* reported that an itinerant prospector walked into the newspaper's office and told of how he first discovered the Abandoned Mine. The man identified himself as Black Jack Gardner ("Black Jack" being the nickname given to numerous outlaws in the Southwest) and said he had wandered into Rattlesnake Canyon, "when my fortunes were at a very low ebb." There he ran into another prospector with a burro as he camped along the San Pedro River, and together they went prospecting in the countryside. One day they spotted a steer and shot it for meat, but when cowboys came by the next day, Gardner and his companion worried they would be accused of rustling. So they headed up into the canyon, where they found "one gold stringer after another" and established the claims. Whether a fraud wandered into the *Star*'s office with this fantasy tale or the editor himself concocted the story is unclear, but the true story of the respectable Branson brothers from Oracle and their discovery of the mine was tossed aside by newspapermen, who preferred a more evocative rendition that sold newspapers to a gullible public.[30]

Deputy Marshal Frank Haynes himself said that most reports he read of the shootout and his own testimony "were distorted to an unbelievable extent," and the only true rendition of what he told reporters appeared in the *Arizona Record* on February 13, 1918, which indeed reflected the testimony he gave under oath on two separate occasions. Frustrated, Haynes stopped talking to the press, but that did not stop the press from attributing to him many erroneous stories.[31]

As the press spun yarns, the citizens of the Gila Valley planned to bury the three fallen officers. A mass meeting was held at city hall on Tuesday, called by the Safford mayor to arrange a funeral for the men who, according to the press, had been "ruthlessly slain by murderous bandits." The following day all businesses in Safford were closed in observance, and an estimated 2,500 people turned out to mourn the deceased at the funeral, held at the largest building in the Gila Valley, Layton Hall. All three lawmen had been killed in their prime—McBride was forty-four, Kempton thirty-nine, and Wootan thirty-six—and left behind three widows to raise twenty children alone. The packed hall was festooned with red, white, and blue bunting, and flowers arrangements were inscribed with the words "Faithful Heroes."[32]

Mormon bishops and elders as well as St. Joseph Stake President Andrew Kimball extolled the virtues of the slain lawmen during the service. Kimball told the audience: "These men were not only gallant officers, patriotic and faithful to the cause of their country but were good Christian citizens, men who had no bad habits, tender and loving fathers and husbands. It is these qualities in the heroic dead officers, more than the horror of the bloody tragedy, that has so upset the people of Graham county that business is near at a standstill and a dark cloud of gloom seems to hover over the county. Never before in the history of the county has anything occurred that seems near so sad." Kimball highlighted McBride's heroism, asserting that when he "discovered that he was forced into a fight he exclaimed in a pleading voice to those unfortunate murderers, 'Boys! Boys! Boys!' as if to say 'stop and realize.' Yet when he saw his pleading was in vain he stood out in the opening and fought like a tiger against overwhelming odds—even after he was mortally wounded, never quitting until the last."[33]

In stark contrast to the elaborate and well-attended funeral for the three lawmen, Jeff Power's body was left unattended at the mine for days. Klondyke residents refused to bury him, perhaps expecting officials to come to autopsy the body, as required by state law. For whatever reason, county attorney Chambers failed to order an inquest, and it was days before he finally authorized Power's burial. Local prospector Al Kountz was asked to perform the task, but no budget was provided for a coffin or burial plot, so Jeff Power's body was laid to rest near the shaft of his beloved mine—no ceremony, no family or friends in attendance, and no fine speeches.[34]

The funeral for the lawmen galvanized an already outraged community against the three fugitives who were characterized by the U.S. marshal, the county attorney, and other public officials as murderers who would rather die than be brought into custody. The press predicted that another deadly "battle will be fought before the fugitives are stopped." Marshal Dillon, who was in charge of capturing them, circulated a wanted poster, printed in both English and Spanish, which highlighted the available reward money and provided photos with descriptions of the three fugitives and the horses and mule they were riding. The frenzied reporting all but guaranteed that most men who joined the growing manhunt would shoot first if they were within sight of the fugitives. The dangerous situation was compounded by the large reward offered for their arrest, which quickly escalated to $5,600, most of which was provided by the Graham County Board of Supervisors, the state of Arizona, and the Cochise-Graham County Cattle Growers Association.[35]

During the first few days of the manhunt, Marshal Dillon and local officials exuded confidence that the Power brothers and Sisson would be caught. The fugitives were sighted as they rode down into Redington on the Sunday of the shootout, and an ad hoc posse of men, which had been alerted by Haynes's quick call to action, came within a half mile of capturing Tom and John and Sisson. Although they managed to elude the posse that first day on the run, hopes for their capture remained high because Harry Wheeler, the sheriff of Cochise County, and Rye Miles, Pima County sheriff, had taken charge of the posses on the ground. They were accomplished lawmen, and both were considered "expert-man hunters" because they had served as Arizona Rangers. Additionally, Wheeler served for years at frontier military posts during the Indian wars. As one journalist put it, the two sheriffs assembled "a strong posse of crack shots. . . . Practically every expert rifle shot in Tucson has joined one or another of the posses."[36]

Over the next few days, however, the trail went cold, and the fugitives were variously reported to be doubling back to the scene of the crime in the Galiuro Mountains, heading to their old home in Doubtful Canyon, or safely lodged with relatives in New Mexico. Three days after the shootout Tucson residents woke to read a frightening headline announcing that the Power-Sisson gang was headed their way. Borrowing from headlines of the war in Europe, it stated that citizens should be on alert for the impending "invasion." The pandemonium was finally put to rest somewhat when posse members found the mule and two horses the fugitives had been riding, so now officials surmised that the three men were on foot and hiding in Cochise Stronghold, the legendary Chiricahua Apache leader's former base of operations in the Dragoon Mountains. The next day they were reported headed toward the Chiricahua Mountains to the east. To prevent

$4,000 REWARD

FOR CAPTURE OF

TOM POWERS

25 years old; dark complexion; smooth shaven; 5 feet 10 inches tall; slender; weight about 165 pounds. Dark hair, trifle curly. Is wearing bandage on forehead, evidently slightly wounded in fight with officers.

JOHN POWERS

JOHN G. POWERS

27 years old; dark complexion; 5 feet 9 inches tall; slender; weight about 165 pounds. Light hair, blue eyes.

TOM POWERS
in Center

TOM J. SISSON

Paroled convict, Arizona State Prison. 49 years old; 5 feet 9¼ inches tall; weight, 165 pounds; dark complexion; black hair; brown eyes; high forehead, deeply wrinkled. Rather stoop shouldered. Fairly good teeth. Lump on left side of head near the ear. Wears 7⅛ hat, and while in prison wore a heavy black beard.

These men killed Sheriff McBride, his under-sheriff, M. R. Kempton, and Posseman Kane Wooten, while resisting arrest on a Federal warrant, charging them with evading the draft. The fight occurred at an abandoned mine near Klondyke, Graham County, Arizona, at 7:30 o'clock Sunday morning, February 10, 1918, and the murderers escaped, riding South on a sorrel horse, a brown horse and a sorrel mule. All animals carried full cowboy equipment. The County of Graham, Arizona, has offered a reward of One Thousand Dollars for the capture, dead or alive, of the three men, or one-third of this amount for either of them.

The Governor of Arizona has issued his proclamation offering a reward of One Thousand Dollars for each of these men subject to the provisions of the Arizona statutes, which authorize officers to use all proper necessary force to effect such apprehension.

The United States Government is expected to add materially to these offers of reward, having been requested by me to do so.

Advise me if any persons answering the description of these men are seen. Use the wires at my expense, Government rate.

Wire or write

JOSEPH P. DILLON, U. S. Marshal

TUCSON OR PHOENIX, ARIZONA

Wanted poster issued by the U.S. Marshal's Office, District of Arizona.
The total reward for the Power brothers and Sisson would reach
$5,600 before the manhunt was concluded.
Courtesy Cameron Trejo Films, LLC.

them from escaping into Mexico, cavalry troops were dispatched to patrol the border just east of Douglas, bloodhounds were brought in to pick up their scent, and several Apache scouts from the San Carlos Reservation took on the task of identifying their trail. The wanted men were trapped in the Chiricahuas, and their capture, officials assured the frightened public, was imminent.[37]

Thousands of years of erosion have transformed the volcanic rock of the Chiricahua Mountains into striking spires, and in more recent memory, the mountains created a natural fortress for Apaches as well as all manner of outlaw. A Tucson newspaper described the mountains as "a domain for a Robin Hood with its running streams, its beautiful forest and its maze of canyons and peaks . . . one place in Arizona where the law is defied." Sheriffs Wheeler and Miles surmised that the Power brothers and Sisson were sleeping during the day and traveling only at night in the rough canyons to avoid detection. After four days without a sighting, the papers announced that the fugitives "were swallowed up in the Chiricahua mountains . . . for the time being safe."[38]

The manhunt grew exponentially as men, equipped with little more than a horse and rifle, volunteered in hopes of gaining the reward money, and soon it became one of the largest in Arizona history. Its enormity created a challenge for Marshal Dillon, who set up his operational headquarters in Douglas near the Mexican border. There were few telegraph stations in the area and the terrain was rugged, so it was difficult to coordinate logistics and communications between Dillon and the sheriffs and deputies reporting to him. The marshal had to find provisions to feed the posse members, as well as continually arrange to ship in fresh horses for the chase and locate cars and trucks to dispatch the needed supplies. The small town of Bowie near the New Mexico border became "a teeming mass of armed and provisioned man hunters and the streets were crowded with autos from the surrounding towns carrying fresh possemen to the front to strengthen the line of guards." Men resorted to wearing white rag bands on their hats identifying themselves as posse members to avoid accidently shooting other searchers they might come across.[39]

Rocket, a trained English bloodhound with a reputation as a killer—he had torn open the throat of a fugitive in a prior engagement—was brought in by Sheriff Rye Miles, but he and the other dogs on the trail had little success. After thirty-six hours bloodhounds have difficulty picking up a scent, and the rain, snow, and sandy desert soil all combined to render their tracking less effective. Mistakes by humans also foiled the dogs. When members of a posse that included Kane Wootan's father, a former federal deputy marshal who should have known better, discovered the fugitives' mounts, they used the saddles themselves before the dogs were brought from Douglas, "so destroying the scent."[40]

The Apache trackers did not have much luck finding the trail, either, as the fugitives, employing tricks Sisson had learned in the military, tied gunny sacks or branches to their shoes to cover their tracks. While the Power brothers and Sisson were holed up in the Chiricahuas without food, water, or horses for days, down below an army of men, sometimes numbering over one thousand soldiers and civilians, created a guard line in a one hundred–mile radius around the mountains. Wheeler seemed reluctant to send posses up into the dangerous region, preferring to cordon off the fugitives in the mountains and starve them out. Some people suggested Wheeler wanted the glory of capturing the men to himself, but Wheeler told the press he was concerned that untrained civilians might get lost, injured, or even killed in the treacherous canyons, a real danger.[41]

Federal authorities tried to locate an "aeroplane" to pursue the criminals from the skies, but the few planes in the area had been requisitioned by the military for the war effort. Although no official ever confirmed that aerial surveillance was used during the manhunt, there were rumors that an airplane was spotted flying near Dos Cabezas and Benson, mounted with lights so it could search at night. If true, the manhunt encapsulated a moment in time when the Old West met the New West. The oldest methods of tracking, bloodhounds, were used in conjunction with the most recent invention, the airplane. "The airmen's search was the only feature suggestive of modernity. Otherwise it might have occurred back in the wild days of the Southwest," offered the editor of the *El Paso Evening Herald*. The *Ogden Standard* further evoked Wild West imagery, reporting that "a posse of 1000 cowboys and a band of Apache Indians" were in close pursuit of the draft evaders.[42]

On February 18, a massive snowstorm moved into the region, thwarting the manhunt. Many posse men opted to hunker down in the saloons of Rodeo, New Mexico, where operation headquarters were relocated and prohibition was not yet the law, or else returned to their homes. Although Sheriff Wheeler remained adamant the men would be captured, much of the initial interest in the manhunt had waned and it was no longer front-page news. Some editors, seeking to explain the manhunt's failure, suggested the murderers had "slipped through the cordon" because they were aided by other slackers in the region, who were rendezvousing in the mountains. It was believed that Tom Kelly, an army deserter loose in the area, was piloting them to their escape, but when he was captured officials could find no evidence he had been in contact with the Powers and Sisson, or any other slackers for that matter.[43]

Although the Kelly story was quickly debunked, the press promoted the idea that there were numerous draft evaders, incited by German agents, hiding in the hills, and massing for an uprising. The prior summer copper mining managers had suggested that German agents were provoking strikes in the camps, and successfully convinced the public to back the Bisbee Deportation, so the notion that draft evaders were planning an attack resonated with the public. At the inquest for the lawmen, county attorney Chambers had pursued this angle as well, asking Jay Murdock if his neighbor, the German prospector Ed Knothe, had persuaded the Power boys to stay out of the army. Murdock responded that Knothe told him "that he thought they were making a mistake" by refusing to register, which apparently convinced the district attorney that Knothe was not a subversive. However, that did not stop rumors that other antiwar agitators were assisting the Power brothers. Reports out of Redington alleged the fugitives were well supplied with food by compatriots who had taken two wagonloads of supplies into the hills. Later accounts claimed they were provisioned by "a veritable nest of slackers settled in the isolated corner of southeastern Arizona and southwestern New Mexico, hiding in the national forest, ready to cross the line on the approach of officers. . . . All of the slackers are said to be well armed and ready to fight capture." Xenophobia was evident as well, as the press suggested that "aliens of all breeds" were among the slackers hiding out in the hills, and calls were made for soldiers to protect the home front.[44]

The murder of three respected lawmen led to speculation over whether justice could truly be served if the fugitives were ever caught alive. During the 1916 election, Arizona voters passed an amendment to abolish the death penalty by the barest of margins: 152 votes out of over 20,800 total votes cast. Proposition 300 had the avid support of liberals like George Hunt, who had been elected as governor the prior fall and was president of the Anti–Capital Punishment Society of America. After the bill's passage, the *Arizona Socialist Bulletin* applauded the progressive legislation, suggesting: "No murderer of any substantial means has ever been legally hung in Arizona. Only murderers who are poor are hung in Arizona." Socialist presidential candidate Eugene Debs declared that the vigilantism and lynching that previously had characterized frontier law enforcement would give way to an "enlightened spirit of the times" in Arizona. But after the brutal killings of McBride, Kempton, and Wootan, numerous newspapers suggested the public was "greatly incensed over the fact that capital punishment has been abolished." A Tucson newspaper reported "that the infuriated cowboys and ranchers . . . deputized for the chase, will endeavor to pull off a necktie party," and there would likely be "two fights, one to capture the men and another to protect them until they can be landed in a secure jail."[45]

By the end of February, the search for Tom and John Power and Tom Sisson was winding down. Sheriff Wheeler was called away on official business, and no new trails were located after the big storm had dropped ten inches of snow on the higher elevations of the region. The last time the pursuers were even close to capturing the fugitives was when their horses were located, just before they entered the Chiricahuas on foot. "In fact," scolded one newspaper editor, "the outlaws have never even been seen by any member of the several posses or the soldiers, and, with the exception of the first trails down Sulphur Springs Valley and across to the Chiricahuas, which might have resulted in the capture of the murderers had the pursuit been continued straight after them, the posses have never been close to the hunted men, who may now be in Mexico."[46]

Amidst all the one-sided reports of the dangerous and remorseless murderers, who no one believed would give up without a fight, only once did a newspaper mention that perhaps the fugitives might have killed in self-defense. Jay Murdock's testimony of Jeff Power's dying words had been ignored by all the newspapers until a small piece, buried on page 2 of the *Tucson Citizen* and almost unnoticed among the more sensational headlines, finally appeared: "Al Kuntz [sic] prospector and trapper from Klondyke who packed out the bodies of the slain officers, says old man Powers told the murderer's nearest neighbors while dying that Kane Wooten shot him, while he had his hands up."[47]

11

CAPTURED

Owing to the intense prejudice existing in this county against them . . .

As the month of February came to an end, the military remained under orders to be on the lookout for Tom and John Power and Tom Sisson, but with the trail cold, only a handful of civilians continued the search. On March 7, 1918, Lieutenant Wolcott P. Hayes, 3rd Squadron, 12th Cavalry, stationed at Fort Hachita, New Mexico, was on border patrol when he received word that the three fugitives had been spotted. Mrs. Barnes Tullos, a ranch woman living near the Mexican border, had seen the wanted posters and recognized the fugitives when they bought provisions from her. She sent one of her sons to Hachita "to give the alarm," and Grant County sheriff Frank Shriver and Deputy Rob McCart picked up the trail and notified command at the nearby fort of the sighting. The lawmen met up with Lieutenant Hayes and the men in his squadron, and together they rode from where the trail had been picked up and headed south to the Mexican border.[1]

Shriver and McCart refused to cross into Mexico, and Hayes did not want to bring too many men with him, because it might "cause a scare if the Mexicans saw a body of cavalry in their country," so the lieutenant took just five of his soldiers across the international line. They split up into two groups of three and continued to follow the tracks toward the Rio Casas. According to Hayes, the fugitives appeared to be wearing cloth or gunny sacks for shoes, quite discernable in the soft desert ground. By noon the lieutenant and his two men were six to eight miles south of the border when Hayes turned around and found himself "looking down three of the biggest gun barrels I had ever seen," poking up from a mesquite bush. Hayes fell off his horse, an automatic reflex he later recalled, and reached for his gun. The three men could have shot him, "but did not. They put their guns down and stood up as I walked up to them." His troopers rode up with rifles ready, but Tom and John Power and Tom Sisson wanted to surrender, not to fight.[2]

Lieutenant Hayes was understandably shocked when the three fugitives he was hunting turned themselves in without firing a shot. The men he found in the desert south of the border bore no resemblance to the desperate murderers everyone living in the Southwest had been reading about for the past twenty-eight days. John Power had been injured during the shootout when a bullet hit the sash of a window and splinters of wood and glass lodged in his left eye and ripped off the bridge of his nose. Without medical assistance his eye became infected, causing him terrible fevers and pain, and Hayes believed the socket was filled with maggots. Tom's left eye was injured as well, filled with shards of glass. All three men were shoeless and covered in scrapes and bruises, starving and dehydrated, having no water and nothing to eat on them but a "dried piece of dead cow." The soldiers offered them what little they were carrying—water and crackers—and signaled the other patrol in the area with rifle fire, then mounted the three weary prisoners on horses because they could walk no farther.[3]

Lieutenant Hayes was curious why the fugitives had not shot him when they had the chance, especially since they had been portrayed in the press as men who had utter disregard for the federal government and the military, preferring to fight to the death rather than submit to the draft. His captives simply told him that "they would not shoot a 'soldier boy.'" However, the Power brothers and Sisson made it clear they would have killed Hayes and his men had they been sheriffs' deputies. The prisoners pleaded with the soldiers not to turn them over to New Mexico or Arizona lawmen, whom they did not trust to bring them in alive. Hayes assured the Power brothers and Sisson that the U.S. Army would protect them and, upon hearing that, the lieutenant reported, "they were very much relieved."[4]

Lieutenant Hayes and his men took the exhausted prisoners back to their camp, cleaned them up a bit, and fed them. Years later the lieutenant recalled: "I really believe they were glad they were caught. . . . I do not believe I ever saw men eat more." They then joined up with Sheriff Shriver and Deputy McCart just north of the border, and when they reached Fort Hachita, officials sent a telegram notifying Sheriff Briggs Stewart, the man who had been named to replace the deceased Frank McBride. By the time Stewart left Safford to pick up his prisoners, reporters from throughout the Southwest were rushing in to cover the capture of the notorious Power-Sisson gang.[5]

The prisoners' concerns that they might be killed if delivered into the hands of county lawmen were well justified. With the abolishment of the death penalty, many residents felt there was insufficient remedy for heinous crimes, and wartime rhetoric seemed to justify vigilantism, allowing "Judge Lynch" to make a reappearance in the Southwest after an absence of many years. Although vigilante justice was prevalent in the Old West, there had been no lynching in Arizona for over thirty years until May 1917, when Van Ashmore was hung by an angry mob of over fifty men wearing handkerchiefs to conceal their identities. Ashmore had befriended a couple travelling along the Apache Trail near Mesa, then shot the husband six times in the back and repeatedly raped the wife. As deputies were transporting him after his capture, dozens of cars intercepted their vehicle in Florence and the armed mob took Ashmore away to "avenge the outrage," hanging him from a telephone pole. Although Arizona newspapers generally decried lynching at this late date, they felt it justified in this case, as did the coroner's jury that ruled that Ashmore was "the victim of justifiable homicide." War propaganda also incited vigilantism, encouraging mobs to take the law into their own hands, as was the case with Frank Little, a union organizer well-known for his anti-war activities in Arizona during the Bisbee Deportation, who had been dragged from his hotel room and lynched the prior August in Butte, Montana. It is no wonder that the Power brothers and Sisson were afraid the sheriffs' deputies would be unable to protect them from mob violence.[6]

Many people later claimed they helped escort the prisoners back to the Gila Valley and told reporters that Tom, John, and Sisson recounted to them lively tales about their close encounters with various posses during the manhunt and the assistance they received from numerous allies in the countryside. But the Power brothers and Sisson later disputed those claims, and most reliable sources noted that the men were subdued and polite after their capture, too exhausted and injured to boast. They said little about their experience on the run, except that they had been on foot since Friday, February 12, when they abandoned their mounts. During their entire twenty-eight days on the run, the men insisted, they had nothing to eat but the "livestock they had killed and only once they obtained bread at a ranch house."[7] Tom Power later recalled how they were never that close to a posse, and how ill his brother was from his eye injury. Several times John was so cold from his fever that he thought he was going to die, so he begged his brother, "Little Tom," and "Big Tom" Sisson to build a fire despite the danger. They also disputed allegations that they were part of a coordinated rebellion against the government, and although army deserter Tom Kelly was arrested for allegedly helping the three men escape, neither he nor anyone else was ever charged with aiding the fugitives. The much discussed nests of slackers were never located in southeastern Arizona.[8]

When Graham County sheriff Briggs Stewart arrived in Hachita on Saturday to pick them up, the prisoners once again expressed concerns that he and his deputies would kill them. Grant County sheriff Shriver claimed he was in charge of the captives and refused to turn the men over to Stewart, demanding authorization from the governor of New Mexico before the men could be returned to Arizona. Shriver had ulterior motives for staying with the three prisoners: he believed he was entitled to the reward money for their capture. The sheriff demanded that he and two of his deputies accompany back to Safford the men who were worth so much alive and nothing dead. A compromise was reached: Shriver would ride in the car with the prisoners back to Safford and Stewart would ride in a separate vehicle, with men assigned to guard the road where it crossed the state line into Arizona.[9]

Although the prisoners had little to say to reporters, they evidently talked more freely in private with Sheriff Shriver, with whom the Power brothers were acquainted from their time growing up in New Mexico. A. P. Hughes, one of Shriver's deputies, who drove the car containing the Power brothers and Sisson, said, "I heard them say that one of the deputies started the shooting first by shooting down their father in cold blood. They then said all they could do was to shoot to protect themselves from getting killed. . . . I will say this, I do not think they are killers for this reason, during the trip from Hachita to Safford the car was full of guns and in reach of the men we had in the car, I often thought if they had been as bad as was said we would have all been dead now."[10]

Officers hoped to sneak the prisoners into the Gila Valley to avoid confrontation with a mob and refused to tell reporters when they were expected in, but the plan failed when two men armed with rifles hailed their caravan a few miles east of Safford. Shriver ordered Deputy Hughes, who was driving, not to stop, so he ran the "car off the road and stepped all the way down on the gas pedal of our Old Jordan car all the way to the Court House in Safford. The people lined the streets of Safford like a parade was in Town. . . . I had the car at over 50 miles an hour right down main street," he recalled.[11] After their arrival in Safford on Saturday afternoon, March 9, John, Tom, and Sisson were escorted into an upper steel cage in the jail of the county courthouse. A doctor was summoned to tend to John's and Tom's wounds, and he pulled glass from both their eyes as well as a wood splinter "one-half inch long and nearly the girth of a pencil" from John's.[12]

News spread quickly when they were returned to Safford, and people drove to town from all over the countryside to get a look at the murderers, who had hardly slept in weeks and were still recovering from their ordeal. Graham County lawmen were careless about the welfare of the three prisoners, placing them on display like animals in a zoo for the remainder of Saturday and all day Sunday. People stood in line for hours to walk through the jail corridor and gawk at them. Even armed relatives of the slain lawmen were allowed within proximity of the captives and, in at least one instance, the jailer disarmed a man as he pulled out his revolver to shoot them. Outside, deputies attempted to disperse the angry mobs of people who spoke openly of planning a lynch party.[13]

While local officers were fumbling the protection of the prisoners in the Safford jail, legal procedures were begun in court to guarantee their safety. The Power brothers sent a message to their brother Charley in New Mexico asking him to hire James Fielder, the noted criminal defense attorney who had defended their father years before against charges lodged by James Gould and James Baird over the sale of the Doubtful Mine. Charley scraped together a couple hundred dollars for Fielder's retainer, a pittance compared to the several thousands of dollars generally needed for a good attorney to defend against a murder charge. When Fielder arrived by train early Wednesday morning, he made a motion for a change of venue for his clients, "owing to the intense prejudice existing in this county against them," and asked to have them immediately removed from Graham County for their safety. Fielder also condemned Sheriff Stewart for allowing the dangerous crowds into the jail the prior weekend. Under the circumstances Graham County attorney William Chambers, anxious "to avoid all danger of a lynching," offered no objections to the motion to move the prisoners to another location.[14]

That night they were taken under cover of darkness to Clifton and delivered into the custody of Greenlee County sheriff Arthur Slaughter. He placed them in three separate cells, no two adjacent to one another, and prohibited journalists from interviewing them. Graham County sheriff Stewart remained defensive about accusations that he failed to protect his prisoners when they had been in his custody in Safford, telling the press that the Power boys and Sisson were removed from his jail because they had criticized "the government, both state and national, as well as the officers and the public in general." Stewart further reported that they expressed no regrets about killing Sheriff McBride or Deputy Wootan, and only felt remorse for killing Undersheriff Kempton because they did not know him.[15]

Sheriff Slaughter, who held the prisoners in his custody in Clifton for several months awaiting trial, reported no such animosity expressed by the Power brothers or Sisson. Although he did not allow them to speak directly to the press, Slaughter relayed the prisoners' story to a reporter for the *Copper Era and Morenci Leader,* Clifton's largest newspaper:

> When the officers reached the Powers home the father of John and Tom Powers went out with his Winchester and asked them what was wanted. The officers first commanded him to throw up his hands. This he did after placing his Winchester between his knees. He was informed that they came after John and Tom. To this the old man asked "for that damned draft?" and when told yes, he replied that they could not get them, and returned to the house with his Winchester. He was shot by Deputy Kempton, through the body, but it was thought the second shot, which was fired by Wootan was the fatal shot. The old man only lived about 30 minutes after he was shot.[16]

The Powers' account, as told to Sheriff Slaughter, was clearly at variance with other testimony provided by Jay Murdock and Frank Haynes. Murdock said Jeff was only shot once, not twice, and by Wootan instead of Kempton, but without an autopsy of Jeff Power's body, it was impossible to know who was telling the truth. According to Henry Allen, Ed Knothe, and Jay Murdock, Jeff was still alive when they arrived at the scene and had lived for over eight hours after the shootout, while the Power brothers suggested their father died before they rode off for the Murdocks' camp. The three men in custody were the best eyewitnesses to the shootout, as Frank Haynes acknowledged that from his position behind the shed, he saw little of the initial action. But the prisoners, of course, were motivated by self-preservation to tell a story that vindicated their actions.[17]

Sheriff Slaughter also revealed comments John Power made about his sister's death, which became fodder for the press as well. Although the coroner's inquest had been inconclusive, after the shootout almost every major newspaper in the Southwest, and even Marshal Dillon, stated unequivocally that Dr. Platt determined Ola's "death was caused by a broken neck." The killings revived rumors that she had met with foul play and the men in her family or Sisson were somehow to blame. John Power allegedly told Slaughter, "'they accuse me of killing her, but the one who killed her will never be known until her slayer is on his death bed, then he will make a confession.'" The reporter for the Clifton paper editorialized, "It will be noticed that John Powers did not deny that it was he who killed the Powers girl," and among the general public it was "presumed that she was aware of certain lawlessness of the trio and it was thought best to put her out of the way."[18]

As they awaited trial during their incarceration at Clifton, the three men slowly recovered. Another doctor was brought in to look at the Power boys' injuries again, and he warned John that he would probably need to have his eye removed because it was so badly infected. John refused to have the operation, so carbolic acid was used to sterilize the wound. The cauterization was effective, halting the infection and saving his life; however, neither he nor his brother Tom ever regained vision in their left eyes.[19]

With the press barred from access to the prisoners, aside from Sheriff Slaughter's sympathetic account of the gunfight, coverage was biased toward the state's case. Their guilt appeared so obvious that the press began to speculate about the inevitable conviction that would follow the trial. Editors lamented the fact that the prisoners would escape the hangman's noose. The editor of the *Arizona Daily Star* complained that the worst fate that awaited the three men if tried in Arizona courts was "knitting socks under the 'honor' system" in state prison. Governor George Hunt had administered many reforms in the Department of Corrections that had come under attack by conservatives. He believed criminals were a product of their environment, over which they had little control, and that humane prison policies could instill a sense of self-respect and good citizenship. He eliminated the striped clothing he believed stigmatized prisoners and halted the practice of placing disruptive prisoners in underground cells where they were stripped down to their underwear, chained to the floor day and night, and fed nothing but bread and water.[20] The prison reform that created the biggest public uproar, however, was the honor system mentioned by the *Star* editor. Hunt put men to work building state roads or on local farms or dairies—not knitting socks, as the newspaper man sarcastically suggested—which allowed them outside the prison walls, where they had a semblance of normal life doing productive work. Hunt believed most criminals could be rehabilitated in such circumstances and he preferred to give them a second chance. But as the governor's numerous opponents liked to point out, those on the honor system, called trustys, avoided the harsh treatment many believed befitted their crimes and occasionally escaped under the lax conditions.[21]

Under public pressure to find a way to assure they were convicted of a capital crime, United States attorney Thomas Flynn investigated whether the killings occurred on the San Carlos Apache Indian Reservation, which would have placed the case under the federal government's jurisdiction and subjected the prisoners to the death penalty. Because he discovered the Power cabin was located over thirty miles away from the reservation and federal deputy marshal Frank Haynes was unharmed during the shootout, the federal government could only prosecute for "resisting an officer and assaulting him or for conspiracy" in violation of the Selective Service Act. Flynn determined it was best to prosecute in state courts, even if the maximum sentence was life in prison.[22]

James Fielder, hired by Charley Power to defend the three men, faced a daunting task. His clients had killed three respected lawmen, and the wartime press printed numerous false assertions about the accused during the period of more than three months between the shootout and the commencement of their trial. Furthermore, Tom Sisson was an ex-convict, while the Power brothers were reviled draft resisters. A handful of people, mostly relatives and friends in Rattlesnake Canyon and Klondyke, believed that the men had acted in self-defense when attacked in their own home, but they were cowered into silence as public indignation mounted against the trio. Tom and John had specifically requested Fielder's services because they grew up in New Mexico hearing their father sing his praises for his "uncanny ability to sway juries and obtain miraculous acquittals when all seemed lost."[23] Given the sentiment against them, the accused murderers needed a miracle.

At fifty-three years of age, Fielder was an experienced criminal defense attorney who had won many difficult cases during his long career. Fielder had served as a United States commissioner in New Mexico, so he was well-versed in federal law, and he successfully defended numerous individuals over the years, the most notorious of whom were members of Black Jack Ketchum's gang, who were charged with robbing a train at Steins Pass in 1897. According to the *Silver City Enterprise,* Fielder's "eloquent argument" and legal gymnastics convinced the jury to turn in a surprising verdict of not guilty, despite overwhelming evidence presented by the county attorney to convict the defendants. In a case that likely informed his strategy for the Power-Sisson trial, in the spring of 1898 Fielder defended Louis L. Lane, charged with killing a constable who was trying to arrest him. Fielder argued that the officer carried no legal arrest warrants for the defendant when he tried to apprehend Lane at his own home. According to witnesses, Lane had been threatened by someone and told to leave town or he would be tarred and feathered. When Lane heard the lawman and his posse approach his home, he fought back, fearing for his life. Fielder's self-defense argument swayed the jury and Lane was acquitted.[24]

Most of Fielder's success stories as a criminal defense attorney were in the distant past by 1918. New Mexico law enforcement had cracked down on the outlaw gangs in the region, so with fewer crimes committed, he was forced to find clients elsewhere. In 1908 he took on the Detroit Copper Company in Greenlee County, Arizona, suing on behalf of residents of Clifton who had suffered losses from floods. Fielder successfully argued the damage was caused by copper tailings from the mining operations, which clogged the river, a problem compounded by the poorly constructed dams Detroit Copper had erected. But his success in winning damage suits against a major copper company did not endear him to corporate interests in Clifton, where he would defend the Power brothers and Sisson ten years later. By the 1910s his legal fees were not paying the bills, and Fielder lost several pieces of property to foreclosure. Despite his changes in fortune, when he ran unsuccessfully for election as district attorney for New Mexico's Sixth Judicial District in 1916, the local newspaper editor said, "We have never heard anything but the highest praise of Mr. Fielder as a lawyer." Even his opponent during the Power-Sisson trial, Graham County attorney William Chambers, suggested that Fielder was "rated as one of the best criminal lawyers of the Southwest."[25]

James Fielder's main strategy was to prove to the jury the three defendants shot at the lawmen in self-defense, only after their father had been gunned down by Kane Wootan while trying to surrender. According to historian Larry Ball, frontier attorneys often used self-defense to counter a murder charge, citing the preeminent Anglo legal authority William Blackstone, who said: "if the party himself, or any of these his relations, be forcibly attacked in his person or property, it is lawful for him to repel force by force. . . . Self-defense . . . is justly called the primary law of nature." On the Southwest frontier, courts often liberally interpreted self-defense, especially when a man was defending his own home.[26]

Fielder also sought to argue that the Power men and Tom Sisson "were not informed by the officers that they were, in fact, officers of the law." Arizona law required arresting officers to identify themselves and present a proper warrant, something Deputy Marshal Haynes admitted had not occurred. It would not take much effort on Fielder's part to prove the Power brothers and Sisson were unaware their assailants were lawmen. "Throw up your hands" was a term used by outlaws and lawmen alike. The defendants did not know Deputy Martin Kempton, and while they were well acquainted with Kane Wootan, he had not been a full-time employee of the sheriff's department for over a year, allowing Fielder to argue that his clients did not know Wootan was there in an official capacity. While the two deputies were in clear view to anyone standing in the doorway or at one of the windows, McBride and Haynes were behind the shed.

From where he stood, Haynes testified he could not make out Jeff Power's face in the dim light of the doorway of the cabin and, since McBride was by his side, Fielder could use Haynes's testimony to argue that under those conditions, the brothers did not recognize Sheriff McBride either.[27]

The third prong of Fielder's defense was to cast doubt on the arrest warrants for all four men living at the Power mining cabin. It was Fielder's belief that state officials could not issue federal warrants, as Graham County justice of the peace U. I. Paxton had for Tom and John Power for violation of the federal Selective Service Act. Furthermore, he would argue that because Sheriff McBride never filed a report on the Power brothers with the U.S. commissioner in Globe, as he was instructed to by the U.S. attorney for Arizona, Tom and John had never received the required official notification that they were in violation of the Selective Service Act. He would also call into question the felony perjury warrants for Jeff Power and Tom Sisson. Fielder knew state law gave officers wide latitude when they held a felony warrant, allowing them to kill a suspect resisting arrest, but the perjury warrants were not issued until February 9, the day before the shootout, allowing Fielder to argue neither Jeff nor Sisson could have possibly known he was wanted by the sheriff. Noting the recent issue date of the perjury warrants (allegedly Fielder would later tell the jury the ink had not yet dried on the warrants for Jeff Power and Tom Sisson) and arguing that the federal warrants for Tom and John were invalid, he was drawing from his previous successful defense of Louis Lane. Lane did not know he was wanted and legal warrants were absent, so the court determined he was free to defend himself and his home when the constable pulled a gun on him during an attempted arrest.[28]

Fielder faced three experienced prosecuting attorneys for the state: Graham County attorney William R. Chambers, Gila County attorney Norman Johnson, and A. R. Lynch. Born and educated in Illinois, Chambers was forty-five and had been practicing law for eleven years when he became the lead prosecutor for the case. Johnson was well known for his ability to question witnesses, and he conducted the bulk of the examinations for the prosecution. Lynch worked on many cases for the Greenlee County Attorney's Office and had served as a delegate to the state's constitutional convention in 1910. The Power-Sisson case was so important to the state that there was talk that Arizona attorney general Wiley E. Jones would join the prosecution's team, but Chambers declined his services, confident he "had plenty of talent" to get a conviction.[29]

After interviewing witness Jay Murdock, who testified at the inquest that Jeff Power was shot while trying to surrender, Chambers realized Fielder had a strong case for self-defense. The prosecution required a strategy that would prove beyond a reasonable doubt the men committed premeditated murder, so Chambers made a trip to the Power cabin in late March to collect evidence and formulate his plan, accompanied by Kane Wootan's brother J. Frank Wootan, Graham County sheriff Briggs Stewart and several of his deputies, and Harry DuBois, a commercial photographer from the Gila Valley. Of course, by that time almost two months had elapsed, and numerous people had disturbed the scene at the cabin. Nevertheless, they inspected the surroundings, collected evidence, took photos, and formulated a strategy to argue for first-degree murder.[30]

As they examined the northeast corner of the cabin where McBride's body had been found, Chambers and his assistants discovered a hole through the chinking between the logs of the shed. From the bullet casings found inside the cabin and the medical examiner's report of McBride's injuries, Chambers concluded that someone had lain on the floor of the shed, punched a rifle through the chinking in the logs, and shot into McBride's knee and stomach. The Power brothers freely admitted shooting Kempton and Wootan—Tom said he shot from the south window while John stood in the east-facing doorway—but claimed McBride was killed by random gunfire, suggesting he might have been hit by friendly fire. Now there was evidence someone in a third location, inside the shed, shot McBride, and only Sisson was unaccounted for during the gun battle.[31]

Chambers decided to drop charges for the deaths of Wootan and Kempton: it was just too easy for the defense to argue the Power boys shot back in self-defense when their father was killed by one of the deputies. Instead, Chambers charged the three defendants only for the murder of Sheriff McBride. The sheriff did not take part in the initial volley of gunfire, so he could not be accused of initiating the attack like Kempton or Wootan, and everyone in the cabin knew who McBride was, so the defendants could not claim they were unaware he was a lawman. Chambers was convinced he could prove "without question Robert F. McBride . . . was deliberately murdered without any excuse whatever."[32]

On the surface Chambers's strategy was surprising, because of the three defendants, Sisson would be the hardest to convict of premeditated murder. At the inquest Henry Allen, Ed Knothe, and Jay Murdock all testified there was no mention of Sisson's role when the Powers spoke at the Murdock camp following the shootout, and Jay claimed John confessed to killing McBride. Furthermore, John and Tom contended for the rest of their lives that Sisson never fired a shot that day, that he never even got out of bed until the shooting had ceased. Despite the testimony denying Sisson played a role in the killings, it is probable that

Chambers believed the jury would discount the testimony of two draft evaders and an ex-convict.[33]

To succeed, both legal teams were forced to rely heavily on the sworn statements of father and son, John and Jay Murdock. Defense attorney Fielder knew these two witnesses could prove self-defense because they heard a dying Jeff Power say that Wootan had killed him while trying to surrender. For the prosecution team of Chambers, Lynch, and Johnson to prove first degree murder, they needed witnesses to testify that all three men had vowed to slay lawmen prior to the shootout, and among all the witnesses interrogated, only Jay Murdock could provide those statements. But after both the defense and prosecution had performed their investigations into the Murdocks, they were no doubt alarmed to discover the two men had dubious pasts and documented instances of lying. Attorneys routinely investigate key witnesses to determine whether they are credible, and as Chambers and Fielder both read through the numerous and lengthy divorce and criminal case files involving the Murdocks as defendants, they must have had qualms about putting either man on the stand. The Bisbee street brawl with Jay's stepfather could be explained by bad blood between relatives, but the other cases that were uncovered were much more damning, and confirmed what many folks in Aravaipa already suspected: the Murdocks were unreliable characters.

The father, John Maddison Murdock, was born in Pope, Arkansas, in 1849 and grew up in Texas, where he married Rebecca Jane McBee, with whom he had seven children, including his son Jay. In 1894, after twenty years of marriage, Rebecca filed for divorce, charging that John had failed to provide properly for her and their children and had been abusive toward them. Murdock's two oldest daughters testified that he was often out of work and refused to find employment, and that he had whipped and verbally abused them, causing one daughter to run away at age fourteen and marry in order to escape his wrath. Rebecca Murdock told the court that she had tolerated her husband's abuse for years until one day, when he was unable to pay his debts, John took out an insurance policy on their home and furniture. According to Rebecca, some of the items on the insurance policy "neither he or I ever had, and he wanted me to swear that I did have this stuff and that it was in this house he aimed to burn the house and get the insurance." When she refused to cooperate, they separated.[34]

After Rebecca left him, John arrived at her house one day and flew into a rage, accusing her of adultery and attacking her with a kitchen knife. Neighbors heard the commotion and stopped him before she was harmed, but Rebecca brought charges against him for attempted murder. After the incident, Rebecca's father told the court, "If I was allowed to say what I thought of the man, it would be to say that the man is certainly crazy." After hearing testimony from numerous witnesses, the judge in the subsequent divorce case ruled the adultery charge was groundless and found for the plaintiff, Rebecca. She was awarded custody of four of their five minor children from their marriage, while John Murdock was awarded custody of twelve-year-old Jay.[35]

Shortly after the divorce John Murdock left New Mexico, where he was still under grand jury indictment for the attempted murder of Rebecca as well as for theft, taking young Jay with him. He eventually relocated to Phoenix and remarried, but his second marriage to Martha Charlton ended in divorce as well in 1903 because, according to his wife, he was "worthless—he was no good to make a living, or anything like that," and expected her children from a previous union to support him.[36] John Murdock took his now-adult son, Jay, to Bisbee, where they worked in the copper mines and came into contact with an attorney who evidently promised John cash if he testified on behalf of a client.

The criminal defense attorney was Starr K. Williams, a man who was often in trouble with authorities for enticing witnesses to give perjured testimony. John Murdock was called to testify for J. P. Chase, charged with murder, who claimed he killed a man on the streets of Bisbee in self-defense. Murdock made statements to corroborate Chase's claim, but the accounts of three other eyewitnesses convinced the jury and the judge it was murder, and the prosecuting attorney dismantled Murdock's testimony, proving he was not in a position to hear or see the confrontation. John Murdock was immediately charged with perjury. A jury found him guilty in August 1910 and sentenced him to three years in the territorial prison. While appealing his case to the Arizona Supreme Court, Murdock pleaded to politicians in his community and to the district judge to commute his sentence on the grounds that he was too old to serve time in prison.[37]

Murdock told the court that he had served in the Confederate Army and when captured in battle had spent time in federal prison, but was paroled by the "personal intervention of President Lincoln and allowed to visit, under military escort, his father, who was dangerously ill at his home in Waco." Murdock continued to explain that his father was a veteran of the Mexican-American War and remained "true to his allegiance to the Union," which is why Lincoln intervened on John's behalf. While awaiting the court's decision, John Murdock also wrote to his representative from Cochise County asking for help, stating he was seventy years old and believed he could not survive a prison sentence.

Representative Billy Graham sent a petition signed by Cochise County residents to Governor George W. P. Hunt, who graciously paroled Murdock while he was sitting in the Tombstone jail awaiting transfer to the territorial prison after the Supreme Court refused to review his case. Many veterans of the Civil War successfully used their prior service to plead for leniency from the courts, but the trouble with Murdock's story was that he was not a veteran. He was actually only sixty years old, not seventy, making him only eleven when the Civil War began. John Murdock's entire story was fabricated to win sympathy from the courts, and he escaped a prison sentence for perjury by perjuring himself once again, this time on a grander scale.[38]

Fielder and Chambers knew of John Murdock's perjury conviction in Cochise County, and the attempted murder charge. They were also aware that his son Jay had recently abandoned his young wife and infant daughter. The attorneys also knew that both Murdock men had trouble hearing. When asked questions by attorneys—John at his perjury trial and Jay at the inquest for the slain lawmen—the court records showed each man had difficulty understanding what was said in a quiet courtroom. At the inquest, Henry Allen, Ed Knothe, and even Jay Murdock himself all stated that it was difficult to understand what was said as John and Tom Power and Tom Sisson rode into the Murdock camp after the shootout. Yet when the attorneys interviewed John and Jay Murdock, the two men with poor hearing somehow had heard much more than the other men present at that pivotal meeting.[39] Prosecutor Chambers and defense attorney Fielder must have had some regrets about placing these two men on the stand, who in peacetime would have had their credibility eviscerated by opposing counsel, but both legal teams needed the Murdocks' testimony.

12

ON TRIAL

I wonder why Kane Wootan shot me with my hands up?

The trial for the murder of Robert Frank McBride opened at nine o'clock on Monday morning, May 13, 1918, at the Greenlee County Courthouse in Clifton. The chamber, which remains in use today and is the oldest functioning courtroom in Arizona, is located on the second floor of the stately structure and has a commanding view of the southern end of town. The large, wood-framed windows would have been opened on that warm spring morning, offering a breeze and a view of the bustling mining community below. As observers filed in, they could not have helped noticing the numerous deputies patrolling outside, assigned by county officials to control the anticipated angry crowds.[1]

Superior Court judge Frank B. Laine, a large and imposing man from a long line of distinguished attorneys, presided over this court. He had practiced law for many years in Clifton and served as the Graham County district attorney before winning election in 1911 as the superior court judge for the newly created Greenlee County. He was known as an impartial justice who could be counted on to dispatch "litigation as rapidly as possible," all while "considering its importance in criminal jurisprudence of Arizona." There were many eyes on him throughout the Power-Sisson trial proceedings, and he would adhere closely to state law to avoid criticism from the many state and federal officials with an interest in the case.[2]

Reconstructing the murder trial for Tom Sisson and John and Tom Power is difficult, because while many of the court records related to the trial—including witness subpoenas, jury instructions, court minutes, evidence, and correspondence—were retained by the clerk of the Greenlee County Superior Court, the actual trial transcripts are missing. Although court reporter Ernest Shortbridge recorded all witness testimony in shorthand, Arizona law dictated that they be transcribed only when a retrial was authorized, which never happened in this case. Over the years since, numerous researchers have spent countless hours digging through archives and courthouse records searching for them, but the transcripts remain unaccounted for. Some of the testimony can be recovered from newspaper articles published in the *Copper Era* and the *Tucson Citizen,* which had reporters in the courthouse at Clifton. In peacetime, coverage would have been very complete, providing verbatim testimony from key witnesses, but during the war, antiwar and anti-draft statements were barred from the press by government censors, so much of the testimony was omitted.[3]

Even when testimony was allowed in print, the two newspapers' accounts of the trial did not always reconcile, and the *Copper Era* and the *Tucson Citizen,* with opposing political agendas, came to different conclusions about the case. Partisanship often dictates how the press covers events, and this trial was no exception. The coverage by the *Copper Era,* a Democratic newspaper published in Clifton and controlled by the Phelps Dodge Corporation, was much more negative towards the Power brothers and Sisson than the *Citizen.* The editor of the *Copper Era,* William B. Kelly, condemned the Power brothers and Sisson as anti-government agitators with an "an abnormal conception of the principle of individual rights," willing "to defy the Federal government by force, and to carry that force to the death." Allan B. Jaynes was the Republican National Committeeman for Arizona and editor and owner of the *Tucson Citizen,* the largest Republican circulation paper in an overwhelmingly Democratic state. Like all newspaper editors at the time, Jaynes too took a dim view of draft evasion and antiwar talk. But as a member of the opposition press, he demonstrated a greater willingness to listen to both sides of the story than editors for the copper press.[4]

After months of editorial rants and erroneous news reports about the shootout and the Power family, as the trial was set to open, editors and court officials realized that it might be impossible to seat a jury that had not been prejudiced by the one-sided coverage. To circumvent the problem, the county called for a special venire of one hundred male voters, hoping that twelve unbiased men could be found among them. The prosecution and defense attorneys interviewed twenty-nine prospective jurors, and everyone was surprised how rapidly jurors were chosen from that group. Although all the veniremen interviewed said they had read accounts of the tragedy, the *Copper Era* suggested, "few had fixed opinions as to the guilt or innocence of the accused." Only one potential juror stated that his opinion "was so fixed that it would be a difficult matter to render a fair and impartial verdict," and he was released. The prosecution carefully screened for any radical labor union members, asking each potential juror if he was a member of the IWW and whether he was opposed to the draft. Ultimately, prosecutor Chambers and his team excluded seven men as unacceptable, most of whom were either southerners or foreign-born naturalized citizens who might have been more sympathetic to draft evaders.[5]

When the selection process wrapped up Monday morning, ten of the twelve jurors chosen worked for copper companies located in Clifton, Morenci, or Metcalf, while only two were ranchers, reflecting the overall occupational breakdown of Greenlee County. Additionally, most of the men who would decide the fate of the Power brothers and Sisson were registered for military service and, as a local paper put it, the fact that two of the defendants "had conspired to evade the draft was one of the chief factors against them and carried much weight with the jury." Defense attorney Fielder made no objections to any of the prospective jurors, even though some had admitted to forming opinions about the case based on press coverage. He was defending two slackers in wartime, in a town where 80 percent of workers were employed by an industry that had effectively used wartime prohibitions on antiwar speech to stymie the labor union movement. Fielder must have realized that selecting an unbiased jury was a quixotic venture in Clifton—or any mining town in the Southwest, for that matter—where the "copper collar" was firmly in place. Instead he settled for casting doubt on whether the proceedings could produce a fair verdict, telling reporters he planned "to establish that the copper companies are interested in the conviction."[6]

With the jury set, the court reconvened on Tuesday morning to hear testimony. The pre-trial publicity attracted a large crowd in the courtroom, many of whom were women who had brought knitting to bide their time during lulls in the proceedings. The press noted that spectators were well-behaved and there was no suggestion that violence might break out, as many had feared. Noticeably absent from the courtroom was Charley Power, who could not offer support to his brothers without risking his own arrest for draft evasion.[7]

The first witness called by the prosecution was Deputy United States Marshal Frank Haynes, who largely repeated his testimony, almost verbatim at times, given the prior February at the coroner's inquest for the slain lawmen. He recounted his trip with the posse from Safford into Klondyke on the evening of February 9, and then up to the Power mine early the next morning. At that point the prosecution entered as exhibits the three original arrest warrants for the defendants. Defense attorney James Fielder quickly objected to the federal warrants for draft evasion for Tom and John. He told the judge his objection "was based on the fact that the warrants which alleged a crime against the United States government were issued by a state officer [Justice of the Peace U. I. Paxton], who was therefore without jurisdiction in the premises." Judge Laine quickly overruled and allowed the warrants. Despite the judge's ruling, Fielder remained adamant the warrants were illegal, entering Exhibits A and B for the defense: the two letters U.S. Marshal Dillon had sent to Frank Haynes directing him to have Paxton fix the draft evasion warrants. Fielder believed these letters demonstrated that a federal official had erred in granting a state officer that authority.[8]

Haynes continued with his account and told jurors what he saw that morning at the cabin, explaining where the lawmen stood while prosecutor Johnson diagrammed his descriptions on a chalkboard for the jury. Haynes said that as he took his position next to McBride on the northeast corner of the cabin, Kane Wootan and Martin Kempton were already at the southeast corner, standing about eight feet from the entrance to the cabin. He heard Wootan give the command to "Throw up your hands" twice, at which point Haynes saw a man in the doorway in front of the two deputies with a rifle held across his breast. After Wootan's command to surrender, Power "dropped the weapon to his right side," and then came McBride's admonishment, "Boys! Boys!"[9] According to Haynes:

> The first shots came from the east door of the cabin, and Jeff Powers fell as soon as shots were fired. Don't know who shot Powers. There was a few seconds intermission between the shots from the door, two close together, then two more, then the firing became more rapid, both from within and without the cabin. Jeff Powers never fired a shot. Two of the shots from the door were fired in the direction of McBride and myself, and two towards Kempton and Wootan. . . . McBride and I took shelter behind northeast corner of the house. By this time shooting became general. I went further up the side of the mountain, on north end of cabin and as I heard shots from within the shed room. I fired into north window. Went back to where I left McBride and saw his body lying at the corner near where he stood, partly north of the cabin with his feet and limbs beyond the corner. I was protected during the firing by the shed at the north of the house, and shots which I believe came from the shed room of the cabin struck the wall of this shed. After seeing McBride down I went up the hills and tried to approach the cabin from another direction, but finding I could not do so returned

to the horses and rode off to the Upchurch ranch for assistance. At the time I left the scene I did not know that Wootan and Kempton were dead.[10]

Each newspaper ran Haynes's statements through its own editorial filters, resulting in wildly conflicting accounts of his testimony. One local newspaper associated with the mining industry claimed Haynes testified that "when ordered to surrender the men refused and started shooting." According to the Associated Press wire story that was widely reprinted throughout the Southwest, "There was no parley between the mountaineers and the officers. The latter advanced boldly into the open towards the cabin. . . . [Jeff Power] was told to hold up his hands and was almost immediately shot. Haynes declares that he attempted to use his gun."[11]

Dr. William Platt took the stand after Haynes. His testimony was critical for the prosecution, because he explained to the jurors how the lawmen died, suggesting the savage nature of the killings. Platt repeated his findings from the inquest that McBride was shot four times: the first three shots pierced his knee, liver, and abdomen, while the fourth shot ran straight through his skull, implying the sheriff was shot at close range, perhaps even executed as he lay on the ground. He told again of how Martin Kempton died from a single gunshot to the back of his head that ripped off part of his jaw, and how Kane Wootan was also shot from behind, evidence that implied the two deputies were killed while trying to flee the gunfight. Then Platt veered from his original testimony. At the inquest he had sworn the mark on Wootan's face "was undoubtedly produced before he died," but now he stated it had been "inflicted after death." Many people concluded from Platt's statement that Wootan had been deliberately kicked in anger, but the mark could also have been made when the bodies were transported to the valley. Under cross-examination by defense attorney Fielder, Platt confirmed that no official examination was ever made of Jeff Power's body.[12]

After the lunch recess photographer Harry DuBois was called to the stand, and several of his photographs of the crime scene, taken weeks after the gun battle, were entered as evidence. The photos, combined with testimony from witnesses who had retrieved the bodies, were used to demonstrate to the jury the positions of the defendants, Jeff Power, and the officers during the gunfight. The key photo for the prosecution was Exhibit 4, taken of the northeast corner of the cabin, where the shed was located and where prosecutor Chambers alleged Tom Sisson was lying on the ground when he shot McBride through the chinking in the logs.[13]

Next to take the stand was Jay Murdock, and the first part of his testimony focused on what he found at the cabin after his arrival following the shootout.

He identified the rifles owned by the Power brothers and Sisson and stated that he found an empty shell in the cabin, which came from one of the defendants' guns. Jay told the jury that the only way McBride, situated at the northeast corner of the cabin, could have been seen from inside was through the hole in the chinking in the shed. Jay also insisted that the two wire screens entered as evidence by the prosecution belonged to the cabin's east and south windows, and after inspecting them, he suggested that bullets had passed through the screens from both inside and outside the cabin. He recounted his testimony from the coroner's inquest in Safford, regarding his conversation with the Power brothers after they and Sisson arrived at his camp that Sunday morning, almost word-for-word. He told the jury that the brothers asked Jay and the others gathered to take care of their father, and said Tom Power told him he had filled his eye with glass when he shot through the window, killing Kane Wootan. But when the prosecutors asked him about Sisson's role, Jay's testimony began to deviate from his statements to the coroner's jury the prior February.[14]

Jay Murdock told the court that after the shootout, John Power told him he had killed Martin Kempton and that Tom Sisson bragged of killing Sheriff McBride, saying he "punched a rifle through the screen and killed McBride" after the deputies shot Jeff Power. Jay's new testimony squared with the district attorney's assertion that McBride was slain by Sisson, rather than by John Power, as Jay had testified earlier. At the same time, Murdock undercut Chambers's argument that someone on the ground of the shed killed McBride, and suggested instead that Sisson shot through a window. Most incendiary of all was Jay's assertion that as the Powers and Sisson rode off after their brief meeting at the Murdock camp, Tom Power said, "'Tell them we will be back in a few days and get more of them.'" There was no record of such a statement made at the inquest; in fact, Henry Allen had testified that John Power only said, "'I'll see you boys in two or three days,'" as the three men left. When John Murdock took the stand next, he corroborated his son's testimony.[15]

Clearly at some point during the inquest or at the trial, or even both times they were under oath, the Murdocks committed perjury. Their testimony was always at odds with the sworn statements of others who were present, such as Knothe and Allen, and it changed each time they were placed on the stand or gave an interview to a newspaper. Given John Murdock's history, it is tempting to speculate that he and Jay were bribed, but both legal teams were aware of John Murdock's perjury conviction and, with so many important figures eyeing the proceedings, it is unlikely either side would take such a risk. It is more plausible that the Murdocks conjured up testimony after succumbing to public pressure to gain a conviction.

Fielder then cross-examined Jay Murdock. Normally, an experienced defense attorney would have taken Murdock to task for his inconsistent statements under oath, but Fielder, of course, could not do so, as he needed his testimony to prove self-defense. He asked Jay to tell the court what Jeff Power said before dying, but before Jay could respond, the prosecution objected to Fielder's line of questioning. The jury was removed from the courtroom as counsel conferred with Judge Laine and Jay Murdock told the judge that Jeff dying words were: "'I wonder why Kane Wootan shot me with my hands up?'"[16]

Prosecutor Chambers had good reason to question the admissibility of Jeff Power's last words because dying declarations are not always allowed in a court of law. The Sixth Amendment of the U.S. Constitution guarantees the right of the accused to be confronted by witnesses against him, but in a murder case when an eyewitness is mortally wounded, dying declarations may be used to either convict or absolve the accused if there are no other witnesses. The legal thinking behind the dying declaration is that the person who knows he is dying, and will shortly be meeting his "creator and heavenly judge," would not lie in such a situation. In *Mattox v. United States,* a case argued before the United States Supreme Court in 1892, the justices ruled that "certain expectation of almost immediate death will remove all temptation to falsehood, and enforce as strict adherence to the truth as the obligation of an oath could impose."[17]

Jeff Power's dying statement that Kane Wootan shot him while he was trying to surrender was acknowledged by the press as "one of the strong cards of the defense," and would have allowed Fielder to argue the defendants justly returned fire, believing they too would be killed if they surrendered to their assailants. When combined with Jay Murdock's testimony that Jeff Power said the officers shot first and Haynes's testimony that the officers failed to identify themselves or present a warrant, the case for self-defense was solid. The time-honored legal notion that a man under attack had "no duty to retreat" was justified in this instance, according to the sympathetic editor of the *Tucson Citizen,* who told readers, "as it is presumed that a 'man's house is his castle' his defense of same is too well recognized to need be dwelt on."[18]

After hearing arguments from Fielder and Chambers, Judge Laine ruled for the prosecution, pronouncing Jeff Power's dying declaration inadmissible as evidence. Without the trial transcripts, we cannot be certain why the judge disallowed the testimony, but it is likely Chambers argued to Judge Laine that dying declarations, which are considered hearsay in a court of law, may only be allowed when the statement can convict or absolve the *defendant* on trial.

Sisson and the Power brothers were on trial for killing Robert Frank McBride, not Kane Wootan for killing Jeff Power, making Jeff's dying statement, "I wonder why Kane Wootan shot me with my hands up?" irrelevant to McBride's murder. When Fielder cross-examined Jay's father, he again tried to introduce Jeff's dying words, but was rebuffed by the judge once more. Frustrated that the foundation of his self-defense strategy was unraveling, Fielder finally attacked the credibility of his witness, forcing John Murdock to admit to the judge and jury his prior perjury conviction in Cochise County.[19]

After the prosecution and defense finished with John and Jay Murdock, court adjourned for the day, and both sides had much to consider. With the arrest warrants for draft evasion declared legal and Jeff's dying declaration barred from the jurors' ears, Fielder had been dealt two staggering blows, but Chambers and his team still had to demonstrate beyond a reasonable doubt that the defendants were lying in wait to murder the officers "with malice aforethought." Without concrete threats, the jury instead might convict them of second-degree murder or manslaughter. With that in mind, the next day the prosecution produced several witnesses—Chambers later claimed at least four, but perhaps as many as seven—who testified that the Power men and Sisson all threatened to kill anyone who came to arrest the Powers for draft evasion.[20]

Unfortunately, press coverage was not specific about what threats were made or by whom because censors were at work, eradicating antiwar sentiments from publications. At this pivotal point in the trial, as prosecutors tried to prove premeditation, we can only speculate about what statements were made, but Chambers later said the witnesses presented "a long list of threats covering a period of several months.'" We do not know what neighbors Joe and Mellie Boscoe said under oath, but after the trial was over, Joe always maintained that on the evening Ola Power died, when he and his wife were summoned to the Power residence at Gold Mountain to assist, Jeff Power told him that if officers came up into Rattlesnake Canyon for his sons, "'they're liable to get more'n they bargained for. We'll be meet'n them on our own ground.'" But there is reason to question the veracity of Joe Boscoe's statements. When Ola died, McBride interviewed the Boscoes about her death, but the sheriff never mentioned the threats allegedly made by Jeff Power in any of his reports to federal authorities that winter, a surprising omission given how eager the sheriff was to apprehend the Power brothers.[21]

John "Sandy" Mangum, a butcher shop owner from Pima, was also called to testify about threats made by the Powers. Although his comments were not reported in the press, he later told many people that when Jeff Power came in his store in the spring of 1917 he condemned the war, threatening, "'If Uncle Sam takes my boys they'll do it over my dead body.'"[22] Again, McBride never mentioned any inflammatory statements to federal agents investigating the Powers, even though he had grown up in Pima and likely knew Mangum. But it is also plausible that Mangum and Boscoe, among others, initially considered threats made by the Powers just so much loose talk. After all, threats were common on the frontier, where many people believed "over my dead body" was a statement of strong opinion rather than evidence of premeditated murder—until, of course, three lawmen were dead and a community demanded retribution.

Gregor and Mary Ann Haby were subpoenaed to testify that day, but it is unclear if they took the stand: family members recall that the couple traveled to Clifton for the trial, but were never placed under oath. As supporters of the Power brothers, they may not have had anything to say that the prosecution wished the jury to hear, and Fielder may have had concerns that their strong German accents would have a more detrimental effect on the jury than any positive statements they could make about the defendants. Nor do we know whether another witness with a heavy German accent, Ed Knothe, or Henry Allen, who also testified that day, corroborated or contradicted the damaging testimony provided by Jay and John Murdock, as the press failed to provide their statements.[23]

Most newspapers printed only the following sanitized summary of what witnesses said that morning: "Evidence was brought into the record showing that in previous conversation with different parties there was a determination on the part of the Powers boys and their father, and Tom Sisson to resist with arms any effort to take the Powers boys for failing to register."[24] Allan Jaynes, the editor and owner of the *Tucson Citizen,* was the only journalist to walk away from the proceedings with a different opinion, convinced the prosecution failed to produce witnesses to demonstrate premeditated murder. He told his readers, "Up to the present, while establishing the fact that the Powers brothers and Sisson killed Sheriff McBride and his deputies, the state has not shown conspiracy aforethought to forcibly resist the officers, nor has the state proven that there was any reason to presume that the defendants knew that the posse were officers or an attacking party. This knowledge, of course, is presumed, but no evidence has been adduced bringing out this act."[25]

Lieutenant Wolcott Hayes, the soldier who captured the defendants in Mexico, was the last man to testify for the prosecution. He identified items that the fugitives had on them when caught, including the rifles, pistols, ammunition, and field glasses they had taken from the lawmen's bodies. Hayes also told the court that although heavily armed, the fugitives did not resist capture. He was asked by prosecutor Johnson about two small vials of strychnine allegedly found among the prisoners' belongings, but Hayes said he did not remember seeing poison at the time of the arrest. By alluding to poison, Chambers and his team established in the minds of the jurors a link between the defendants and the unsolved death of Ola May Power. On that ominous note, the prosecution rested its case at two o'clock on Wednesday, May 15, and the court recessed for thirty minutes while James Fielder conferred with his clients and prepared to present his defense.[26]

Neighbors and family members friendly to the Powers, like the Bleaks, the Morgans, and the Salazars, who might have dispelled any notions the Powers were dangerous, were never summoned as witnesses for the defense. State law at the time required defendants to pay for the transportation and lodging costs of witnesses traveling to Clifton to testify for their defense, and apparently, because the Powers and Sisson had so little money to pay their attorney, Fielder was unable to subpoena witnesses. Fielder called only two men to testify on behalf of the defendants: John Murdock and John Power. Murdock was an intriguing choice, because Fielder had already informed the jury that John was a convicted perjurer, but Fielder needed someone besides the defendants to testify that they fired in self-defense. With Murdock on the stand, he tried a third and final time to get the dying statement of Jeff Powers into the record, but Judge Laine again sustained the prosecution's objection.[27]

Fielder's last hope was John Power, who took the stand Wednesday afternoon and quickly turned the tide of public opinion in his favor. At age twenty-eight, John was a good looking, fair-haired, strongly built man, who still wore a gauze bandage wrapped over his injured eye and around his head. Fielder undoubtedly hoped his appearance would impress upon jurors that John too had been attacked and horribly wounded while defending his own home. The *Tucson Citizen* described John as "a strong witness for the defense. . . . He said that after his father was shot down he fired at both groups of officers, that the fusillade was of a minute's duration and that when the firing ceased he carried his father in."[28]

The next day, however, when John Power took the stand again, his testimony unraveled under prosecutor Norman Johnson's cross-examination. When shown the cabin's wire screens and canvas curtains, which were entered as evidence, John, in an obvious move to suggest the crime scene had been tainted before officials inspected it, said they looked "too new" to be from the cabin's windows. Furthermore, John stated that he and Tom carried his father to the mine after the shootout, contradicting the earlier testimony of Henry Allen and the Murdocks that they had found Jeff at the arrastra and carried him to the tunnel long after the Powers and Sisson had fled. Finally, when he was asked about Tom Sisson's role in the gun battle, John said the former soldier shot no one: "'He was in bed when it started . . . and stayed there all the time the shooting was going on.'" The press concluded that putting John Power on the stand was a mistake, because it appeared he lied under oath in "an obvious attempt to absolve Sisson of any blame in connection with the officers' death." John "there and then destroyed whatever confidence and goodwill he may have gained in previous testimony, there was too much proof of Sisson's guilt."[29]

With little hard evidence and no eyewitnesses except the defendants to argue for self-defense, Fielder was forced to rely on his legendary oratorical skills. His lengthy closing remarks lasted the remainder of Thursday's session and carried over into Friday's, in what one reporter called "a vain effort to save his clients." We do not know, of course, what Fielder spoke of for hours. No doubt he reminded the jury of the prejudicial coverage of the case in the press and alluded to his suspicions that the copper companies were working behind the scenes to gain a conviction. He surely reminded the jury that John Murdock was a convicted perjurer whose testimony should be dismissed, but did he point out that Jay Murdock's testimony at the trial differed from his own statements under oath at the inquest? Did he mention that Dr. Platt too had changed his testimony since the inquest about whether Kane Wootan had been kicked in the face before or after death?[30]

Fielder would have told the jury to discount Jay Murdock's testimony that Tom Power allegedly said after the shootout, "'tell them we will be back in a few days and get more of them.'" Even if Tom had made such in statement, it was spoken in anger just after his father had been killed and could not provide evidence of premeditated murder. He no doubt reminded jurors that the men in the cabin were not informed the officers were there to arrest them, and as an experienced litigator, he would have itemized all the irregularities in the aftermath of the shootout: that relatives and friends of the deceased lawmen moved their bodies and collected evidence, that two months elapsed before an official examination was conducted at the crime scene, and that county officials failed to perform an autopsy on Jeff Power's body. Even by the standards of 1918, the investigation was shoddy.

Undoubtedly, Fielder spent a considerable amount of time during his closing arguments casting doubt on the testimony of Frank Haynes, challenging jurors to consider the deputy marshal's ambiguous statement: "The first shots came from the east door of the cabin, and Jeff Powers fell as soon as shots were fired. Don't know who shot Powers." Fielder must have asked the jury if they thought Jeff Power's own sons would initiate a confrontation if their father was standing in the open and exposed to men who were pointing rifles at him, or if they had shot their father by accident in that first round.[31] Several witnesses testified that there was a break in the action after the initial volley of gunfire, as both sides took their positions and reloaded. Although all four of the lawmen were alive and uninjured at that point, they failed yet again to identify themselves and not one of them called out to the men inside to surrender, common practice by officers, especially when suspects were surrounded.

The son and grandsons of Jane Power had demonstrated no prior disposition to draw first blood in a confrontation, and it was more likely that a jittery, half-frozen deputy shot first when he spotted Jeff Power walking out of his doorway with rifle in hand. The jury was not made aware of the Power family's prior runs-in with James Gould and Wayne Brazel, which could have easily ended in bloodshed but where calmer heads had prevailed, because fear of reprisals kept them from revealing those incidents. Nor did Fielder have access to the numerous classified federal investigations filed by agents of the U.S. Department of Justice that produced no verified intelligence that the Powers ever threatened to kill officers. Even as the trial began, the assistant U.S. attorney for Arizona, John Langston, presented his findings to United States attorney general Thomas Gregory, which concluded that the only case the federal government had against the Power brothers and Sisson was "for resisting an officer and assaulting him or for conspiracy . . . to violate the Selective Service Law."[32] Federal officials knew they could not prove in a court of law that the Power brothers had threatened the lives of anyone before February 10, 1918.

After Fielder concluded his remarks, prosecutor Norman Johnson then addressed the jury, and while the newspapers also failed to record his comments, he undoubtedly presented the defendants as remorseless murderers who had fled the scene of their crime—an assignation of their guilt—and who had brutalized the bodies of their victims, kicking in Kane Wootan's face and shooting Frank McBride in the head as he lay dying. The prosecution placed the blame for the death of McBride squarely on Sisson, who, Johnson argued, shot the sheriff from the shed, allowing him to avoid the "many rumors concerning matters of self-defense that the defendants could prove" for the deaths of Kempton and Wootan.[33] Johnson certainly provided the jury with a summary of the threats

made by the Powers to others prior to the shootout, but above all else it was Jay
Murdock's testimony of Tom Power's statement, "'Tell them we will be back in
a few days and get more of them,'" allegedly made just after his father had been
killed, that the prosecution believed proved first-degree murder. As Graham
County attorney Chambers later revealed, he was certain the case turned on
statements the state introduced that were allegedly made by each of the defendants
"less than an hour *after* the crime was committed showing the vindictive and
premeditated character of the murder"[34] (author's emphasis).

With closing statements wrapped up on Friday morning, the judge prepared
to instruct the jury. Fielder, still convinced that Judge Laine had ruled incorrectly
on the federal warrants for Tom and John Power, asked the judge to direct the
jury to ignore them, because they "were not and are not lawful warrants." Laine
once again rejected Fielder's assertion. After an adjournment for lunch, Judge
Laine spent almost an hour and a half giving the jury his instructions, which
highlighted the legal points of the trial and quoted extensively from Arizona
statutes. Laine provided the definitions for first- and second-degree murder, as
well as manslaughter, from the penal code, allowing jury members to make their
own determination as stipulated by state law. As requested by the prosecution, he
pointed out Arizona law allowed public officers to defend themselves if accused
felons resisted arrest. Acknowledging that much of the evidence presented by the
state was circumstantial, Judge Laine provided the jury with a lengthy description of how circumstantial evidence could be given the "same weight as direct
evidence" if it allowed the jury to "exclude every reasonable hypothesis other
than that of guilt."[35]

Judge Laine's instructions were balanced, addressing points raised by the
defense as well as the prosecution. Acknowledging the fact that John Murdock
was a convicted perjurer and his son, Jay, had made contradictory statements
under oath, the judge told jurors, "If you believe from the evidence in this case
that any witness sworn in the case has intentionally or willfully sworn falsely
to any material fact in the case, you are at liberty to disregard" that testimony.
The issue of self-defense also loomed large, so Judge Laine told jurors, "The
right of self-defense is allowed to the citizen as a shield, and not as a sword, and
in the exercise of this right a person must act honestly, and in good faith." He
presented the circumstances that accounted for justifiable homicide, including
"when committed in defense of habitation, property or person." He stated that
a person, if assaulted, "may exercise a reasonable degree of force to repel an
attack," but then, circling back to the prosecution's assertion that McBride had

not initiated the attack, Laine told jurors that no one could "provoke an attack in order that he may have an apparent excuse for killing his adversary." The judge told the jury that if they believed from the evidence that the deceased, Frank McBride, "made the first hostile demonstration against the defendants" and "was about to inflict upon them great bodily injury, then the defendants were justifiable in acting upon those appearances in that belief, and if necessary to prevent great bodily injury to themselves, and acting under the influence of those fears alone, they fired the fatal shots that killed the deceased, they were justified in so doing."[36]

Members of the jury retired to deliberate just before three o'clock on Friday afternoon. If they failed to return a guilty verdict, Chambers planned to immediately charge the three defendants for the murder of Martin Kempton, and if again unsuccessful, then yet another trial would be called for the murder of Kane Wootan. Deputy U.S. Marshal Frank Haynes, who was present in the courtroom, held federal warrants for all three defendants, including Tom Sisson, on draft evasion charges issued by the U.S. commissioner. Regardless of the verdict, they would not walk out free men that day.[37]

Less than thirty minutes later the jury returned to the courtroom, and the foreman read the unanimous verdict: "Guilty of murder in the first degree." According to the press, "The defendants received the verdict stoically, without betraying any emotion. . . . Thus the curtain is rung down on the final act in the Galiuro Mountain tragedy." But journalists who believed the convicted murderers would never be heard from again once they were behind prison bars underestimated the Power brothers. In fact, the curtain was just rising for the last act of their saga.[38]

13

THE BIG HOUSE ON THE GILA

Each is a desperate character.

Tom and John Power had spent their entire lives along the Gila River. They were born in the town of Gila, located near its source in New Mexico, and then as young men they lived in Rattlesnake Canyon, where the snowmelt from the Galiuros drained into the Gila each spring. Now they were ordered by Judge Laine to live out their natural lives along its banks. On Monday, May 20, Judge Laine sentenced Thomas Jefferson Power Jr., John Grant Power, and Thomas Joseph Sisson to life in prison, the toughest penalty available to him. The three convicted murderers were transported that evening to the Arizona State Prison at Florence, located about sixty miles southeast of Phoenix and often referred to as the Big House on the Gila. While the river was a constant in their lives, everything else had been torn from the brothers: their family, their freedom, even their gold mine. Tom and John would not let go of their past lives easily and, like their father and grandmother before them, would continue to fight to reclaim whatever they could from behind bars.[1]

The state penitentiary was a progressive institution for its day, allowing inmates many rights. The medieval practices employed at the territorial prison at Yuma, where Wiley Morgan served, or even at Leavenworth, the military prison where most draft resisters were sent after court martial, had been abolished at Florence by progressive governor George Hunt. Prisoners were no longer required to wear stigmatizing striped clothing and were given opportunities for exercise in the yard, where they could join the baseball or basketball team or train in the boxing ring. When visitors were present, the prison yard was a wholesome, serene place where inmates played cards, checkers, or dominoes, but when visiting hours ended, things quickly became more spirited as the games shifted to blackjack, poker, or craps. Contraband, including alcohol, marijuana, and narcotics to numb the boredom and degradation of prison existence, was readily available for a price.[2]

Although corporal punishment and the silent rule were no longer employed, and men were no longer chained to the floor in the "snakes," it was still an unpleasant place to live. Prison guards kept troublemakers in unheated cells in solitary confinement with nothing but bread and water for up to thirty days. Inmates had one another to fear as well. First-time offenders like Tom and John Power were greeted in the prison yard with a chorus of "fish, fish, fresh fish." New arrivals were assigned to cut wood in the prison yard during their first week on the inside to toughen them up for the physical work ahead. They were then usually placed in the largest cellblock, where dozens of men were crowded together with little guard supervision. Older, hardened convicts used the "fresh fish" to satisfy their sexual appetites, knowing full well "the code of the underworld meant death to squealers."[3]

Convicted murderers like the Power brothers and Tom Sisson, however, were separated out from the general prison population and assigned to Cell House One, where guards kept constant watch over the most dangerous inmates. John and Tom would be cellmates for the remainder of their time in prison, while Tom Sisson was assigned to another cell in the same building. In 1918 state voters reinstated the death penalty, largely because the public was so outraged by the vicious killings of McBride, Kempton, and Wootan. So John and Tom and Sisson would witness the execution of numerous fellow inmates at the gallows, located exactly thirteen steps from Cell House One.[4]

Even within their high-security living arrangements the three men came under special scrutiny when they first arrived, because Graham County attorney William Chambers had warned prison officials about the "vindictive" nature of the murderers. "Each is a desperate character and would kill a guard without the slightest hesitation," he noted in their official prison record. During their first few years at the Florence facility, the Power brothers and Sisson worked in the prison kitchen, laundry, or dairy, where they came under constant surveillance. They were given the opportunity to attend classes to learn to read or write and enhance their educations, but there is no record of Tom Sisson or either of the brothers taking advantage of the opportunity to attend the prison school. They did learn occupational skills like woodworking and metalworking, producing belt buckles, spurs, and horse bits that were sold to local ranchers or in the prison gift shop, and they received a small percentage of the proceeds.[5]

Better-educated inmates convicted of white-collar crimes, including forgery and fraud, were employed as clerical workers in the prison office and often helped fellow convicts with limited educations write letters to family, attorneys, or the parole board. The Power brothers and Sisson used their services often to plead for their release. A library provided newspapers, magazines, and other reading material, all paid for by the state, as well as outdated law books. Tom Power, who was the most literate of the three men, spent hours trying to figure out how he could gain release from their sentence. Of course, he only had Arizona statutes at his disposal, so without access to the four hundred pages of special legislation that governed the Selective Service Act, he soon grew frustrated trying to understand the laws that had locked him up.[6]

Even before the Power brothers were dispatched to the state prison, they had instructed their attorney to petition for a retrial. As soon as the guilty verdict was read in the courtroom James Fielder, convinced the judge had ruled incorrectly on the federal warrants for draft evasion, walked out of the Greenlee County Courthouse and told reporters he had filed a petition for a motion for a new trial and, if denied, he would bring the case before the state supreme court. One of the most baffling aspects of the Power-Sisson murder trial was that Fielder's request for a new trial was ignored. Perhaps Fielder failed to file the supporting documents needed to review the case, because the three convicted men had run out of money to pay him, or else the court clerk simply failed to follow up on the retrial petition. Whatever the reason, despite Fielder's petition, the case was never reviewed, and even if it had been, it was unlikely a retrial would have been granted. Fielder had been incorrect in assuming the warrants were illegal, and throughout the Power-Sisson proceedings Judge Frank Laine's rulings closely adhered to state law. Many had observed the Power-Sisson trial, including officials at the U.S. Department of Justice and the state attorney general's office, because county, state, and federal politicians had no intention of allowing the three defendants to go free on a technicality.[7]

In the early 1900s, the average time served by inmates convicted of first-degree murder in Arizona was only seven years, but hiring attorneys to gain a retrial or parole was expensive. It cost thousands to hire a top-rated lawyer to defend a murder charge, and even more for a retrial, money the Power brothers and Sisson did not have. Unlike their uncle Wiley Morgan, who had cattle and land to sell to pay for his appeals when he was convicted, the brothers had only their inheritance from their father—his meager personal belongings and the mine—and that was threatened by a pending suit initiated by the widows of the three slain lawmen, Clara McBride, Sena Kempton, and Laura Wootan. Even before the Power brothers

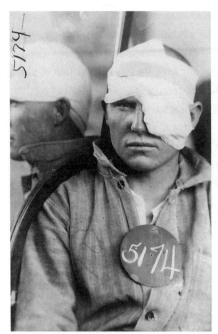 

(Left) John Power as he appeared when he first arrived at the Arizona State Prison
at Florence in May 1918, still wearing a bandage from injuries
sustained during the gunfight three months earlier.
Courtesy Pinal County Historical Museum.

(Right) Tom Power turned twenty-five just days before his incarceration
for murder at the Arizona State Prison at Florence.
Courtesy Pinal County Historical Museum.

and Sisson were captured in March 1918, the widows filed a writ of attachment
on Tom and John Power's property and Jeff Power's estate to obtain $150,000 in
damages for the wrongful deaths of their husbands.[8]

During a special session held in the summer of 1918, the state legislature
appropriated $17,500 in compensation—$7,500 to Clara McBride and $5,000 each
to Sena Kempton and Laura Wootan—for the loss of their husbands in the line of
duty. The money was placed in a trust to allow them a small income and to protect
it from creditors, but the sum was not nearly enough to take care of their families.
Among the three widows, Sena Kempton alone had the financial resources to
raise the surety bond to launch a lawsuit against the Powers, forcing them to
reduce their claim on the Powers from the original $150,000 to just $35,000.[9]

Clara McBride, expecting her eighth child at the time of her husband's death, had debts totaling $1,000 to pay off, forcing her to register as an indigent with the county so she could receive a small monthly stipend until she could dispose of assets. Laura Wootan, pregnant with her fifth child, was left with Kane's debts to banks and merchants, which totaled almost $19,000. Kane had already liquidated much of his cattle and most of his real property prior to his death, retaining only his mortgaged house in Safford and a parcel in Pinal County and leaving only what remained of his cattle to pay off debts. To make matters worse, the price of beef had fallen in recent years. His estate was executed by his older brother J. Frank, who raised about $11,000 in sales from the estate, far short of what he needed to satisfy creditors. In addition to all of Laura Wootan's other problems, the Central Cattle Loan Company successfully sued Kane Wootan's estate, proving the deceased had cheated and defrauded the bank when he failed to properly brand his herd as stipulated in his loan agreement.[10]

As the widows' lawsuit went forward, John and Tom Power reached out to their brother, Charley, to save the mine from seizure. Charley scraped together a few hundred dollars to pay an attorney, who filed paperwork trying to establish that John retained rights to the claim, but without success. Charley was almost broke after paying Fielder's fee, and did not have the retainer money needed to launch a countersuit to retain his one-third share of his father's estate, which was threatened by the widows' lawsuit. He also could not return to Arizona to file a claim on the estate himself for fear of being arrested for draft evasion. His attempts to negotiate a sale of the Power mine in the summer of 1918 all failed because of the litigation, and the widows won their lawsuit by default when Charley and his incarcerated brothers failed to appear in court. Tom and John were incensed when they discovered that the mine, for which they had sacrificed so much, was awarded to the families of the men who had killed their father.[11]

Despite the legal victory for the widows, it was not easy getting cash out of Jeff Power's estate. The sheriff's auction of personal items netted only $636: Jeff's Ford touring car fetched just over $300, while sentimental items like Ola's fiddle and John's guitar sold for only a few dollars each. In November 1918 the nine mining claims held by John and Jeff Power went up for auction, and newspaper editors who had heard so much about their value estimated them to be worth at least ten thousand dollars, and perhaps as much as one hundred thousand dollars. But the war was at an end and ore prices had dropped, so no one could justify a large investment in a marginal operation in an inaccessible location, especially since many of the early claims about its potential were undoubtedly exaggerated. Additionally, five people had died violently at the mine, including Commodore Perry Tucker in 1912 and Jeff Power and the three officers in 1918, leaving many people to believe the mine was jinxed. There were no bidders for the Powers' claims at the sheriff's auction, so the court valued them at $2,500, the price Jeff and John had paid for their shares of the Abandoned and Burro claims, and awarded them to the widows. John Power, seemingly unable to come to terms with the fact he was no longer a free man, fumed at this defeat, writing to prison officials, "I have some personal property that I ought to be looking after and mining property that I ought to be attending to for it is going to rack because I am unable to attend matters pertaining to it."[12]

His brothers' trial and the lawsuit had a devastating effect on Charley Power as well, who not only lost his inheritance, but also faced prison time if caught for failing to register for the Selective Service. Up until then, Charley had avoided the draft by remaining in hiding, but his brothers' notoriety placed him in jeopardy. On September 12, 1918, the final draft registration day of the war, the government expanded the age requirement to include all men between eighteen and forty-five and intensified its enforcement efforts. Charley could no longer avoid registration, but if he filled out the questionnaire with his correct birthday, February 9, 1889, officials would have evidence that Charley too had been a slacker who failed to submit in June 1917. Instead, when Charley reported to his polling precinct on September 12, he told the registrar he was born on February 9, 1881, thereby making himself eight years older than he really was and putting him over the legal draft age of thirty in June 1917. He would continue to perpetuate the deceit about his age on federal forms for the rest of his life.[13]

The draft registrar came to call on Charley's brothers, housed at the Arizona State Prison at Florence, on that very same day. Prisoners were required by federal law to register, but were considered "morally unfit" to serve. Both Tom and John stubbornly told the registrar they "refused to submit." Their continued defiance of the Selective Service Act stifled any sympathy for their plight at a time when public tolerance of draft evaders was almost non-existent. Major campaigns involving the American Expeditionary Forces began during the summer of 1918, and newspaper columns were filled with stories of local boys like their cousin and close companion, George Morgan, who had been transported in July to the front lines in France with his field artillery outfit.[14]

As the need for fresh troops mounted, federal officials began to realize that bringing in evaders one-by-one was costly, inefficient, and dangerous, and therefore authorized slacker raids all over the country in the spring of 1918. Just after the Power brothers arrived at prison, one of these roundups was held on a Saturday night in Phoenix, supervised by U.S. Marshal Joseph Dillon, who orchestrated local police and sheriff's deputies as they arrested any man found in public without a draft card on his person. In scenarios that would play out in every city in the country, men were hauled from theaters, restaurants, soda fountains, stores, dance halls, and poolrooms, and detained in jail until they could prove they were registered. Although only about 5 percent of those arrested turned out to be delinquents or deserters, the raids continued until September 1918, when the largest roundup was held in New York City. Around seventy-five thousand men were arrested during three days of raids, some of whom were elderly or disabled and clearly disqualified from service, but nevertheless were forced to sit for days in local prisons with insufficient food, water, and sanitary facilities. As historian Gerald Shenk notes, the wartime slacker raids "demonstrated the fragility of Constitutional guarantees against unreasonable searches and arrests without probable cause or warrants."[15]

The slacker raids drove many men out of the cities and into the countryside to hide, and fears mounted among the public that numerous resisters were gathering strength for a rebellion in rural areas. In the summer of 1918, confused rumors of dangerous evaders in rural Arkansas stirred up public anxiety and led to armed encounters with lawmen in what has become known as the Cleburne County War. In one incident eerily similar to the Power case, a sheriff, two deputies, and two additional civilian posse members arrived at the home of alleged draft evaders just before sunrise on a Sunday. They slipped into the Adkisson family barn, where brothers Bliss and Hardy Adkisson, conscientious objectors, were hiding. The Adkissons were Russellites, known today as Jehovah's Witnesses, who were not exempt from military service despite their pacifist beliefs. One version of the story asserts that Hardy Adkisson was fired upon by posse members as he ran from the barn, and that his father, Tom, fired back, fatally wounding one of the officers. But conflicting testimonies cast doubt as to who fired first.[16]

The Adkisson men escaped, so the local sheriff enlisted more than one hundred posse men and the Arkansas governor sent in National Guard troops with machine guns to attempt to arrest them, as well as other deserters and delinquents believed to be hiding in the woods and protected by sympathetic family members and neighbors. Angry lynch mobs formed, motivated by Council of Defense members who alarmed the community by suggesting that dozens of dangerous slackers were roaming the countryside. The Adkissons eventually turned themselves in, with the father Tom conceding "gruffly that they would have surrendered earlier to the soldiers, but 'we were afraid to start towards them for fear the other mob would cut us off.'" The dying posse member identified Tom Adkisson as his assailant and, while he admitted firing in self-defense, Tom was neither apologetic nor repentant: "'I am a conscientious objector to war, as I believe a man must be allowed to follow the dictates of his conscience.'" Tom Adkisson was found guilty of voluntary manslaughter and sentenced to two years in state prison, while his son Bliss was found guilty of second-degree murder and sentenced to twenty years.[17]

In his definitive study of the draft during World War I, John Whiteclay Chambers estimates between twenty and twenty-five men died in similar skirmishes between draft resisters and lawmen in the mountains of Arizona, Arkansas, Nevada, Texas, North Carolina, and elsewhere, but that number is probably low. Because these arrests fell under various jurisdictions, both state and federal, no comprehensive study of draft evader violence has been conducted, making it difficult to compare the incidents. But historians have noted that local culture often determined how harshly resisters were punished. Juries in the rural regions of Arkansas or Oklahoma, where many residents opposed conscription, were reluctant to hand out harsh judgments, and judges were quick to overturn decisions. Bliss Adkisson was released from state prison in less than two years, far short of his twenty-year sentence. One juror, who served during the trial of draft evaders who took part in the Green Corn Rebellion in Oklahoma in August 1917, voiced his belief that the "defendants ought to be 'given a good scare but probably not convicted.'"[18]

Most delinquents and deserters who killed soldiers or federal officers, along with conscientious objectors or vocal dissenters who refused to support the military, were court martialed by the military and sent to federal prison. Because these inmates were considered "dangerous enemies of the state," many were placed in solitary confinement, beaten, and tortured, and some were even killed by guards: at least seventeen dissenters perished in prison during the war, and many more were driven insane by their circumstances. Wartime prisoners overtaxed the prison systems at Leavenworth, where most were housed: normal capacity was 1,700, but by the early part of 1919, well after the armistice was signed, over 4,000 prisoners wreaked havoc on the facility.[19] Federal officials began to reexamine the policy that had placed so many men, often well educated and with no prior convictions, in federal prison. In the spring of 1919 the government instituted a program of amnesty for conscientious objectors, and the program was later extended to political dissenters as well. In 1920 Warren G. Harding campaigned to return the nation to "normalcy," and once elected president he began the process of releasing antiwar dissidents held in federal prison, even those who had killed officers while resisting the draft and been sentenced to death. Civil libertarians successfully challenged in court and dismantled some of the more noxious sections of the Espionage Act that inhibited free speech.[20]

The amnesty granted to draft evaders and the changing political climate did not go unnoticed by John and Tom Power, and once they earned enough money selling items in the prison gift shop, they hired attorneys to obtain their freedom. Those lawyers soon discovered that the trial transcripts had vanished, which meant the parole board could not review their case to determine if any irregularities occurred during the original proceedings. The largest obstacle to their release, however, was their sentence of life in prison, which under state law meant they were unable to petition for parole. Their only hope was to request that their sentence be commuted to a term shorter than life, and for that to occur, they would need the support of numerous individuals, from prison guards to family members to community leaders and state officials, even the governor.[21]

The first step in the process of clemency was to earn the trust of prison guards, who could recommend to the warden prisoners they felt were worthy of a hearing with the Arizona Board of Pardons and Paroles. Despite the warnings by Graham County attorney William Chambers that the Power brothers and Sisson were dangerous and likely to kill guards, prison officials quickly realized the three convicted murderers were not threats. By 1923 all three inmates were granted trusty status and put to work on the honor system outside the prison walls. John Power and Tom Sisson worked on the road crew constructing state highways, while Tom Power was assigned to the prison farm. The freedom proved too tempting for Tom Power, however. With nothing but a life behind bars to look forward to, he escaped with another convicted murderer on December 16, 1923. Evidently, the two inmates had some help obtaining access to an automobile, and drove to San Diego. They were captured there without incident almost a month later, and Tom spent six days in solitary for punishment before returning to the general prison population, where he told guards he just "wanted to see what the country looked like."[22]

Tom disturbed no one while on the run, but following his escape some folks in the Gila Valley demanded that prison officials remove John Power and Tom Sisson from the road gang, because they allegedly had "threatened the lives of a number of people." The prison superintendent, Scott White, denied they were a problem, insisting instead that John and Sisson were "excellent and faithful workers and responsible men" and assured Graham County residents there was no reason "to fear that either of them would attempt to molest any person." Tom Power had not committed any additional crimes during his escape, and his behavior remained otherwise exemplary, so less than two years after his escape he regained trusty status and was assigned to work at the assistant warden's residence. Shortly after, prison guards began agitating again for a commutation hearing and members of the Arizona State Board of Pardons and Paroles, aware of other draft evasion cases under review, agreed to schedule a hearing for the end of 1926.[23]

The parole board was comprised of three members: the state attorney general, the superintendent of public instruction, and a non-elected official, selected by the other two members, who served as the chairman. Before coming to a decision, the members of the board considered each inmate's behavior, any irregularities in his trial proceedings, and whether he had job offers and a place to live on the outside. With the trial transcripts gone, little was left to review, but the Power brothers had offers for work from relatives and friends outside, and Sisson had a military pension to draw from. The board also considered whether respected citizens could attest to a prisoner's good character and if significant numbers opposed his release. To gain release, the trio had to convince leaders in the counties where their crime occurred and where they were convicted to agitate for their freedom, an impossible task given the ill will remaining in Graham County.[24]

The three slain lawmen belonged to prominent families capable of rallying powerful politicians to their side. When word of the planned hearing reached the Gila Valley, reaction was swift. Nate Kempton, Martin Kempton's brother, gathered hundreds of signatures on a petition asking the board to deny parole. William Chambers, who had become county superior court judge since prosecuting the Power brothers and Sisson, sent a scathing letter to the parole board stating he did not believe they deserved a hearing: "Any pardon of these men would be an outrage upon justice and would turn loose upon society two of the most desperate criminals ever convicted of murder in this State." With such unified opposition, the board decided not to hear their case.[25]

The drumbeat for their release continued through the 1930s from inside the state prison. The captain of the prison yard, A. G. Walker, was Kane Wootan's brother-in-law and McBride's former constable in Klondyke, and he was quite familiar with the Power-Sisson case. Walker wrote to the parole board to say that while he believed the Powers were ultimately responsible for the deaths of the three lawmen because they did not heed the draft, he still felt Tom and John Power deserved a hearing, as they had "paid dearly with the best years of their lives for what I understood was not a premeditated crime." Another guard said of the three men, "You would never take them to be murderers. They committed their murder during war times. . . . I would like to see these boys free again as they are all likable fellows and I believe they will make good if given one more chance by the state." Even strangers who met the men in prison were impressed with them and offered to take up their cause. David Harlin, who owned oil fields in Oklahoma and worked closely with inmates he felt deserved a second chance, wrote often to the parole board, offering to find the Power brothers employment as oil rig drillers if they were released.[26]

The parole board discussed their case behind closed doors on five separate occasions during the 1930s, each time eliciting loud protests from residents of the Gila Valley that could not be countered by the handful of Power supporters on the outside. The city attorney for Miami, Arizona, wrote to the board: "Many other prisoners with a more dastardly crime have either escaped or have been granted paroles, and I see no reason why the Power Brothers should not be paroled at this time," but the trickle of Power support was overwhelmed by a torrent of mail and phone calls from angry Gila Valley residents demanding they remain locked up "for all time."[27] The three families of the lawmen were never united in their opposition to the release of the prisoners, but the most vocal and best-organized among them wanted to keep the men incarcerated, so the Power brothers and Sisson could do little but petition the board, only to receive rejection after rejection.

Newspaper articles and official reports had often been wildly inaccurate following the shootout and during their trial, and as the years wore on, the assertions made by many descendants of the sheriff and his deputies became even more inflamed. Members of the McBride family insisted that the Powers had a long criminal history and had transformed their mining cabin into a "fortress," with "drilled holes at intervals in the walls for aiming and firing guns" to ambush the unsuspecting officers. Jeff Power, they alleged, was fully dressed and wearing a six-shooter when he stepped outside the door of the cabin, and when ordered to surrender, he "pulled his hat down with his left hand" and whirled around toward his sons, a prearranged signal to them to open fire.[28]

Those accounts offered by the lawmen's families did not reconcile with the views held by residents of Aravaipa who knew the Powers, and who began to question why the families of the lawmen worked so hard to prevent a hearing.

John and his father, Jeff, may have been unsociable, but most knew Tom was a fun-loving, likeable young man and Ola had been a sweet, well-mannered young lady. The family spent both time and money to help develop the region, building a road and improving a mine many people hoped would stimulate the local economy—not exactly outlaw behavior. Their trial took place when emotions ran strong against slackers, but even after tempers had cooled, so many official documents went missing that no one could retrace the testimony to verify if the original proceedings had been fair.

Behavioral scientists tell us that humans continually seek order in their lives and often try to connect the dots in incongruous situations, just to find the sense of order they crave. Soon after the trial stories appeared in the canyon that allowed residents to reconcile the deadly shootout with the reclusive family they knew. After the Wham robbery took place in the Gila Valley in 1889, rumors suggested the stolen payroll money was hidden in a chicken coop owned by one of the defendants. Similarly, tall tales circulated in Graham County, and continue to this day, that "'someone' paid to have the Power trial transcript disappear," and those transcripts and other missing official records were buried in the yard of one of the lawmen's relatives.[29]

No one was more responsible than Jay Murdock for contributing to the growing body of contradictory and conspiratorial stories about the shootout. Until his death in 1956 Murdock spent many hours talking to reporters, writers, and Graham County residents about his memories of the Power family. Jay's accounts of what he witnessed on February 10, 1918, changed many times over the years and were often at odds with the recollections of others who knew the Powers well and with the public records, but they nevertheless became the foundation for the Power shootout story. Despite his inconsistencies, Sheriff McBride's son Darvil called Jay "a man of astute judgment," and Graham County historian William Ryder Ridgway used interviews with Murdock as the basis for several publications on the shootout. Most of the key participants, like Deputy Marshal Frank Haynes, as well as attorneys James Fielder, Norman Johnson, and William Chambers, were dead by the late 1930s, so they could not challenge Murdock's new narratives, allowing him to shape the legacy of the Power family.[30]

As Murdock wrote to Tom and John in 1931, "If there is one man in this world that knows that you boys should NOT be in prison it is me. In the thirteen years that you boys have been in there, I have been helping you in every way I can by telling everyone the exact truth about the fight. And you have lots of friends and sympathizers." It was difficult, however, to know what the "exact truth" was according to Jay Murdock. He told people sympathetic to the Powers that Sheriff Frank McBride killed Undersheriff Martin Kempton accidentally while shooting at John Power. Then Murdock told the families of the lawmen a very different version, saying that when he visited with the prisoners, "They boasted that each got their man, Sisson joking that he did his fighting from the kitchen. Tom has admitted that he killed Wootan, so it remains that John killed Kempton." There is much truth buried within Jay Murdock's recollections that has found its way into print over the years, but they also contain many falsehoods that became the basis for much of the folklore surrounding the shootout.[31]

From inside prison, Tom and John Power added stories of their own, telling anyone who would listen that greed, rather than valid criminal warrants, brought the law to their doorstep. Playing on suspicions harbored by many non-Mormons since the Wham payroll robbery, the brothers claimed McBride had tried to buy their mining claims on several occasions and, when their father turned him down, the sheriff came up to kill them. If they had not taken flight after the shootout, Tom and John argued, another posse would have come along and finished them off. No doubt the Power brothers, remembering how they had lost the Doubtful Mine in legal proceedings initiated by influential men in New Mexico in 1910, believed the same scenario was playing out as powerful men from the Gila Valley stole their mine. With these statements, the Power brothers began transforming what had been a battle over the draft into a battle over the mine, and visitors or guards carried their conspiracy theories back to Klondyke. Many of those rumors were printed in local newspapers, which reported that "whisperings were indulged that certain interests" coveted the Power Mine because Jeff and John had been offered one hundred thousand dollars for it by a large mining corporation, and the only reason why the deal was not closed "was because the prospective buyer would not take the money up to their cabin in the hills and count it out in dollars and cents." Other stories suggested that the Power brothers had resisted the draft for fear of leaving their father alone, because so many people wanted to steal their valuable mine. "As they knew only the law of force, and depended largely upon their rifles to protect themselves from those whom they imagined desired to despoil them of their holdings . . . it would require the combined physical strength of the entire Powers clan to hold this property."[32]

The clumsy handling of the arrest by the lawmen sparked vigorous debates in both Aravaipa and the Gila Valley. Many wondered why the lawmen surrounded the cabin at dawn on a Sunday, a tactic commonly used against dangerous criminals, not to arrest suspects wanted for nonviolent crimes. Lupe Salazar, son of Aravaipa pioneers Epimenio and Crespina Salazar, told friends that Kane Wootan had asked him to accompany the posse to arrest the Power brothers, but Lupe "adamantly refused to go" to arrest his friends under such dangerous conditions. To Aravaipa residents, the only explanation for their carelessness was that Haynes, McBride, Kempton, and Wootan were all drunk. Liquor and frontier violence often went hand in hand, so unsurprisingly, stories were told that whiskey bottles were found strewn on the trail up to the cabin, and the lawmen were so inebriated when they arrived that they could barely stand up.[33] Like the insinuation that greedy lawmen planned to steal their mine—a mine deemed so worthless that no one bid for it when it came up for auction—charging the officers with intoxication can be viewed as a calculated move to restore the reputations of the convicted murderers and defame the deceased sheriff and undersheriff who had vigorously enforced prohibition.

Frank Haynes came under special scrutiny, as he was the sole survivor among the officers. Despite his many successful years bringing dangerous criminals to justice, members of the McBride family suggested that he "had never done anything in particular to prove his prowess as an officer." Even his former boss and father-in-law, Sheriff Henry Thompson, allegedly challenged his judgment, asking him, "'Frank, what were you thinking of? You must have wanted to commit suicide. Had you waited until daylight and when they were all out working you would have had no trouble.'" The deputy marshal was often portrayed as a coward who ran even before the first shot was fired, but it could also be suggested that it was good judgment and instincts gained from years as an officer, not cowardice, that led him to take cover and exit the hopeless situation they had stumbled into at the cabin.[34]

Outside of Graham County, Haynes's solid reputation as a law officer remained intact. Clifford C. Faires, the military intelligence officer assigned to reporting on the Power brothers during World War I, later became Gila County Superior Court judge, and Frank Haynes served as Judge Faires's probation officer for fifteen years and as his hunting companion for even longer. The judge noted that while Haynes was disparaged in Graham County after the shootout, in Gila County his credibility was never undermined "with those who knew him best." The shootout, trial, and negative publicity had a profound effect on Haynes, who never mentioned his involvement to his only child or spoke of it to friends. Faires recalled, "I respected his silence. His wife informed me that he was so moved by the tragic experience that he never referred to it after the trial."[35]

Defense attorney James Fielder was also criticized as incompetent. The consensus in Aravaipa was he was washed up by the time he took the case, and "time had dealt this once able barrister a staggering blow. Age, ill health and John Barleycorn, like boring termites, had left but a hollow shell of the man they had selected to defend them." Power neighbor Merrel Haby quipped that Fielder "was quite a spiritualist, that is with the spirits that soar downward, and I think that he was pretty spirited up when he tried their case." Tom Power later confirmed Fielder was a heavy drinker and they could always smell whiskey on him during the trial, but Tom did not blame their conviction on drunkenness. Instead, he claimed Fielder was corrupt and had accepted a bribe of three hundred thousand dollars from the Mormon Church to lose the case, a claim he made with no evidence at all.[36]

A thorough investigation of all the folklore and conspiracy theories related to the Power case would fill volumes, but dissecting the distortions only distracts from the more important question of why legend supplanted fact in this case. Historians and behavioral scientists have suggested that mythology preserves history, especially among homogenous cultural groups isolated from others. It is tempting to blame the disparate shootout stories on the two conflicting cultural groups involved—Mormons versus southerners—and many writers have done so, even occasionally falsely asserting that Deputy Kane Wootan was a Latter-day Saint, but the two groups were too interwoven by the 1910s and revealed frayed tribal bonds. Mormons living in Aravaipa sided with the Power family, while many non-Mormons in the Gila Valley felt the miners at the cabin were in the wrong, an indication that geography rather than religion forged the different versions of the shootout story. Zola Webster, a young Mormon woman helping her father run their ranch near Klondyke at the time of the shootings, knew both Jane and Ola Power well and believed the entire family to be "fine people." She was appalled when she heard the horrible rumors about Ola, which she claimed had "not a word of truth to them. She was a beautiful, sweet young girl, just as proper as a girl could be." Webster made a point of attending the trial in Clifton. Even though she was engaged to a serviceman who was about to be shipped overseas to war, after hearing testimony that only told the lawmen's side of the story, she walked away from the courthouse in Clifton wondering: "'Where was the other side of the story? It certainly wasn't told at the trial.'" Likewise, Henry Allen, the young Latter-day Saint ranch hand, always sided with the Powers against the lawmen, who he insisted were drunk when they arrived at the cabin. "I know damn well all those officers were drunk when they went in. I found the whiskey bottles, four pint bottles, on the trail."[37]

While it was easy to blame greedy or drunken officers for bungling the arrest or to assert that the Powers were blood-thirsty criminals, it was difficult to accept the more likely explanation that wartime propaganda and regulations fostered by the federal government precipitated the tragedy. There was much kindling for this fire: preexisting tensions and suspicions between the residents of the Gila Valley and Aravaipa, the stubborn nature of the Power men, a persistent and energetic sheriff intolerant of slackers, and, of course, the unsolved death of Ola May, which placed Frank McBride and Jeff Power at odds with one another. But it was the wartime rhetoric characterizing draft evaders as dangerous enemies of the state that created the tinderbox setting and ultimately led to the horrific outcome.

As legal authorities noted during the war, especially in mining communities, "overzealous prosecutors, super-patriotic juries fired up by the copper press, and biased judges combined to punish scores of people for opening their mouths in the wrong place and at the wrong time." Even the prosecutor who put them away for life, William Chambers, later told his son he believed in 1918 "the Power brothers could not have received a fair hearing anywhere in the country." Chambers believed the testimony that was key to obtaining the first-degree murder conviction was Tom Power's statement made just after witnessing the shooting of his own father: "'Tell them we will be back in a few days and get more of them.'" If Chambers's assessment was correct, then the war indeed had warped the way justice was administered in the United States, allowing statements made after a killing to prove premeditation. Likewise, the testimony of a convicted perjurer like John Murdock would never have been tolerated in peacetime. As George Bernard Shaw noted, "During the war the courts in France, bleeding under German guns, were very severe; the courts in England, hearing but the echoes of those guns, were grossly unjust; but the courts of the United States, knowing naught save censored news of those guns, were stark, staring, raving mad."[38]

The press originally portrayed the Power men as agitators and vocal opponents of the war, but soon folklore formed in Aravaipa that countered that image, suggesting they were just uninformed about the draft because they lived in an isolated canyon. It is possible the family, living far from the war news buzzing in towns, did not realize just how dangerous it had become to defy the draft, but the brothers always insisted they knew of the requirement. Tom and John provided many different excuses as to why they failed to comply, but the tale that became part of local legend was that the brothers traveled into Redington in Pinal County to volunteer for the military when the nation first entered the war. There the local postmaster turned them away, saying the army did not require their services. This version ignores the fact that military authorities had made quite clear registration requirements to all Americans: Power cousins, neighbors, and friends all understood the need to register at their polling precinct, which was in Klondyke, not Redington. Despite the numerous notices posted in every newspaper and at all post offices and public buildings, Tom, John, and even Charley Power in New Mexico all failed to comply with regulations. More importantly, the numerous communications between Sheriff McBride and federal officials dating back to June 1917 established that Tom and John were not confused about their duty, but rather, "positively refused to register from the first."[39]

As the Power brothers and Sisson launched petitions for a hearing from prison, and their supporters in Aravaipa constructed alternative narratives to recast their image, the rest of the country turned to more pressing problems. Life in Aravaipa was changing rapidly. A prolonged drought drove out many ranchers, including Wiley Morgan, who was forced to go back to cowboying for others. J. Frank Wootan was forced out by hard times as well in the late 1920s, relocating with other family members to Willcox. Declines in the ranching industry were harbingers of deteriorating economic conditions. The Great Depression hit Arizona hard and the state budget was slashed, allowing conditions to become precarious at the state prison. The superintendent had to let many of the guards go, and sleep-out trustys ran off every night or so. Often the warden did not have funds for gasoline or repairs for prison vehicles, so not much of an effort was made to catch the escapees. By 1938, runaways happened so often that the Phoenix and Tucson papers kept a daily box score, infuriating Warden Gene Shute.[40]

Tom and John Power joined the inmate exodus, escaping from the prison dairy with another convicted murderer on December 28, 1939. When asked by reporters why the Power brothers had escaped, Warden Shute stated the men were frustrated with the repeated denials for clemency. The warden recently had petitioned for a hearing, but parole board chairman Walter Hofmann refused to recommend it because the citizens of Safford, "still bitter over the massacre of their lawmen almost a generation ago, had immediately demanded that the brothers should never appear before a parole board for the rest of their natural lives."[41]

A description of Tom and John Power and the third escapee was sent out to county sheriffs and police departments, but no search was organized because all three men were, according to the warden, "green as gourds" about the ways of the world, and John Power was so badly crippled with arthritis he could barely walk. Evidently, the brothers used earnings from their metal and leather goods to pay for outside help to reach Mexico, where they lived for a while, bribing local officials not to extradite them. They were unable to get work permits, so when their funds ran low, they decided to return to the United States. As they waded across the Rio Grande just outside of El Paso, they were apprehended by a customs patrol agent. When they were returned to the prison at Florence after four months of freedom, they were reunited with their devoted friend Tom Sisson, who was now seventy years old. Sisson had promised the guards he would never try to escape, and he kept his word through the years. He was spending increasingly more time in the hospital for a variety of ailments, especially heart disease. If the three convicts were ever to have their case reheard, it would have to be soon, before it was too late. But any serious attempts to gain their freedom would have to wait, as the United States prepared once again to enter a global conflict, requiring all young men to register for the draft.[42]

14

CLEMENCY

Are you men enough?

Liquor store racks and prison libraries were overflowing with true-crime magazines prior to World War II. The formula was simple: find a lurid murder case,
add a detailed police investigation report and photos of scantily clad women, and
churn out sensational stories that appealed to young men and sold millions of
copies each month. In prison, Tom Power was an avid reader of the genre, and
he always dreamed of seeing the Power side of the shootout published in such a
magazine, where the lawmen would be exposed as greedy individuals who would
stop at nothing to steal the Power mine and who gunned down his father while
he was trying to surrender. Tom got his wish to see his life story in print in 1941,
when two of the most popular true-crime magazines ran pieces on the Power
shootout in the Galiuro Mountains.[1] They did not, however, tell the version of
the story that Tom wanted to read, so he and his brother John would spend the
next two decades trying to recast their images.

True-crime magazines portrayed protagonists in black-and-white terms, and
the two wartime pieces on the Power cabin affair were no exception. *True Detective*
ran a story in March 1941 titled "Kinsmen of Disaster," based on the old newspaper
accounts of the shootout, manhunt, and trial. It also included interviews with
Mormons from the Gila Valley, notably Sandy Mangum, the butcher who had
testified against the Power brothers at the trial. The same month, *Real Detective*
magazine ran a similar story, titled "Bloody Trail of the Sharp Shooting Draft
Dodgers." In both stories, Jeff Power plays the leader of an outlaw gang who
waltzes in and out of saloons with pistols strapped to his waist, mouthing off

threats to everyone he meets. Like his brother-in-law, Wiley Morgan, who was transformed by folklorists into a gunslinger, Jeff becomes a stock character straight out of a dime novel who horsewhips the would-be lover of his daughter "Oala," causing her to fall off a horse and break her neck. Sheriff McBride plays the hero, who calls Jeff a "sniveling, mean, stubborn pack rat," and carefully follows procedure to obtain legal warrants to arrest the draft evaders hiding in the hills before being mercilessly cut down by the cruel Power gang. As the *Real Detective* author warned his audience, "As thousands of men are being drafted into the armed services, the old problem of slackers and draft dodgers comes to the fore again . . . we present the story of the Power clan who refused to do their duty as American citizens and who terrorized the Southwest for months, cutting a wide and bloody swath of bombings, murder and pillage across two states."[2]

As young American men made ready to serve in yet another world war, it was obviously a difficult time to start a campaign to release draft evaders convicted of murder. The Power brothers and Tom Sisson continued to impress guards with their behavior, but they had to impress the parole board and governor as well if they wanted to win their release. Perhaps because the chairman of the parole board, Walter Hofmann, was a Protestant minister who had served as prison chaplain for years, John Power joined the only religious organization that met officially at the prison, the St. Dismas Catholic Men's Club, and converted to Catholicism. A member of a long line of nonreligious Power men had found faith at last. It is uncertain whether John's conversion was genuine or a ploy to advance his case with the parole board. Don Dedera, who met the Power brothers in 1958, believed the brothers were "clutching at straws" as they entered their fifties and wanted to legitimize their reputations to win over Reverend Hofmann, but John was an active member of the Catholic men's club for at least a decade, serving as vice president of the club's advisory board. In his 1951 petition for a commutation of sentence he included a statement alluding to his newfound faith: "during my confinement I have studied the Bible and thoroughly and completely believe in the word of GOD, and am trying my best to follow the precepts laid down by the MASTER. Under the circumstances I am of the opinion that I am completely and fully reformed and rehabilitated so far as it is humanly possible."[3]

When the war was over and Americans returned to a peacetime footing, the Powers and prison officials resumed their Sisyphean effort to arrange for a clemency hearing, knowing that time was running out for the three prisoners. After a lifetime of physical labor, they were slowing down and showing signs of health problems, spending more time in the prison hospital or the chronic yard for

inmates with persistent illnesses than working outside the walls. Tom, the youngest, remained the healthiest of the three, still able to pick cotton during World War
II and take care of the prison's cattle, but by the 1950s he was increasingly assigned
to indoor jobs that were less strenuous, and he spent a good portion of 1953 and
1954 in the prison hospital. John too was assigned to the cotton crew as a trusty in
1942, but he was unable to perform the work and requested to be returned to the
prison, even though it meant he was unable to earn time off from his sentence. The
two brothers were allowed to live in a little shack outside the prison walls, where
they hung beef jerky to dry, grew vegetables in a small patch, served as grooms
for the prison horses, and worked at their outdoor shop making spurs, bridle bits,
and belt buckles. Tom Sisson could no longer work by the 1950s and was in and out
of the hospital with heart problems. The army veteran was entering his eighties
and walked with a crutch and cane. It became clear to everyone at the prison he
would soon serve out Judge Laine's sentence of life in prison.[4]

John Power stepped up his letter writing campaign to have their sentences
commuted, alluding to the urgency of his case: "It will take me a little while to
get adjusted to civilian life again and I haven't too many years left to do this in."
Clemency was only offered when men had the promise of work on the outside,
and while the brothers continued to receive jobs offers, if they became too old
to work, they would be unable to support themselves. Sisson had a military
pension to live on, but the Power brothers had nothing. The lawmen's widows
had confiscated all their assets, and most of their prison earnings went to hiring
attorneys. Corrections officials, noting either the men would need to be released
soon or they would die in custody, scheduled a public hearing for December
16, 1952, their first since entering prison in 1918, and notifications went out to
officials in Graham County.[5]

The families of the lawmen once again launched a barrage of letters, telegrams,
telephone calls, and petitions to stop the planned hearing. Judges, state representatives, and lawyers sent messages to the parole board asserting that the three
inmates were beyond redemption. The current Graham County superior court
judge, Benjamin Blake, reported that some members of the families in the Gila
Valley were threatening to revive the charges for the murders of both Martin
Kempton and Kane Wootan if the Powers and Sisson were released. Officers of
several American Legion posts telegraphed Governor Howard Pyle to notify him
that their veteran members were "unalterably opposed to any parole or reduction
of sentence being granted to the Powers brothers for reasons that they murdered
to evade the draft," and had been "in rebellion against their own Government."[6]

The protests fell on deaf ears because parole board chair Hofmann was determined to review the case. The hearing was held in the trusty mess hall at the prison, with about twenty members of the lawmen's family in attendance. Power family members living in New Mexico were not notified of the hearing, so there were no witnesses, aside from prison guards and the prisoners themselves, to speak on their behalf. Board chairman Walter Hofmann oversaw the proceedings, and testimony was heard for two hours. Jesse Udall, a prominent Graham County attorney, was hired by members of the McBride, Kempton, and Wootan families, and he told the board the families were not there out of vindictiveness, but because they believed the three men had "no place in society." Ignoring the fact that Tom Sisson had a guaranteed income from his federal pension and the Power brothers had been offered employment, Udall argued the three men were past the age where they could work and support themselves, so they should remain in prison.[7]

Both Tom and John Power spoke at the hearing, outlining their version of what happened on February 10, 1918. They maintained that living in their remote canyon, they knew little of the war "or their obligation to register for the draft except what they learned through occasional reading of newspapers." They insisted that they had never threatened anyone, did not know the men outside the cabin that morning were officers, and had fired back only in self-defense. John Power told the board the same story he adhered to his entire life: "We didn't have any idea who it was. They killed our father in cold blood. They were trying to kill us. We fired only five shots. We think we killed Wootan and Kempton. McBride probably was killed by stray bullets. Tom Sisson crawled under the bed and didn't shoot."[8]

The timing still was not right for their release. America was again at war, drafting young men to fight in Korea, and Senator Joseph McCarthy warned the public that Communist agents had infiltrated the highest levels of government. The Cold War resurrected the same sense of insecurity experienced during the Great War, and Americans felt the need to rally around and defend their government. The fearful atmosphere was reinforced by a more local event. During their hearing news made its way to the prison that Thomas Kane Wootan Jr., who had been born just after his father was killed in 1918, had been shot by two gunmen while he was making a routine traffic stop as a state highway patrolman. While his wound was not life-threatening, the incident, along with what one reporter called the "unyielding opposition to clemency" by the families of the officers, proved too much for the Power brothers and Sisson to overcome. Six weeks later the board denied their bid to have their sentences commuted.[9]

Despite the defeat, the hearing raised tremendous awareness for the plight of the three convicts. Even members of the lawmen's families, who had fought against their release for decades, noticed the frailty of the prisoners, all crippled by arthritis after a lifetime of physical labor. Sheriff McBride's son Darvil admitted they "elicited pity among us. Certainly it was not a pleasant thought that they might die behind bars." The hearing also highlighted discord within the ranks of the families who were not united in their opposition to the release of the Power brothers and Sisson. One of Martin Kempton's sons, Glenn, was just thirteen years old at the time of his father's death, and initially he said he felt "a bitterness and a hatred toward the confessed slayer of my Father," but as time went by, he found consolation in his faith. "One day while reading the New Testament, I came to Matthew, fifth chapter, verses 43 to 45," which says, "You have heard that it was said, 'Love your neighbor and hate your enemy.' But I tell you, love your enemies and pray for those who persecute you, that you may be children of your Father in heaven." Kempton told LDS apostle Spencer Kimball: "Here it was, the words of the Savior saying we should forgive. This applied to me. I read those verses again and again and it still meant forgiveness."[10]

About thirty years after the shootout, Glenn Kempton visited the state prison and asked to meet with Tom Power. The two men talked at length, and when they finished Kempton shook Power's hand and said, "With all my heart, I forgive you for this awful thing that has come into our lives." Kempton's story of forgiveness has become an important part of Mormon teachings in southeastern Arizona, but as historian Catherine Ellis has suggested, "it seems important to recognize that in granting someone forgiveness, really you are saying, 'I am right, you are wrong, and I forgive you.'"[11]

Despite the appearance of cracks in the phalanx against clemency, the Power brothers made little progress toward their release. Tom Sisson always let them take the lead, rarely saying a word in his own defense, because, as a repeat offender, it was more difficult for him to argue for a commutation. Yet he had garnered so much trust among the guards over the decades that he was allowed free access to his own rifle to go hunting for wild burros to provide food for the prison dogs. In January 1956, at age eighty-seven, Sisson finally succumbed to the heart disease that had plagued him for years. Tom and John refused to allow their comrade be buried in the prison cemetery and arranged instead for his interment at the Florence city cemetery. Former Warden Alva Weaver filled out the application for a military headstone for the old veteran and, because he and everyone else at the prison had heard endless stories of Sisson's role in the Indian wars, wrote "Indian Scout" on the form to denote Sisson's military grade and branch of service. The paperwork was sent to military authorities in Washington for review, and when the form was returned, "Indian Scout" had been crossed out and replaced with the correct title: "private."[12]

Although with one swift motion of a red pen, government officials had exposed Sisson's small lie about his military exploits, no one seemed to notice. In fact, with his passing, the stories about him, the brothers, and the shootout grew more outrageous, proliferating and finding their way into print. Rob Brotherton has noted that the Communist witch hunts of the 1950s stimulated a spike in conspiracy theories in the United States that "hit fever pitch." He argues that "we have innately suspicious minds. We are all natural-born conspiracy theorists," and it is precisely at that time that new theories were published that contradicted earlier versions of what happened at the cabin. When she heard of Sisson's passing, Elizabeth Lambert Wood, who had spent many happy hours hiking in the Galiuro Mountains as a young woman, listening to Jay Murdock's stories about the shootout, decided to weave them together in a slim volume. The book, titled *The Tragedy of the Powers Mine: An Arizona Story*, portrays the Powers as the victims of greedy, drunken lawmen. Wood's own son was killed in action during World War I, so she focused on the bitter anguish caused by conscription and military service. In her version, Charley's grandmother pleads with him to volunteer for the army against his father's wishes, and when he signs up and is shipped overseas for active duty, his father will no longer speak his name. Of course, Jane died two years before the country entered World War I and Charley had evaded the draft, but the book presented to the wider public a new narrative, based on attitudes long held by people living in Aravaipa: that the Power brothers were not defiant slackers, but instead were controlled and dominated by their father. The most important contribution of Wood's book was her assertion that a feud existed between John Power and Kane Wootan. Hard feelings festered between them for years, she wrote, and the shootout was a result of Wootan's determination to kill the entire Power family.[13]

Wood's book motivated many Power supporters who had remained quiet over the decades to come forward to work for their release. What had been discussed in the canyons of Aravaipa was now reported to the governor and the parole board. Governor Ernest McFarland heard from a member of the Morgan family, who insisted "that these boys were purely justified in killing those officers as they just rode up in the yard and shot their daddy down in cold blood murder."[14] Zola Webster, the Mormon rancher who had attended the trial and believed the Power side of the story had not been told then, had since married Marcus Claridge, the nephew of a prominent LDS Graham County politician. The couple continued to ranch in Aravaipa, and in the 1930s Zola became a leader in the county Republican Party. At that time the party had little clout in state politics, but by the 1950s demographic changes in Arizona had occurred as a result of World War II, and increasingly voters elected Republicans to office. Claridge, who had worked hard for the party during the lean years, now was on a first-name basis with many of the men who occupied seats on the parole board or sat in the governor's office, and she routinely pleaded the Power case to them. Other Latter-day Saints would join the cause as well, including attorney Glen L. Randall, who performed hundreds of hours of pro bono legal work for the Power brothers in the 1950s.[15] While their work behind the scenes was beneficial, what was needed to counteract the opposition to their release emanating from the Gila Valley was a public investigation that would force the parole board to act.

In the fall of 1958 Don Dedera, who wrote the most popular editorial column for the *Arizona Republic,* the state's largest circulation newspaper, was at the state prison to write a story about one of the inmates. After completing his interview, Warden Frank Eyman approached Dedera and suggested he talk to the Power boys, as they were still called by prison guards, because he believed they had a story Dedera would find interesting. As a former Marine and reporter who had worked the police beat for an urban newspaper, Dedera was guarded in his approach to convicted felons, who he knew would tell him "that every convict is wholly innocent, is wrongfully incarcerated, and needs only another chance to prove it." Although Dedera had never heard of the Power brothers, he had tremendous respect for Warden Eyman, so he listened patiently to John and Tom as they told their "well-rehearsed" story of injustice at the hands of Graham County officers.[16]

Despite his reservations about the authenticity of their story, certain aspects of their first meeting struck the columnist, especially the fact that the brothers had spent four decades in prison and, in all that time, had only been granted one formal parole hearing. According to Dedera, John, "slumped over like a turtle," barely said a word the entire interview, but Tom was well-spoken and impressed the reporter with his knowledge of the law. Leadership in the prison considered the brothers exemplary prisoners, and Sisson had served his entire life sentence without a minute's grief for the guards, yet he was never considered fit for release. Dedera wondered why these two men were still incarcerated when so many others who had committed similar crimes had been paroled, so he decided to investigate their story.[17]

Dedera soon discovered that the Power brothers had hired many lawyers over the years who believed that the trial, conducted in wartime, did not conform to "present standards of criminal justice." One attorney went so far as to state the trial had been a "legal monstrosity." Yet, according to those same legal experts, the Power brothers were their own worst enemies, unrealistically demanding complete exoneration because they refused to shoulder any blame for the shootout. According to more than one attorney whom they had fired over the years, had they been less stubborn, "they would not now be in prison."[18]

When Dedera returned to the prison for a follow-up interview, the brothers gave him a paper bag filled with one hundred dollar bills, explaining to him that each time they hired an attorney they had to pay him a retainer. Dedera laughed and told them to keep their money. He did not intend to retry the case in court, he said, but rather hoped to present both sides of the story in his newspaper columns, allowing society the opportunity to reevaluate their case. Dedera then traveled to Graham County to interview anyone still living with firsthand knowledge of the events and to examine remaining case records. The oral histories that had percolated in isolated Aravaipa for forty years were now presented to a statewide audience in his column, "Coffee Break."[19] The Power boys had finally found their champion.

Dedera's first column about the shootout appeared on November 10, 1958, and primed his readers for much incendiary material to follow: "America was at war with the Central Powers. T. J. Power was at war with the people around him," began the series. Dedera's Jeff Power was a domineering and "obstinately independent" man who refused to allow his boys to serve in the war. "The Power boys wanted to join up," according to Dedera, but their father's reply was, "'I'll see you in hell first!'" His sons were not to blame for their predicament, the columnist argued; they were victims of circumstance. Dedera offered the Power brothers' version of the shootout in his second column: "They say they were asleep when the officers surrounded their cabin. . . . They woke when a belled mare ran past the front of the cabin. Old Tom [Jeff Power], thinking a mountain lion was after the mare, stepped outside dressed in long johns and carrying his rifle." When Kane Wootan shouted, "'Throw up your hands!'" he complied, responding, "'Don't shoot!'"[20]

Within the next six days, four more columns appeared in which Dedera told his readers what he had gleaned from his investigation. Dedera expressed his doubts about some of the claims made by the Power brothers, especially their suggestion that "they were railroaded by a stacked jury, unfair judge, perjured testimony, and inept counsel," noting that "much of society had judged them guilty before the trial began. But the Power boys were given their rights." Then, building on Elizabeth Lambert Wood's book and stories he heard from longtime residents of Aravaipa, Dedera confirmed that a feud existed between the Wootans and the Powers. Although he was unsure what caused the "bad blood" between the two families—people he interviewed in Aravaipa suggested Kane Wootan either had been spurned by Ola Power before she died or had sparred with the Power brothers over grazing rights—Dedera alleged that the draft charges were trumped up to give Wootan the opportunity to get even with the Power brothers. He quoted Tucson journalist J. F. Weadock, who had also investigated the case and concluded that Jeff Power, "in his stubborn attitude toward the draft, coupled with Kane Wootan's desire for vengeance . . . juggled the two boys into a mess which was not of their making."[21]

The origins of the feud narrative can be found in the rough treatment locals gave the Power family when they first arrived in Aravaipa, something Lee Solomon, a distant relative of the Wootan family and a primary source of the feud story, called the "little trouble." Everyone freely acknowledged that the Power family was not welcomed in Aravaipa, but, of course, residents were suspicious of any additional outsiders who threatened already scarce resources. The early stories of the chousing of their cattle were vague regarding the identity of their tormenters, but as the folklore took root and evolved, Kane Wootan became the designated ringleader, allegedly exchanging harsh words with Jeff Power and chasing off his cattle. For years, people wondered why Deputy Kane Wootan shot Jeff Power that morning, with some suggesting that because he borrowed a rifle with a hair trigger, he might have fired accidentally, and others speculating that he might have panicked when Jeff Power walked outside with rifle in hand. Once the feud scenario was introduced, those benign explanations gave way to a more sinister plot, allegedly engineered by Kane Wootan to exterminate the Power family. For Dedera and others whom he would rally to the cause of freeing the brothers, draft evasion was not the primary reason behind the shootout; rather, it was driven by "a personal grudge."[22]

Lee Solomon was the leading proponent of the theory that Kane Wootan's antipathy toward the Powers instigated the gunfight. Although the Solomons were related by blood and marriage to the Wootans, the relationship was strained, and the Solomons were apparently closer to the Powers than the Wootans. When Sam and Jane Power lived in Gillespie County, Texas, from the 1860s to 1890, Lee Solomon's father and mother, David Lee Solomon and Jane "Dee" Wootan Solomon, were their friends. After both families moved to Arizona, the next generation, including Lee Solomon and his sisters, Delila, Madge, and Roxie, continued their friendship with the Power family. As a young man Lee Solomon himself had punched cattle with Charley, John, and Tom Power, as well as his relative Kane Wootan in Aravaipa. His sister Delila, who went by Lila, married Kane Wootan's father, Black Bill, in 1909 after his divorce from his first wife, Sarah, so she was Kane's stepmother at the time of the shootout. Years later her marriage to Wootan also ended in divorce, adding to the existing acrimony between the Solomons and Wootans. Relatives now began to superimpose complex family squabbles on the shootout story.[23]

The Solomon siblings suggested that Kane Wootan taunted Tom Power at the Klondyke store when he first arrived, and then bribed girls with boxes of chocolate to ignore Tom at a school dance, though Tom Power never mentioned those incidents in his version of events, a book titled *Shoot-Out at Dawn*. Lee Solomon, who ran a ranch in Oracle at the time of the shootout, also told Dedera that Kane Wootan had boasted to him that if he killed the Powers he would be elected sheriff. Solomon said, "I did my best to talk him out of going on the posse trip. I reminded him that he had a feud with the boys, that he did not like them; that they did not like him. Kane said before long he would give me a good job as chief deputy. 'You don't know how to play politics. I am going to ride into the Power place. I'll be the first man there. I'll shoot the hell out of them! And from there, I'll be elected sheriff of Graham County.'"[24] Dedera received corroboration on the feud story from Glenn Kempton, Undersheriff Martin Kempton's son, who told him it was "common knowledge that Kane Wootan had had disputes with the Power family, that the Wootan family had conflicting claims with the Powers, and that Kane Wootan and John Power had long carried on a personal vendetta."[25] Dedera's columns inspired other journalists to pursue the story, and assured that the oral histories of conspiracy and deception were no longer confined to Graham County, but were read by a statewide audience each morning over coffee.

It is possible that the feud became a way for some people living in Aravaipa—for whom feuds were an intrinsic part of their southern heritage—to understand how such an unfortunate event could have occurred in their midst, but it is problematic on many levels. Both the Power brothers and the Wootans acknowledged that there were occasions prior to the shootout when the two families had their disagreements, but as Tom later stated, "I would not have thought that our brushes with the Wootans were cause enough for them to try to kill us." Tom and John Power had always maintained Sheriff McBride wanted their gold mine, but after conferring with visitors to the prison in the 1950s, they began to entertain the possibility that the shootout had been precipitated by a feud with the Wootans.[26]

The public records do not support a feud. There were no civil suits or injunctions filed by either side over water or land rights in Graham County. Neither Kane nor any other Wootan owned property near the Power Mine, Gold Mountain, or Power Garden Place, and Kane Wootan had moved to Safford a year prior to the shootout, far from Rattlesnake Canyon. Even Frank Haynes testified under oath that as the posse rode up to where the Powers lived at Gold Mountain in the early morning hours of February 10, 1918, Wootan told him he had not been that way for five or six years, making it unlikely that he had much contact with the family during that period. The notion that Kane Wootan wanted the position of sheriff also does not stand up to scrutiny. At the time of his death he was involved in foreclosure and legal proceedings that would have disqualified him from running for public office, and his indebtedness would have made it impossible to post the ten thousand dollar bond required if elected. The most convincing evidence that the feud was not real can be found in the Bureau of Investigation reports and U.S. marshal records for the Power case. It is clear from the correspondence between Sheriff McBride and federal officials from the period of June 1917 to January 1918 that Kane Wootan played no role in orchestrating the arrest of the Power brothers. He was never mentioned once in those reports; rather, it was Sheriff McBride who was determined to bring to justice every slacker in his jurisdiction.[27]

The brothers had always blamed McBride for the tragedy, tapping into long-held prejudices that Mormons stole and murdered and then conspired to cover up their crimes. But their accusations that the sheriff was willing to kill for their mine fell on deaf ears. McBride had been a respected, honest public servant, and his family and friends were too numerous and powerful to allow such accusations to stand. If the Power brothers were ever to go free, their supporters knew they would have to find someone else to blame in order to win over public opinion. Kane Wootan was an easier target. According to Jay Murdock, he had usurped the leadership of the posse, striding up to the cabin before his superior officers were in position, initiating confrontation, and shooting Jeff Power. More importantly, his reputation had been tarnished by his financial problems. Wootan had fallen on hard times prior to his death, and the bank's lawsuit against him claiming fraud cast doubt on his integrity. His wife, Laura, died in 1925, so she was unable to defend his honor, as longer-lived Clara McBride so ably did for her slain spouse. Some of Kane's brothers, most notably J. Frank, continued to battle the accusations launched by Power supporters, but among the three lawmen, Kane Wootan was the easiest on which to cast suspicion. Despite their initial doubts, the Power brothers eventually became convinced by the Solomons and others that Kane Wootan had plotted against them.[28]

The families of the deceased lawmen quickly disputed the feud claims. Opal Wootan Shepard, Kane's daughter, chastised Dedera for writing "horrible things" about her father. She insisted no one in the Wootan family knew anything about "bad blood" between the families, and suggested instead that the Solomons were trying to discredit the Wootans by creating the myth of the feud. The sheriff's son, Darvil McBride, also denied that a feud was to blame, saying, "Such a story has been kicked around quite a bit since the affair, but has been proved to be only imagination . . . manufactured by those who must always weave intrigue and romance into any controversial and 'old west' affair."[29]

Whatever the source, real or imagined, the Wootan-Power feud narrative was a powerful corrective to previous accounts of the shootout, and it immediately captured the public's imagination. Dedera likened the reaction to his columns about the feud to "poking a broom handle into a hornet's nest." The men who had once been portrayed by the press as the "monsters of 1918" were suddenly transformed by Dedera "into kindly old men" who had paid sufficiently for whatever role they had played in the shootout.[30] Dozens of letters poured into the *Arizona Republic*'s office, most addressed to Dedera's boss, Eugene Pulliam. Pulliam was arguably one of the most powerful figures in state politics at the time, a conservative largely responsible for the victories of many of Arizona's Republican politicians in the 1950s and 1960s. Day after day, as angry letters arrived addressed to the editor-in-chief and publisher of the *Arizona Republic*, Pulliam remained silent. He could have pulled the story at any time, but he instead said nothing directly to Dedera, and sent his secretary Mary Freeman to his star columnist each day with a new stack of letters. She would inform him in her "professorial" manner, "Mr. Pulliam requests you produce answers for these," and Dedera dutifully sat down at his typewriter and responded to each and every one. To the lawmen's outraged relatives who wrote to him, Dedera acknowledged, "Personally, I am not convinced that the Power brothers should be released. That is a decision for society." The case could not be retried because so many documents had vanished and witnesses had died, but as he went on to say, "society, I believe, is on trial. Our way of justice has an issue before it." These men had been in prison longer than anyone else in Arizona history, for a crime that "from the outset was fraught with controversy and confusion and contradiction. Others convicted of similar crimes had been released, why not them?"[31]

About a week after Dedera's first six columns appeared, aspiring writer Marguerite Buchanan visited the Power brothers in prison on Thanksgiving Day with her Aunt Madge Solomon Miller and Uncle Lee Solomon. Tom and John explained to her their side of the story, just as they had to Dedera, and she was surprised they displayed "no vengeful attitude, no rankling of malice toward fellow mankind." Before long she joined forces with Don Dedera to create a "committee" to free the Power brothers, consisting of her many Solomon uncles and aunts. Several Mormons soon joined the campaign, playing an integral role within the informal group: attorney Glen Randall continued to provide legal work, while Zola Webster Claridge tapped into her Republican connections. Throughout the decades the lawmen's families had solicited the support of politicians and judges to keep the Power brothers in prison. Now Don Dedera and his ad hoc committee would employ the same tactics to obtain their release.[32]

The group provided the backing that the Power brothers, bereft of powerful friends or finances, needed. Members wrote letters to newspaper editors and state politicians, discussed the matter over lunch with prominent citizens, and strategized about how to overcome the resistance to clemency. Marguerite Buchanan received advice from Robert Morrison, a former state attorney general and close friend of parole board chairman Walter Hofmann, who was familiar with the case. Morrison told her that when he investigated the Power case several years before, "the greatest factor against the boys" was "the HUE and CLAMOR from the Wootan faction." Morrison soon set up a meeting for her with Hofmann, as well as the other two parole board members, Superintendent of Public Instruction W. W. Dick and the new attorney general, Wade Church, to get a sense of what was needed to gain clemency. Church, Hofmann, and Dick told her that appeals by attorneys and the Powers were insufficient. The board wanted to hear from citizens of good character who would speak for the Powers. Dedera's columns unleashed those voices. Letters poured in from ministers, long-lost friends, politicians, judges, and most importantly, members of the lawmen's families. Lila Solomon Wootan, Kane's stepmother, wrote to Governor Paul Fannin, suggesting bluntly: "My relative opened fire on them. The boys have been imprisoned unjustly."[33]

Attorney General Church agreed to investigate the case, and made the startling discovery that someone pretending to be employed by his office had tried to defraud the Power brothers. A "Mr. Smith" told the brothers he needed one thousand dollars if they wanted the attorney general's office to reopen the case. Staffers quickly tracked down the culprit and forced him to return the brothers' payment, but the incident piqued Church's interest. He was a Harvard

Law School graduate, a Democrat who had clerked for United States Supreme Court justice Felix Frankfurter and worked as the director of the Arizona State Federation of Labor. Of course Frankfurter, before becoming a justice on the highest court, was appointed by President Woodrow Wilson to investigate the Bisbee Deportation in Arizona. Undoubtedly, his clerk Wade Church had heard numerous stories about the extremely explosive conditions Frankfurter found in southeastern Arizona during World War I, allowing Church to understand how a miscarriage of justice might have been carried out in the Power case. The attorney general made it clear to Dedera's committee that he was sympathetic to freeing the Power brothers.[34]

In March 1960 the parole board announced it would hold a public hearing the following month for the Power brothers. Dedera picked up the story in his columns once again, expressing his opinion that the brothers had little chance for success in their bid for freedom because, as he noted, "Hate is strong. Mercy is weak." Even though several wardens and some members of the Kempton family were willing to forgive John and Tom, Dedera told his readers, "the same hard core of embittered and vengeful Graham County citizens has served notice that they again will protest clemency for the Powers." Based on the stories he had heard in Aravaipa about the "clannish" Mormons in the Gila Valley, who colluded to hide any evidence that would convict one of their own, Dedera hinted that many believed a Mormon conspiracy kept the brothers from gaining a release. Tapping into more than a century of suspicion between the Gentiles and Saints of Graham County, established during the anti-polygamy campaigns and the federal investigation into the Wham payroll robbery, Dedera suggested, "So intense has been the hatred of the [Gila Valley] group, there is a fear, unjustly founded as it may be, that the wrath of a church group will fall upon any politician who dares to help the Power boys."[35]

The assertion that a Mormon conspiracy was keeping the Power brothers in prison struck a raw nerve. As one Aravaipa resident later told a researcher: "The Mormons got them. Them kinda things will happen around here." And finger-pointing at the Mormon Church was not confined to residents of Aravaipa. Lemuel Mathews, a justice of the peace in Casa Grande in 1918 and later an attorney in Yuma, wrote to Don Dedera expressing the "greatest respect for the Mormon church," but noted that early on in Arizona, Mormons had "their trouble," and it was not "until around 1920 did people of other religious faiths of Arizona have the respect for Mormons as they do now.... They felt early after the Powers boys were convicted that they should oppose clemency and stood strong as a unit against" it. John Power himself, drawing on stories he undoubtedly heard from his father and grandmother about the deaths of the Baker-Fancher emigrants from Arkansas as they traveled through Utah, stated emphatically that the shootout was "a little Mountain Meadows Massacre. The Mormons knew how rich that mine was, and they come out here to kill us and get it."[36]

There was no evidence Mormons conspired to cover up evidence and keep the Powers locked away. Among the lawmen only McBride and Kempton were Latter-day Saints, while Kane Wootan and Frank Haynes were not, even though Wootan was often mislabeled a Mormon in much of the pro-Power mythology. Nor were any of the federal officers who approved the warrants or the posse members of the Mormon faith. Dedera himself quickly pointed out in his next column that not all Mormons were against the Power brothers, but in fact, many were working behind the scenes to secure their release, like Zola Webster Claridge and Glen Randall. Trying to lay to rest the rumor of a conspiracy, Dedera proclaimed: "Anybody who says the Mormon Church holds the Power boys' prison key is a liar." Despite his comments to the contrary, Dedera's columns were, in his own words, "political dynamite," and laid bare anti-Mormon sentiments. But they also forced the LDS church to end its silence about the Power case.[37]

From his personal interactions, Dedera had nothing but respect for the Mormon people, but more importantly "battering an established institution" was diametrically opposed to his personal philosophy. Years later the columnist admitted that his only regret regarding his handling of the story was attacking the Mormon Church, but at the same time, as he noted, there was "no bigger gorilla in the room. . . . In retrospect, I'm not sure I was as objective as I should have been. The disparity of justice seemed so gross my reportage was more in the form of a crusade to see them released. But then, mine was a signed column, and if folks didn't want to agree with my opinion, they didn't have to." He believed that if there was any truth to the suggestion the church had a policy to keep them behind bars, "maybe it was the key to unlock the prison door." He knew from long acquaintances with so many of the LDS faith that they would not "need much of a nudge to save their reputation," and he was correct.[38]

Newspapers around the state took up the story, and most expressed sympathy for the plight of the "mild-mannered, soft-spoken old gents" who had spent more time in state prison than anyone else. *Tucson Daily Citizen* journalist Bob Wood presented his own findings after interviewing both sides, noting that the Power brothers continued to argue their father had been shot in cold blood without warning from the officers. When asked if he held a grudge against the families,

Tom responded: "'How can we hate or be bitter against the people who have fought to keep us here so long when we don't know them, have never seen them. Once we are out, we'll leave people alone, if they just leave us alone. They've taken our property; we have nothing to go back to.'" The brothers continued to claim they did not understand the draft registration process and were unaware they were required to sign up until a week after the draft date. Wood concluded, "to backwoods boys, the draft was a strange, sinister thing which they felt was no part of their existence." The McBrides, Kemptons, and the Wootans continued to claim "the lawmen walked into a trap and were gunned down," and it was clear the decades that had passed since had dulled their anger only slightly. Sheriff McBride's son Darvil told Wood, "'We still believe in what we have stood for all these years. The Powers were guilty, the officers innocent. We don't hate anyone, but we will never forget. The McBrides would never look up the brothers, but if we met them face to face, who knows what would happen.'" Kane Wootan's brother J. Frank, who at eighty-three remained an imposing figure, stated: "'I would have felt like shooting them down once. Maybe I'm past that now.'"[39] Those expressions of deep-seated animosity only helped the Power cause.

Dedera's columns and the other articles that appeared in the statewide press created a sea change in public opinion, and members of the McBride and Kempton families, sensing the brothers might be released at the scheduled hearing, began intense negotiations with members of the parole board and the governor. The children of McBride and Kempton expressed fears that if released, Tom and John Power might harm them or their elderly mothers. They asked for a special audience with the governor to gain his assurance that if their sentences were commuted, the brothers would remain on parole, so their every move would be monitored on the outside. While the Kemptons and McBrides attempted to adjust to the notion the men might be freed, J. Frank Wootan refused to relent, and suggested to the parole board that Don Dedera had been bribed to write his columns in defense of the Power brothers. To avoid an unpleasant encounter, board chair Hofmann told Dedera he could not attend the hearing. When Tom and John heard the decision, they announced they would boycott unless Dedera was allowed in. The board relented and Dedera, after engaging in a heated exchange with J. Frank Wootan outside the hall, entered the trusty mess and sat down on the picnic benches, where roughly one hundred people had gathered to hear testimony on April 20, 1960.[40]

It was a warm afternoon, and the evaporative coolers did little to cool things down in the packed hall. The three members of the parole board were present,

Arizona Republic columnist Don Dedera (left) had a heated discussion
with Kane Wootan's brother J. Frank Wootan prior to the clemency
hearing for the Power brothers, held on April 20, 1960.
*Courtesy Arizona State Library, Archives and Public Records,
History and Archives Division, mg92_B5_F132_I36.*

as were the two prisoners dressed in their denim gray and blue uniforms. Lee
Solomon came to testify, along with three former prison wardens, Ted Mullan,
Alva Weaver, and Lorenzo Wright. Attorney Glen Randall, who had been released
by the brothers over a difference of opinion, was there to speak for them in an
unofficial capacity. The Wootans and McBrides had retained Wilford Rene
Richardson to represent them, and he was accompanied by Alvin Krupp, the
current Graham County attorney. Two cousins of the inmates, Bill and Joe
Morgan, had traveled from New Mexico to attend. In the back of the room were
reporters for the local dailies and wire services as well as a television cameraman,

Tom Power asked descendants of the lawmen for forgiveness at his hearing in 1960,
held at the Arizona State Prison at Florence. Parole board members
W. W. Dick (wearing a white shirt) and Walter Hofmann
(wearing a dark jacket) are seated behind him.
Courtesy Arizona State Library, Archives and Public Records,
History and Archives Division, mg92_B5_F132_I37.

but the din was so loud and the acoustics so poor that it was difficult to hear what
was said. Parole board chair Hofmann quickly set the tone for the hearing: "In
no sense will we have a retrial here today. The boys have no attorney. They have
told their story. They simply want to spend the few years they have left to them
as free men. That is the decision we will make here today."[41]

Attorney Richardson was the only representative who spoke against their
release, and he told the board members that the families believed John and
Tom Power did not merit parole because they "still believe they were victims of
a miscarriage of justice, and that they have an antisocial attitude. If there is any
resentment, it has been generated by the press with slanted stories." Next up were a
series of witnesses who spoke for the brothers. Former warden Ted Mullan stated
that the men had paid for any crime they had committed and should be given

the chance for freedom, and he would personally accept responsibility for their actions on the outside. "After 42 years, people who come down here to protest must be filled with hatred. Hatred has no part here." The next former warden to speak, Alva Weaver, concurred: "Give them a chance. Men have been released from here who committed the same crime or worse. . . . There is no revenge on their hearts. . . . Let these white-haired old men breathe free air before they die." Glenn Kempton spoke of his prison meeting with Tom Power and explained he had no animosity, just a deep sense of sorrow for the unfortunate chain of events. His brother, Albert Kempton, followed him, similarly expressing his belief that they should be granted freedom, as did Lee Solomon and others.[42]

The last speaker was Lorenzo Wright, who had served as prison warden in the 1930s and was a former stake president for the LDS church in Maricopa County, the most populous county in the state. As the portly, white-haired man many called "Mr. Mormon" rose, he addressed the Latter-day Saint families in attendance. "It is with humility and humbleness that I stand here. I'm related to both of these wonderful families, the Kemptons and the McBrides. Never better people lived in this world. I love them all." He then turned to the wider audience and said, "God has said, if you will not forgive, he will not forgive you. . . . The killings were a horrible thing. If they paroled today, it will hold no jurisdiction over what God has for them. This board won't satisfy him. They will have to face their God."[43]

As Wright finished, Richardson requested permission from the board to speak again, and then addressed the sixty-seven-year-old Tom and seventy-year-old John, who could only walk with the aid of crutches. "I don't like the allusion that the families have not forgiven the Power brothers. But there are two widows of the slain officers who are mortally afraid the Power boys will come after them." The brothers broke their composure for the first time, smiled, and shook their heads. Richardson continued, "If it were made clear that these prisoners think they made a tragic mistake, the situation might be different. But they believe they were not wrong, that they were right."[44]

Lorenzo Wright arose once more and in a roaring voice confronted the prisoners, demanding: "Are you men enough? I have come here to speak in your behalf. If you are not men enough to ask forgiveness and to forgive, then I withdraw my support." When he received no response from Tom or John, he repeated the challenge, asking: "Are you men enough?" Tom, in a shaking voice, mumbled a barely audible, "We are." Wright demanded he repeat his answer, which Tom did in a more convincing tone, adding, "We hold no hatred for anybody. We are

The spurs presented to Don Dedera by Tom and John Power upon their release
in 1960. During their forty-two years in prison, the brothers made
many similar items and sold them to pay for their legal counsel.
Courtesy Cameron Trejo Films, LLC.

not much acquainted with the families. We hold no bitterness. We will forgive
and would like to be forgiven. What happened 42 years ago is out of our control
now. We are sorry about all that happened, but there is nothing we can do about
that. I thank all of you." The audience erupted with applause, the stomping of
feet, and wild cheering. Veteran journalist Bob Thomas, whose story went out
on the news wires, wrote it was "one of the most spine-tingling experiences I've
ever covered as a reporter."[45]

After Tom spoke, it took more than a minute for Chairman Hofmann to
restore order in the room so that John Power could address the crowd. John
had doggedly insisted on their innocence for over four decades, firing countless
attorneys who wanted to settle for something less than complete exoneration.
He had never been much for talk, and the words he chose at that moment were
characteristically concise: "I hold no hatred for anybody. I beg for forgiveness."
Don Dedera was flabbergasted, later telling his readers, "Those who knew him
would more expect the San Francisco Peaks to topple into Lake Mary than to
hear John Power, in a voice loud and free, beg forgiveness of the people he had

considered his tormentors for 42 years." Again the room erupted in jubilation as everyone tried to congratulate the two men. Even J. Frank Wootan, who had stubbornly opposed their release until the end, humbly offered his hand to each of the brothers. An hour later, John and Tom were called into the assistant warden's office and notified that the board had commuted their sentence to time served. The next day, Republican Governor Paul Fannin signed the papers for their release.[46]

A few days later John and Tom Power walked out of the gates of the Arizona State Prison and greeted the man they considered their liberator, Don Dedera. They presented him with a pair of spurs they had made in prison, decorated with their signature metalwork design. Tom told him, "We knowed you wuz a dude, so we made 'em so's you could wear 'em in parades." Indeed, Dedera was no real cowboy, but he had ridden to their rescue nonetheless. His coverage of the Power story earned him numerous accolades, including an Arizona Press Club Award in 1958 and recognition from *Newsweek* magazine. His managing editor, Oren Fifer, even encouraged him to apply for a Pulitzer Prize, which he opted not to do. For Dedera, those spurs made by the brothers were the honor he coveted most in his long career in journalism. "No gift before or since ever has meant so much to me."[47]

15

REDEMPTION

A story from which myths were woven

John and Tom Power mustered out of prison with new Levi jeans, cowboy hats, boots that they had purchased, and $12.50 in pay on April 27, 1960. John was so elated by his impending freedom that on the morning of his release, he left without his shiny new black cowboy boots and was forced to return to his shack at the prison to retrieve them. Warden Frank Eyman laughed, saying, "He's so excited. I finally had to dress him. He got his boots but he forgot his socks." Even then, he failed to put on a clean shirt, still wearing a soiled work shirt as journalists snapped photos of the brothers leaving the prison gates. Tom too was thrilled, writing to Don Dedera shortly after his release, "I surely am enjoying this 'free world' . . . thanks to you!"[1]

When the celebrations of their newfound freedom finally abated, reality settled in. Each man had some savings from the sale of the items they had made and sold in prison—John about two thousand dollars and Tom about one thousand—and Tom Sisson had bequeathed John his military pension, worth about ten thousand dollars, but additional income would be hard to find. They were prohibited by the terms of their commutation from receiving any paychecks for participating in television, magazine, or newspaper interviews or publishing their story. They had little education, and as young men they had performed only manual labor, but now they were too old. They soon became dependent upon the goodwill of the same folks who had worked so hard to free them. Initially, Lee Solomon moved them to his AC Ranch in Yavapai County, and later they cared for the horses at various dude ranches and summer camps, including Bud Brown's Friendly

Pines Camp near Prescott. Don Dedera always chuckled at the thought of Tom and John wrangling ponies at Friendly Pines, because, as he said, one day they were "incarcerated as convicted murderers," and shortly afterwards they were "caring for, with surpassing gentleness, the kiddies of Phoenix's first families."[2]

The work they found was only seasonal, and, as Tom noted, "this ranglin dudes is pretty hard work for an old cow poke." The brothers were tired of each other after spending so much time together for four decades, so they often went their own ways. John spent much of his time in Silver City, New Mexico, working at a spur and bridle shop on a ranch, living with old friends and members of the Morgan family, and visiting his childhood home in Gila, where he erected a barbed-wire barricade to keep the cattle from grazing on his mother's grave. Tom found work shoeing horses in Scottsdale, Arizona, for a while, but as a friend observed, "God knows that's a tough job for a young man and certainly no position for a 67 year old man."[3]

Don Dedera soon discovered that keeping an eye on the parolees was full-time work that drove him and his "committee of care givers nuts." After missing so much of life, Tom wanted to travel to places like Disneyland, and when he turned seventy, he wanted a birthday party—something he had never had—so Dedera arranged for a cake, party hats, and presents. Tom was also constantly talking to movie producers and book publishers about signing deals, which would have voided the terms of his probation. John remained consumed with getting the mine back in operation, but the terms of their parole prevented them for returning to Klondyke. Concern grew among the caregivers that the brothers might do something wrong that would send them back to prison. No one in the group worried about the two old men committing a violent act, but they were so poor they might steal a loaf of bread. Tom and John always needed money, a better job, and a ride somewhere, but most of all they wanted a pardon.[4]

Both men were dissatisfied with the terms of their release. They demanded their names be cleared of all wrongdoing and their voting rights reinstated, and they did not want to report to a parole officer each month, but instead to return to the Galiuro Mountains to reclaim their mine. Don Dedera and the rest of the committee took up their cause once again, writing letters of support to the parole board and to newspaper editors. They won a partial victory when they were released from their parole restrictions in 1963 and allowed to return to Klondyke to reopen the mine. In the 1950s, after years of labor that yielded no gold discoveries, the lawmen's widows and their partners had abandoned the Power mine in Kielberg Canyon, but other individuals, including Charley Power, soon reclaimed them. After his brothers' parole restrictions were lifted and they could return to Graham County, Charley deeded over the claims to John, who then moved into the old mine shaft, bringing everything he owned—some bedding, clothing, and handmade tools. However, in their final years, Tom and John had neither the physical strength nor the financial resources to reopen the claims, and even if they had, the mine is unlikely to have ever produced for them. Between 1915 and 1922 only fifty-three ounces of gold was produced in the Rattlesnake Mining District. John P. Wilson, a historian and archaeologist familiar with the area, concluded that the Powers, lacking basic understanding of the geology of gold mining, had been "wildly optimistic about the value of their holdings." Another observer concurs: "the only thing harder to wrest from the land than gold is the rumor of gold. No one would do more to prove the truth of this statement than the Power family."[5]

Still unsatisfied with the conditions of their release, they continued to petition for a full pardon, but the board turned down their request in January 1968. Don Dedera criticized the denial in one of his columns: "One must wonder what need of society is served in the refusal of the State Board of Pardons and Paroles to recommend a pardon for John and Tom Power. Fifty years—a half century!—ago this winter, in a mountain gunfight that began with the bushwhacking of their father, the Power boys killed an Arizona sheriff and two possemen." The brothers had demonstrated eight years of exemplary behavior since leaving prison, Dedera scolded, but board's answer was still "no, no, no." He reminded his readers that the two elderly men would still be in prison if the board had not been "shaken by publicity and political pressure."[6]

That year the nation's newspapers were filled with stories of Vietnam War protests and young men burning their draft cards. Distrust of government was at a new high, creating a very different national climate from the one in which the brothers were first convicted of murder. The unpopularity of the war in Southeast Asia shattered the public's conviction that all draft dodgers were criminals. During the Powers' years in prison, as the country fought two world wars and the Cold War, there was little sympathy for a couple of aging slackers, but Vietnam changed all that. A steady stream of letters supporting a pardon arrived, addressed to the governor and members of parole board members, until January 1969, when a date was finally set to hear their pardon plea.[7]

The board unanimously approved their pardon, issuing a statement that they had led "an exemplary life in their community and have conducted themselves as law abiding citizens since their release from the Arizona State Prison." On

January 25, 1969, Republican Governor Jack Williams signed their pardon, summing up the prevailing attitude toward the brothers in a public statement:

> I have put my signature to these documents with some concern. But that concern is outweighed by a feeling that justice will be served by this action. This feeling is supported by recommendations from the sheriffs of Cochise, Graham and Greenlee counties and from other county and judicial officers, that the Power brothers be granted pardon. The consensus of their views is that the debt of these men to society has been fully paid; that it is right and just to return their civil rights, and the rights of citizenship, to them. My hope is that this action will not, by any stretch, be taken as condoning draft-dodging or attacks upon official authority. The full circumstances of this situation, the exemplary life conducted by John and Thomas Power since their sentences were commuted by (former) Gov. Paul Fannin, and their present age, all combine to lead me to believe that their full pardon will service justice.[8]

Years later, after he had left office, Williams became more philosophical about his pardon of the Power brothers, stating, "The dramatic gun battle in Keilberg [*sic*] Canyon . . . was a story from which myths were woven. . . . Who will ever know the rights and wrongs of it?"[9]

When the pardon went through, John and Tom were living in the Gila Valley in a cluttered shack, with old yellowed linoleum peeling off the floor and paint peeling from the walls. They expressed relief that their campaign of fifty-two years was finally concluded. John told the reporter who had arrived to get their reaction to the pardon, "'it's the last step. We've been waiting for it for a long time.'" To the end, the two refused to admit guilt, continuing to tell the same story they had told for over half a century about the lawmen who arrived on that frozen dawn in 1918. John was emphatic: "'They was out to kill us, they weren't trying to arrest us. Hell, we didn't even know they wanted us. They just started shooting, shot down our daddy in the doorway. You'd fight back too, wouldn't you, if they shot down your Pa?'"[10]

Their release and pardon did little to stop the proliferation of tall tales in Graham County. Roderick J. Roberts Jr., who lived in the Gila Valley off and on during the 1960s and 1970s, became familiar with the many different versions of the shootout, and was intrigued with how the stories offered by residents in communities along the Gila River varied from those offered by inhabitants of Aravaipa or the Sulphur Springs Valley, so he interviewed five hundred people,

When their parole restrictions were finally lifted in 1963, Tom (left) and
John Power finally returned to their old home. This photo was taken
in 1970 at the Klondyke store, just prior to Tom's death.
Courtesy Pinal County Historical Museum.

asking them only if they knew about the shootout. Although all were familiar with
the story, over 70 percent refused to talk to him, and almost all the remaining folks
agreed to speak only if their names were withheld because they feared reprisals.
When he sought old newspaper articles from the local publisher or official records
at the county courthouse, he was curtly refused cooperation. Roberts commented,
"I knew that I had stumbled upon a narrative that had a deep significance to the
community in which it circulated." The interviews were later incorporated into
his doctoral dissertation in the field of Folklore at the University of Indiana.[11]

When the brothers were pardoned, they were finally released from the requirement that they could not profit from their story, and Tom agreed to have John
Whitlatch, a friend and Gila Valley businessman, write down the stories he
and John had told numerous Aravaipa residents over the years in a book called
Shoot-Out at Dawn. Tom's book makes many outlandish claims and demon-
izes anyone who ever had a hand in their arrest or conviction, perpetuating
the far-fetched notion that greedy lawmen plotted to kill the Power family for
their mine and ignoring entirely the fact that the brothers had evaded the draft.
Despite its failings, it remains the most popular version of the shootout story

because it captures the sense of injustice the brothers felt about their conviction and lengthy incarceration. Darvil McBride offers a much more reasoned and accurate version of events in his book *The Evaders,* published in 1984, but often retreats to the McBride family's assertion that the Powers initiated the shooting and insinuates incorrectly that they had an outlaw past.[12]

Numerous accounts of the shootout continued to appear in print, including several in the true detective genre that reversed the narratives of the original articles published during World War II and which must have delighted Tom Power. *Cavalier* and *Front Page Detective* published stories in the early 1960s that featured Lee Solomon's version of the feud, with him telling reporters: "It was a one-sided affair. . . . Kane Wootan was badgering them. I told Kane a hundred times to leave the boys lone. But he had a bad temper and his hate was deep and bitter." Lee Solomon's niece Marguerite Buchanan became Marguerite Noble after she was widowed and remarried, and published a novel, *Filaree,* which incorporated elements of the feud story she had heard from her aunts and uncles. Loosely based on the ranching experiences of her mother, who struggled to raise a family in Gila County at the turn of the century, the story features a feud between an evil deputy sheriff named Ted Neeson—a bully despised by everyone—and a good-natured, handsome cowboy named Ike Talbot. When Neeson goes gunning for Talbot, he shoots and misses. Talbot, in self-defense, returns fire, killing the deputy. After the killing he tells the woman he loves that he must leave, because the deputy he killed has lots of powerful relatives in town: "'They're a mean outfit. And the sheriff is wantin' reelection. . . . I can't wait for no trial, and 'twouldn't be a fair trial no how. It'll be prison for me if I stay.'" He leaves to hide out in the mountains until things cool down, eluding the law and eventually riding off to Silver City, where he finds protection among friends.[13]

The folklore that began to find its way into the press, academic research, and literature in the 1950s redeemed the reputations of the Power brothers, but it focused primarily on the question of who shot first on February 10, 1918. The only four men who were in a position to know who initiated the gunfight—Jeff Power, Frank McBride, Martin Kempton, and Kane Wootan—all died that day. The more crucial question, however, was why four lawmen felt compelled to travel sixty-plus miles over rough roads and trails by car and on horseback in the dead of winter to arrest four men for nonviolent crimes. The only answer that adequately explains the shootout is that fever-pitch wartime emotions, not greed or a feud, caused this tragedy.

Jeff Power, like his ancestors, had clawed out a living in unforgiving terrain, continually forced to defend what little he had from predators, both human and non-human. He inherited his distaste for war from his family's experiences during the Civil War, while his years of combating aggression in Texas and New Mexico instilled in him a populist bent, sentiments he would pass on to his own three sons. Life in Rattlesnake Canyon brought him a temporary reprieve from the clamor of the outside world, until the draft of World War I threatened his ability to develop the mine, leaving him with the prospect of losing everything he had: his sons and his ability to earn a living. He was wary of government and eschewed society, an outcast even among the numerous outcasts living in the canyon, but the Great War required the assistance of every able-bodied person and would not allow him or his family to remain in isolation. As historian Eduardo Obregón Pagán has said about Jeff Power, "As Americans we like to mythologize about the rugged individualist, but the truth of the matter is the rugged individualist is celebrated only in certain times for certain reasons. As a nation when we need to band together, we need to band together, and that individualist will pay the cost for who they are."[14]

Since the nation's founding Americans have debated how to balance the rights of individuals against the power of the federal government, but during World War I the pendulum swung so decisively toward national security to preserve order that protests were drowned out, especially in the Southwest, where strikes threatened to disrupt the production of war materiel. Wartime legislation cast aside constitutional protections on free speech, and dissidents like the Powers were cavalierly branded dangerous anarchists. Forgetting his nation's long history of rejecting conscription, one newspaper editor wrote of the Power brothers in 1918, "These men were outlaws, they had repudiated the draft."[15] While it was never clear whether they took up arms to resist the draft or simply to defend their home, the public had automatically assumed it was the former. Most instances of armed draft resistance occurred among outspoken dissidents who were conscientious objectors or had political motivations, but the Powers were not religious or political, nor were they foreign born, Mexican-Americans, Socialists, labor radicals, or members of any other marginalized groups in the Southwest that became special targets for persecution during the war. Perhaps that is what makes this incident so startling: the war conflated animosities to the point that even the white, native born, apolitical Power family, living miles from civilization, became caught up in accusations of treachery against the United States government.

In southwestern mining towns, where rabid, pro-war copper corporations controlled local news, citizens received a steady diet of news that there was something "dangerously wrong" with the brains of slackers like the Power brothers. In peacetime witnesses like John and Jay Murdock would never have been allowed to take the stand because of their questionable characters and documented instances of lying, yet their conflicting and likely perjured statements were consumed whole by jurors, as was much of the circumstantial and contradictory evidence in the case. The haphazard investigation of the crime scene by authorities and the biased coverage of the shootout in the press reflected the common assumption that the three defendants were guilty of murder long before Judge Frank Laine banged his gavel to open their trial in Clifton. Tilden Scarborough, who had grown up with Tom Power in Gila and bootlegged with him in Globe before becoming an attorney, understood how topsy-turvy the world was in 1918: "I followed the proceedings of their trial and conviction closely, and have no criticism of the verdict and the judgment of the court. However, the undisputable fact is that the country was at high tension at the time of their arrest and conviction. The world was at war, and evasion of the draft law was fresh in the jurors' minds, without which it is doubtful if a first-degree verdict would have been rendered."[16]

The Power shootout should have been forgotten long ago, an obscure side story to World War I history. Instead, the story was kept alive precisely because enough people believed the outcome was unjust. At the time of the trial the public wanted vengeance, but could find none because the death penalty could not be administered. The Power brothers and Tom Sisson wanted a retrial or clemency hearing, but were denied legal recourse by the united efforts of the lawmen's relatives. With crucial documents lost or stolen, a review of the case could only take place in the court of public opinion, where rumors soon replaced the few facts left behind. Stubborn attitudes prevailed as both sides refused to accept responsibility. In the end, only the death of Sisson and the advanced ages of the Power brothers brought the story to light outside of Graham County and the state prison system, and even then the path to the release of John and Tom Power was paved with distortions that transformed a straightforward case of draft evasion into a tale of feuds and conspiracies. It was not until 2008, ninety years after the gunfight, that enough time had passed to allow for the publication of the first study to place blame squarely on the war rather than the participants, Barbara Brooks Wolfe's *Power, Passion, and Prejudice: Shootout in the Galiuro Mountains*.

Prior to their incarceration neither Tom nor John had registered to vote, and once that privilege was reinstated with the pardon in 1969, they drove over sixty miles from Aravaipa to Safford to register. They joined the Republican Party and then voted in the primary on September 8, 1970. Numerous prominent Republicans, like Zola Claridge and Eugene Pulliam, had paved the way for their release, and two Republican governors, Fannin and Williams, had granted them their freedom and reinstated their rights as citizens, which likely had an impact on the brothers' choice of political party. Whether they also chose the party of Abraham Lincoln because of a deep-rooted family affiliation with the GOP, going back several generations to the Civil War, is anyone's guess.[17]

Three days after voting for the first time in his life, Tom Power, age seventy-seven, died suddenly on his brother John's seventy-ninth birthday. The cause of death was ruled a heart attack, and he was buried the next day at Klondyke near his sister, Ola, and grandmother, Jane. At the funeral, his brother John sat in a place of honor at the foot of the casket. Also in attendance were many of the folks who had helped the brothers find work and places to stay since their release, as well as former prison guards they had befriended over the years. After the funeral John remained in Klondyke, and often was so destitute he was forced to live in his pickup truck.[18]

Despite the tranquility offered by the canyon, John's lifelong friends noticed marked paranoid tendencies since his release and commented that they increased without his brother Tom to comfort him. Ever since Ola's death in 1917, John had been convinced someone was trying to kill the family. After his release from prison he constantly tested his drinking water for poison. He broke down often and cried when he thought about the tragic circumstances surrounding the deaths of Ola and his father, and he became inconsolable when he talked about how his father never had a proper burial.[19]

In 1972 John exhumed his father's remains at the mine and reburied them with the rest of the family in Klondyke. Ray Luster knew the brothers his whole life—Luster's father had been superintendent of the prison farm where the brothers worked—and was owner of the Safford funeral home, so he helped John erect granite tombstones on the graves of family members. On his grandmother's grave, John inscribed: "killed by run away horse and buggy accident." He never explained why, but somehow a distraught John became convinced that his brother's death was not a result of natural causes, and instead engraved Tom's marker: "poisoned in l.a., calif."[20] Hundreds of pages had been written defending John's actions at the cabin, but none as potent as the handful of words he etched in stone for his father and sister. Jeff's marker reads, "shot down with hands up in his own door," while Ola's epitaph is, "poisoned by unknown person."

Charley was the next Power sibling to die, in 1973 at age eighty-four. Because of his brothers' notoriety, following the shootout, Charley was forced to live his life in the shadows. In the 1920s he resided near his Morgan relatives in Alma, New Mexico, working as a ranch hand and farm laborer, but at some point in the middle of the Great Depression he moved to Bell County, Texas, just north of his birthplace in the Hill Country, where he worked as a driller in the oil fields. There is no evidence he ever married or had any children, and he apparently died alone in Monticello, New Mexico. Many people have suggested that Charley was estranged from his brothers after the shootout, and that might have been true. Although the two men had contact in the 1960s when Charley deeded the mine to John, neither Tom nor John ever mentioned Charley in interviews. In addition, John erected monuments on the gravesites of all his beloved family members, but Charles Samuel Power is buried in an unmarked pauper's grave.[21]

After Charley's death, John was the sole surviving grandchild of Sam and Jane Power. Although he was without close kin, he had numerous friends in Klondyke, including those from his youth, like Lupe Salazar and Merrel Haby. The three aging "patriarchs" of Klondyke, as one journalist called them, hiked together each day in the wilderness as far as their arthritic bodies would allow. These canyon dwellers were a "different breed" of men, the journalist wrote, who "were born in the outdoors, lived in the outdoors, and, hopefully, they will die in the outdoors." John Power continued to tell everyone he met that he knew there was still gold in the Power Mine, and he was itching to go prospecting again soon. But he remained reluctant to answer many of the more perplexing questions about the shootout and refused to speak of Ola's death.[22]

Wade Cavanaugh, a journalist who covered eastern Arizona for the *Arizona Republic* in the 1950s and 1960s and had attended the Power brothers' parole hearing in 1960, began researching material for a book on the shootout, tracking down and interviewing those involved who were still alive. Cavanaugh became close friends with John Power in his waning years and spent many hours asking him questions about his family, the shootout, and the mine.[23] In the middle of March 1976, the two men were sitting around a small campfire when John began to speak in a quiet, emotional voice:

> You asked about Ola several times in the past few months. . . . It was an accident. We had an argument 'cause she wanted to run off and get married to this guy. We didn't like him, didn't think he was good for her. She wouldn't listen. She went out and got on her horse to go up to where the

car was at the Haby's in Klondyke. I wanted her to stay but she wouldn't. I tried to rope her off the horse. She raised her hand to knock back the rope but she missed and it got tangled in her neck. The horse kept runnin' but she got pulled off. I didn't know it was around her neck. I didn't think she was hurt. She had been pulled off lots of times before, we all had. I carried her into her bed, she was cryin' and moaning. I didn't know what was wrong, dad and Tom came in, and he told Tom [Sisson] to ride over to Boscoe's for help.[24]

Of course, Ola died before the Boscoes arrived, so the Power men and Sisson came to a decision. "How could we tell anybody, who'd believe us? They was lookin' for Tom and me anyway, nobody would have believed us, nobody." After a few moments of reflection, he told Cavanaugh, "Don't put that in your book, please, at least not 'til after I'm gone." He was still worried, after fifty-eight years, that he would be prosecuted for his sister's death.[25]

A few weeks later, on April 5, 1976, John died alone in his sleep in his trailer, parked near the Klondyke post office. He had been suffering from the flu, and when he failed to pick up his mail, friends went looking for him and found him dead. Longtime friends like the Salazars and Claridges attended his funeral service, and Wade Cavanaugh provided the eulogy. After a reading of the 23rd Psalm, "The Lord is my shepherd . . . ," and a prayer, John was laid to rest next to his grandmother Jane; father, Jeff; sister, Ola; and brother Tom. He had chosen the words for his own tombstone: "Rest in Peace."[26]

It would be easy to dismiss John's confession to Cavanaugh regarding Ola's killing as just another tale concocted by a journalist trying to sell a book or hoping to put his own spin on the Power legend. After all, Cavanaugh's story dovetails nicely—perhaps too nicely—with John's last known words about Ola, spoken after his capture in 1918, when he allegedly told Sheriff Art Slaughter, "'They accuse me of killing her, but the one who killed her will never be known until her slayer is on his death bed, then he will make a confession.'" I must admit my own skepticism about the veracity of Cavanaugh's story, but after wading through mountains of contradictory stories for years in the pursuit of the truth about the Power shootout, I have become cynical, and question the validity of all new material that surfaces. The Cavanaugh story is especially problematic, because all that remains is an unpublished manuscript. The tape recordings and most of the transcripts of his original interviews have disappeared—true to form for so many documents associated with the Powers. Although I have my doubts, like

Don Dedera had his doubts when he first heard the brothers tell their story in prison, something rings true about John's confession to Cavanaugh. According to Cavanaugh's daughter, he cherished his friendship with John Power, never would have done any harm to him, and never told anyone about the confession. She was unaware of it herself until 2015, when she read her deceased father's unpublished manuscript for the first time. She was initially reluctant to allow the confession to be made public, because she did not want to tarnish John's image, but she relented when she realized that publishing it might indeed allow him to truly rest in peace.[27]

The death of John Power marked the end of the family born of Sam and Jane Power. Although there are descendants of Sam's siblings living scattered across the West, not one of his own grandchildren—Charles, John, Tom, or Ola—ever married or had children of his or her own. All that is left are the buildings they occupied in Rattlesnake Canyon, and even those are quietly being reclaimed by nature. The process of depopulating Aravaipa Canyon began in the 1920s, when drought devastated the ranching industry in southeastern Arizona. Decline continued in 1930s during the Great Depression and after passage of the Taylor Grazing Act, which ended the open range system. The last mining operation in the region and the Klondyke post office both closed in the mid-1950s, and by then all herds of goats were gone. While cattle ranching and farming continued, most families tended to remain on the east end of Aravaipa, where electricity and telephone lines were available, far from Rattlesnake Canyon.[28]

In 1969 Aravaipa Canyon was designated a primitive area by the Bureau of Land Management, and in the 1980s more than 77,000 acres of land in the Coronado National Forest were designated the Galiuro Wilderness. The Wilderness Act, passed by Congress in 1965, created a preservation system to provide "an area where the earth and its community of life are untrammeled by man, where man himself is a visitor who does not remain." Restrictions were placed on grazing and hunting, and new construction was banned to protect the canyon from over use. Today only about a dozen people inhabit the ghost town of Klondyke, located just outside the Galiuro Wilderness. The Klondyke store is closed, but a guesthouse caters to the numerous hikers who come for the wildlife, flora, and breathtaking scenery. It remains a difficult hike into Rattlesnake Canyon, which is inaccessible to vehicles. The steep grade at what is now called "Powers Hill" by the United States Forest Service is a challenge for pack animals and humans alike. The Power family's old haunts are now even more separated from civilization than they were in the 1910s.[29]

The Power stamp mill, which was never operational,
still stands on Rattlesnake Creek.
Photo taken by the author in 2014.

The Power cabin in Kielberg Canyon, located in the Galiuro Wilderness,
is listed on the National Register of Historic Places.
Photo taken in 2014. Courtesy Steve Porter.

At the lovely clearing in the canyon that the Power family called Garden Place, the original structures occupied by the family are long gone, save a lone log cabin built by Pete Spence, which now serves as a tack room.[30] A few miles up the trail at Gold Mountain, a handful of dilapidated structures still stand. In the summer of 2014 the Oak Fire threatened this portion of the Coronado National Forest, so firefighters cleared brush from the area, exposing additional cabin ruins. Perhaps someday an archaeologist with the forest service will identify the saloon where the Power men lived and the small cabin inhabited by Ola when she died. The stamp mill that the Power men and Sisson hauled into the canyon just prior to the shootout never became operational, but it remains standing silently near Rattlesnake Spring, its timbers split and metal parts rusted. The boiler to power the stamp mill, which Jeff Power was waiting for when he died, never arrived; the vehicle hauling it broke down somewhere between the Gila River and Aravaipa Creek, and it laid abandoned for years before someone finally carted it away.[31]

The mining cabin in Kielberg Canyon where Thomas Jefferson Power, Sheriff Robert Franklin McBride, and deputies Martin Robert Kempton and Thomas Kane Wootan lost their lives still remains and is listed on the National Register of Historic Places. In the 1980s a group of volunteers based in Tucson performed much-needed restoration work on the cabin.[32] When the Oak Fire threatened the structure, firefighters cleared the brush around it and shrouded it with flame-resistant material, saving it from destruction. The chinking, shed, windows, and screens are long gone, the log poles are sagging, and the roof is collapsing, but the Power cabin, like the folklore that engulfs it, endures.

ABBREVIATIONS

ADOC	Arizona Department of Corrections
AHS	Arizona Historical Society, Tucson
ASLAPR	Arizona State Library, Archives and Public Records, Phoenix
ASU	Arizona Collection, Hayden Library, Arizona State University Libraries, Tempe
AZ v. Sisson	State of Arizona v. Thomas J. Sisson, John Power, and Thomas Power, Greenlee County Superior Court Criminal case no. 438a
BLM GLO	Bureau of Land Management, Government Land Office, U.S. Department of Interior
Copper Era	Copper Era and Morenci Leader
DOJ	United States Department of Justice
FBI	Federal Bureau of Investigation
GCC	Grant County (New Mexico) Clerk
GCRO	Graham County (Arizona) Recorder's Office
MID	United States Military Intelligence Division
NARA	National Archives and Records Administration
NMSRCA	New Mexico State Records Center and Archives
NPS	National Park Service
NRHP	National Register of Historic Places
Noble	Noble, Marguerite Collection
PBRN	Power Brothers Research Notebook
RG	Record Group
TSLAC	Texas State Library and Archives Commission
USGS	United States Geological Survey

NOTES

PREFACE

1. The Owens-Blevins shootout, which occurred in Holbrook in 1886, was part of the larger Pleasant Valley War and left three dead.
2. Richard Slotkin, *The Fatal Environment: The Myth of the Frontier in the Age of Industrialization, 1800–1890* (New York: Atheneum, 1985), 29–30.
3. Don Dedera, "Coffee Break," *Arizona Republic* (Phoenix), November 14, 1958.
4. United States Marshals' Collection, AHS Tucson; Bob Thomas, *Arizona Republic*, January 26, 1969.
5. The U.S. attorney records for Arizona are held at NARA Riverside, CA, but include only correspondence between 1899 and 1910. Whoever removed documents from the U.S. Marshals Collection did so selectively, leaving behind letters that discussed men who were hiding out in the hills near Klondyke but did not mention the Powers by name. Documentation related to the manhunt, and authorization for a wanted poster and for witness expenses are all that remain. The materials were in the possession of the marshal's office until U.S. Marshal Archie M. Meyer donated them to the Arizona Historical Society in 1959.
6. See, for example, Elizabeth Lambert Wood, *The Tragedy of the Powers Mine: An Arizona Story* (Portland: Metropolitan Press, 1957); William Ryder Ridgway with Milton Bean, *The Power Family of Graham County, Arizona* (Texicanwife Books, 2012); Thomas Cobb, *With Blood in Their Eyes* (Tucson: University of Arizona Press, 2012); Tom Power and John Whitlatch, *Shoot-Out at Dawn: An Arizona Tragedy* (Phoenix: William F. McCreary, 1981); Fred McClement, "The Bullet That Has Never Stopped Burning," *Cavalier* (August 1961): 26–58.
7. Harold E. Herbert interview with the author, October 27, 2015.

CHAPTER 1

1. Larry J. Griffin and Peggy G. Hargis, eds., *The New Encyclopedia of Southern Culture*, vol. 20: *Social Class* (Chapel Hill: University of North Carolina Press, 2012), 368; Roderick J. Roberts Jr., "'The Powers Boys,' An Historical Legend: Its Formation and

Function" (PhD diss., University of Indiana, 1974), 287, 289, 293; Gladys Stewart, as told to Leva Kempton, "The McBride Story—'Clara and Frank,'" 12.

2. Robert V. Hine and John Mack Faragher, *Frontiers: A Short History of the American West* (New Haven: Yale University Press, 2007), 62.

3. Tom Power interview, Noble, box 5, Power Brothers folder 131, ASLAPR; U.S. Census, 1820: Falmouth, Pendleton, Kentucky, 28; R. Gerald Alvey, *Kentucky Bluegrass Country* (Jackson: University Press of Mississippi, 1992), xiv; David Hackett Fischer, *Albion's Seed: Four British Folkways in America* (New York: Oxford University Press, 1989), 638.

4. U.S. Census, 1840: Salem, Washington, Indiana; Drew R. McCoy, *The Elusive Republic: Political Economy in Jeffersonian America* (Chapel Hill: University of North Carolina Press, 1980), 13.

5. Alvey, *Kentucky Bluegrass Country*, 28; U.S. Census, 1830: Anderson, Kentucky.

6. Sarah McStotts Oborne, emails to the author, December 18, 2014, and February 3, 2015; U.S. Census, 1830: Anderson, Kentucky.

7. Alvey, *Kentucky Bluegrass Country*, 28.

8. Lewis Collins, *History of Kentucky* (Covington, KY: Collins & Co., 1874), xxi, 15; Alvey, *Kentucky Bluegrass Country*, 28.

9. U.S. Census, 1850: Salem, Washington, Indiana; BLM GLO, May 1, 1845, Docs. IN2850.136 and IN2860.086; *History of Benton, Washington, Carroll, Madison, Crawford, Franklin, and Sebastian Counties, Arkansas* (Chicago: Goodspeed Publishing, 1889), 508, 693–94. The portion of Crawford County the Powers settled in was annexed to Sebastian County after their arrival.

10. S. Charles Bolton, *Arkansas, 1800–1860: Remote and Restless* (Fayetteville: University of Arkansas Press, 1998), 167; Jeannie M. Whayne, Thomas A. DeBlack, George Sabo, and Morris S. Arnold, *Arkansas: A Narrative History* (Fayetteville: University of Arkansas Press, 2002), 135.

11. Bolton, *Arkansas*, 167; *History of Benton*, 693–94; Roberts, "'The Powers Boys,'" 310.

12. *History of Benton*, 693–94; Whayne, *Arkansas*, 128, 138; Bolton, *Arkansas*, 157; BLM GLO, Accession Nr: AR 1820_.124, March 1, 1855, http://www.glorecords.blm.gov/ (accessed March 9, 2015); Will Bagley, *Blood of the Prophets: Brigham Young and the Massacre of Mountain Meadows* (Norman: University of Oklahoma Press, 2002), 55.

13. *History of Benton*, 508; Whayne, *Arkansas*, 130.

14. Robert Caro, *The Years of Lyndon Johnson*, vol. 1, *The Path to Power* (New York: Alfred A. Knopf, 1982), 5–8; U.S. Census, 1860: Center, Sebastian, Arkansas.

15. John Mack Faragher, *Women and Men on the Overland Trail* (New Haven: Yale University Press, 1979), 31; Whayne, *Arkansas*, 133–34; Bagley, *Blood of the Prophets*, 7, 9, 38, 66, 240; Daniel J. Herman, *Hell on the Range: A Story of Honor, Conscience, and the American West* (New Haven: Yale University Press, 2010), 28–29; Roberts, "'The Powers Boys,'" 315.

16. U.S. Census, 1860: Visalia, Tulare, California; *Internal Revenue Service Assessment Lists for California, 1862–1912*; BLM GLO, Accession Nr: CA1400_.148; Edith Sparks, *Capital Intentions: Female Proprietors in San Francisco, 1850–1920* (Chapel Hill:

University of North Carolina Press, 2006), 125; U.S. Census, 1870: Santa Rosa, Sonoma, California.

17. Thomas Sheridan, *Arizona: A History,* 2nd ed. (Tucson: University of Arizona Press, 2012), 77; service records of Private Thomas J. Power, Office of the Adjutant General, NARA, RG 94, Union Soldiers Compiled Service Records, 1861–1865, M533 roll 5.

18. Alvin R. Lynn and J. Brett Cruze, *Kit Carson and the First Battle of Adobe Walls: A Tale of Two Journeys* (Lubbock: Texas Tech University Press, 2014), 75; Richard H. Orton, *Records of California Men in the War of the Rebellion, 1861–1867* (Sacramento: State Printing Office, 1890), 75; Darlis A. Miller, *The California Column in New Mexico* (Albuquerque: University of New Mexico Press, 1982), 21.

19. Sheridan, *Arizona,* 77–78; Orton, *Records of California Men,* 68–86.

20. Application for removal of charge of desertion for Thomas J. Power/s, case no. 12046, Office of the Adjutant General, NARA, RG 94, Union Provost Marshals' File of Papers Relating to Individual Civilians, 1861–1866, Enlisted Branch, 1886, roll 221.

21. Ibid.; service records of Joseph S. Anderson, Office of the Adjutant General, NARA, RG 94, Union Soldiers Compiled Service Records, 1861–1865, M533 roll 1.

CHAPTER 2

1. Tom Power interview, Geneology [*sic*], Noble, ASLAPR; U.S. Census, 1860: Center, Sebastian, Arkansas. Tom Power told friends his mother's grandmother was Cherokee, but that claim is dubious.

2. Tom Power interview, Noble; U.S. Census, 1880: District 4, Gillespie, Texas. Ridgway, *The Power Family,* 21, notes that Jeff "told tales of his youth and young manhood which he spent on a ranch near Fredericksburg, Texas." Officials did not record births in rural areas of Texas until decades later.

3. Frederick Law Olmsted, *A Journey Through Texas* (Austin: University of Texas Press, 1978), 275–76.

4. Myron P. Gutmann and Kenneth H. Fliess, "The Determinants of Early Fertility Decline in Texas," *Demography* 30 (August 1993): 443–45; Sandra L. Myres and Emily K. Andrews, "A Woman's View of the Texas Frontier, 1874: The Diary of Emily K. Andrews," *Southwestern Historical Quarterly* 86 (July 1982): 52, 57; Rodman L. Underwood, *Death on the Nueces* (Austin: Eakin Press, 2000), 68.

5. Martin Donell Kohout, "Gillespie County," *Handbook of Texas Online,* https://tshaonline.org/handbook/online/articles/hcg04 (accessed June 1, 2017); Caro, *Path to Power,* 5, 8, 18.

6. Underwood, *Death on the Nueces,* 63; Jan Wrede, *Trees, Shrubs, and Vines of the Texas Hill Country: A Field Guide* (College Station: Texas A&M University Press, 2010), 3–7.

7. Caro, *The Path to Power,* 5–8; Joseph S. Hall, "Horace M. Hall's Letters from Gillespie County, Texas, 1871–1873," *Southwestern Historical Quarterly* 62 (January 1959): 338; Stanley S. McGowen, "Battle or Massacre? The Incident on the Nueces, August 10, 1862," *Southwestern Historical Quarterly* 104 (July 2000): 64.

8. Underwood, *Death on the Nueces,* 12, 15.

9. Claude Elliott, "Union Sentiment in Texas, 1861–1865," *Southwestern Historical Quarterly* 50 (April 1947): 450–52; McGowen, "Battle or Massacre?" 64; Underwood, *Death on the Nueces,* 15–16, 105, 109; George Q. Flynn, *Conscription and Democracy: France, Great Britain and the United States* (Westport, CT: Greenwood Press, 2001), 14. In the North, Abraham Lincoln faced similar challenges to the Enrollment Act of 1863, which required all men between the ages of twenty and forty-five to sign up to fight for the Union cause. The federal draft allowed men three choices: they could fight, they could find a substitute, or they could pay a three hundred dollar fee to be exempted. About 85 percent of those drafted avoided the battlefield, some by using the legal means available to them, others by running away. Only 8 percent of the Union Army was conscripted.

10. McGowen, "Battle or Massacre?" 193; Elliot, "Union Sentiment in Texas," 464; Underwood, *Death on the Nueces,* 15–16, 21, 91; Flynn, *Conscription and Democracy,* 10.

11. Underwood, *Death on the Nueces,* 21–24, 91; David Johnson, *Mason County "Hoo Doo" War, 1874–1902* (Denton: University of North Texas Press, 2006), 2, 14; Elliot, "Union Sentiment in Texas," 462, 466.

12. Matthew Salafia, *Slavery Borderland: Freedom and Bondage along the Ohio River* (Philadelphia: University of Pennsylvania Press, 2013), 2; Interview with Thomas Jefferson Power, Power Brothers Papers, AHS; California Voter Registrations, Ventura County, Camarillo Precinct, 1900–1924, accessed February 11, 2015, Ancestry.com; NARA records of Confederate and Union soldiers provide no evidence that Sam Power of Texas enlisted or was drafted in any capacity during the Civil War.

13. Joe Baulch, "The Dogs of War Unleashed: The Devil Concealed in Men Unchained," *West Texas Historical Association Yearbook* 73 (n. d.): 135–37.

14. Tom Power interview, Noble.

15. Flynn, *Conscription and Democracy,* 14.

16. A. M. Gibson, *The Life and Death of Colonel Albert Jennings Fountain* (Norman: University of Oklahoma Press, 1965), 53–54; Caro, *Path to Power,* 18; Underwood, *Death on the Nueces,* 12; Johnson, *Mason County,* ix.

17. Johnson, *Mason County,* x, 1–2, 14, 15; Underwood, *Death on the Nueces,* 105–7; J. Frank Dobie, "The First Cattle in Texas and the Southwest Progenitors of the Longhorns," *Southwestern Historical Quarterly* 42 (January 1939): 171–72; Walter L. Buenger, *Secession and the Union in Texas* (Austin: University of Texas Press, 1984), 17; Caro, *Path to Power,* 20–21; O. C. Fisher, *It Occurred in Kimble* (Houston: Anson Jones Press, 1937), 204; Peter R. Rose, *The Reckoning: The Triumph of Order on the Texas Outlaw Frontier* (Lubbock: Texas Tech University Press, 2012), xv, xxi; Herman, *Hell on the Range,* 283; Thomas P. Slaughter, *The Whiskey Rebellion: Frontier Epilogue to the American Revolution* (New York: Oxford University Press, 1986), 72.

18. "Coal Creek," *Handbook of Texas Online,* June 15, 2010, http://www.tshaonline.org/handbook/online/articles/rbcft (accessed July 17, 2017); Texas General Land Office, Patent No. 706, vol. 3, file number 000168, TSLAC; Gillespie County Deed Record, vol. M, pp. 606–7, TSLAC. James G. Burnham was the original landholder of the Coal Creek property. Sam Power's name does not appear on the 1867 voter registration roster for Texas, an indication he may have fled the region during Reconstruction.

19. Llano County Probate Minutes, case no. 347, book 6, pp. 194–96, TSLAC; Martin Donell Kohout, "Willow City, TX," *Handbook of Texas Online*, June 15, 2010, https://tshaonline.org/handbook/online/articles/hnw51 (accessed July 16, 2017); Ridgway, *Power Family,* 53, 78.

20. Kohout, "Willow City."

21. Selected U.S. Federal Census Non-population Schedules, 1880 Agricultural Census for Gillespie County, Texas; *State of Texas v. S. B. Powers,* Gillespie County Justice Court Docket (Precinct 4), 1876–1888, vol. 1, p. 231, TSLAC. The justice ordered Sam to be held in the custody of the constable until costs and fine were paid, which did not happen until G. Harrison paid the county treasurer the $2.05 fine and $2.80 in court costs on Sam's behalf on November 9, 1886.

22. Judith N. McArthur, "Woman's Christian Temperance Union," *Handbook of Texas Online*, June 15, 2010, http://www.tshaonline.org/handbook/online/articles/vaw01 (accessed July 17, 2017). Frances Willard toured Texas between 1881 and 1883, establishing the first local chapters of the Texas Woman's Christian Temperance Union in sixteen towns.

23. Graham County Great Register of Electors, Klondyke Precinct, 1914, ASLAPR; Barbara Brooks Wolfe, *Power, Passion, and Prejudice: Shootout in the Galiuro Mountains* (Tucson: Imago Press, 2008), 23; Ridgway, *Power Family,* 22; Johnson, *Mason County,* 2.

24. Tom Power interview, Noble; Wrede, *Trees, Shrubs, and Vines,* 3–7; Caro, *Path to Power,* 5–8; Gillespie County Deed Records, vol. R, p. 242, vol. 2, pp. 104–6, TSLAC.

25. Ridgway, *Power Family,* 21; U.S. Census, 1900: Upper Gila, Grant, New Mexico; U.S. Census, 1910: Willcox, Cochise, Arizona.

26. Caro, *Path to Power,* 31; Power, *Shoot-Out at Dawn,* 7; Margaret Haby, "Wiley Marion Morgan," *Arizona National Ranch Histories of Living Pioneer Stockmen,* vol. 9, Betty Acomazzo, comp. and ed. (Phoenix: Arizona National Livestock Show, Inc., 1987), 45–56; Tom Power interview, Geneology [*sic*], Noble. William Jefferson Bybee, the brother of Amanda Bybee, Wiley and Mattie's mother, enlisted in the Confederate Army in 1862 in Texas.

27. Llano County Tax Rolls, 1856–98, reel 1150001, TSLAC.

28. James B. Heckert-Greene, "Oxford, TX," *Handbook of Texas Online*, June 15, 2010, http://www.tshaonline.org/handbook/online/articles/hno24 (accessed July 17, 2017); Llano County Probate Minutes, Samuel Power, case no. 347, book 6, pp. 194–96, Deed Record, book 39, pp. 611–14 and book 41, pp. 308–9, TSLAC. Besides his small real estate holdings, Sam Power owned only a horse, an old buggy, three hogs, some mules, and his blacksmith tools when he died. His total estate was valued at just over eleven hundred dollars by the probate judge before his debts were paid.

CHAPTER 3

1. Daisy Willeford, "Wiley Marion Morgan," in *The Heritage Writing Project: The Pioneer People and Their Land, Here between the Santa Catalina and Galiuro Mountains, Arizona,* vol. 3, no. 1 (Aravaipa, AZ: Central Arizona College, 1988), 33.

2. Laura Barry, *Willcox: The First 100 Years* (Willcox, AZ: The Arizona Range News, 1980), 70–71; "Sierra Bonita Ranch," *Arizona Daily Star* (Tucson), December 17, 1972.

3. Willeford, "Wiley Marion Morgan," 33; Haby, "Wiley Marion Morgan," 45.

4. Marc Simmons, *Massacre on the Lordsburg Road: A Tragedy of the Apache Wars* (College Station: Texas A&M University Press, 1997), 51; Bob Alexander, *Desert Desperadoes: The Banditti of Southwestern New Mexico* (Silver City, NM: Gila Books, 2006), 17; Laverne McCauley and Terrell T. Shelley, *Pioneer Families of Grant County, New Mexico: A History of the Hooker-Shelley Families and the 916 Ranch* (Baltimore: Gateway Press Inc., 1987), xi; Robert J. Tórrez, *Myth of the Hanging Tree: Stories of Crime and Punishment in Territorial New Mexico* (Albuquerque: University of New Mexico Press, 2008) 6, 160; John A. Milbauer, "Population Origins and Ethnicity in the Silver City Mining Region of New Mexico, 1870–1890," *International Social Science Review* 60, no. 4 (Autumn 1984): 160; *Silver City Enterprise,* January 2, 16, 1891.

5. U.S. Census, 1900: Upper Gila, Grant, New Mexico; *Silver City Enterprise,* August 26, 1904; Tom Power interview, Noble.

6. Grant County Deed Records, book 28, p. 50, GCC.

7. Ida Foster Campbell and Alice Foster Hill, *Triumph and Tragedy: A History of Thomas Lyons and the LCs* (Silver City, NM: High-Lonesome Books, 2003), 119–20; Paul H. Carlson, ed., *The Cowboy Way: An Exploration of History and Culture* (Lubbock: Texas Tech University Press, 2000), 2–5; Power, *Shoot-Out at Dawn,* 7; C. L. Sonnichsen, *Billy King's Tombstone: The Private Life of an Arizona Boom Town* (Caldwell, ID: The Caxton Printers, Ltd., 1942), 143; Ridgway, *Power Family,* 23; Bob Alexander, *Sheriff Harvey Whitehill: Silver City Stalwart* (Silver City, NM: High-Lonesome Books, 2005), 237–39.

8. *Deming Headlight,* November 1, 1890; Ridgway, *Power Family,* 24; Sonnichsen, *Billy King's Tombstone,* 143; *Western Liberal* (Lordsburg), January 6, 1905. Local newspaper editors criticized partner Angus Campbell, who was a county commissioner, for being dishonest and claimed the two partners had too much influence over local government.

9. *Old Fort West Ditch Co. v. Jefferson Power et al.,* Grant County District Court Civil case no. 2455, Docket D, 1891, p. 326, NMSRCA; Power, *Shoot-Out at Dawn,* 7; Ridgway, *Power Family,* 24; Cattle Sanitary Board of New Mexico, *Brand Book of the Territory of New Mexico* (Las Vegas, NM: Cattle Sanitary Board of New Mexico, 1907), 36. There is no evidence that it was a widow who sold the property, rather Jane purchased from a husband and wife, Eli and Emma Latham.

10. *Silver City Enterprise,* January 2, 1891; *New Mexico Territory v. Jane Power* and *New Mexico Territory v. L. Childress* [Childers], Grant County District Court Criminal case nos. 3676 and 3677, Docket Book G, 1893, p. 358, NMSRCA.

11. Gibson, *The Life and Death of Colonel Albert Jennings Fountain,* 246; David Lavender, *The Southwest* (Albuquerque: University of New Mexico Press, 1980), 241; Power, *Shoot-Out at Dawn,* 9.

12. Larry D. Ball, *Desert Lawmen: The High Sheriffs of New Mexico and Arizona, 1846–1912* (Albuquerque: University of New Mexico Press, 1992), 211–12.

13. Robert W. Larson, *New Mexico Populism: A Study of Radical Protest in a Western Territory* (Boulder: Colorado Associated University Press, 1974), xi, 113, 242; *Arthur S. Clark v. Jane and T. J. Powers,* Grant County District Court Civil case nos. 3178, 3265, Docket E, pp. 404, 575, 1896, NMSRCA; Ridgway, *Power Family,* 32; Power, *Shoot-Out at Dawn,* 7.

14. U.S. Census, 1900: Upper Gila, Grant, New Mexico; *Silver City Enterprise,* March 5, 1897; Ridgway, *Power Family,* 22; Power, *Shoot-Out at Dawn,* 7–8; Manuscript, Wade Cavanaugh Collection.

15. Power, *Shoot-Out at Dawn,* 8; Ridgway, *Power Family,* 22. The grave is also marked by a footstone, simply engraved with her initials, "M. P." "Lonely Graves Stirs Arizona History," Power Brothers papers, Power cabin restoration file, states that John Power erected the monument on his mother's grave after his release from prison in 1960, but the distinctive style of the gravestone places it in the nineteenth century, not the mid-twentieth. Furthermore, Wade Cavanaugh's interview with John indicates he only cleaned up the gravesite and erected barbed wire to keep cattle from roaming over it. Manuscript, Cavanaugh Collection.

16. Power, *Shoot-Out at Dawn,* 8–9; Ridgway, *Power Family,* 22.

17. See, for example, Grant County Deed Records, book 28, p. 50, GCC; U.S. Census, 1900: Upper Gila, Grant, New Mexico; Ridgway, *Power Family,* 9, 22, 52; Millie Wootan Barnes interview, *Power's War* transcripts.

18. Carlson, *Cowboy Way,* 1; Ridgway, *Power Family,* 25, 30, 32.

19. Ridgway, *Power Family,* 31–32; Tom Power interview, Noble; Wolfe, *Power, Passion,* 21–22. The Bybees were Lutheran.

20. Power, *Shoot-Out at Dawn,* 9; *New Mexico v. Jeff Powers* and *New Mexico v. Charles Powers,* Grant County, District Court Criminal case nos. 5219, 5220, serial no. 13372, box no. 13372, and Court Journal, roll 16, 1894, NMSRCA; Foster, *Triumph and Tragedy,* 167; 1910 Census: Mangas, Grant, New Mexico. Turman lived with William H. Moss and Benjamin F. Crawford, deputies involved with murders believed to be ordered by Lyons.

21. Robert N. Mullin, ed., *Maurice Garland Fulton's History of the Lincoln County War* (Tucson: University of Arizona Press, 1968), 8, 24; Robert M. Utley, *High Noon in Lincoln: Violence on the Western Frontier* (Albuquerque: University of New Mexico Press, 1987), 21–27, 172–73.

CHAPTER 4

1. Patrick Q. Mason, *The Mormon Menace: Violence and Anti-Mormonism in the Postbellum South* (New York: Oxford University Press, 2011), 5, 283; Herman, *Hell on the Range,* 28; C. L. Sonnichsen, *I'll Die Before I'll Run: The Story of the Great Feuds of Texas* (Lincoln: University of Nebraska Press, 1988), xv; Bertram Wyatt-Brown, *Southern Honor: Ethics and Behavior in the Old South* (New York: Oxford University Press, 1982); Slotkin, *Fatal Environment,* 16; Richard Maxwell Brown, *No Duty to Retreat: Violence and Values in American History and Society* (New York: Oxford University Press, 1992), vi. In 1921 the United States Supreme Court upheld the doctrine of no duty to retreat.

2. Tom Power interview, Noble.

3. Prisoner Record 1585, ADOC, ASLAPR; Willeford, "Wiley Marion Morgan," 33; Patricia Joan Morgan Fuson, telephone interview with the author, April 21, 2013; Ball, *Desert Lawmen,* 209; Lynn R. Bailey, *The "Unwashed Crowd": Stockmen and Ranches of the San Simon and Sulphur Spring Valleys, Arizona Territory, 1878–1900* (Tucson: Westernlore Press, 2014), 207–8; *Graham Guardian* (Safford), March 31, 1916, March 20, 1918.

4. Fuson interview; *Tombstone Prospector,* September 26, 1899; *Tombstone Prospector,* September 26, 1899.

5. *Tombstone Prospector,* September 26, 1899; *Arizona Territory v. Wiley Morgan,* Cochise County Superior Court Criminal case no. 3886, box 25, 1899, ASLAPR; Willeford, "The Morgan Case," in *The Heritage Writing Project,* 34.

6. *Tombstone Epitaph,* December 17, 1899; *Arizona Territory v. Wylie M. Morgan,* Arizona Territorial Supreme Court case no. 150, 1901, ASLAPR; *Arizona Territory v. Wiley M. Morgan,* Cochise County Superior Court, ASLAPR; *Tombstone Epitaph,* December 17, 1899; *Arizona Republican* (Phoenix), September 25, 1899. Wiley claimed Mitchell made him go up to Duncan's place because they were all under obligation of the Stock Growers' Association, whose members were required to assist in the conviction of cattle thieves.

7. In the 1900 census, Wiley Morgan is listed twice: U.S. Census: Yuma, Yuma, Arizona Territory, roll 48, p. 1B and p. 12A; Fuson interview.

8. Willeford, "The Morgan Case," 34; Daniel G. Moore, *Enter Without Knocking* (Tucson: University of Arizona Press, 1969), 29–30; *Tombstone Epitaph,* May 5, 1901, June 15, December 14 & 18, 1902, June 17, 1903. Hereford and Hazard were Morgan's other attorneys.

9. *Arizona Territory v. Wiley Morgan,* Arizona Supreme Court, ASLAPR; *Bisbee Daily Review,* December 14, 1901; Diana Hadley, Peter Warshall, Don Bufkin, *Environmental Change in Aravaipa, 1870–1970: An Ethnoecological Survey,* Cultural Resource Series Monograph No. 7 (Phoenix: Bureau of Land Management, 1991), 75.

10. *Bisbee Daily Review,* December 14, 1901. While the case was appealed to the Supreme Court, Morgan was released on bail.

11. Arthur L. Campa, "Folklore and History," *Western Folklore* 24, no. 1 (January 1965): 1.

12. Sonnichsen, *Billy King's Tombstone,* 170, 173–75; Jane Eppinga, "Cochise County Attorney Allen R. English," *Arizona Capitol Times,* November 14, 2014.

13. Haby, "Wiley Marion Morgan," 45; *Mary Graham v. Wiley M. Morgan,* Graham County Superior Court Civil case no. 1112, 1910, ASLAPR; *Bisbee Daily Review,* January 31, 1913; *Graham Guardian,* September 24, 1913; Joanne Collins, telephone interview with the author, May 5, 2013.

14. Tom Power interview, Noble.

15. See for example, Grant County Records of Deeds, book 28, p. 50, GCC.

16. Heidi J. Osselaer, "On the Wrong Side of Allen Street: The Businesswomen of Tombstone, 1878–1884," *Journal of Arizona History* 55 (Summer 2014): 145–66; Melanie Sturgeon, "'Belgian Jennie' Bauters: Mining-Town Madam," *Journal of Arizona History* 48, no. 4 (Winter

2007): 349–74; Donna Guy, "The Economics of Widowhood in Arizona, 1880–1940," in *On Their Own: Widows and Widowhood in the American Southwest, 1848–1939,* Arlene Scadron, ed. (Urbana: University of Illinois Press, 1988), 195–223.

17. Herman, *Hell on the Range,* 287; Slotkin, *Fatal Environment,* 16; Kathleen P. Chamberlain, *In the Shadow of Billy the Kid: Susan McSween and the Lincoln County War* (Albuquerque: University of New Mexico Press, 2013), 3–4, 218.

18. Ridgway, *Power Family,* 24; Bob Wootan, T. K. Wootan, and Joe Wootan, interview, AHS.

19. Bob Wootan et al. interview, AHS; Tom Power interview, Noble.

20. Cochise County Accession No. 246060, Document No. 08312, BLM GLO; Katherine Benton-Cohen, *Borderline Americans: Racial Division and Labor War in the Arizona Borderlands* (Cambridge, MA: Harvard University Press, 2009), 177.

21. Cochise County Deeds of Mines, book 24, p. 82, ASLAPR; Grant County Deeds of Mines, book 52, pp. 8–9, GCC; Power, *Shoot-Out at Dawn,* 9; Robert N. Mullin, *The Strange Story of Wayne Brazel* (Canyon, TX: Palo Duro Press, 1970), 28.

22. Kathy Weiser and Dave Alexander, "New Mexico Legends: Steins—A Railroad Ghost Town," September 2016, http://www.legendsofamerica.com/nm-steins.htm (accessed June 18, 2017); Mullin, *The Strange Story of Wayne Brazel,* p. 28; Wolfgang E. Elson, *Kimball Mining District of Hidalgo County* (Albuquerque: University of New Mexico Press, 1965), 189. The name of the major was Enoch Steen, but his name is often misspelled "Steins" on landmarks.

23. *Western Liberal,* March 17, 1911, August 20, 1915; Grant County Records of Deeds, book 42, p. 433, book 47, pp. 211–2, 384, GCC; Grant County Miscellaneous Records, book 47, p. 48, GCC; Grant County Deeds of Mines, book 52, pp. 285–86, GCC; Gibson, *The Life and Death,* 265, 277; Leon C. Metz, *Pat Garrett: The Story of a Western Lawman* (Norman: University of Oklahoma Press, 1974), 294.

24. *New Mexico v. Jeff Power,* Grant County District Court Criminal case no. 5807, Docket Book I, p. 151, 1910, NMSRCA; Grant County District Court Records, Court Journal, roll 17, 1907–1912, NMSRCA; *Silver City Independent,* September 13, 1910; Power, *Shoot-Out at Dawn,* 9–10. It is unclear why Baird and Gould only named Jeff Power, and not his mother, in the charges, since both held the property.

25. *M. J. Power and C. S. Power v. J. Gould et al.,* Cochise County, Bowie Justice Precinct 7, case no. 6177, 1910, ASLAPR; Lynn R. Bailey and Don Chaput, *Cochise County Stalwarts: A Who's Who of the Territorial Years,* vol. 2 (Tucson: Westernlore Press, 2000), 12; *Arizona Republican,* February 8, 1910.

26. Metz, *Pat Garrett,* 283–84, 298; *Daily Arizona Silver Belt* (Miami), May 5, 1909; Colin Rickards, *Sheriff Pat Garrett's Last Days* (Santa Fe: Sunstone Press, 1986), 47.

27. *Santa Fe New Mexican,* November 2, 1909, May 31, 1910; *Western Liberal,* February 24, 1911; *Tombstone Epitaph,* July 31, 1910; Cochise County Mortgages, book 23, pp. 186–88, ASLAPR; *Western Liberal,* March 3, 1914; William A. Keleher, *The Fabulous Frontier: Twelve New Mexico Items,* rev. ed. (Albuquerque: University of New Mexico Press, 1962), 246. The total capitalization for the Long S. was one hundred and fifty thousand dollars, but the paid-up capital was forty thousand dollars.

28. *M. J. Power and C. S. Power v. J. Gould et al.*

29. Ibid.

30. Ridgway, *Power Family,* 26; Wolfe, *Power, Passion,* 21; McBride, *Evaders,* 103.

31. Grant County Miscellaneous Deeds, book 47, pp. 620–22, GCC; Ridgway, *Power Family,* 21; BLM GLO, Cochise County patent no. 246060; Cochise County School Census, District 13, Willcox, 1910, ASLAPR; Power, *Shoot-Out at Dawn,* 10. Jane sold the ranch for twelve hundred dollars. The school census recorded the ages of the Power children incorrectly as John, eighteen, Tom, sixteen, and Ola, fifteen. The 1910 census lists the Powers residing both in Doubtful Canyon and in Willcox.

32. Ridgway, *Power Family,* 27, calls it the Dunlap Ranch; Graham County Deeds of Mines, book 9, p. 194, GCRO.

33. Ridgway, *Power Family,* 22–23; Mason, *The Mormon Menace,* 5.

CHAPTER 5

1. Hadley, *Environmental Change,* 1, 80, 271–72; Edward Abbey, "In the Land of 'Laughing Waters,'" *New York Times,* January 3, 1982. The word "aravaipa" is ascribed to the Pima and Papago languages as well.

2. Hadley, *Environmental Change,* 35–36, 49–50, 101, 371, notes evidence of Salado, Hohokam, and Mogollon occupation in Aravaipa; Chip Colwell-Chanthaphonh, *Massacre at Camp Grant: Forgetting and Remembering Apache History* (Tucson: University of Arizona Press, 2007), 47, 57; Eleanor Claridge, *Klondyke and the Aravaipa Canyon* (Safford, AZ: D & M/Kopy Kat Printing, 1989), 10, 27; Roberts, "'The Powers Boys,'" 94; Ian W. Record, *Big Sycamore Stands Alone: The Western Apaches, Aravaipa, and the Struggle for Place* (Norman: University of Oklahoma Press, 2008), 23, 44, 52. The Tsè jinè clan refers to the Galiuros as "the place known as Dark Rocks."

3. Hadley, *Environmental Change,* 1, 71–78, Appendix II, 13.

4. Claridge, *Klondyke,* 21, 168; U.S. Census, 1910: Klondyke and Aravaipa precincts, Graham, Arizona Territory; Douglas Preston, *Cities of Gold: A Journey Across the American Southwest* (New York: Simon & Schuster, 1992), 157; Biographical information, box 1, folder 1, Ming Family Papers, AHS. Klondyke was established in 1907, with John F. Greenwood serving as the first postmaster. Although today the city of Klondike in the Yukon is spelled with an "i," in the early twentieth century it was usually spelled "Klondyke."

5. *Arizona Daily Star,* April 19, 2015; Frank S. Simons, *Geology of the Klondyke Quadrangle, Graham and Pinal Counties, AZ,* U.S. Department of Interior, Geological Survey professional paper (Washington, DC: Government Printing Office, 1964), 461.

6. Hadley, *Environmental Change,* 103–5, 114–17; John P. Wilson, *Islands in the Desert: A History of the Uplands of Southeastern Arizona* (Albuquerque: University of New Mexico Press, 2000), 169–71; William P. Blake, "The Geology of the Galiuro Mountains, Arizona, and of the Gold-Bearing Ledge Known as Gold Mountain," *Engineering and Mining Journal* 73 (April 1902): 546–47; S. C. Creasey et al., "Mineral Resources of the Galiuro Wilderness and Contiguous Further Planning Areas, Arizona," *USGS*

Bulletin 1490 (Washington, DC: Government Printing Office, 1981), 69–72; Simons, *Geology of the Klondyke,* 461. Production was of such low quality and work was so irregular that labor unions failed to organize mine workers in the Rattlesnake District, unlike other mining camps in the Southwest.

7. Oran A. Williams, "Settlements of the Gila Valley in Graham County, 1879–1900" (master's thesis, University of Arizona, 1937), 29; Roberts, "'The Powers Boys,'" 70, 72, 74.

8. Hadley, *Environmental Change,* 241–42.

9. Ibid., 84–85, Appendix II, 4, 14; *Graham Guardian,* September 8, 1905, March 19, July 9, 1915.

10. Hadley, *Environmental Change,* 141, 284, Appendix II, 2–3.

11. C. S. Power homestead application, no. 190, July 7, 1911, Crook National Forest, U.S. Forest Service, Tucson. Many versions of this story have been told; see, for example, Manuscript, Cavanaugh Collection; "Before I Die," Noble, ASLAPR; Don Dedera, "Coffee Break," *Arizona Republic,* April 10, 1960.

12. Tom Power interview, Noble; Public Lands Visitor Center, "Galiuro Wilderness," http://publiclands.org/visitorcenter/exhibits.php?e=Lands&s=Galiuro (accessed February 21, 2015), suggests Galiuro is an Anglo corruption of the Spanish word "Calistro"; *Bisbee Daily Review,* February 14, 1918.

13. Thomas Cobb interview, *Power's War* transcripts.

14. Ridgway, *Power Family,* 27, 29; C. S. Power homestead application, U.S. Forest Service, Tucson; Hadley, *Environmental Change,* 72–73, 92, 99, 106, 238; Wolfe, *Power, Passion,* 22.

15. Hadley, *Environmental Change,* 163–64; "The Power Boys," Noble, ASLAPR; Wolfe, *Power, Passion,* 21; *Bisbee Daily Review,* February 14, 1918; *Jeff Clayton v. John Power and Tom Sisson,* Graham County Superior Court Criminal case no. 308, book 5, 1916, ASLAPR; Sonnichsen, *Billy King's Tombstone,* 159.

16. Graham County Deeds of Mines, book 9, p. 194, GCRO; Graham County Location of Mines, book 21, pp. 470–71, book 13, pp. 446–51, book 14, p. 470–85, GCRO; Sonnichsen, *Billy King's Tombstone,* 144, 147, 159; Leon C. Metz, *The Encyclopedia of Lawmen, Outlaws, and Gunfighters* (New York: Checkmark Books, 2003), 70, 200; Laurence J. Yadon, *Texas Outlaws and Lawmen, 1835–1935* (Gretna, LA: Pelican Publishing Co., 2008), 89.

17. Ridgway, *Power Family,* 34-35; U.S. Census, 1940: Precinct 5, Graham, Arizona; Wilson, *Islands in the Desert,* 171. Knothe arrived in the United States in 1890 and became a citizen in 1896 in New England, before moving to Arizona. Over the many years he worked his mine, ultimately sinking two shafts, he achieved modest success and scraped together a few small shipments of gold ore.

18. Ridgway, *Power Family,* 21; Graham County Location of Mines, book 23, pp. 382–84, 452–53, book 24, pp. 345–46, GCRO. *Catherine Murdock v. James J. Murdock,* Cochise County Superior Court Civil case no. 424, 1913, ASLAPR; J. Frank Wootan interview, AHS; Manuscript, Cavanaugh Collection.

19. *Bisbee Daily Review,* July 27, 1905; *Owen E. Murphy JP Territory of Arizona v. Nathan V. Braley,* Cochise County Superior Court Criminal case no. 590, 1905, ASLAPR; Bob Wootan et al., interview, AHS.

20. *Catherine Murdock v. James J. Murdock,* Cochise County Superior Court Civil case no. 424, box 16, folder 796, 1913, ASLAPR; *Bisbee Daily Review,* August 4, 1908, August 11, 1910; *Copper Era* (Clifton), January 3, 1913; Wood, *Tragedy of the Power Mine,* 27.

21. Sale of Branson Mine 1 and 2 in Graham County Deeds of Mines, book 9, p. 194 and Locations of Mines, book 21, pp. 470–71, book 13, pp. 446–51, book 14, pp. 470–85, GCRO; *Daily Arizona Silver Belt,* April 3, 1910; Power, *Shoot-Out at Dawn,* 10; Ridgway, *Power Family,* 27.

22. Hadley, *Environmental Change,* 75, 102; F. L. Kirby to Arthur Ringland, August 22, 1911, September 19, 1911, October 1, 1911; Ringland to C. S. Power, February 13, 1912, C. S. Power homestead application, U.S. Forest Service, Tucson.

23. Ringland to Power, October 12, 1912; Kirby to Ringland, October 1, 1911, U.S. Forest Service, Tucson; Hadley, *Environmental Change,* 125; Herman, *Hell on the Range,* 282; Coronado National Forest, "Galiuro Wilderness," U.S. Forest Service, https://www.fs.usda.gov/recarea/coronado/recarea/?recid=25456 (accessed July 18, 2017). The Galiuro Mountains became part of the Crook National Forest in 1910, just after Charley bought the Branson Mine, so the Powers were grandfathered in and could not be evicted.

24. Wolfe, *Power, Passion,* 21–22; Ridgway, *Power Family,* 29, 87; Graham County Deeds to Chattel Mortgages, book 3, p. 106, GCRO; Roberts, "'The Powers Boys,'" 329; J. Frank Wootan interview, AHS; Records of the Forest Service, Grazing Permits for Graham County, Arizona, NARA.

25. Tom Power interview, Noble; Ridgway, *Power Family,* 30–31; Wolfe, *Power, Passion,* 22-23; Roberts, "'The Powers Boys,'" 310.

26. Ridgway, *Power Family,* 30–31; U.S. Census, 1910: St. Maries, Shoshone, Idaho.

27. Fuson interview; Tom Power interview, Noble; Haby, "Wiley Marion Morgan," 33; Power, *Shoot-Out at Dawn,* 11.

28. U.S. Census, 1860: Precinct 1, Medina, Texas; Wolfe, *Power, Passion,* 24; Roberts, "'The Powers Boys,'" 302; Opal Lines Neeson to Dedera, April 12, 1960, PBRN, ASU.

29. Hadley, *Environmental Change,* Appendix II, 3; Ridgway, *Power Family,* 42, 52; U.S. Census, 1910: Gila, Grant, New Mexico Territory; Claridge, *Klondyke,* 79.

30. Roberts, "'The Powers Boys,'" 302; Great Registers of Electors, Klondyke Precinct, 1910–1918, ASLAPR.

31. Roberts, "'The Powers Boys,'" 306, 308, 310; Manuscript, Cavanaugh Collection.

32. Wolfe, *Power, Passion,* 23; Claridge, *Klondyke,* 15, 79; "Texas, Muster Roll Index Cards, 1838–1900," Ancestry.com; W. E. Wootan, "Black Bill Wootan Tells His Experiences," *Frontier Times,* August 1927: n. p.

33. *Graham Guardian,* October 9, 1908, January 13, June 7, 1911; Graham County 1916 Great Register of Electors, Klondyke precinct, ASLAPR.

34. *Graham Guardian,* July 18, 1913, August 14, 1916; *J. F. Greenwood v. Millie Wootan et al.,* Graham County Superior Court Civil case no. 285, 1916, ASLAPR; Claridge, *Klondyke,* 167.

35. Thomas Kane Wootan, Graham County Probate case no. 119, 1918, ASLAPR; *Graham Guardian,* July 19, 1912, March 19, 1915.

36. Wootan Probate, ASLAPR; *Graham Guardian,* June 19, 1914; Graham County Deeds of Chattel Mortgages, book 2, pp. 183, 276, book 3, pp. 8–9, 113, 269, GCRO; Ball, *Desert Lawmen,* 200.

CHAPTER 6

1. Robert Howard Sayers, "Mormon Cultural Persistence in the Vicinity of Graham County, Arizona, 1879–1977" (PhD diss., University of Arizona, 1979), 87–88.

2. Bagley, *Blood of the Prophets,* 7, 38–39, 41; Gordon S. Wood, "Evangelical America and Early Mormonism," in *The Mormon History Association's Tanner Lectures: The First Twenty Years,* eds. Dean L. May and Reid L. Neilson (Urbana: University of Illinois Press, 2006), 15; Stewart, "The McBride Story—'Clara and Frank,'" McBride Family Collection, 1; Sayers, "Mormon Cultural Persistence," 54–55, 83–84; Oran A. Williams, "Settlements of the Gila Valley in Graham County, 1879–1900" (master's thesis, University of Arizona, 1937), 29; Roberts, "'The Powers Boys,'" 70, 72, 74. Frank McBride was born in 1875 in Eden, Utah.

3. Williams, "Settlements of the Gila Valley," 2–4, 7, 34; George L. Cathcart, "Religious Belief as a Cultural Value: Mormon Cattle Ranchers in Arizona's Little Colorado River Valley" (master's thesis, Arizona State University, 1995), 5–6; James H. McClintock, *Mormon Settlement in Arizona: A Record of Peaceful Conquest of the Desert* (Tucson: University of Arizona Press, 1985), 242–44; Larry D. Ball, *Ambush at Bloody Run: The Wham Paymaster Robbery of 1889* (Tucson: Arizona Historical Society, 2000), 58.

4. Richard S. Van Wagoner, *Mormon Polygamy: A History,* 2nd ed. (Salt Lake City: Signature Books, 1989), 1, 3, 86; Wood, "Evangelical America and Early Mormonism," 18–21; Bagley, *Blood of the Prophets,* 9.

5. C. A. Teeples, "First Pioneers of the Gila Valley," in *Let Them Speak for Themselves: Women in the American West, 1849–1900,* ed. Christiane Fischer (Hamden, CT: Archon Books, 1990), 74–78; Williams, "Settlements of the Gila Valley," 20, 31; Edward Leo Lyman, "Elimination of the Mormon Issue, 1889–1894," *Arizona and the West* 24, no. 3 (Autumn 1982): 211–15.

6. Lyman, "Elimination of the Mormon Issue," 205; Cathcart, "Religious Belief as a Cultural Value," 5; Sheridan, *Arizona,* 205–6; *Pioneer Town: Pima Centennial History* (Pima, AZ: Eastern Arizona Museum & Historical Society Inc. of Graham Co., 1979), 31–32; Sayers, "Mormon Cultural Persistence," 75, 87.

7. *Salt Lake Tribune,* January 7, 1880; Lyman, "Elimination of the Mormon Issue," 206; Roberts, "'The Powers Boys,'" 75.

8. Williams, "Settlements of the Gila Valley," 31, 33–34, 40; Van Wagoner, *Mormon Polygamy,* 125; John Q. Cannon, *The Life of Christopher Layton* (Salt Lake City: The Deseret New Press, 1911), 190–91, 208; Lyman, "Elimination of the Mormon Issue," 211–15. President Abraham Lincoln initiated the first anti-polygamy law, but little enforcement was attempted until after the Civil War.

9. Williams, "Settlements of the Gila Valley," 40–44, 67; Heidi J. Osselaer, *Winning Their Place: Arizona Women in Politics, 1883–1950* (Tucson: University of Arizona Press, 2009), 8; *Apache Chief* (St. Johns, AZ), May 30, 1884; Lyman, "Elimination of the Mormon Issue," 206, 208–9; Ball, *Ambush at Bloody Run,* 58–59; *Arizona Laws,* 1885, no. 87, sec. 2, 214, Arizona State Library.

10. Connie Huber and Gregory S. Porter, "The 1884 Journal of Frank McBride," Robert Franklin McBride, www.porter-az.com/albums/RFMcBride/RFMcBride.htm (accessed April 16, 2015); Williams, "Settlements of the Gila Valley," 40, 61, 67; Lyman, "Elimination of the Mormon Issue," 206, 208; Stewart, "'Clara and Frank,'" 2. Cleveland's gubernatorial appointee in Arizona, C. Meyer Zulick, dismantled the test oath law in 1887.

11. Williams, "Settlements of the Gila Valley," 53–58, 61; Ball, *Ambush at Bloody Run,* 43, 73.

12. Ball, *Ambush at Bloody Run,* 157, 168–69.

13. Ibid., 190–93, 196–97, 205–6, 218. Both Wilfred Webb and Jacob Burns were removed from their official positions by the U.S. Postmaster General. Jacob Burns was Ruth Burns McBride's brother and Wilfred Webb was married to Ruth's sister. Wilfred's brother, Leslie Webb, along with two other men, confessed to the 1894 stagecoach robbery, and they were sentenced to federal prison at San Quentin. Ira Kempton, father of McBride's undersheriff, Martin Kempton, had the misfortune to be the stage driver on two separate occasions when it was robbed, and he identified one of the robbers as Jake Felshaw, one of the original Wham robbery defendants.

14. William R. Ridgway interview, AHS; Rosemary Drachman Taylor, *Bar Nothing Ranch* (New York: McGraw Hill Book Co., 1947), 8, 26; George H. Kelly, comp., *Legislative History: Arizona, 1864–1912* (Phoenix: Manufacturing Stationers Inc., 1926), 265, 230, 232, 373; *Arizona Republican,* February 8, 1909. Webb's political career unraveled in 1912 when he was caught dallying with an actress (who later became his wife) rather than delivering Arizona's presidential electoral votes in Washington, DC, and when his ranch was declared insolvent and taken by the bank.

15. Stewart, "'Clara and Frank,'" 3; D. Michael Quinn, "The Mormon Church and the Spanish-American War: An End to Selective Pacifism," *Pacific Historical Review* 43, no. 3 (August 1974): 354; Van Wagoner, *Mormon Polygamy,* 153, 164, 173; Cathcart, "Religious Belief as a Cultural Value," 5; Bagley, *Blood of the Prophets,* 9; Raymond Haberski Jr., *God and War: American Civil Religion since 1945* (New Brunswick, NJ: Rutgers University Press, 2012), 69; Thomas W. Simpson, *American Universities and the Birth of Modern Mormonism, 1867–1940* (Chapel Hill: University of North Carolina, 2016), 1; Chronicling America, "About *Graham Guardian,*" Library of Congress, http://chroniclingamerica.loc.gov/lccn/sn95060914/ (accessed June 18, 2017); *Graham Guardian,* December 9, 1898, August 3, 1900, November 3, 1911; Lyman, "Elimination of the Mormon Issue," 210, 223–26; Williams, "Settlements of the Gila Valley," 75; Robert H. Hellebrand, "General Conference Addresses during Times of War," in *War & Peace in Our Time: Mormon Perspectives,* eds. Patrick Q. Mason, J. David Pulsipher, and Richard L. Bushman (Salt Lake City: Greg Kofford Books,

2012), 129–32; Quinn, "The Mormon Church," 342–66. Quinn notes there were some dissenters in the LDS Church during the Spanish-American War, most notably Brigham Young Jr., but most vocal resistance was halted during that war.

16. Williams, "Settlements of the Gila Valley," 11, 18, 20, 29; *Pioneer Town*, 31–32, 42; Roberts, "'The Powers Boys,'" 83; Stewart, "'Clara and Frank,'" 3.

17. Stewart, "'Clara and Frank,'" 5–10; *Arizona Republican*, February 8, 1909; *Graham Guardian*, July 25, 1902; Darvil B. McBride, *The Evaders or Wilderness Shoot-Out* (Pasadena, CA: Pacific Book & Printing, 1984), 9–10.

18. Karen Underhill Mangelsdorf, "The Beveridge Visit to Arizona in 1902," *Journal of Arizona History* 28, no. 3 (Autumn 1987): 253–56.

19. *Congressional Record*, 57th Cong., 2d sess., 1411, Library of Congress; Sayers, "Mormon Cultural Persistence," 68; Osselaer, *Winning Their Place*, 7–10, 33–34; Herman, *Hell on the Range*, xv.

20. Harry David Ware, "Alcohol, Temperance, and Prohibition in Arizona" (PhD diss., Arizona State University, 1995), 95, 112; Christina Rabe Seger, "The Economics of Vice: Prohibition Along the Mexico-Arizona Border, 1915–1933," 2, AHS.

21. Sayers, "Mormon Cultural Persistence," 83–84; *Graham Guardian*, July 19, 1910, July 19, 1912; August 4, 1916; Kelly, *Legislative History*, 265.

22. Ball, *Desert Lawmen*, 74, 179, 202, 298, 303–5; *Graham Guardian*, September 29, 1911; Jane Eppinga, *Arizona Sheriffs: Badges and Bad Men* (Tucson: Rio Nuevo, 2006), 176.

23. *Graham Guardian*, September 22 & 29, October 27, November 3, 1911; Jo Connors, *Who's Who in Arizona* (Tucson: Press of the *Arizona Daily Star*, 1913), 778; U.S. Census, 1910: Lebanon, Graham, Arizona; "Membership of The Church of Jesus Christ of Latter-day Saints, 1830–1848," accessed July 18, 2017, Ancestry.com.

24. *Eastern Arizona Courier*, June 4, 2014; *Graham Guardian*, October 27, 1911, July 7, 1912, January 5, 1913; Ball, *Desert Lawmen*, 31. Alger, perhaps acknowledging his lack of experience in law enforcement, crossed the political aisle and went outside the Mormon community to name Republican Ned Ussher of Solomonville, the deputy for the previous sheriff, as his second in command.

25. "Union Church at Klondyke," *Graham Guardian*, July 9, 1915; Roberts, "'The Powers Boys,'" 271–72, 283, 355.

26. Huber and Porter, "The 1884 Journal of Frank McBride"; *Graham Guardian*, September 20, 24, 26, 1913; *State of Arizona v. Wiley Morgan*, Graham County Superior Court Criminal Register of Actions, case nos. 136, 137, and 138, Graham County Courthouse, ASLAPR; Samuel L. Pattee, comp., *Revised Statutes of Arizona, 1913, Penal Code* (Phoenix: The McNeil Co., 1913), sect. 297, allowed minors under the age of sixteen in a saloon if accompanied by a parent. Wiley Jr. was in attendance with his father, so McBride was a bit overzealous enforcing the law in that instance.

27. Graham County Great Register of Electors, 1912, Klondyke precinct, ASLAPR.

28. *Graham Guardian*, November 14, 1913; *Bisbee Daily Review*, January 31, 1913.

29. Osselaer, *Winning Their Place*, 64–65; *Graham Guardian*, November 14, 1913.

30. *Graham Guardian*, October 10 & 23, December 12, 1913.

31. *Graham Guardian,* February 7, September 26, October 23, December 5, 1913, and June 19, August 21, October 9, 1914, and February 5, 1915. Although both men were ranger deputies, McBride's monthly salary was $125 and Wootan's was only $50.

32. *Graham Guardian,* April 10, 1914, February 5, March 19, 1915.

33. *Graham Guardian,* March 21, 1913, August 21, October 9, 1914.

34. Hadley, *Environmental Change,* 241; Sayers, "Mormon Cultural Persistence," 89; *Graham Guardian,* September 22, 1911, February 7 & 13, March 8, 12, 26, May 22, 1914, February 5, April 23, 1915; Stewart, "'Clara and Frank,'" 11. The distance from Safford to Klondyke was thirty-two miles, according to the *Arizona Record* (Globe), February 12, 1918. The driving record at the time was two hours and fifty minutes to drive from the Grand Reef Mine located near Klondyke to Fairview in the Gila Valley.

35. *Graham Guardian,* March 19, 1915.

36. Stewart, "'Clara and Frank,'" 11–12; *Graham Guardian,* April 23, 1915.

37. *Graham Guardian,* February 12, 1909, March 31, April 7, May 19, 1916. Frank Richardson, a non-Mormon with a long history of law enforcement, also ran in the primary.

38. *Graham Guardian,* April 7, August 4, September 22, October 19 & 20, 1916. There was speculation that Richardson only entered the race to draw votes away from Alger, and that McBride had promised him five hundred dollars or the undersheriff position if he won. McBride was forced to address those rumors of a "frame-up" between himself and Richardson, which he did in a forthright way, emphatically denying the allegations. Tom Power falsely asserted that he helped McBride win the Democratic primary in Klondyke in his book *Shoot-Out at Dawn,* 20.

39. *Graham Guardian,* November 3, December 22, 1916, and January 5 & 26, 1917; Martin Kempton interview, *Power's War* transcripts; Ball, *Desert Lawmen,* 24–25; U.S. Census, 1910: Township 6, Graham, Arizona.

40. *Graham Guardian,* July 3, 1914, March 2, May 18, July 20, August 17, 1917; U. I. Paxton's Ledger Book, p. 13, GCRO.

41. Arizona Livestock Sanitary Board Minutes, September 5, 1916, vol. 1, p. 77, ASLAPR; Graham County Deeds to Chattel Mortgages, book 3, pp. 151, 167, 191, 222, GCRO; Closed Files 5173-4, ADOC, ASLAPR; Wootan Probate, ASLAPR; Millie Wootan Barnes interview, *Power's War* transcripts. The records do not provide the reason for the termination of Wootan, but the Livestock Sanitary Board called for the resignation of several deputies that session, so perhaps it was a cost-cutting decision.

42. *Graham Guardian,* February 23, March 2 & 9, 1917.

43. *Graham Guardian,* February 9 & 23, March 2 & 9, June 29, July 19, August 24, September 28, November 2 & 30, December 28, 1917, March 9, 1918; McBride, *The Evaders,* 58; *Arizona Bulletin* (Solomonville), February 22, 1917. The county paid over $765 to a detective agency to track down bootleggers in March 1918.

44. *Graham Guardian,* January 26, February 26, 1917; *John Power v. J. D. Clayton,* Graham County Civil case no. 307, 1916, ASLAPR; Stewart, "'Clara and Frank,'" 11–12. According to court records, McBride visited with the Powers on January 17, 1917, to return the equipment from Clayton.

CHAPTER 7

1. *Bisbee Daily Review*, July 19, 1911.
2. Power, *Shoot-Out at Dawn*, 10. The mines were called both "Abandon" and "Abandoned" in public records. John Power staked claims on the Gold Leaf 1 and 2 and the Lee 1 and 2, and Jeff purchased a share of the Retrieve Mine. Graham County Record of Mines, book 23, pp. 48–49, 352–53, Graham County Deeds of Mines, book 9, p. 277, GCRO.
3. John Hernandez, "Kielberg Canyon in the Galiuro Mountains—how did it get its name?" CopperArea.com, December 27, 2013, http://www.copperarea.com/pages/kielberg-canyon-in-the-galiuro-mountains-how-did-it-get-its-name-2/ (accessed May 22, 2015).
4. Graham County Deeds of Mines, book 9, p. 281, book 18, pp. 228–31, GCRO; Graham County Record of Mines, book 13, pp. 446–51, book 14, pp. 470–85, book 15, p. 128, book 16, p. 97, book 18, pp. 228–31, book 21, pp. 470–71, GCRO; Power Cabin, National Register of Historic Places, National Park Service, U.S. Department of Interior, August 3, 1975, https://npgallery.nps.gov/NRHP/AssetDetail?assetID=11f7b3a9-33c3-4f49-93d1-5d97e79b1d81 (accessed November 15, 2014), hereafter cited as Power cabin nomination form.
5. Ridgway, *Power Family*, 34–37; Power, *Shoot-Out at Dawn*, 10–11; *R. C. Elwood v. J. F. Greenwood*, Graham County Superior Court Civil case no. 23, 1912, ASLAPR; Power cabin nomination form; Graham County Deeds of Mines, book 8, p. 231, book 16, pp. 97–98, GCRO. Fred Golden of Globe also purchased a share in the mine, but quickly sold his stake to Richard C. Elwood, a miner and an investor located in Miami in Gila County.
6. Barbara Schmidt, "Mark Twain Quotations," http://www.twainquotes.com/Miner. html (accessed July 19, 2017); Ridgway, *Power Family*, 34-36; Power, *Shoot-Out at Dawn*, 10; Graham County Index to Mines, book 8, p. 279, book 16, pp. 97–98, ASLAPR.
7. *Graham Guardian*, January 26, February 2, 1912; Power, *Shoot-Out at Dawn*, 10; Ridgway, *Power Family*, 34–37.
8. Graham County Real Estate Deeds, book 2, pp. 84–85, GCRO; Graham County Deeds of Mines, book 9, pp. 232, 281, 288, GCRO; Ridgway, *Power Family*, 39.
9. Graham County Deeds to Chattel Mortgages, book 2, pp. 208, 274, 283, book 3, pp. 2, 15, GCRO; Graham County Real Estate Deeds, book 22, pp. 84–85, GCRO; Graham County Deeds of Mines, book 9, p. 233, GCRO; Power, *Shoot-Out at Dawn*, 16; Ridgway, *Power Family*, 34–39. Jeff Power pledged two hundred head of cattle as collateral to borrow $1,250 from the Sulphur Springs Valley Bank. Neill is variously spelled Neil, Neal, and Niel in records.
10. *Graham Guardian,* February 12 & 13, 1914, March 19, April 9, 1915, and November 21, 1916.
11. *Graham Guardian*, February 12, 1915.
12. Power, *Shoot-Out at Dawn*, 15–16; World War I Selective Service Draft Registration Card, 1917–1918, M 1509, for Charles S. Power (hereafter cited as WWI Draft Card),

NARA; Graham County Proof of Labor, book 4, pp. 257, 292, GCRO. Although many people have argued that Charley was still living in Rattlesnake Canyon when the United States entered the war in 1917, the proof of labor affidavits failure to mention him, indicating Charley was not present when the Power family was building a road to the mine in 1915 and 1916.

13. Henriette E. Miller to Howard Pyle, December 9, 1952, Closed Files 5173-4, ADOC, ASLAPR; Power, *Shoot-Out at Dawn*, 15–16; *Graham Guardian*, March 19, 1915, June 29, 1917; Seger, "The Economics of Vice," 4–8.

14. *Bisbee Daily Review*, February 14, 1918; Ridgway, *Power Family*, 40; Graham County Proof of Labor, book 4, p. 257, GCRO; Power cabin nomination form. Road construction for 1915 was performed by John, Tom, T. J. Power, and Tom Sisson. The number of miles between the Power mine and the Aravaipa Road, according to the National Park Service, is twenty-one miles, but others have suggested it was only sixteen miles.

15. U.S. Census, 1880: Livonia, Sherburne County, Minnesota; Thomas J. Sisson, Register of Enlistments in the U.S. Army, 1798–1914, Records of the Adjutant General, RG 94, roll M233, NARA; R. P. Page Wainwright, *The First Regiment of Cavalry* (Washington, DC: United States Army Regimental Press, 1906), 20, 22; Larry D. Ball, *Tom Horn in Life and Legend* (Norman: University of Oklahoma Press, 2014) 53; *Silver City Enterprise*, May 20, 1892; Ridgway, *Power Family*, 40–44.

16. U.S. Census, 1900: Precincts 3, 9, and 11, Cochise, Arizona Territory; homestead patent no. 338555, BLM GLO; Ridgway, *Power Family*, 41; Tom Sisson, Application for Headstones for U.S. Military Veterans, 1925-1941, microfilm publication M1916, 596118, Office of the Quartermaster General, RG 92, NARA.

17. Ridgway, *Power Family*, 41; Graham County Record of Deeds, book 20, p. 145, GCRO; *Arizona Territory v. Thomas J. Sisson*, Graham County Superior Court Criminal case no. 214, 1914, ASLAPR; *Sisson v. State*, 16 Ariz. 170, 141 p. 713; *Graham Guardian*, February 4, 1910, October 3, 1913. Sisson was granted a certificate of reasonable doubt by the trial judge in his case, but nevertheless lost his appeal to the Supreme Court of Arizona.

18. Prisoner Record 4355, ADOC, ASLAPR; Wolfe, *Power, Passion*, 25; David R. Berman, *George Hunt: Arizona's Crusading Seven-Term Governor* (Tucson: University of Arizona, 2015), 72–73, 87; Ridgway, *Power Family*, 41–42; Roberts, "'The Powers Boys,'" 333; *Graham Guardian*, July 17, 1914. In November 1914, the month after his release, Arizona voters passed an initiative that created a Board of Pardons and Paroles with the power to determine which convicted felons would be paroled, limiting the governor's power.

19. Ridgway, *Power Family*, 42–43; Roberts, "The Powers Boys," 302–3; *Bisbee Daily Review*, February 14, 1918. J. Frank Wootan interview, AHS, suggests she died in August 1915.

20. Graham County Deeds of Mines, book 9, p. 281, book 4, p. 257, GCRO; Graham County Chattel Mortgages, book 3, p. 106, GCRO; Graham County Bill of Sales, book 4, pp. 332–33, GCRO; *T. J. Power v. Jeff Clayton*, Graham County Superior Court Civil case nos. 287, 307, 1916, ASLAPR; *Graham Guardian*, February 5, 1915; Roberts, "'The

Powers Boys,'" 334. Jeff Power paid $450 for the used stamp mill. War embargoes on Argentine beef drove up beef prices in Arizona to twenty-five dollars a head.

21. *Graham Guardian*, October 22, 1915. Charles Jones and Joe Mulheim were well-known mining investors in the Warren District of Cochise County.

22. Power, *Shoot-Out at Dawn*, 16–17; Graham County Deeds of Mines, book 9, p. 288, GCRO; *Graham Guardian*, February 12, 1915; *Bisbee Daily Review*, April 16, 1916; *Tombstone Prospector*, August 12, 1918. We can only speculate why John paid half of what Jeff paid earlier. It may have been because several speculators had visited and passed on the opportunity to buy, so Bauman was willing to sell at a lower price.

23. Roberts, "'The Powers Boys,'" 302, 334; Ridgway, *Power Family*, 40; *Graham Guardian*, May 7, 1920; Graham County Great Register of Electors, 1916, Klondyke precinct, ASLAPR.

24. Manuscript, Cavanaugh Collection; McBride, *The Evaders*, 13.

CHAPTER 8

1. *Graham Guardian,* October 6, 1916, May 25, June 1 & 8, July 13, 1917; WWI Draft Cards for Klondyke Precinct and Bonita Precinct, Graham County, Arizona, NARA.

2. John Whiteclay Chambers, *To Raise an Army: The Draft Comes to Modern America* (New York: The Free Press, 1987), 184, 210–11; W. S. Gifford to the Arizona State Council of Defense, May 22, 1917, Council of Defense records, box 5, folder 72, ASLAPR; *Graham Guardian,* June 8, July 13, 1917; *Bisbee Daily Review,* June 7, 1917. In most locations, men who failed to appear on June 5, 1917, had until the following Saturday to register.

3. Jeanette Keith, *Rich Man's War, Poor Man's Fight: Race, Class, and Power in the Rural South During the First World War* (Chapel Hill: University of North Carolina Press, 2004), 84.

4. H. C. Peterson and Gilbert C. Fite, *Opponents of War: 1917–1918* (Madison: University of Wisconsin Press, 1957), 3–5, 24; Hendrick A. Clements, *The Presidency of Woodrow Wilson* (Lawrence: University Press of Kansas, 1992), 138–40.

5. James F. Willis, "The Cleburne County Draft War," *Arkansas Historical Quarterly* 26, no. 1 (Spring 1967): 24; Peterson and Fite, *Opponents of War,* 21; Keith, *Rich Man's War,* 3; Daniel G. Donalson, *Espionage and Sedition Acts of World War I: Using Wartime Loyalty Laws for Revenge and Profit* (El Paso: LFB Scholarly Publishing LLC, 2012), 2.

6. Chambers, *To Raise an Army,* 184; Stewart Halsey Ross, *Propaganda for War: How the United States Was Conditioned to Fight the Great War of 1914–1918* (Jefferson, NC: McFarland, 1996), 177, 196–98; Clemens P. Work, *Darkest Before Dawn: Sedition and Free Speech in the American West* (Albuquerque: University of New Mexico Press, 2005), 87–88, 97; Keith, *Rich Man's War,* 4.

7. Chambers, *To Raise an Army,* 73–74, 181–83, 211; Keith, *Rich Man's War,* 84; Flynn, *Conscription and Democracy,* 3–4.

8. Theodore Kornweibel, *Investigate Everything: Federal Efforts to Compel Black Loyalty During World War I* (Bloomington: Indiana University Press, 2002), 87–88; Keith, *Rich Man's War,* 84–85; Chambers, *To Raise an Army,* 73, 181–83.

9. Chambers, *To Raise an Army*, 211; William Haas Moore, "Prisoners in the Promised Land: The Molokans in World War I," *Journal of Arizona History* 14, no. 4 (Winter 1973): 281–82, 285; Report on Molokans, Federal Bureau of Investigation, Old German files, case nos. 186233, 186733, September 17, 1918, NARA, available on Fold3.com (hereafter cited as FBI); Lillian Schlissel, ed., *Conscience in America: A Documentary History of Conscientious Objection in America, 1757–1967* (New York: E. P. Dutton & Co. Inc., 1968), 128; David R. Henderson, "From 'Porous' to 'Ruthless' Conscription, 1776–1917," *The Independent Review* 14, no. 4 (Spring 2010): 587–98; Keith, *Rich Man's War*, 130; Stephen M. Kohn, *Jailed for Peace: The History of American Draft Law Violators, 1658–1985* (Westport, CT: Greenwood Press, 1986), 25–27; Robert C. Cottrell, *Roger Nash Baldwin and the American Civil Liberties Union* (New York: Columbia University Press, 2000), 52, 66, 72, 88.

10. Chambers, *To Raise an Army*, 212; Bert Conaway to Tom Campbell, October 4, 1917, Sam B. Bradner to Herbert Hoover, September 15, 1917, Council of Defense records, ASLAPR.

11. *Selective Service Regulations*, 2nd ed. (Washington: Government Printing Office, 1918), sect. 135–36, 140; Keith, *Rich Man's War*, 128; Gerald E. Shenk, *"Work or Fight!": Race, Gender, and the Draft in WWI* (Gordonsville, VA: Palgrave MacMillan, 2005), 2, 5.

12. Shenk, *"Work or Fight,"* 5, 38; Kornweibel, *Investigate Everything*, 73; Moore, "Prisoners in the Promised Land," 289–96; Christopher C. Gibbs, *The Great Silent Majority: Missouri's Resistance to World War I* (Columbia: University of Missouri Press, 1988), 33; Keith, *Rich Man's War*, 128.

13. Keith, *Rich Man's War*, 183; Willis, "Cleburne County," 38. Kornweibel, *Investigate Everything*, 88; H. B. Mock to C. L. Keep, FBI case no. 4092, November 24, 1917, NARA; Chambers, *To Raise an Army*, 211–14.

14. *Selective Service Regulations*, sect. 131–35; R. F. McBride to J. P. Dillon, June 21, 1917, United States Marshals' records for the District of Arizona, AHS.

15. U.S. Marshals Service, "Arizona District Marshals," Department of Justice, www.usmarshals.gov/district/az/general/history.htm (accessed October 14, 2014); *Graham Guardian*, March 24, 1911.

16. Kornweibel, *Investigate Everything*, 73–77, 85; F. R. Raymond, FBI case no. 27221, October 22, 1917, McCaleb report, FBI case no. 18531, August 8, 1917, NARA.

17. Keith, *Rich Man's War*, 184–85; Willis, "Cleburne County," 26; C. C. Faires to Robert Barnes, August 25, 1917, H. J. Brown to Dillon, August 15, 1917, U.S. Marshals' records, AHS.

18. *Graham Guardian*, May 25, 1917; Loyd Ericson, "Eugene England's Theology of Peace," in *War & Peace in Our Time*, eds. Patrick Q. Mason, J. David Pulsipher, and Richard L. Bushman (Salt Lake City: Greg Kofford Books, 2012), 176; Lynne Watkins Jorgensen, "Begging to Be in the Battle: A Mormon Boy in World War I," *Journal of Mormon History* 29, no. 1 (Spring 2003): 107–11; William J. Breen, *Uncle Sam at Home: Civilian Mobilization, Wartime Federalism, and the Council of National Defense, 1917–1919* (Westport, CT: Greenwood Press, 1984), 99; report of McCaleb, FBI case

no. 69042, November 22, 1917, NARA. Throughout its early history, the LDS church had practiced "selective pacifism," asserting its right to not participate in war.

19. Shenk, "*Work or Fight,*" 2; Chambers, *To Raise an Army,* 182; Sheridan, *Arizona,* 185; Keith, *Rich Man's War,* 84; Kornweibel, *Investigate Everything,* 86–90; *Graham Guardian,* August 24, September 7, 1917; *Arizona Bulletin,* June 7, 1917; *Arizona Record,* December 8, 1917; McCaleb to John E. Green, FBI case no. 4092, December 11 & 13, 1918; R. F. McBride to McCaleb, October 4, 1917, Robert L. Barnes to R. F. McBride, October 12, 1917, FBI case no. 69042, NARA; Final List of Deserters and Delinquents for Graham County, 1919, Office of the Provost Marshal General, NARA.

20. *Graham Guardian,* March 2, 1917 and August 24, 1917; report of McCaleb on B. C. Hatfield, FBI case no. 76653, October 18, 1917; R. F. McBride to McCaleb, FBI case no. 69042, October 4, 1917, NARA.

21. Ball, *Desert Lawmen,* 209; Report on Henry Williams and Clay Clark, FBI case no. 47534, August 11, 16, 25, 1918, September 17, 1917, NARA; Faires to Barnes, August 16 & 25, September 7, 1917, U.S. Marshals' records, AHS. Williams and Clark were cattle rustlers, not slackers, so the federal posse was cancelled. In the correspondence of the U.S. attorney for Arizona, there seemed to be no consensus as to what legal grounds constituted authorization for a posse for draft delinquents.

22. R. F. McBride to Dillon, June 21, 1917, and J. H. Langston to Dillon, June 22, 1917, U.S. Marshals' records, AHS; Bob Thomas, *Arizona Republic,* January 26, 1969; Don Dedera, "Coffee Break," *Arizona Republic,* November 10, 1958; Power, *Shoot-Out at Dawn,* 20; Ridgway, *Power Family,* 121; U.S. Census, 1900: Upper Gila, Grant, New Mexico and Willcox, Cochise, Arizona; WWI Draft Card for Charles S. Power, Socorro, New Mexico, NARA. Charley could not feign ignorance of the draft, as his Morgan cousins living near him also signed up. Either his recent return to New Mexico after a decade of living in Arizona allowed the twenty-eight-year-old some degree of anonymity or else the local sheriff was not as motivated to locate slackers as Sheriff McBride.

23. Keith, *Rich Man's War,* 3, 84, 86–87, 97–98; Ridgway, *Power Family,* 44–45.

24. Ross, *Propaganda for War,* 246; Report of Bledsoe, FBI case no. 18668, July 19, 1918, NARA; *Graham Guardian,* June 22, October 19, November 16, 1917, January 4, March 20, 1918; Keith, *Rich Man's War,* 128; Schlissel, *Conscience in America,* 130; Shenk, "*Work or Fight,*" 2.

25. Ridgway, *Power Family,* 121; McBride, *The Evaders,* 35, 104; Manuscript, Cavanaugh Collection.

26. Peterson and Fite, *Opponents of War,* 20, 30; Powers, *Broken,* 83–84, 86; Donalson, *Espionage and Sedition Acts,* 2. The Espionage Act went into effect June 15, 1917.

27. Keith, *Rich Man's War,* 11, 128, 175, 200; *Arizona Republican,* August 7, 1917, January 3, 1918; Report of McCaleb, FBI case no. 111375, January 3, 1918, Report of Theodore T. Swift, FBI case no. 69042, March 7, 1918, NARA.

28. Sheridan, *Arizona,* 190–91; Schlissel, *Conscience in America,* 128–30; Peterson and Fite, *Opponents of War,* 9, 30.

29. Sheridan, *Arizona,* 191–92; Frederick C. Giffin, *Six Who Protested: Radical Opposition to the First World War* (Port Washington, NM: Kennikat Press, 1977), 125; Shenk,

*"Work or Fight,"*105; Keith, *Rich Man's War,* 86; William H. Lyon, *Those Old Yellow Dog Days: Frontier Journalism in Arizona, 1859–1912* (Tucson: Arizona Historical Society, 1994), 86; David R. Berman, *Radicalism in the Mountain West, 1890–1920* (Boulder: University Press of Colorado, 2007), 278.

30. Peterson and Fite, *Opponents of War,* 50–51; Berman, *Radicalism,* 273–76; *Bisbee Daily Review,* February 18, 1918.

31. *Bisbee Daily Review,* August 28, 1917; *Arizona Record,* July 6, 1917; *Arizona Republican,* October 2, 1917, February 13, 1918; *Copper Era,* November 2, 1917; Report of McCaleb, FBI case no. 18531, August 8, 1917, NARA; FBI Radical Activities report 8000-377098, NARA. In Jerome the response against the unions was similar, but much smaller in scale, and only about seventy-five strikers were deported out of the county.

32. Benton-Cohen, *Borderline Americans,* 218, 221–26, 234–35; Shenk *"Work or Fight,"* 2; Peterson and Fite, *Opponents of War,* 30; Keith, *Rich Man's War,* 140–41.

33. Chambers, *To Raise an Army,* 212; Keith, *Rich Man's War,* 85–86, 97–81; Report of August 12, 1917, box 88, MID, Evasion of Military Service, NARA; Frederick C. Luebke, *Bonds of Loyalty: German Americans and World War I* (DeKalb: Northern Illinois University Press, 1974), 267.

34. Report of August 12, 1917, MID, NARA; Report of H. B. Mock, FBI case no. 53467, August 14, 1917, NARA; WWI Draft Card for Tilden Edward Scarborough, Gila County, Arizona, NARA.

35. *El Paso Herald,* March 15, 1918; Report of McCaleb, FBI case no. 8532-284, November 22, 1917, NARA; *Graham Guardian,* September 7, 1917.

36. Reports of McCaleb, FBI case nos. 27221, 69042, July 9, 19, 1917, November 22, 1917, Barnes to McCaleb, FBI case no. 76653, October 18, November 4, 5, 1917, NARA.

37. Don Dedera interview, June 18, 2015; Henry Allen transcript, Cavanaugh Collection.

CHAPTER 9

1. *Graham Guardian,* December 14, 1917; Stewart, "'Clara and Frank,'" 12.

2. Graham County Coroner's Report for Ola May Power, December 8, 1917, in Ridgway, *Power Family,* 146–47. The coroner's jurors were Albert Kountze, L. C. Flick, W. S. Allbritton, J. T. Sanford, J. P. Weathersby, and W. S. McClintock. The inquest report for Ola Power vanished from Graham County records years ago, but copies have turned up in several private collections, and because all copies appear the same, it is safe to say they are copies of the authentic original.

3. *Graham Guardian,* December 14, 1917; Ridgway, *Power Family,* 48–49, 146–47; Power, *Shoot-Out at Dawn,* 24; Report of Albert Whipple, Closed Files 5173-4, ADOC, ASLAPR. Depending on the source, the Boscoes lived seven, ten, or twelve miles from the Powers at Gold Mountain.

4. Wolfe, *Power, Passion,* 166; Ridgway, *Power Family,* 48–49, 146–47.

5. Ridgway, *Power Family,* 49, 51.

6. Ibid., 146–47; Report of Albert Whipple, Closed Files 5173-4, ADOC, ASLAPR; Power, *Shoot-Out at Dawn,* 21.

7. Ridgeway, *Power Family,* 146–47; *Graham Guardian,* March 9, 1918. Although Ola's lab report cannot be found in public records, the County Board of Supervisors report noted payment of forty dollars to the Pathological Laboratory for work performed, and since hers was the only death at that time in Graham County, it therefore seems likely the tests were conducted. Testing for poisons had been routinely performed in Arizona for about ten years prior to Ola's death.

8. Ridgway, *Power Family,* 50–56; Power, *Shoot-Out at Dawn,* 21; Roberts, "'The Powers Boys,'" 302–3.

9. Stewart, "'Clara and Frank,'" 13; Roberts, "'The Powers Boys,'" 304; Ridgway, *Power Family,* 51–54; Wolfe, *Power, Passion,* 41–42; *Arizona Bulletin,* February 14, 1918; Manuscript, Cavanaugh Collection. The *Gila Valley Farmer* ran a story about Ola's death, according to a Pima resident, with "lurid implications on its pages" accusing her brothers "of breaking her neck to hide earlier crimes against her person." Those rumors "reached the law and Dr. Platt." All copies of the *Gila Valley Farmer* published from late 1917 to early 1918 have vanished from local historical societies and archives.

10. *Graham Guardian,* December 14, 1917; Roberts, "'The Powers Boys,'" 183, 286, 288; *Bisbee Daily Review,* February 12, 1918; *Copper Era,* March 15, 1918; Neeson to Dedera, April 12, 1960, PBRN, ASU; Manuscript, Cavanaugh Collection; Ridgway, *Power Family,* 52.

11. Wolfe, *Power, Passion,* 166–67; Power, *Shoot-Out at Dawn,* 21; Ridgway, *Power Family,* 199; *Clara McBride et al. v. John T. Power, Tom Power, and the estate of Jeff T. Power, deceased,* Graham County Superior Court Civil case no. 521, 1918, ASLAPR. When the lawmen's widows sued the Power family, a complete inventory was taken of the contents of the Power property and no canned goods were listed.

12. *Arizona Bulletin,* February 14, 1918; Arizona Genealogy Birth and Death Certificates, "Ala May Power," Arizona Department of Health Services, filed February 8, 1918, http://genealogy.az.gov/azdeath/017/10170469.pdf (accessed September 19, 2013); Report of McCaleb, FBI case no. 69042, December 18, 1917, NARA. Almost all the information on the death certificate for Ola May Power was incorrect, including the date of her death, her age, and place of birth. Even her name was misspelled "Ala" May, indicating that whoever filled out the paperwork did not know her and had no contact with her family. No member of the Power family signed the document.

13. Report of McCaleb, FBI case no. 111375, January 3, 1918, NARA.

14. Darvil McBride to Eugene Pulliam, November 17, 1958, PBRN, ASU; Report of Albert Whipple, U. I. Paxton to Walter Hofmann, December 1, 1952, Closed Files 5273-4, ADOC, ASLAPR; Selective Draft Law Cases, United States Supreme Court, 38 S. Ct. 159, 245 U.S. 366 (1918), http://biotech.law.lsu.edu/cases/nat-sec/selective-draft.htm (accessed July 18, 2017).

15. Dillon to Frank Haynes, January 25, 1918, *AZ v. Sisson; Arizona Republic,* December 17, 1952. The justice court records for this period from Graham County have disappeared from the county courthouse, but a copy of the Justice Court Record of Actions can be found in PBRN, ASU.

16. McBride, *The Evaders,* 53; *Graham Guardian,* June 29, 1906; *Daily Arizona Silver Belt,* January 5, 1909; Appointment and Oath of Office for Frank Haynes as Deputy

Marshal in the Territory of Arizona, Records of the U.S. Marshals Service, RG 527, NARA, https://research.archives.gov/id/295746 (accessed March 15, 2013).

17. *Daily Arizona Silver Belt*, January 3, 1909. For a small sampling of Haynes's exploits as a lawman, see: *Daily Arizona Silver Belt*, April 2, 1909, January 20 and December 26, 1911, and October 6, 1916; *Arizona Republican*, December 27, 1911, January 18, 1912, August 28, 1917; *Arizona Sentinel and Yuma Weekly Examiner*, June 27, 1912, May 13, 1913; Report on Frank Raymond, FBI case no. 27221, October 22, 1917, NARA; Gila County Justice Court Register of Actions, 1914–1918, Gila County Historical Society, Globe.

18. Dillon to Haynes, January 28, 1918, *AZ v. Sisson*; Dillon to the U.S. Attorney General, September 17, 1917, U.S. Marshals' records, AHS. In the letter Dillon outlined how the posse would be paid and admonished Haynes to keep expenses to a minimum, a common theme in all of Dillon's instructions to his deputies and a reflection of the Department of Justice's tight budget for such cases.

19. Faires to Barnes, August 25, 1917, U.S. Marshals' records, AHS.

20. G. W. Shute, "Tragedy of the Grahams," *Arizona Cattlelog* (April 1960): 32–33. Although the letter has long since vanished, Gene Shute, who was the warden at the Arizona State Prison at Florence in the 1930s and 1940s, claimed to have read it when it was still in his prison files and published the contents, as they read here, in an article he wrote in 1960. Both Henry Allen and Jay Murdock verified that they saw the letter and independently confirmed the letter's contents.

21. Ridgway, *Power Family*, 56.

22. McBride, *The Evaders*, 40–42; Manuscript, Cavanaugh Collection. Only Tom Power denied the existence of the letter, and said, "We never got no letter," Tom Power interview, Noble. Henry Allen later stated that he, not Murdock, gave Jeff Power the letter. Regardless of what happened, the consensus was that the letter was delivered to Jeff Power the last week of January.

23. Reports by David Ross, FBI case nos. 10794, 203795, 92005, 4092, 114188, 135166, NARA; Report by Ross on the "Powell" brothers, FBI case no. 53467, August 14, 1917, NARA.

24. Report by Ross on the Power brothers, FBI case no. 53467, February 8, 1918, NARA.

25. Tom Power and John Power arrest warrants, *AZ v. Sisson*; Graham County Justice of the Peace, Register of Actions, 1918, PBRN, ASU. Paxton originally issued the warrants on a federal commissioner's form, but since he was a state, not a federal, officer, Flynn instructed him to cross out in two places the lines that read "United States Commissioner" as issuing agent, replacing it with "Justice of the Peace in and for Graham County."

26. Dillon to Haynes, January 25 & 28, 1918, *AZ v. Sisson*; Inquest of Robert F. McBride, Martin R. Kempton, and Thomas K. Wootan, 51–52, Power Brothers Collection, AHS (hereafter cited as "Inquest of McBride"); Statement by W. R. Chambers, Closed Files 5173-4, ADOC, ASLAPR.

27. Ball, *Desert Lawmen*, 209; Inquest of McBride, 52; Dillon to Haynes, January 25 & 28, 1918, *AZ v. Sisson*.

28. Haynes to Dillon, telegram, February 10, 1918, DOJ, box 2148, straight numerical file no. 186233-940, NARA (hereafter cited as Power-Sisson DOJ file); Millie Wootan Barnes interview, *Power's War* transcripts; Report of Albert Whipple, Closed Files 5173-4, ADOC, ASLAPR; *Central Cattle Loan Co. v. Estate of T. K. Wootan,* Graham County Superior Court Civil case no. 522, box 23, folders 542 and 543, 1919, ASLAPR; Pima County Deeds of Mortgages, book 42, pp. 214–16, ASLAPR; *Reginald Soule v. Kane Wootan et al.,* Pima County Register of Actions and Fee Book, Civil case no. 6328, vol. 13, p. 536, 1917, ASLAPR.

29. Inquest of McBride, 52; *Graham Guardian,* April 28, 1916, July 20, December 28, 1917; Stewart, "'My Father Was the Sheriff,'" 1; Graham County Probate Records for Martin Kempton, box 20, folder 784, case no. 117, 1918, ASLAPR, corroborates Kempton family stories that he paid off all his debts prior to joining the posse.

30. *Graham Guardian,* February 9 & 22, 1917, February 8, 1918; *Arizona Bulletin,* July 19, 1917; Chronicling America, "About *Graham Guardian.*"

31. *Graham Guardian,* February 15, 1918; Stewart, "'My Father Was the Sheriff,'" 3; Inquest of McBride, 53; *Copper Era,* May 17, 1918; Ridgway, *Power Family,* 61–62.

32. Inquest of McBride, 53–55; Pattee, comp., *Revised Statutes of Arizona,* Title 5 PC 858, p. 170; Roberts, "'The Powers Boys,'" 302; *Bisbee Daily Review,* February 14, 1918. At the inquest of the lawmen, Haynes testified they left their horses 75 *rods* from the cabin. Newspaper coverage of the trial reported it as 75 *yards.*

33. Inquest of McBride, 55; "Proposed Plan of the Restoration and Preservation of the Historic Power Cabin," Power Brothers papers, 1918–1990, AHS.

34. Inquest of McBride, 56; Power, *Shoot-Out at Dawn,* 27.

35. Inquest of McBride, 56–58; *Copper Era,* May 17, 1918.

36. Inquest of McBride, 56–59; *Copper Era,* May 17, 1918.

37. *Copper Era,* May 17, 1918; *Arizona Record,* February 13, 1918. Haynes claimed he shot only three times, twice at the door at the beginning of the gunfight and once at the window on the west side of the cabin near the end of the exchange.

CHAPTER 10

1. Ira E. Gilpin to Dedera, March 28, 1960, PBRN, ASU; Inquest of McBride, 62–63.

2. Haynes to Dillon, telegram, February 10, 1918, Power-Sisson DOJ file.

3. Ibid.; *Nogales Oasis,* February 16, 1918.

4. Dillon to the Attorney General Thomas Gregory, February 11, 12, 1918, telegram, Acting Attorney General Davis to Dillon, February 13, 1918, telegram, Power-Sisson DOJ file; *Tucson Citizen,* February 12, 1918; *Arizona Republican,* February 13, 1918.

5. *Arizona Gazette* (Phoenix), February 11, 1918.

6. Ibid.

7. Inquest of McBride, 52–56; *Arizona Record,* February 13, 1918,

8. Inquest of McBride, 2–4, 13, 20–21, 40–41, 44–45.

9. Ibid., 2, 5–6, 14, 21–23, 42; McBride, *The Evaders,* 33, 44; Ridgway, *Power Family,* 57. Red Nuttal and Solomon E. Rhea were also present, and Rhea testified at the trial, but

evidently neither man heard or saw anything of significance. Henry Allen claimed the three men rode up two hours after the gunfight, while Jay Murdock said it was only thirty minutes later.

10. Inquest of McBride, 5–6, 22, 47.

11. Ibid., 8, 22–23, 47.

12. Ibid., 24–30.

13. *Bisbee Daily Review,* February 14, 1918; Power, *Shoot-Out at Dawn,* 21, 23; Roberts, "'The Powers Boys,'" 302.

14. McBride, *The Evaders,* 104; Manuscript, Cavanaugh Collection; Power, *Shoot-Out at Dawn,* 21; Wolfe, *Power, Passion,* 35; Inquest of McBride; Ridgway, *Power Family,* 44–45, 121. Charges under the Espionage Act were never filed against anyone in the Power household, nor were Tom or John listed among the delinquents and deserters for Graham County in records housed at NARA Riverside, CA and College Park, MD.

15. Inquest of McBride, 7–8; Power, *Shoot-Out at Dawn,* 39.

16. Inquest of McBride, 8–9, 35; Ridgway, *Power Family,* 75–79.

17. Inquest of McBride, 9–10, 36–40, 49; *Arizona Bulletin,* February 14, 1918; Thomas Pickering Pick, *Surgery: A Treatise for Students and Practitioners* (New York: Longmans, Green, and Co., 1899), 784. Haynes never mentioned that Jeff Power spoke, contradicting Jay Murdock's suggestion that Power said, "We give up."

18. Inquest of McBride, 14–19; McBride, *The Evaders,* 79; Wolfe, *Power, Passion,* 53; Ridgway, *Power Family,* 85–86; *Graham Guardian,* September 22, 1916; McBride, *The Evaders,* 83.

19. Inquest of McBride, 67–68.

20. Ibid., 68–70.

21. Ibid., 71–74; Murder complaints for Thomas J. Sisson, Tom and John Power, *AZ v. Sisson*; Pattee, comp., *Revised Statutes of Arizona,* Title 5, Sect. 859 and 860. Several other relatives and friends of the deceased lawmen testified, providing the court with the ages of each man as well as evidence that each man had been robbed of his money. The county recorder testified that his records showed that each of the slain officers was duly appointed by the county.

22. Report of C. C. Faires, February 12, 1918, case no. 10101-623, box 2495, Correspondence of the MID, 1917–41, NARA.

23. Ibid. The report also falsely claimed the Power family was still in the ranching business.

24. *Tucson Citizen,* February 13, 1918; *Bisbee Daily Review,* February 12, 13, 14, 1918; *El Paso Herald,* February 21, 1918; *Casa Grande Dispatch,* February 15, 1918; *Daily Arizona Silver Belt,* February 11, 1918; *Arizona Republican,* February 16, 1918. Only the *Bisbee Daily Review,* February 14, 1918, corrected the false information about Maricopa Slim and others.

25. *Tucson Citizen,* February 13, 1918; *Arizona Daily Star,* February 20, 1918.

26. *Bisbee Daily Review,* February 20, 1918.

27. *Arizona Range News* (Willcox), February 15, 1918; *Ogden Standard,* February 18, 1918; *Arizona Daily Star,* February 20, 1918.

28. *Tucson Citizen,* February 21, 1918; *Coconino Sun* (Flagstaff), March 8, 1918; *El Paso Herald,* February 14, 1918; *Western Liberal,* February 15, 1918; *Arizona Republican,* February 14, 1918; Suspect List for February 1918, box 2126, 9140-5862/1, Correspondence of the MID, NARA; *Arizona Daily Star,* February 12, 1918. Tom Sisson and Tom and John Power were all listed as "wanted for evading draft."

29. *Western Liberal,* February 15, 1918.

30. *Copper Era,* June 14, 1918; *Bisbee Daily Review,* June 16, 1918; Graham County Deeds of Mines, book 18, p. 231, GCRO. James T. Branson was the Oracle postmaster.

31. *Arizona Record,* February 13, 1918.

32. *Graham Guardian,* February 15, 1918; *Arizona Bulletin,* February 14, 1918 (estimate of two thousand attendees).

33. *Graham Guardian,* February 15, 1918; Ridgway, *Power Family,* 98; *Daily Arizona Silver Belt,* February 13, 1918.

34. *Tucson Citizen,* February 12, 14, 20, 1918; *Bisbee Daily Review,* February 12, 1918; *El Paso Herald,* February 11, 1918; McBride, *The Evaders,* 81; Ridgway, *Power Family,* 86; Pattee, comp., *Revised Statutes of Arizona,* Title 24, Sect. 1379; *Arizona Gazette,* February 12, 1918, erroneously reported that Jeff Power's body was buried as well.

35. *Arizona Republican,* February 12, 1918; *Phoenix Gazette,* February 11 & 12, 1918; Deputy Willits to Dillon, February 16, 1918, U.S. Marshals' records, AHS; *Bisbee Daily Review,* March 21, 1918; *Arizona Daily Star,* February 11 & 16, 1918; *Graham Guardian,* February 15, March 22, 1918; *Copper Era,* March 15, 1918; *Western Liberal,* February 15, 1918; *El Paso Herald,* February 11 & 14, 1918; *Arizona Record,* February 13, 1918; Dillon to Gregory, telegrams, February 11 & 12, 1918, Power-Sisson DOJ file. The state offered the maximum amount allowed by law, one thousand dollars, and Graham County also offered that much, while the local cattlemen's association offered fifteen hundred dollars and the federal government offered two hundred dollars. Initially, four thousand dollars was awarded, hence the number on the wanted poster.

36. Davis to Dillon, two telegrams, February 13, 1918, Power-Sisson DOJ file; Bill O'Neal, "Captain Harry Wheeler: Arizona Lawman," *Journal of Arizona History* 27, no. 3 (Autumn 1986): 298; D. N. Willits to Dillon, February 26, 1918, U.S. Marshals' records, AHS; *Arizona Republican,* February 13, 1918.

37. *Tucson Citizen,* February 13 & 14, 1918; *El Paso Herald,* February 13, 1918; *Daily Arizona Silver Belt,* February 13, 1918; *Arizona Republican,* February 14, 1918; *Bisbee Daily Review,* February 16, 1918; *Arizona Daily Star,* February 14, 1918.

38. *Tucson Citizen,* February 16, 20, 21, 1918; *Arizona Daily Star,* February 15, 1918.

39. *Tucson Citizen,* February 16, 20, 21, 1918; *Arizona Republican,* February 17, 1918; *Copper Era,* February 22, 1918.

40. *Tucson Citizen,* February 16, 1918; Ball, *Desert Lawmen,* 206; *Arizona Republican,* February 20, 1918.

41. *Arizona Republican,* February 17, 1918; *Tucson Citizen,* February 20, 1918; *Copper Era,* February 22, March 15, 1918; *Arizona Range News,* February 22, 1918, suggested that after only eight hours, the scent was lost by the dogs. In the decades following the

manhunt, many reporters suggested as many as three thousand men participated, but contemporary accounts never indicated more than a thousand men were involved, seven hundred of whom were soldiers stationed on the border to prevent an invasion from Mexico during the war.

42. *El Paso Daily Herald,* February 14 & 19, 1918; *Arizona Daily Star,* February 15, 1918; *Tucson Citizen,* February 12 & 14, 1918; *Ogden Standard*, February 18, 1918.

43. *Arizona Republican,* February 16, March 1, 1918; *Bisbee Daily Review,* February 19, March 3, 1918.

44. Inquest of McBride, 37–38; Willis "The Cleburne County," 25; Keith, *Rich Man's War,* 184; *Copper Era,* February 22, 1918; *Arizona Daily Star,* February 14 & 18, 1918; *Arizona Republican,* February 14, 16, 18, 20, 1918; *Daily Arizona Silver Belt,* February 11, 1918; *El Paso Herald,* February 14, 1918; *Arizona Range News,* February 15, 1918.

45. Berman, *George Hunt,* 67; Berman, *Radicalism,* 223; *Tucson Citizen,* February 16, 1918; *Arizona Gazette,* February 14, 1918; *Arizona Record,* February 12, 1918.

46. *Bisbee Daily Review,* February 20 & 27, 1918; *Graham Guardian,* February 22, March 1, 1918; *Copper Era,* March 15, 1918. The *Arizona Bulletin,* February 14, 1918, published the inquest of McBride, Kempton, and Wootan in its entirety, yet newspaper editors ignored the testimony from Jay Murdock stating Jeff Power had been shot down while trying to surrender.

47. *Tucson Citizen,* February 20, 1918.

CHAPTER 11

1. *Western Liberal,* March 15, 1918; *Silver City Enterprise,* March 15, 1918.

2. Ridgway, *Power Family,* 206–8; *Silver City Enterprise,* March 15, 1918; *Copper Era,* May 17, 1918. Hayes and his men were about fifteen miles southeast of the international border when they found the fugitives.

3. Ridgway, *Power Family,* 206–7.

4. Ibid.

5. Ibid.; *Arizona Range News,* March 15, 1918; *Graham Guardian,* March 15, 1918.

6. *Border Vidette* (Nogales), May 12, 1917; *Graham Guardian,* May 11, 1917; *Bisbee Daily Review,* May 8, 1917.

7. *Arizona Range News,* March 15, 1918; Ridgway, *Power Family,* 113; Power, *Shoot-Out at Dawn,* 159; *Silver City Enterprise,* March 15, 1918; *Copper Era,* March 15, 1918. They also told reporters they killed and roasted rabbits over a campfire. The *Arizona Daily Star,* February 15, 1918, confirmed that their campfire was found about a mile from Dos Cabezas and that they received bread from a lone woman.

8. Roberts, "'The Powers Boys,'" 317–18; *Tombstone Epitaph,* March 10, 1918; *Copper Era,* March 15, 1918; *Silver City Enterprise,* March 15, 1918; *Bisbee Daily Review,* March 10, 1918; Ridgway, *Power Family,* 80; Power, *Shoot-Out at Dawn,* 56; *Arizona Republican,* February 15, 1918; McBride, *The Evaders,* 99.

9. *Silver City Enterprise,* March 15, 1918; *Copper Era,* March 8 & 15, 1918; *Arizona Republican,* March 10 & 11, 1918; *Western Liberal,* March 15, 1918; *Graham Guardian,* March 15, 1918.

After months of legal wrangling, Shriver was denied the reward money and it was awarded to Lieutenant Hayes's men.

10. A. P. Hughes to Walter Hofmann, November 16, 1952, Closed Files 5173-4, ADOC, ASLAPR.

11. Ibid.; *Arizona Record*, March 9, 1918; *Bisbee Daily Review*, March 9, 1918; *Arizona Republican*, March 9 & 10, 1918; *Graham Guardian*, March 15, 1918; *Silver City Enterprise*, March 15, 1918. Newspapers reported that the trip back to the Gila Valley was uneventful.

12. D. McBride to Pulliam, November 17, 1958, PBRN, ASU.

13. *Graham Guardian*, March 15, 1918; Power, *Shoot-Out at Dawn*, 52; McBride, *The Evaders*, 99–100.

14. Grant County District Court Records, roll 17, Court Journal case no. 5807, 1910, NMSRCA; W. R. Chambers to Board of Pardons and Paroles, November 24, 1926, Governor George Hunt papers, 1923–33, box 3, folder 23, ASLAPR; McBride, *The Evaders*, 100; Change of venue, *AZ v. Sisson*; Pattee, comp., *Revised Statutes of Arizona*, para. 1001; *Copper Era*, March 15, 1918; Dedera to D. McBride, November 19, 1958, PBRN, ASU; Ridgway, *Power Family*, 116. Many thought the case would be tried in Tucson, but state law provided "that in transferring a case on a change of venue it must be sent to the county seat which is most accessible to the county seat from which the case originated." U. I. Paxton told Don Dedera that Howard McBride, the sheriff's brother, tried to kill the Power brothers, while Jay Murdock said Martin Kempton's brother Nate pulled a gun on the prisoners while in jail. However, neither man was charged.

15. *Bisbee Daily Review*, March 10, 1918; *Weekly Journal-Miner*, March 13, 1918; *Tombstone Epitaph*, March 10 & 17, 1918; *Copper Era*, March 15, 1918.

16. *Copper Era*, March 15, 1918. It is surprising that the statement condemning the draft made it through censors.

17. Inquest of McBride, 9–10, 34–36, 49–50.

18. *Arizona Bulletin*, February 14, 1918; *Coconino Sun*, March 15, 1918; *Arizona Republican*, February 16, 1918; *Bisbee Daily Review*, February 20, 1918; *Copper Era*, March 15, 1918.

19. Roberts, "'The Powers Boys,'" 318; Power, *Shoot-Out at Dawn*, 53; *Copper Era*, March 22, 1918; *Arizona Republican*, March 10, 1918; *Bisbee Daily Review*, March 20, 1918. Before the procedure John Power could see some light, but after, he was completely blind in his left eye.

20. *Arizona Record*, February 12, 1918; *Phoenix Gazette*, February 14, 1918; *Arizona Daily Star* editorial reprinted in the *Tombstone Epitaph*, March 17, 1918; Berman, *George Hunt*, 66.

21. *Copper Era*, March 15, 1918; Karen Holiday Tanner and John D. Tanner, "Scott White, Arizona Lawman," *Journal of Arizona History* 49, no. 1 (spring 2008): 20. An editorial in the *El Paso Herald*, March 15, 1918, also denounced Hunt for his progressive prison policies, asserting that convicted murderers in Arizona were "condemned to a long and peaceful life in Florence prison."

22. Langston to Gregory, May 14, 1918, Power-Sisson DOJ file. The shootout occurred on U.S. Forest Service land, which, according to the U.S. attorney general, did not fall under federal jurisdiction for a criminal case.

23. Ridgway, *Power Family*, 188.

24. *The Eagle* (Lordsburg), September 25, October 16, 1895, March 3 & 9, 1898; *Western Liberal*, October 11, 1918; *Silver City Enterprise* quotation in Jeffrey Burton, *The Deadliest Outlaws: The Ketchum Gang and the Wild Bunch* (Denton: University of North Texas Press, 2009), 122–25; Larry D. Ball, *The United States Marshals of New Mexico and Arizona Territories, 1846–1912* (Albuquerque: University of New Mexico Press, 1978), 206.

25. *Deming Graphic*, October 9, 1908, May 17, 1912; *Daily Arizona Silver Belt*, March 12, 1907; *Western Liberal*, July 14, 1916; Chambers to Board of Pardons and Paroles, November 24, 1926, Hunt papers, ASLAPR; *Clifton-Morenci Mining Journal*, May 26, 1918.

26. *Copper Era*, May 17, 1918; *Tucson Citizen*, May 16, 1918; Ball, *Desert Lawmen*, 180–81; William Blackstone, *Commentaries on the Laws of England*, ed. J. W. Ehrlich (San Carlos, CA: Nourse, 1959), 450; Brown, *No Duty to Retreat*, vi.

27. *Bisbee Daily Review*, May 18, 1918; Power, *Shoot-Out at Dawn*, 23; Pattee, comp., *Revised Statutes of Arizona*, Title 5, PC 859-60, Title 8, PC 180 (2).

28. Pattee, comp., *Revised Statutes of Arizona*, Title 8, PC 179 (2); Wolfe, *Power, Passion*, 138.

29. Minutes of Greenlee County Superior Court, March 13, 1918, ASLAPR; *Graham Guardian*, March 29, May 10, 1918; Richard Sloan, *History of Arizona*, vol. 3, *Biographical* (Phoenix: Record Publishing Co., 1930), 524; David Ling, Greenlee County attorney, took no part in the proceedings, according to *Copper Era*, May 17, 1918, because the burden of prosecution shifted to the Graham County attorney. There were rumors that Chambers really turned down Wiley Jones's offer to assist because the attorney general had a drinking problem.

30. *Graham Guardian*, March 29, 1918; R. H. Chambers to W. Ryder Ridgway, January 22, 1970, William Ryder Ridgway Collection.

31. Inquest of McBride, 15; Ridgway, *Power Family*, 200.

32. W. R. Chambers to Board of Pardons and Paroles, June 20, 1933, Closed Files 5173-4, ADOC, ASLAPR.

33. Inquest of McBride, 5, 23, 48; *Copper Era*, May 17, 1918; Power, *Shoot-Out at Dawn*, 28.

34. *Rebecca J. Murdock v. John M. Murdock*, Eddy County District Court Civil case no. 189, box 13347, 1894, NMSRCA.

35. Ibid.

36. *John M. v. Martha J. Charlton Murdock*, Maricopa County Superior Court Civil case no. 4077, 1903, ASLAPR. Additionally, John Murdock had fraudulently transferred the family home into his father's name to protect it from creditors. Unfortunately, those cases are missing from Eddy County records, because Murdock fled New Mexico before the cases went to trial.

37. *Arizona Territory v. J. M. Murdock*, Arizona Territorial Supreme Court 1801, 1910, ASLAPR; *Bisbee Daily Review*, December 5 & 19, 1906, August 7, 1910, June 7, 1912.

38. *AT v. J. M. Murdock*; *Bisbee Daily Review*, December 17, 1901, August 7, 1910; *Copper Era*, June 7, 1912; *Tombstone Epitaph*, January 9, 1910, June 2, 1912.

39. *Catherine Murdock v. James J. Murdock*, Cochise County Superior Court Civil case no. 424, 1913, ASLAPR; *Arizona Territory v. J. M. Murdock*; *Arizona Republican*, May 18, 1918; WWI Draft Card for Jay Murdock, Graham County, Arizona, NARA; *Copper Era*, May 17, 1918.

CHAPTER 12

1. *Tucson Citizen,* May 16, 1918, noted that the additional protection for the defendants was unneeded and "perfect order prevails."

2. Wolfe, *Power, Passion,* 133; *Copper Era,* May 17, 1918; Connors, *Who's Who in Arizona,* 505.

3. Harriet Sweeting to John Whitlatch, April 10, 1969, *AZ v. Sisson*; Report of Albert Whipple, Closed Files 5173-4, ADOC, ASLAPR. Several of the photos used as evidence in the file remain in private hands, part of the Ryder Ridgway Collection and were recently published in a book, *The Power Family of Graham County, Arizona,* but most of the photos taken by DuBois are missing. See Wolfe's *Power, Passion, and Prejudice,* 12–13, for her description of efforts to recover the trial transcripts.

4. *Copper Era,* May 17, 1918; Lyon, *Those Old Yellow Dog Days,* 86; J. Morris Richards, *"Ink by the Barrel": Arizona's Hall of Fame Newspaper Men and Women* (Tempe: Arizona Historical Foundation, 1992), n. p.; Estelle Lutrell, *Newspapers and Periodicals of Arizona, 1859–1911* (Tucson: University of Arizona, 1950), 18.

5. *Copper Era,* April 19, May 17, 1918; Jurors' list, *AZ v. Sisson; Tucson Citizen,* May 15, 1918. Newspapers reported thirty-two veniremen were interviewed, but the Minutes of the Greenlee County Superior Court, May 13, 1918, put the number at twenty-nine. During the jury selection process, the prosecution lodged opposition to seven potential jurors, including the man who stated he could not be impartial. Richard Stephens, born in England, a wholesale liquor dealer married to a German wife, was disqualified by the prosecution, as was Samuel Forbes born in Belfast, Ireland, and Carl Peterson born in Sweden. Southerners dismissed included Jasper A. Wish, born in Texas, and Luther Pringle, born in Kentucky.

6. *Tucson Citizen,* May 15, 16, 1918; *Clifton-Morenci Mining Journal,* May 16, 23, 1918; jurors' list, *AZ v. Sisson*; Greenlee Minutes, Miscellaneous, 1911–1948, p. 957, ASLAPR; Benton-Cohen, *Borderline Americans,* 234–6; Chambers to Board of Pardons and Paroles, November 24, 1926, Hunt papers, ASLAPR. Many of the jurors worked in middle management positions for the mining companies—Joseph Goolsby was a smelter superintendent, C. M. Bishop was a squad foreman, Simeon Spriggs a purchasing agent, Dan Grant a mine foreman, George Kiddie an assayer. Only four jurors were laborers, Jessie E. Dart and C. A. Lennox were miners, E. A. Wood, who served as jury foreman, was a painter, and J. Lippets was a carpenter.

7. *Copper Era,* May 17, 1918; *Clifton-Morenci Mining Journal,* May 16, 1918.

8. Ibid.; Exhibits A and B, *AZ v. Sisson*; Greenlee Minutes, p. 958, ASLAPR; Pattee, comp., *Revised Statutes of Arizona,* Title 8, PC 179 (2).

9. *Arizona Republican,* May 18, 1918.

10. *Copper Era,* May 17, 1918. The *Copper Era* said Jeff Power shifted his rifle, while the *Tucson Citizen,* May 16, 1918, offered a more benign version, saying he "dropped the weapon to his right side."

11. *Clifton-Morenci Mining Journal,* May 16, 1918; *Bisbee Daily Review,* May 14 & 18, 1918; *Tucson Citizen,* May 14, 1918.

12. *Tucson Citizen,* May 16, 1918; Inquest of McBride, 70; Wolfe, *Power, Passion,* 137; *Copper Era,* May 17, 1918; Greenlee Minutes, p. 958, ASLAPR.

13. Greenlee Minutes, p. 958, ASLAPR; *Tucson Citizen,* May 17, 1918; Ridgway, *Power Family,* 200–1.

14. *Graham Guardian,* September 17, 1918; *Copper Era,* May 17, 1918; *Tucson Citizen,* May 16 & 17, 1918; Roberts, "'The Powers Boys,'" 319.

15. *Tucson Citizen,* May 16, 1918; Statement by W. R. Chambers, Prisoner Records 5173-4, ADOC, ASLAPR. Inquest of McBride, 7; *Copper Era,* May 17, 1918; Shute, "Tragedy of the Grahams," 36. In the years to come, however, Jay's testimony would be embellished by others, who claimed John said they were coming back in a few days to get more of "'them damned sons of bitches.'"

16. Inquest of McBride, 7; *Copper Era,* May 17, 1918.

17. Aviva Orenstein, "Her Last Words: Dying Declarations and Modern Confrontation Jurisprudence," *Illinois Law Review* (2010): 1412–8; "The Admissibility of Dying Declaration," *Fordham Law Review* 38, no. 3 (1970): 509–10.

18. *Copper Era,* May 16 & 17, 1918; Richard Maxwell Brown, "Western Violence: Structure, Values, Myth," *Western Historical Quarterly* 24, no. 1 (February 1993): 15; *Tucson Citizen,* May 16, 1918.

19. *Copper Era,* May 16 & 17, 1918; *Tucson Citizen,* May 16, 1918.

20. Pattee, comp., *Revised Statues of Arizona, 1913,* Title 8, PC 180 (2); W. R. Chambers to Board of Pardons and Paroles, June 20, 1933, Closed Files 5173-4, ADOC, ASLAPR.

21. Chambers to Board of Paroles and Pardons, November 24, 1926, Hunt papers, ASLAPR; Ridgway, *Power Family,* 49.

22. McBride, *The Evaders,* 104; Ridgway, *Power Family,* 121.

23. Witness subpoenas, *AZ v. Sisson;* Pamela Pollock interview with author in Clifton, March 11, 2015; Interview with Thomas Jefferson Power, Power Brothers Papers, AHS.

24. *Copper Era,* May 17, 1918.

25. *Tucson Citizen,* May 17, 1918.

26. *Copper Era,* May 17, 1918.

27. Greenlee Minutes, p. 595, ASLAPR; Witness subpoenas, *AZ v. Sisson; Copper Era,* May 17, 1918.

28. *Tucson Citizen,* May 15, 16, 17, 1918; Prisoner Record 5174, ADOC, ASLAPR.

29. *Tucson Citizen,* May 15, 17, 1918; *Copper Era,* May 17, 1918.

30. *Clifton-Morenci Mining Journal,* May 23, 1918; *Copper Era,* May 17, 1918.

31. *Copper Era,* May 17, 1918.

32. Langston to Gregory, May 14, 1918, NARA.

33. W. R. Chambers to Board of Board of Pardons and Paroles, June 20, 1933, Closed Files 5173-4, ADOC, ASLAPR; *Graham Guardian,* September 17, 1918.

34. Statement of W. R. Chambers, Closed Files 5173-4, ADOC, ASLAPR.

35. Instructions to the jury, *AZ v. Sisson.*

36. Ibid.

37. Greenlee Minutes, p. 960, ASLAPR; Langston to Gregory, May 14, 1918, Gregory to Thomas Flynn, May 9, 1918, Power-Sisson DOJ file; *Copper Era,* May 17, 1918; *Graham*

Guardian, May 17, 1918. Clearly Sisson was not guilty of draft evasion, but he was listed in the federal records as a draft evader—an indication of just how ineffective government intelligence gathering was at that time.

38. *Copper Era,* May 17, 1918.

CHAPTER 13

1. *Clifton-Morenci Mining Journal,* May 23, 1918; Statement of Tom Sisson, Sentence, *AZ v. Sisson.* While the three convicted murderers remained lodged in the Greenlee County courthouse jail for the weekend, pending sentencing by Judge Laine on Monday, Judge Laine asked each man to swear out a statement, which Tom and John Power refused to do. However, Tom Sisson opted to say: "I am not guilty of the crime. I plead with the court for mercy." Laine responded that he had no alternative "in view of the fact the jury has found you guilty . . . I have no discretion in this matter. I can only pass the sentence that the law provides." State law required a minimum sentence of twenty years for first-degree murder.

2. Moore, *Enter Without Knocking,* 38, 43.

3. Tanner and Tanner, "Scott White," 20, 26, 37–38, 48, 50; Berman, *George Hunt,* 69; Moore, *Enter Without Knocking,* 35–37, 44.

4. Moore, *Enter Without Knocking,* 32; *Border Vidette,* June 8, 1918; Dedera interview, June 18, 2015. The death penalty was restored on December 5, 1918, and nineteen executions by hanging occurred before the gas chamber replaced the gallows in the 1930s.

5. Statement of W. R. Chambers, Closed Files 5173-4, Prisoner Records 5172-4, ADOC, ASLAPR; Power, *Shoot-Out at Dawn,* 84, 86; Moore, *Enter Without Knocking,* 32.

6. J. H. Sanders, "Restrictions on Prisoners' Mail," *Journal of the American Institute of Criminal Law and Criminology* 4, no. 6 (March 1914): 920; Moore, *Enter Without Knocking,* 86, 90; Power, *Shoot-Out at Dawn,* 80, 86, 88; Dedera interview, January 16, 2013. Items sold for one dollar in the gift shop, and prisoners received fifteen cents for each item sold.

7. Harriet Sweeting to John Whitlatch, April 10, 1969, *AZ v. Sisson; Copper Era,* May 17, 1918; Motion Dockets for Arizona Supreme Court, vol. 2, 1914–18, Calendars of Arizona Supreme Court, 1912–21, ASLAPR; Notice by defendants of intention to file motion for new trial, *AZ v. Sisson; Daily Arizona Silver Belt,* May 18, 1918; Greenlee County Criminal Register of Action, case 438a, 1918, pp. 66–68, Greenlee County Superior Court Clerk.

8. Power, *Shoot-Out at Dawn,* 87–88; *Copper Era,* June 14, 1918; *Sena Kempton v. Tom and John and the estate of Thomas Jefferson Power,* Graham County Superior Court Civil case no. 500, 1918, ASLAPR; *Clara McBride v. Tom and John and the estate of Thomas Jefferson Power,* Graham County Superior Court Civil case no. 501, 1918, ASLAPR; *Laura Wootan v. Tom and John and the estate of Thomas Jefferson Power,* Graham County Superior Court Civil case no. 499, 1918, ASLAPR.

9. Kempton Probate, ASLAPR; *Kempton v. Power; Tombstone Prospector,* August 12, 1918. Since the defendants were tried for the death of Clara's husband, she alone was

awarded the $35,000 judgment, but evidently there was some arrangement with the two other widows to share the proceeds.

10. *Graham Guardian,* March 29, May 14, 1918; Huber and Porter, "Notebook Entries by Frank & Clara McBride," Robert Franklin McBride, http://www.porter-az.com/albums/RFMcBride/RFMcBride.htm (accessed April 19, 2015); Wootan Probate, ASLAPR.

11. Graham County Proof of Labor, book 5, p. 529, GCRO; John Power to Charles S. Power, November 28, 1919, Closed File 5173, ADOC, ASLAPR; *Bisbee Daily Review,* June 16, 1918.

12. *Tombstone Prospector,* August 12, 1918; *Copper Era,* August 16, 1918; Sheriff's Return of Execution, *McBride v. Power*; Graham County Proof of Labor Performed, books 4–6, GCRO; Roberts, "'The Powers Boys," 330; Statement of John Power, December 31, 1919, Closed File 5173, ADOC, ASLAPR. All three families performed the annual assessment work on the mines for a few years until Lyman was hired to manage the mine through the 1950s.

13. WWI Draft Card for Charles S. Power, Socorro County, New Mexico, NARA; Social Security file for Charles S. Power, 525-22-7849, Social Security Administration.

14. *Graham Guardian,* June 1, 1917, August 9, 1918; Prisoner Records 5173-4, entry for September 12, 1918, ADOC, ASLAPR; Lists of Outgoing Passengers, 1917–1938, Records of the Quartermaster General, Roll 453, NARA. On the same day, Tom Sisson, Prisoner Record 5172, submitted the following statement in his record: "Tom and John Powers refused to register today I thought that this was not right and I tried to convince them of the wrong attitude which they were taking and that in these days of trouble it is the duty of every loyal American to stand by his country but they would not listen. Unfortunately I am too old to register and would be only too glad to do my part for our country. I would like the record to show my attitude in this matter." In 1931, Sisson filed a notarized document refuting he ever made the statement, claiming someone else submitted the statement without his knowledge.

15. *Arizona Service Bulletin,* vol. 1, no. 2, June 1, 1918, Council of Defense, box 5, folder 72, ASLAPR; Kornweibel, *Investigate Everything,* 77, 85, 98; Athan Theoharis, *The FBI and American Democracy: A Brief Critical History* (Lawrence: University Press of Kansas, 2004), 105; Chambers, *To Raise an Army,* 213; Shenk, "*Work or Fight,*" 114.

16. Willis, "Cleburne County," 25–28.

17. Ibid.; Keith, *Rich Man's War,* 184–85.

18. Chambers, *To Raise an Army,* 212; U.S. Census, 1920: Faulkner, Arkansas; Keith, *Rich Man's War,* 98.

19. Kohn, *Jailed for Peace,* 25–29; Keith, *Rich Man's War,* 128–30, 184; Work, *Darkest Before Dawn,* 180; Moore, "Prisoners in the Promised Land," 296, 299. No draft evaders or deserters convicted of killing an officer were executed. Several were sentenced to death, but were reprieved by President Wilson.

20. Wilfred L. Ebel, "The Amnesty Issue: A Historical Perspective," *Parameters: The Journal of the US Army War College* 4, no. 1 (1974): 74. Today the Espionage Act is still used in the war on terror, "not to prosecute spies, but to go after government officials who talked to journalists," according to the *New York Times,* January 1, 2017.

21. "Board of Pardons and Paroles, State of Arizona, Rules and Regulations of the Board," (August 1933), 6–9, Arizona State Library.

22. Prisoner Records 5172-4, ADOC, ASLAPR; *Arizona Republican,* December 18, 1923, January 16, 1924.

23. Phil C. Merrill to George Hunt, June 22, 1926, Scott White to George Hunt, June 28, 1926, Governor Hunt papers, box 3, folder 23, ASLAPR; Tanner and Tanner, "Scott White," 20; *Arizona Republican,* January 16 & 18, 1924; Prisoner Record 5173, ADOC, ASLAPR; Moore, *Enter Without Knocking,* 50. The typical punishment for escaping was thirty days in the snakes, so Tom's sentence was light.

24. *Graham Guardian,* November 26, 1926; Chambers to Board of Pardons and Paroles, November 24, 1926, Hunt papers, ASLAPR. Initially, the subpoenas, warrants, instructions to the jury, and even the sentencing documents went missing from the case file. Only after repeated requests by attorneys, authors, and state investigators were the court documents discovered somewhere in the Greenlee County Superior Court office, but the trial transcripts were never located.

25. *Graham Guardian,* November 24 & 26, 1926; Chambers to Board of Pardons and Paroles, November 24, 1926, Hunt papers, ASLAPR; *Arizona Daily Star,* April 27, 1960; *Phoenix Gazette,* December 20, 1966.

26. April 10, 1931 petition signed by thirteen guards and twenty-eight prisoners, A. G. Walker to Arthur La Prade, October 4, 1934, David Harlin to John L. Sullivan, March 8, 1935, David L. Harlin to Board of Pardons and Paroles, telegram, June 12, 1935; Harlin to Tom Power, March 1, 1939, both in Closed Files 5173-4, ADOC, ASLAPR; "The Big House on the Gila, written by an Ex-Convict—Centering Around Life and Conditions Inside the Walls of the Arizona State Prison at Florence, Arizona" (n.p., 1933), 58, ASLAPR; Ira F. Walker to Dedera, February 27, 1961, PBRN, ASU.

27. Roberts, "'The Powers Boys,'" 302; George F. Senner to Barry Petersen, March 30, 1932, John B. Hart to Board of Pardons and Paroles, November 30, 1931, William Delbridge to Lin B. Orme, Closed Files 5173-4, ADOC, ASLAPR.

28. Roberts, "'The Powers Boys,'" 149–51, 271–72; Milford W. Kempton to Paul Fannin, April 19, 1960, Governor Paul J. Fannin papers, 1959–1965, Pardons and Parole File, ASLAPR; William G. Montierth to Dedera, November 11, 1958, D. McBride to Pulliam, November 17, 1958, PBRN, ASU; McBride, *The Evaders,* 5–6.

29. Ball, *Ambush at Bloody Run,* 205–6; Bob Thomas, *Arizona Republic,* January 26, 1969; Rob Brotherton, *Suspicious Minds: Why We Believe Conspiracy Theories* (New York: Bloomsbury Sigma, 2015), 13; Slotkin, *Fatal Environment,* 407–8.

30. McBride, *The Evaders,* 73. Jay Murdock's stories are the foundation of Ryder Ridgway's writings, found in articles for the *Eastern Arizona Courier* and published in Glenn Burgess, ed., *Mt. Graham Profiles,* vol. 1, *Ryder Ridgway Collection* (Safford, AZ: Graham County Historical Society, 1978) and in Ridgway's *The Power Family of Graham County.*

31. Jay Murdock to Tom and John Power, September 7, 1931, Closed Files 5173-4, ADOC, ASLAPR; McBride, *The Evaders,* 74–79.

32. Moore, *Enter Without Knocking,* 54; *Tombstone Prospector,* August 12, 1918; *Copper Era,* August 16, 1918; Interview with Thomas Jefferson Power, Power Brothers papers,

AHS; John Power to Fred O. Wilson, October 27, 1949, Closed File 5173, ADOC, ASLAPR.

33. Roberts, "'The Powers Boys,'" 268, 273, 274, 281, 288–89; John Power to F. O. Wilson, October 27, 1949, Lydia Armstrong to Ernest McFarland, September 27, 1957, Closed Files 5173-4, ADOC, ASLAPR; Claridge, *Klondyke*, 167; Manuscript, Cavanaugh Collection; Elizabeth Lambert Wood to Dedera, November 16, 1958, PBRN, ASU; Howard Morgan interview, *Power's War* transcripts; Elliott West, *The Saloon on the Rocky Mountain Mining Frontier* (Lincoln: University of Nebraska Press, 1979), 19. If Allen testified about the liquor at the trial, reporters failed to mention it. Nor did he mention finding liquor bottles on the trail when he testified at the inquest. Many people later said they told the lawmen beforehand not to go up to the Power cabin without an escort by a local, including Wiley Morgan and Lupe Salazar. However, Frank Haynes's testimony never indicated that the posse members spoke to anyone in Klondyke before arriving at the Upchurch ranch after dark the night before the shootout.

34. McBride, *The Evaders*, 53; Shute, "Tragedy of the Grahams," 36; Ridgway, *Power Family*, 60.

35. Faires to Dedera, November 18, 1958, PBRN, ASU; Robin Willett, email to author, February 3, 2014.

36. Ridgway, *Power Family*, 118; Roberts, "'The Powers Boys,'" 273, 306, 319; Power, *Shoot-Out at Dawn*, 92. The 1920 census shows Fielder was still practicing law and had a mortgage on his home, despite Tom Power's contention he paid off his mortgage with the bribe.

37. Slotkin, *Fatal Environment*, 16; Roberts, "'The Powers Boys,'" 1–3; Junietta Claridge, "We Tried to Stay Refined: Pioneering on the Mineral Strip," *Journal of Arizona History* 16, no. 4 (Winter 1975): 407–9, 425; Manuscript, Cavanaugh Collection.

38. Work, *Darkest Before Dawn*, 180–81; Thomas E. Johnson to E. D. McBryde, David Roer, and Mickey Williams, September 14, 1987, Power cabin restoration file, Power Brothers papers, AHS; Shute, "Tragedy of the Grahams," 36; *Copper Era*, May 17, 1918; Statement of W. R. Chambers, Prisoner Records 5173-4, ADOC, ASLAPR.

39. Ridgway, *Power Family*, 44–45; Wolfe, *Power, Passion*, 38; Power, *Shoot-Out at Dawn*, 21; R. F. McBride to Dillon, June 21, 1917, U.S. Marshals' records, AHS.

40. Willeford, "Wiley Marion Morgan," 33; Moore, *Enter Without Knocking*, 48, 128.

41. Moore, *Enter Without Knocking*, 98–99; *Arizona Republic*, December 29, 1939.

42. *Arizona Republic*, December 29, 1939, April 17, 1940; *Graham Guardian*, December 29, 1939; Moore, *Enter Without Knocking*, 55, 98–99, 128; Shute, "Tragedy of the Grahams," 36; U.S. Customs Patrol Agent Mayberry to Governor Osborn, February 21, 1940, Closed Files 5173-4, Prisoner Records 5172-4, ADOC, ASLAPR.

CHAPTER 14

1. John Marr, "The Long Life and Quiet Death of True Detective Magazine," August 19, 2015, http://gizmodo.com/the-long-life-and-quiet-death-of-true-detective-magazin-1725094095 (accessed July 18, 2017); Dedera interview, June 18, 2015.

2. Chester Channing, "Kinsmen of Disaster," *True Detective* 35 (March 1941): 14–16, 95; Joe H. Graham, "Bloody Trail of the Sharp Shooting Draft Dodgers," *Real Detective* (March 1941): 50.

3. T. Power to Walter Hofmann, September 6, 1941, Lin B. Orme to Walter Hofmann, August 4, 1941, J. Power to Joseph Conway, June 23, 1941, J. Power to D. C. Mangum, January 11, 1943, petition by J. Power, October 1, 1951, Closed Files 5173-4, ADOC, ASLAPR; Dedera interview, June 18, 2015.

4. Prisoner Records 5172-4, ADOC, ASLAPR; *Arizona Republic,* April 22, 1960; *Tucson Daily Citizen,* April 28, 1960.

5. J. Power to F. O. Wilson, October 27, 1949, January 21, December 19, 1951, Closed Files 5173-4, ADOC, ASLAPR; *Graham Guardian*, November 21, 1952.

6. Petition protesting release, December 10, 12, 1952, Chester J. Peterson to Hofmann, November 26, 1952, Benjamin Blake to Howard Pyle, December 8, 1952, Oscar C. Cole to Hofmann, November 28, 1952, J. F. Wootan to Pyle, December 11, 1952, Earl D. Hawthorne to Pyle, December 12, 1952, Elmo Hughes to Hofmann, December 15, 1952, Wilford R. Richardson to Board of Pardons and Paroles, December 15, 1951, Closed Files 5173-4, ADOC, ASLAPR.

7. *Graham Guardian,* November 21, December 16 & 19, 1952; Mrs. P. E. Morgan to McFarland, February 15, 1955, Closed Files 5173-4, ADOC, ASLAPR.

8. Clairborne Nuckolls, *Arizona Republic,* December 17, 1952; Dedera, "Coffee Break," *Arizona Republic,* November 11, 1958; Bob Wood, "Hate Simmers," *Phoenix Gazette,* PBRN, ASU.

9. Mark Fenster, *Conspiracy Theories: Secrecy and Power in American Culture* (Minneapolis: University of Minnesota Press 1999), 3; *Tucson Citizen,* December 16, 1952; Nuckolls, *Arizona Republic,* December 17, 1952.

10. McBride, *The Evaders,* 111; Spencer W. Kimball, *The Miracle of Forgiveness* (Salt Lake City: Deseret Book Co., 1969), 291–93.

11. Kimball, *The Miracle of Forgiveness,* 289–93; Catherine H. Ellis, email to author, May 1, 2014.

12. Power, *Shoot-Out at Dawn,* 112; Prisoner Record 5172, ADOC, ASLAPR; Tom Sisson, Application for Headstones for U.S. Military Veterans, NARA.

13. Brotherton, *Suspicious Minds,* 17, 19; E. L. Wood to Dedera, November 16, 1958, PBRN, ASU; Wood, *Tragedy of the Powers Mine,* 17–18, 46, 51.

14. Mrs. P. E. Morgan to McFarland, February 15, 1955, Closed Files 5173-4, ADOC, ASLAPR; Roberts, "'The Powers Boys,'" 272–73.

15. Claridge, "We Tried to Stay Refined," 424–25; Zola Claridge to Paul Fannin, April 17, 1960, Fannin papers, Pardons and Parole File, ASLAPR; Glen L. Randall to Harriet Sweeting, May 18, 1957, *AZ v. Sisson*; Dedera interview, June 18, 2015.

16. Dedera interview, January 16, 2013.

17. Ibid.

18. Ibid.; Richard H. Hertzberg to Hofmann, January 15, 1960, Closed Files 5173-4, ADOC, ASLAPR.

19. Dedera interviews, January 16, 2013, June 18, 2015.

20. Dedera, "Coffee Break," *Arizona Republic,* November 10, 11, 1958.

21. Ibid., November 13 & 14, 1958.

22. Dedera to D. McBride, November 19, 1958, PBRN, ASU; Power, *Shoot-Out at Dawn,* 23; Roberts, "'The Powers Boys,'" 294, 300, 338, 342.

23. "The Power Boys," Thanksgiving 1958, Noble, ASLAPR.

24. WWI Draft Card for David Lee Solomon, Pima County, Arizona, NARA; Dedera to D. McBride, November 19, 1958, PBRN, ASU; Dedera "Coffee Break," *Arizona Republic,* April 10, 1960; Power, *Shoot-Out at Dawn,* 23; Roberts, "'The Powers Boys,'" 342–43.

25. Dedera to D. McBride, November 19, 1958, PBRN, ASU; Roberts, "'The Powers Boys,'" 316, 371; Ridgway, *Power Family,* 52.

26. Power, *Shoot-Out at Dawn,* 118; Interview with Thomas Jefferson Power, Power Brothers Papers, AHS.

27. Inquest of McBride, 54; Wootan Probate, ASLAPR.

28. Power, *Shoot-Out at Dawn,* 84, 89–91; Millie Wootan Barnes interview. After Laura Wootan died, her five orphaned children were separated and sent to be raised by relatives.

29. Shepard to Dedera, April 11, 1957, D. McBride to Pulliam, November 17, 1958, PBRN, ASU.

30. Dedera interview, January 16, 2013; Roberts, "'The Powers Boys,'" 149–51.

31. Dedera interview, June 18, 2015; Dedera to D. McBride, November 19, 1958, PBRN, ASU.

32. "The Power Boys," Thanksgiving 1958, Noble; Dedera interview, June 18, 2015.

33. RE: Tom and John Power, January 24, 1959, Noble, ASLAPR; Marguerite Buchanan to Fannin, July 10, 1959, Closed Files 5173-4, ADOC, ASLAPR; Lila Solomon Wootan to Fannin, April 5, 1960, Fannin Papers, Pardons and Parole File, ASLAPR.

34. Report of Albert Whipple, Wade Church to Alva Weaver, August 21, November 23, 1959, Weaver to Hofmann, November 23, 1959, Thomas J. Power to Weaver, November 24, 1959, Closed Files 5173-4, ADOC, ASLAPR; Wade Church obituary, *Arizona Republic,* December 11, 2002.

35. Dedera, "Coffee Break," *Arizona Republic,* March 23, 31,1960. For examples of those suspicions, see, Ball, *Ambush at Bloody Run,* 205–6, 216–17; Roger D. Launius and John E. Hallwas, *Cultures in Conflict: A Documentary History of the Mormon War in Illinois* (Logan: Utah State University Press, 1995), 2; Roberts, "'The Powers Boys,'" 271–72.

36. Roberts, "'The Powers Boys,'" 103, 271–72, 310, 315; Lemuel P. Mathews to Dedera, December 10, 1958, PBRN, ASU; Della Meadows interview, AHS.

37. Dedera, "Coffee Break," *Arizona Republic,* March 31, 1960; Roberts, "'The Powers Boys,'" 271–72, 279.

38. Dedera interviews, January 16, 2013, June 18, 2015; Dedera to D. McBride, November 19, 1958, PBRN, ASU.

39. Bob Wood, "Two in Notorious Gun Fight," *Tucson Daily Citizen,* April 14, 1960.

40. Z. Claridge to Fannin, April 17, 1960, Closed Files 5173-4, ADOC, ASLAPR; Millie Wootan Barnes interview; Cavanaugh hearing notes, Cavanaugh Collection.

41. Dedera, "Parole Board Says Commute Sentence," *Arizona Republic,* April 21, 1960; Dedera, "Coffee Break," *Arizona Republic,* April 24, 1960; Cavanaugh hearing notes, PBRN, ASU; *Arizona Daily Star,* April 22, 1960.
42. Cavanaugh hearing notes, PBRN, ASU; *Arizona Daily Star,* April 22, 1960.
43. Dedera interview, January 16, 2013; *Tucson Citizen,* April 21, 1960; *Phoenix Gazette,* April 21, 1960.
44. *Tucson Citizen,* April 21, 1960; *Phoenix Gazette,* April 21, 1960.
45. Ibid.; Cavanaugh hearing notes, Cavanaugh Collection.
46. Cavanaugh hearing notes, Cavanaugh Collection; *Arizona Republic,* April 22 & 24, 1960; *Tucson Citizen,* April 21, 1960; *Graham Guardian,* April 22, 1960. The San Francisco Peaks are the highest mountain range in Arizona, towering around 12,000 feet above nearby Lake Mary in Flagstaff.
47. Dedera to Cavanaugh, May 27, 1976, Orien W. Fifer to Dedera, November 23, 1958, PBRN, ASU.

CHAPTER 15

1. *Arizona Daily Star,* April 22 & 28, 1960; T. Power to Dedera, June 30, 1960, PBRN, ASU.
2. Frank Eyman to Hofmann, December 7, 1959, Closed Files, 5173-4, ADOC, ASLAPR; *Arizona Daily Star,* April 28, 1960; Dedera to Cavanaugh, August 17, 1976, Dedera Collection, ASU; T. Power to Dedera, July 1, 1961, PBRN, ASU; Dedera interview, June 18, 2015.
3. Dedera, "Coffee Break," June 5, 1962, *Arizona Republic;* T. Power to Dedera, May 24, 1960, PBRN, ASU; E. W. Duhame to Robert W. Pickrell, December 19, 1960, Closed Files 5173-4, ADOC, ASLAPR.
4. Power, *Shoot-Out at Dawn,* 154; Dedera interview, June 18, 2015; "Before I Die," Noble.
5. Dedera, "Coffee Break," *Arizona Republic,* January 31, 1968; J. Power to Wade Church, May 18, 1960, ADOC, ASLAPR; *Arizona Daily Star,* May 24 1960; T. Power to Dedera, April 28, 1960, PBRN, ASU; Duhame to Pickrell, December 29, 1960, Marcella Maize to Pickrell, December 29, 1960, Closed Files 5173-4, ADOC, ASLAPR; *Arizona Daily Star,* December 20, 1964, November 23, 1975; Grant County Deeds of Mines, book 141, p. 20, GCC; Interview with Thomas Jefferson Power, Power Brothers papers, AHS; *Tombstone Prospector,* August 12, 1918; Simons, *Geology of the Klondyke Quadrangle,* 461; Wilson, *Islands in the Desert,* 170–72; "Guns and Gold: History of the Galiuro Wilderness," ASU; John C. Lacy, email to author, May 1, 2013; Public Lands Visitor Center, "Galiuro Wilderness"; John Power was interviewed by the Forest Service ranger at Willcox in 1974, when the NPS was assessing the nomination of the cabin to the NRHP, and he verified the lack of gold production from the mine. "Mr. Power stated their family never shipped any ore from their Abandoned Claims and never realized any income from these claims."
6. "Pardon Board Denies Bid," *Arizona Republic,* January 27, 1968; complete discharge from parole, May 9, 1963, Closed Files 5173-4, ADOC, ASLAPR; *Arizona Republic,* May 16, 1963: Dedera, *Arizona Republic,* June 5, 1962.

7. Prisoner Records 5173-4, ADOC, ASLAPR; see, for example, Marguerite Buchanan, letter to editor, *Arizona Republic,* February 3, 1968.

8. *Arizona Republic,* January 26, 1969.

9. "Pardoning of the Power Brothers," Dedera Collection, Box 85, Folder 2, ASU.

10. Interview with Thomas Jefferson Power, Power Brother papers, AHS; *Arizona Republic,* January 26, 1969.

11. Roberts, "'The Powers Boys,'" 3, 100, 105, 152–53.

12. Power, *Shoot-Out at Dawn,* 118; McBride, *The Evaders,* 5, 66-67.

13. McClement, "The Bullet that Has Never Stopped Burning," 58; Geraldine McClung, "Hate Dies Hard," *Front Page Detective* (September 1960): 34; Marguerite Noble, *Filaree: A Novel of an American Life* (Albuquerque: University of New Mexico Press, 1979), 85–86.

14. Slaughter, *The Whiskey Rebellion,* 25–26, 72; Interview with Thomas Jefferson Power, Power Brothers papers, AHS; Eduardo Obregón Pagán interview, *Power's War* transcripts.

15. *Tombstone Epitaph,* March 17, 1918.

16. T. Edward Scarborough to State Board of Pardons and Paroles, February 16, 1932, Closed Files 5173-4, ADOC, ASLAPR.

17. Wolfe, *Power, Passion,* 163; Power, *Shoot-Out at Dawn,* 166, 168; September 12, 1970, newspaper clipping, Cavanaugh Collection.

18. Manuscript, Cavanaugh Collection; *Tucson Daily Citizen,* September 12, 1970; *Eastern Arizona Courier,* September 16, 1970; Roberts, "'The Powers Boys,'" 146; *Arizona Daily Star,* November 23, 1975.

19. Roberts, "'The Powers Boys,'" 316, 387; *Arizona Daily Star,* December 20, 1964.

20. Williams, "The Power Brothers' Story," 19; Interview with Thomas Jefferson Power, Power Brothers papers, AHS.

21. U.S. Census, 1940: Dwyer, Grant, New Mexico; Social Security Administration records for Charles S. Power, 525-22-7849; Roberts, "'The Powers Boys,'" 335; Nancy Hough, "Charles Samuel 'Charley' Power," Find a Grave, August 21, 2010, http://findagrave.com/cgi-bin/fg.cgi?page=gr&GSln=power&GSfn=charles&GSiman=1&GScid=1965360&GRid=23604949& (accessed November 19, 2013). John Power said his brother Charley lost a hand in a drilling accident while in Texas, but if so, he failed to file for disability with the Social Security Administration.

22. *Arizona Daily Star,* November 23, 1975.

23. Cavanaugh to Dedera, December 9, 1975, introduction written by Dedera, PBRN, ASU.

24. Manuscript, Cavanaugh Collection.

25. Ibid.

26. Newspaper clippings, n. d., Funeral Program for John Power, Cavanaugh Collection.

27. *Copper Era,* March 15, 1918; Colleen Cavanaugh DeRose, email to author, July 6, 2016.

28. Hadley, *Environmental Change,* 166, 300.

29. Claridge, *Klondyke,* 73; The Wilderness Act, Public Law 88-577 (16 U.S.C. 1121-36) September 3, 1964, Section 2(c). Additional acres were added later, and today the Galiuro Wilderness consists of approximately ninety thousand acres.

30. Power cabin nomination form. The two cabins standing today at Power Garden were built after the Power family left.

31. Manuscript, Cavanaugh Collection; Ridgway, "'The Powers Boys,'" 302.

32. Power cabin nomination form.

SELECTED BIBLIOGRAPHY

PRIMARY SOURCES

Archival and Manuscript Collections

Arizona Collection, Hayden Library, Arizona State University Libraries, Tempe
    Don Dedera Papers, 1955–2008
    Power Brothers Research Notebook
    "Guns and Gold: History of the Galiuro Wilderness"
Arizona Historical Society, Tucson
    Della Meadows Interview
    Ming Family Papers
    Power Brothers Papers, 1918–1990
    William R. Ridgway Interview
    Christina Rabe Seger, "The Economics of Vice: Prohibition Along the Mexico-Arizona Border, 1915–1933"
    United States Marshals' Records for the District of Arizona, 1892–1927
    Bob Wootan, T. K. Wootan, and Joe Wootan Interview
    J. Frank Wootan Interview
Arizona State Library, Phoenix
    Arizona Laws (1885)
    "Board of Pardons and Paroles, State of Arizona, Rules and Regulations of the Board" (August 1933)
Arizona State Library, Archives and Public Records, History and Archives Division, Phoenix
    Arizona State Council of Defense Records, 1916–1938
    Arizona Livestock Sanitary Board Minutes, Volume 1, 1912-1934
    Arizona Territorial and State Supreme Court Records
    "The Big House on the Gila, written by an Ex-Convict—Centering Around Life and Conditions Inside the Walls of the Arizona State Prison at Florence, Arizona," 1933

Cochise County
    Bowie Justice Court Records
    Deeds of Mines
    Mortgages
    Superior Court Records
    Willcox School Census
Department of Corrections Records, 1875–2008
Council of Defense Records, 1916–1938
Governor Paul J. Fannin Papers, 1959–1965
Graham County
    Great Register of Electors (1910–1918)
    Index to Mines
    Probate Cases
    Superior Court Records
Greenlee County Superior Court Records
Governor George W. P. Hunt Papers, 1859–1934
Maricopa County Superior Court Records
Marguerite Noble Collection, Box 5, Folder 131, "Power Brothers"
Pima County Superior Court Records
Central Arizona College, Aravaipa
    "The Heritage Writing Project: The Pioneer People and Their Land, Here between
        the Santa Catalina and Galiuro Mountains, Arizona," vol. 3, no. 1, 1988
Gila County (Arizona) Historical Society, Globe
    Justice Court Registers of Actions
Graham County (Arizona) Recorder's Office, Safford
    Bills of Sales
    Deeds to Chattel Mortgages
    Deeds of Mines
    Location of Mines
    Miscellaneous Deeds
    Proof of Labor
    Real Estate Deeds
    Record of Deeds
    Record of Mines
    U. I. Paxton's Ledger Book
Grant County (New Mexico) Clerk, Silver City
    Deeds of Chattel Mortgages
    Deeds of Mines
    Miscellaneous Deeds
    Probate Records
    Quit Claim Deeds
    Records of Deeds

Greenlee County (Arizona) Superior Court Clerk, Clifton
    Criminal Register of Action
New Mexico State Record Center and Archives, Santa Fe
    Eddy County District Court Records
    Grant County District Court Records
Texas State Library and Archives Commission, Austin
    Gillespie County
        Justice Court Dockets
        Deed Records
    Llano County
        Tax Rolls
        Deed Records
        Probate Minutes
    Texas General Land Office Patents

United States Government Collections

National Archives and Records Administration, College Park, MD
    Records of the Department of Interior, Bureau of Land Management, General
        Land Office Records, RG49, available at glorecords.blm.gov
    Records of the Department of Justice, RG 60
        General Records
        FBI Reports, Old German Files, available at Fold3.com
    Records of the War Department, Military Intelligence Division, 1918–1947, RG 165
National Archives and Records Administration, Riverside, CA
    Records of the Forest Service, Grazing Permits, Graham County, Arizona, RG 95
    Records of the Office of the Provost Marshal General, Selective Service System
        Deserter and Delinquent Records, Graham County, Arizona, RG 163
National Archives and Records Administration, Washington, DC
    Records of the Office of the Adjutant General, RG 94
    Records of the Bureau of the Census, 1790–1940, RG 29, available at FamilySearch.org
    Records of the Office of the Quartermaster General, RG 92
    Records of the Social Security Administration, RG 47
    World War I Selective Service System Draft Registration Cards, 1917–1918, M1509,
        available at Ancestry.com
United States Forest Service, Tucson
    Crook National Forest Records, Homestead Application for Charles S. Power

Unpublished Sources Privately Held

Wade Cavanaugh Collection, Colleen DeRose
Power's War Transcripts, Cameron Trejo Films LLC, 2014
William Ryder Ridgway Collection, Maxine Bean
Gladys Stewart, as told to Leva Kempton, "The McBride Story—'Clara and Frank,'"
    and "The McBride Story—'My Father was the Sheriff,'" McBride Family Collection

SECONDARY SOURCES

Articles, Books, Theses, and Dissertations

"The Admissibility of Dying Declaration." *Fordham Law Review* 38, no. 3 (1970): 509–10.

Alexander, Bob. *Desert Desperadoes: The Banditti of Southwestern New Mexico*. Silver City, NM: Gila Books, 2006.

———. *Sheriff Harvey Whitehill: Silver City Stalwart*. Silver City, NM: High-Lonesome Books, 2005.

Alvey, R. Gerald. *Kentucky Bluegrass Country*. Jackson: University Press of Mississippi, 1992.

Bagley, Will. *Blood of the Prophets: Brigham Young and the Massacre of Mountain Meadows*. Norman: University of Oklahoma Press, 2002.

Bailey, Lynn R. *The "Unwashed Crowd": Stockmen and Ranches of the San Simon and Sulphur Spring Valleys, Arizona Territory, 1878–1900*. Tucson: Westernlore Press, 2014.

Bailey, Lynn R., and Don Chaput. *Cochise County Stalwarts: A Who's Who of the Territorial Years*, vol. 2. Tucson: Westernlore Press, 2000.

Ball, Larry D. *Ambush at Bloody Run: The Wham Paymaster Robbery of 1889*. Tucson: Arizona Historical Society, 2000.

———. *Desert Lawmen: The High Sheriffs of New Mexico and Arizona, 1846–1912*. Albuquerque: University of New Mexico Press, 1992.

———. *Tom Horn in Life and Legend*. Norman: University of Oklahoma Press, 2014.

———. *The United States Marshals of New Mexico and Arizona Territories, 1846–1912*. Albuquerque: University of New Mexico Press, 1978.

Barry, Laura. *Willcox: The First 100 Years*. Willcox, AZ: Arizona Range News, 1980.

Baulch, Joe. "The Dogs of War Unleashed: The Devil Concealed in Men Unchained." *West Texas Historical Association Yearbook* 73 (n. d.): 126–41.

Benton-Cohen, Katherine. *Borderline Americans: Racial Division and Labor War in the Arizona Borderlands*. Cambridge: Harvard University Press, 2009.

Berman, David R. *George Hunt: Arizona's Crusading Seven-Term Governor*. Tucson: University of Arizona Press, 2015.

———. *Radicalism in the Mountain West, 1890–1920*. Boulder: University Press of Colorado, 2007.

Bieter, John P., Jr. *Showdown in the Big Quiet: Land, Myth, and Government in the American West*. Lubbock: Texas Tech University Press, 2015.

Blackstone, William. *Commentaries on the Laws of England*. Edited by J. W. Ehrlich. San Carlos, CA: Nourse, 1959.

Blake, William P. "The Geology of the Galiuro Mountains, Arizona, and of the Gold-Bearing Ledge Known as Gold Mountain." *Engineering and Mining Journal* 73 (April 1902): 546–47.

Bolton, Charles S. *Arkansas, 1800–1860: Remote and Restless*. Fayetteville: University of Arkansas Press, 1998.

Breen, William J. *Uncle Sam at Home: Civilian Mobilization, Wartime Federalism, and the Council of National Defense, 1917–1919*. Westport, CT: Greenwood Press, 1984.

Brotherton, Rob. *Suspicious Minds: Why We Believe Conspiracy Theories.* New York: Bloomsbury Sigma, 2015.

Brown, Richard Maxwell. *No Duty to Retreat: Violence and Values in American History and Society.* New York: Oxford University Press, 1992.

———. "Western Violence: Structure, Values, Myth." *Western Historical Quarterly* 24, no. 1 (February 1993): 4–20.

Buenger, Walter L. *Secession and the Union in Texas.* Austin: University of Texas Press, 1984.

Burgess, Glenn, ed. *Mt. Graham Profiles.* Vol. 1 of *Ryder Ridgway Collection.* Safford, AZ: Graham County Historical Society, 1978.

Burton, Jeffrey. *The Deadliest Outlaws: The Ketchum Gang and the Wild Bunch.* Denton: University of North Texas Press, 2009.

Campa, Arthur L. "Folklore and History." *Western Folklore* 24, no. 1 (January 1965): 1–5.

Campbell, Ida Foster, and Alice Foster Hill. *Triumph and Tragedy: A History of Thomas Lyons and the LCs.* Silver City, NM: High-Lonesome Books, 2003.

Cannon, John Q. *The Life of Christopher Layton.* Salt Lake City: Deseret News Press, 1911.

Carlson, Paul H., ed. *The Cowboy Way: An Exploration of History and Culture.* Lubbock: Texas Tech University Press, 2000.

Caro, Robert. *The Years of Lyndon Johnson.* Vol. 1, *The Path to Power.* New York: Alfred A. Knopf, 1982.

Cathcart, George L. "Religious Belief as a Cultural Value: Mormon Cattle Ranchers in Arizona's Little Colorado River Valley." Master's thesis, Arizona State University, 1995.

Cattle Sanitary Board of New Mexico. *Brand Book of the Territory of New Mexico.* Las Vegas, NM: Cattle Sanitary Board of New Mexico 1907.

Chamberlain, Kathleen P. *In the Shadow of Billy the Kid: Susan McSween and the Lincoln County War.* Albuquerque: University of New Mexico Press, 2013.

Chambers, John Whiteclay. *To Raise an Army: The Draft Comes to Modern America.* New York: The Free Press, 1987.

Channing, Chester. "Kinsmen of Disaster." *True Detective* 35 (March 1941): 14–19, 95–96.

Claridge, Eleanor. *Klondyke and the Aravaipa Canyon.* Safford, AZ: D & M/Kopy Kat Printing, 1989.

Claridge, Junietta. "We Tried to Stay Refined: Pioneering in the Mineral Strip." *Journal of Arizona History* 16, no. 4 (Winter 1975): 405–26.

Clements, Hendrick A. *The Presidency of Woodrow Wilson.* Lawrence: University of Kansas Press, 1992

Cobb, Thomas. *With Blood in Their Eyes.* Tucson: University of Arizona Press, 2012.

Collins, Lewis. *History of Kentucky.* Covington, KY: Collins & Co., 1874.

Colwell-Chanthaphonh, Chip. *Massacre at Camp Grant: Forgetting and Remembering Apache History.* Tucson: University of Arizona Press, 2007.

Connors, Jo, comp. *Who's Who in Arizona.* Tucson: Press of the Arizona Daily Star, 1913.

Cottrell, Robert C. *Roger Nash Baldwin and the American Civil Liberties Union.* New York: Columbia University Press, 2000.

Creasey, S. C., J. E. Jinks, F. E. Williams, and H. C. Meeves. "Mineral Resources of the Galiuro Wilderness and Contiguous Further Planning Areas, Arizona." In *United*

States Geological Survey Bulletin 1490. Washington, DC: Government Printing Office, 1981.

Dobie, J. Frank. "The First Cattle in Texas and the Southwest Progenitors of the Long-horns." *Southwestern Historical Quarterly* 42 (January 1939): 171–97.

Donalson, Daniel G. *Espionage and Sedition Acts of World War I: Using Wartime Loyalty Laws for Revenge and Profit.* El Paso: LFB Scholarly Publishing LLC, 2012.

Eastern Arizona Museum & Historical Society. *Pioneer Town: Pima Centennial History.* Pima: Eastern Arizona Museum & Historical Society Inc. of Graham Co., 1979.

Ebel, Wilfred L. "The Amnesty Issue: A Historical Perspective." *Parameters: The Journal of the US Army War College* 4, no. 1 (1974): 67–77.

Elliott, Claude. "Union Sentiment in Texas, 1861–1865." *Southwestern Historical Quarterly* 50 (April 1947): 449–77.

Elson, Wolfgang E. *Kimball Mining District of Hidalgo County.* Albuquerque: University of New Mexico Press, 1965.

Eppinga, Jane. *Arizona Sheriffs: Badges and Bad Men.* Tucson: Rio Nuevo, 2006.

Faragher, John Mack. *Women and Men on the Overland Trail.* New Haven: Yale University Press, 1979.

Fischer, David Hackett. *Albion's Seed: Four British Folkways in America.* New York: Oxford University Press, 1989.

Fisher, O. C. *It Occurred in Kimble.* Houston: Anson Jones Press, 1937.

Flynn, George Q. *Conscription and Democracy: France, Great Britain and the United States.* Westport, CT: Greenwood Press, 2001.

Gibbs, Christopher C. *The Great Silent Majority: Missouri's Resistance to World War I.* Columbia: University of Missouri Press, 1988.

Gibson, A. M. *The Life and Death of Colonel Albert Jennings Fountain.* Norman: University of Oklahoma Press, 1965.

Giffin, Frederick C. *Six Who Protested: Radical Opposition to the First World War.* Port Washington, NM: Kennikat Press, 1977.

Graham, Joe H. "Bloody Trail of the Sharp Shooting Draft Dodgers." *Real Detective* (March 1941): 50–55, 92–94.

Griffin, Larry J. and Peggy G. Hargis, eds. *Social Class.* Vol. 20 of *The New Encyclopedia of Southern Culture.* Charlotte: University of North Carolina Press, 2012.

Gutmann, Myron P. and Kenneth H. Fliess. "The Determinants of Early Fertility Decline in Texas." *Demography* 30 (August 1993): 443–57.

Guy, Donna. "The Economics of Widowhood in Arizona, 1880–1940." In *On Their Own: Widows and Widowhood in the American Southwest, 1848–1939,* edited by Arlene Scadron. Urbana: University of Illinois Press, 1988.

Haberski, Raymond, Jr. *God and War: American Civil Religion since 1945.* New Brunswick, NJ: Rutgers Univeristy Press, 2012.

Haby, Margaret. "Wiley Marion Morgan" and "The Morgan Case." In *Arizona National Ranch Histories of Living Pioneer Stockmen,* vol. 9, compiled and edited by Betty Accomazzo. Phoenix: Arizona National Livestock Show, Inc., 1987.

Hadley, Diana, Peter Warshall, and Don Bufkin. *Environmental Change in Aravaipa, 1870–1970: An Ethnoecological Survey.* Cultural Resource Series Monograph No. 7. Phoenix: Bureau of Land Management, 1991.

Henderson, David R. "From 'Porous' to 'Ruthless' Conscription, 1776–1917." *Independent Review* 14, no. 4 (Spring 2010): 587–98.

Herman, Daniel J. *Hell on the Range: A Story of Honor, Conscience, and the American West.* New Haven: Yale University Press, 2010.

Hine, Robert V. and John Mack Faragher. *Frontiers: A Short History of the American West.* New Haven: Yale University Press, 2007.

History of Benton, Washington, Carroll, Madison, Crawford, Franklin, and Sebastian Counties, Arkansas. Chicago: Goodspeed Publishing, 1889.

Johnson, David. *Mason County "Hoo Doo" War, 1874–1902.* Denton: University of North Texas Press, 2006.

Jorgensen, Lynne Watkins. "Begging to Be in the Battle: A Mormon Boy in World War I." *Journal of Mormon History* 29, no. 1 (Spring 2003): 107–34.

Keith, Jeanette. *Rich Man's War, Poor Man's Fight: Race, Class, and Power in the Rural South during the First World War.* Chapel Hill: University of North Carolina Press, 2004.

Keleher, William A. *The Fabulous Frontier: Twelve New Mexico Items.* Revised ed. Albuquerque: University of New Mexico Press, 1962.

Kelly, George H., comp. *Legislative History, Arizona 1864–1912.* Phoenix: Manufacturing Stationers, 1926.

Kimball, Spencer W. *The Miracle of Forgiveness.* Salt Lake City: Deseret Book Company, 1969.

Kohn, Stephen M. *Jailed for Peace: The History of American Draft Law Violators, 1658–1984.* Westport, CT: Greenwood Press, 1986.

Kornweibel, Theodore. *Investigate Everything: Federal Efforts to Compel Black Loyalty During World War I.* Bloomington: Indiana University Press, 2002.

Larson, Robert W. *New Mexico Populism: A Study of Radical Protest in a Western Territory.* Boulder: Colorado Associated University Press, 1974.

Launius, Roger D. and John E. Hallwas. *Cultures in Conflict: A Documentary History of the Mormon War in Illinois.* Logan: Utah State University Press, 1995.

Lavender, David. *The Southwest.* Albuquerque: University of New Mexico Press, 1980.

Luebke, Frederick C. *Bonds of Loyalty: German Americans and World War I.* DeKalb: Northern Illinois University Press, 1974.

Lutrell, Estelle. *Newspapers and Periodicals of Arizona, 1859–1911.* Tucson: University of Arizona Press, 1950.

Lyman, Edward Leo. "Elimination of the Mormon Issue from Arizona Politics, 1889–1894." *Arizona and the West* 24, no. 3 (Autumn 1982): 205–28.

Lynn, Alvin R., and J. Brett Cruze. *Kit Carson and the First Battle of Adobe Walls: A Tale of Two Journeys.* Lubbock: Texas Tech University Press, 2014.

Lyon, William H. *Those Old Yellow Dog Days: Frontier Journalism in Arizona, 1859–1912.* Tucson: Arizona Historical Society, 1994.

Mangelsdorf, Karen Underhill. "The Beveridge Visit to Arizona in 1902." *Journal of Arizona History* 28, no. 3 (Autumn 1987): 243–60.

Mason, Patrick Q. *The Mormon Menace: Violence and Anti-Mormonism in the Postbellum South*. New York: Oxford University Press, 2011.

Mason, Patrick Q., J. David Pulsipher, and Richard L. Bushman, eds. *War & Peace in Our Time: Mormon Perspectives*. Salt Lake City: Greg Kofford Books, 2012.

McBride, Darvil B. *The Evaders or Wilderness Shoot-Out: The Story of the Power Affair*. Pasadena: Pacific Book & Printing, 1984.

McCauley, Laverne and Terrell T. Shelley. *Pioneer Families of Grant County, New Mexico: A History of the Hooker-Shelley Families and the 916 Ranch*. Baltimore: Gateway Press Inc., 1987.

McClement, Fred. "The Bullet That Has Never Stopped Burning." *Cavalier* (August 1961): 26–29, 55–58.

McClintock, James H. *Mormon Settlement in Arizona: A Record of Peaceful Conquest of the Desert*. Tucson: University of Arizona Press, 1985.

McClung, Geraldine. "Hate Dies Hard." *Front Page Detective* (September 1960): 35–37, 60–62.

McCoy, Drew R. *The Elusive Republic: Political Economy in Jeffersonian America*. Chapel Hill: University of North Carolina Press, 1980.

McGowen, Stanley S. "Battle or Massacre? The Incident on the Nueces, August 10, 1862." *Southwestern Historical Quarterly* 104 (July 2000): 64–86.

Metz, Leon C. *Pat Garrett: The Story of a Western Lawman*. Norman: University of Oklahoma Press, 1974.

———. *The Encyclopedia of Lawmen, Outlaws, and Gunfighters*. New York: Checkmark Books, 2003.

Milbauer. John A. "Population Origins and Ethnicity in the Silver City Mining Region of New Mexico, 1870–1890." *International Social Science Review* 60, no. 4 (Autumn 1985): 160–65.

Miller, Darlis A. The *California Column in New Mexico*. Albuquerque: University of New Mexico Press, 1982.

Moore, Daniel G. *Enter Without Knocking*. Tucson: University of Arizona Press, 1969.

Moore, William Haas. "Prisoners in the Promised Land: The Molokans in World War I." *Journal of Arizona History* 14, no. 4 (Winter 1973): 281–302.

Mullin, Robert N., ed. *Maurice Garland Fulton's History of the Lincoln County War*. Tucson: University of Arizona Press, 1968.

———. *The Strange Story of Wayne Brazel*. Canyon, TX: Palo Duro Press, 1970.

Myres, Sandra L. and Emily K. Andrews. "A Woman's View of the Texas Frontier, 1874: The Diary of Emily K. Andrews." *Southwestern Historical Quarterly* 86 (July 1982): 49–80.

Noble, Marguerite. *Filaree: A Novel of an American Life*. Albuquerque: University of New Mexico Press, 1979.

Olmsted, Frederick Law. *A Journey Through Texas*. Austin: University of Texas Press, 1978.

O'Neal, Bill. "Captain Harry Wheeler: Arizona Lawman." *Journal of Arizona History* 27, no. 3 (Autumn 1986): 297–314.

Orenstein, Aviva. "Her Last Words: Dying Declarations and Modern Confrontation Jurisprudence." *Illinois Law Review* (2010): 1412–18.

Orton, Richard H. *Records of California Men in the War of the Rebellion 1861–1867.* Sacramento: State Printing Office, 1890.

Osselaer, Heidi J. "On the Wrong Side of Allen Street: The Businesswomen of Tombstone, 1878–1884." *Journal of Arizona History* 55 (Summer 2014): 145–66.

———. *Winning Their Place: Arizona Women in Politics, 1883–1950.* Tucson: University of Arizona Press, 2009.

Pattee, Samuel L., comp. *Revised Statutes of Arizona, 1913, Penal Code.* Phoenix: The McNeil Co., 1913.

Peterson, H. C., and Gilbert C. Fite. *Opponents of War: 1917–1918.* Madison: University of Wisconsin Press, 1957.

Pick, Thomas Pickering. *Surgery: A Treatise for Students and Practitioners.* New York: Longmans, Green, and Co., 1899.

Power, Tom, with John Whitlatch. *Shoot-Out at Dawn: An Arizona Tragedy.* Phoenix: William F. McCreary, 1981.

Preston, Douglas. *Cities of Gold: A Journey Across the American Southwest.* New York: Simon & Schuster, 1992.

Quinn, Michael D. "The Mormon Church and the Spanish-American War: An End to Selective Pacifism." *Pacific Historical Review* 43, no. 3 (August 1974): 342–66.

Record, Ian W. *Big Sycamore Stands Alone: The Western Apaches, Aravaipa, and the Struggle for Place.* Norman: University of Oklahoma Press, 2008.

Richards, J. Morris. *"Ink by the Barrel": Arizona's Hall of Fame Newspaper Men and Women.* Tempe: Arizona Historical Foundation, 1992.

Rickards, Colin. *Sheriff Pat Garrett's Last Days.* Santa Fe: Sunstone Press, 1986.

Ridgway, William Ryder, with Milton Bean. *The Power Family of Graham County, Arizona.* Texicanwife Books, 2012.

Roberts, Roderick J., Jr. "'The Powers Boys,' An Historical Legend: Its Formation and Function." PhD diss., University of Indiana, 1974.

Rose, Peter R. *The Reckoning: The Triumph of Order on the Texas Outlaw Frontier.* Lubbock: Texas Tech University Press, 2012.

Ross, Stewart Halsey. *Propaganda for War: How the United States Was Conditioned to Fight the Great War of 1914–1918.* Jefferson, NC: McFarland & Co., 1996.

Salafia, Matthew. *Slavery Borderland: Freedom and Bondage Along the Ohio River.* Philadelphia: University of Pennsylvania Press, 2013.

Sanders, J. H. "Restrictions on Prisoners' Mail." *Journal of the American Institute of Criminal Law and Criminology* 4, no. 6 (March 1914): 920–24.

Sayers, Robert Howard. "Mormon Cultural Persistence in the Vicinity of Graham County, Arizona, 1879–1977." PhD diss. University of Arizona, 1979.

Schlissel, Lillian, ed. *Conscience in America: A Documentary History of Conscientious Objections in America, 1757–1967.* New York: E. P. Dutton & Co. Inc., 1968.

Selective Service Regulations. 2nd ed. Washington, DC: Government Printing Office, 1918.

Shenk, Gerald E. *"Work or Fight!": Race, Gender, and the Draft in World War One.* Gordonsville, VA: Palgrave MacMillan, 2005.

Sheridan, Thomas. *Arizona: A History*. 2nd ed. Tucson: University of Arizona, 2012.

Shute, G. W. "Tragedy of the Grahams." *Arizona Cattlelog* (April 1960): 32–37.

Simmons, Marc. *Massacre on the Lordsburg Road: A Tragedy of the Apache Wars*. College Station: Texas A&M Press, 1997.

Simons, Frank S. *Geology of the Klondyke Quadrangle, Graham and Pinal Counties, AZ*. United States Department of Interior, Geological Survey professional paper 461. Washington, DC: Government Printing Office, 1964.

Simpson, Thomas W. *American Universities and the Birth of Modern Mormonism 1867–1940*. Chapel Hill: University of North Carolina Press, 2016.

Slaughter, Thomas P. *The Whiskey Rebellion: Frontier Epilogue to the American Revolution*. New York: Oxford University Press, 1986.

Sloan, Richard. *Biographical*. Vol. 3 of *History of Arizona*. Phoenix: Record Publishing Co., 1930.

Slotkin, Richard. *The Fatal Environment: The Myth of the Frontier in the Age of Industrialization, 1800–1890*. New York: Atheneum, 1985.

Sonnichsen, C. L. *Billy King's Tombstone: The Private Life of an Arizona Boom Town*. Caldwell, ID: The Caxton Printers, Ltd., 1942.

———. *I'll Die Before I'll Run: The Story of the Great Feuds of Texas*. Lincoln: University of Nebraska Press, 1988.

Sparks, Edith. *Capital Intentions: Female Proprietors in San Francisco, 1850–1920*. Chapel Hill: University of North Carolina Press, 2006.

Sturgeon, Melanie. "'Belgian Jennie' Bauters: Mining-Town Madam." *Journal of Arizona History* 48, no. 4 (Winter 2007): 349–74.

Tanner, Karen Holiday and John D. Tanner. "Scott White, Arizona Lawman." *Journal of Arizona History* 49, no. 1 (Spring 2008): 1–26.

Taylor, Rosemary Drachman. *Bar Nothing Ranch*. New York: McGraw Hill Book Co., 1947.

Teeples, C. A. "First Pioneers of the Gila Valley." In *Let Them Speak for Themselves: Women in the American West, 1849–1900*, edited by Christiane Fischer. Hamden, CT: Archon Books, 1990.

Theoharis, Athan. *The FBI and American Democracy: A Brief Critical History*. Lawrence: University Press of Kansas, 2004.

Tórrez, Robert J. *Myth of the Hanging Tree: Stories of Crime and Punishment in Territorial New Mexico*. Albuquerque: University of New Mexico Press, 2008.

Underwood, Rodman L. *Death on the Nueces*. Austin: Eakin Press, 2000.

Utley, Robert M. *High Noon in Lincoln: Violence on the Western Frontier*. Albuquerque: University of New Mexico Press, 1987.

Van Wagoner, Richard S. *Mormon Polygamy: A History*. 2nd ed. Salt Lake City: Signature Books, 1989.

Wainwright, R. P. Page. *The First Regiment of Cavalry*. Washington, DC: United States Army Regimental Press, 1906.

Ware, Harry David. "Alcohol, Temperance, and Prohibition in Arizona." PhD diss., Arizona State University, 1995.

West, Elliott. *The Saloon on the Rocky Mountain Mining Frontier.* Lincoln: University of Nebraska Press, 1979.

Whayne, Jeannie M., Thomas A. DeBlack, George Sabo, and Morris S. Arnold. *Arkansas: A Narrative History.* Fayetteville: University of Arkansas Press, 2002.

Williams, Mickey. "The Power Brothers' Story." *Arizona Sheriff* (October 1972): 19–26.

Williams, Oran A. "Settlements of the Gila Valley in Graham County, 1879–1900." Master's thesis, University of Arizona, 1937.

Willis, James F. "The Cleburne County Draft War." *Arkansas Historical Quarterly* 26, no. 1 (Spring 1967): 24–39.

Wilson, John P. *Islands in the Desert: A History of the Uplands of Southeastern Arizona.* Albuquerque: University of New Mexico Press, 2000.

Wolfe, Barbara Brooks. *Power, Passion, and Prejudice: Shootout in the Galiuro Mountains.* Tucson: Imago Press, 2008.

Wood, Elizabeth Lambert. *The Tragedy of the Powers Mine: An Arizona Story.* Portland: Metropolitan Press, 1957.

Wood, Gordon S. "Evangelical America and Early Mormonism." In *The Mormon History Association's Tanner Lectures: The First Twenty Years,* edited by Dean L. May and Reid L. Neilson. Urbana: University of Illinois Press, 2006.

Wootan, W. E. "Black Bill Wootan Tells his Experience." *Frontier Times* (August 1927): n. p.

Work, Clemens P. *Darkest Before Dawn: Sedition and Free Speech in the American West.* Albuquerque: University of New Mexico Press, 2005.

Wrede, Jan. *Trees, Shrubs, and Vines of the Texas Hill Country: A Field Guide.* College Station: Texas A&M University Press, 2010.

Wyatt-Brown, Bertram. *Southern Honor: Ethics and Behavior in the Old South.* New York: Oxford University Press, 1982.

Yadon, Laurence J. *Texas Outlaws and Lawmen, 1835–1935.* Gretna, LA: Pelican, 2008.

INDEX

References to illustrations appear in italic type.

abandoned mines, 52, 70, 79–80, 81, 86.
    See also Power Mine
Adelsverein, 12–13
Adkisson family, 175–76
agriculture. *See* farmers
airplanes, 138
alcohol consumption, 5, 7, 13, 19, 26,
    36, 38, 41, 76, 83, 170; and James
    Fielder, 183; and Power family, 19–20;
    and Power-Sisson posse, 182, 183,
    192, 260n33. *See also* bootleggers;
    prohibition; saloons
Alger, Thomas, 71, 73, 74, 75–76, 239n24,
    240m38
Allen, Henry: death of Ola Power, 103,
    108; McBride letter, 111, 248n20,
    248n22; and Power shootout, 111, 122,
    124–28, 130, 146, 151, 154, 160, 165, 183,
    250n9; and Power-Sisson trial, 163,
    260n33
American Indians, 3, 7–8, 9; in Arizona,
    44–45, 83, 138; in New Mexico, 9–10,
    22; as scouts, 84, 135, 137, 138, 191–92; in
    Texas, 12, 17. *See also names of specific
    tribes*
American Red Cross, 93, 98, 99, 103
Apaches, 9, 22, 23, 39–40, in Aravaipa,
    44–45, 51, 83; in Gila Valley, 62, 63; as
    scouts, 137, 138

Aravaipa Canyon (Ariz.), 37, 44–47, 51,
    53, 83, 234nn1–2; community life in,
    47–48, 51, 55, 57, 59, 71, 74–75; federal
    government in, 45, 53–54, 219, 236n23;
    folklore in, 152, 181–82, 184, 185, 192, 194,
    195, 196, 200, 211, 215; Great Depression
    in, 185, 217, 219; law enforcement in,
    71, 72, 73–74, 76, 77–78, 114; Mexican
    settlers, 45, 47–48; mining in, 46–47,
    52–53, 55, 62, 79–82, 86–88; and
    Mormons, 48, 59, 71–72, 74–75, 183,
    192–93, 200; outlaws in, 51–52, 76, 83;
    politics in, 74, 75, 76; prohibition in,
    72–73, 77; ranching in, 45–55, 112, 185,
    193, 219; transportation in, 44, 47, 74,
    83. *See also* Rattlesnake Canyon (Ariz.)
Aravaipa Creek, 44, 45, 46, 58, 221
Aravaipa Road, 44, 74–75, 83, 242n14
Aravaipa Wilderness Area, 219
Arizona: American Indians in, 44–45,
    83, 138; labor unions in, 99–101, 102,
    139, 143, 200, 235n6; mining in, 46,
    47, 52, 81–2, 99, 149, 153; Mormons
    in, 62–64, 65, 69; and Progressivism,
    69–70, 85, 100, 139, 169, 253n21; and
    prohibition, 69–73, 76, 82–83, 182;
    statehood movement, 34, 69; and
    woman suffrage, 72; and World War I,
    89, 92–94, 99–101

Arizona Board of Pardons and Paroles, 171, 242n18; and Power clemency, 177–79, 185, 188, 189, 190–91, 192, 193, 199–200, 202–07; and Power pardon, 210–211; and Power parole, 208–10

Arizona Republic, and release of Power brothers. *See* Dedera, Don; Pulliam, Eugene

Arizona State Prison at Florence, 84–85, 169–71, 174, 191, 193, 207, 248n20; escapes, 177–78, 185–86; honor system, 147, 177–78, 185, 189; solitary confinement, 147, 170, 177, 259n23. *See also under* Power brothers (Tom and John); Sisson, Thomas Joseph

Arizona Territorial Prison at Yuma, 34–35, 84, 169

Arkansas: and Civil War 12, 15; draft resistance in, 175–76; John Murdock in, 152; Power family in, 3, 5–8, 9, 10, 11, 12, 13, 55, 201. *See also* Baker-Fancher wagon train

Armer, Thomas, 95, 96–97, 111

Ashurst, Henry, 100

automobiles, 55, 58, 74, 77, 115

Baird, James A., 40–41, 42, 145

Baird, Mary, 40

Baker-Fancher wagon train, 7–8, 201

Baldwin, Roger Nash, 92

Battle of the Nueces (Texas), 15

Bauman, Al, 52, 79, 80, 81, 86, 243n22

Benton-Cohen, Katherine, 101

Beveridge, Albert J., 69

Bielaski, Alexander Bruce, 94

Billy King's Tombstone (Sonnichsen), 36

Billy the Kid, 41, 43

Birdno, John, 70, 71, 116

Bisbee, Ariz., 52, 81, 86, 126, 152, 53

Bisbee Deportation, 100–101, 102, 139, 143, 200

Blackstone, William, 149

Bleak, Joseph, 29, 104, 107

Bleak family, 58–59, 88, 104, 127, 164

bloodhounds, 137–38

Bonita, Ariz., 59, 71, 82, 88

bootleggers, 45, 82, 95; and McBride, 73, 75, 77–78, 117, 240n43; and Tom Power, 82–83, 102, 215. *See also* prohibition

Bowie, Ariz., 40, 42, 137

Boscoe, Joseph 104, 106, 109, 162, 163, 218, 246n3

Boscoe, Mellie, 105, 106, 108, 162, 218, 246n3

Branson, George and James T., 43, 53, 80, 133, 251n30

Brazel, Jesse Wayne, 41–42, 43, 59, 166

Breniman, Charles, 102, 123

brothels. *See* prostitution

Brotherton, Rob, 192

Bryan, William Jennings, 89

Buchanan, James, 8

Bureau of Investigation (BI), U.S. Department of Justice, 94–95, 99, 100, 101; and Power brothers, 102, 103, 109–10, 112–13, 123–24, 126, 197, 257n37

Burns, Jacob, 66, 116, 238n13

Burro Mine. *See* abandoned mines; Power Mine

Butterfield Overland Stage, 7, 39–40

California Gold Rush, 6–7

California: migration to, 6, 7, 8, 14; Power family in, 8–9

California Volunteers, 9–10. *See also* Union Army

Campa, Arthur L., 36

Campbell, Angus, 24, 230n8

Campbell, Thomas, 88, 100

Camp Grant. *See* Fort Grant

capital punishment, 15, 139, 143, 147–48, 170, 177, 215, 257n4. *See also* vigilantism

Carson, Christopher "Kit," 9–10

Catholics, 13, 44, 48, 64, 188

cattle ranching, 7, 17, 22–23, 24, 42, 45, 68; in Aravaipa, 45, 46, 47–50, 53–55, 62, 71, 75, 112, 185, 193, 219; associations, 33, 38, 59, 71, 73, 135; branding, 55, 84; cowboys, 17, 22–23, 24; McBrides and, 68, 71, 73, 74, 75; Morgans and, 20, 21, 22, 23, 32–34, 35, 36, 37, 39, 40, 46–47, 56–57, 82, 185, 217; Mormons and, 64; overgrazing, 48, 219; Powers and, 18, 24, 26–28, 29–30, 37, 38, 39, 40, 43, 48, 49, 51, 53–55, 57, 58, 59, 79, 85, 196, 227n2, 234n31, 250n23; and roundups, 23, 26, 48, 54–55; and rustling, 12, 18, 23, 26–27, 33–34, 38, 41, 59, 71, 73, 75, 77, 120, 127, 133; in Southwest, 22–28, 30, 31, 32–34, 36, 39, 40, 42, 50, 64; in Texas, 13, 17, 18, 19, 20, 21; Wootans and, 60–61, 77; during World War I, 92. *See also names of specific cattle ranches;* goat ranching; Livestock Sanitary Board

Cavanaugh, Wade, 217–19, 231n15

censorship. *See under* World War I

Chamberlain, Kathleen, 38

Chambers, John Whiteclay, 176

Chambers, William R., 77, 180; arrest of Power brothers and Sisson, 110, 145; and lawmen's inquest, 124, 125–26, 130, 134, 139; post-trial comments of, 170, 177, 178, 184; and Power-Sisson trial, 149, 150–52, 154, 157, 159, 160, 161–62, 164, 167, 168, 254n29

Cherokees, 12, 30, 227n1

Childers, Lem, 27

Chiricahua Mountains (Ariz.), 137

Chiricahuas. *See* Apaches

Church, Wade, 199–200. *See also* Arizona Board of Pardons and Paroles

civil liberties. *See* World War I

Civil War, 7, 8; in Arkansas, 12, 15; and conscription, 11, 13, 14, 16, 91, 97, 228n9; and John Murdock, 153–54; and Power family, 8, 9–10, 15–16, 97,

214, 216, 228n9, 228n14; in Southwest, 9–10, 40; in Texas 11, 12, 13–15, 16, 60

Clanton, Laura Jane and Phineas, 51

Claridge, Marcus, 193, 218

Claridge, Zola Webster, 183, 192–93, 199, 201, 216, 218

Clayton, Jeff, 51, 78, 118, 240n44

clemency. *See* Arizona Board of Pardons and Paroles; Power brothers; Sisson, Thomas Joseph

Cleveland, Grover, 65, 238n10

Clifton, Ariz., 47, 52, 64, 70, 71, 145–46, 147, 149, 155, 157; newspapers in, 156–57. *See also* Power-Sisson trial

Cobb, Thomas, 50

Cochise County, Ariz. *See* Bisbee Deportation; Doubtful Canyon (Ariz., N.Mex.)

Cold War, 190, 192, 210

Comanches, 5, 9, 12, 13, 15, 16–17

Committee on Public Information (CPI), 90

communalism. *See* United Order of Enoch

Confederate Army, 9, 11, 14–16, 153, 228n12, 229n26

Confederate States of America (CSA), 9, 12, 14, 97

conscientious objectors. *See under* conscription in World War I

conscription in World War I, 88–89, 90, 102–3; conscientious objectors, 90, 91–93, 94, 95, 97, 175–77, 214; draft boards, 89, 91, 93, 96, 111–12; economic impact of, 92; foreign born and, 92, 95–96; opposition to, 89, 91–93, 96–97, 101–2, 123, 175–76; quotas, 96, 102; registration for, 88–89, 174; Selective Service Act, 91, 94, 95–96, 97, 102, 110, 114, 148, 150, 166, 171, 174. *See also* Bureau of Investigation (BI); Civil War; deserters; slackers conspiracy theories, 101, 181–83, 192, 196, 200–201

Copper Creek (Ariz.), 44, 46

Copper Era and Morenci Leader, coverage of Power-Sisson trial, 146, 156–57

Copper Hill Mine, 83, 102

copper mining. *See* mining, placer; mining corporations

coroner's inquests, 41, 43; for C. P. Tucker, 81; for Graham County lawmen, 124–29, 130, 139, 150–52, 154, 157, 159, 160, 165, 249n37, 252n46; for Jeff Power, 134; for Ola Power, 104–7, 109, 146, 246n2, 247n7

Councils of Defense, 89, 175

cowboys. *See* cattle ranching

Cox, William Webb, 41

crime, 7, 18, 23, 51–52; in Aravaipa, 51–52, 62, 77–78; in Gila Valley, 43, 62, 63, 66–67, 76, 77, 116–17, 180, 181, 238n13; in Southwest, 18, 23, 26–7, 28, 40–41, 43, 51–52, 133, 137; in Texas, 17, 18, 60. *See also* cattle ranching; true crime magazines

Crook (Coronado) National Forest, 45, 53, 221

Crowder, Enoch, 88, 91

death penalty. *See* capital punishment

Debs, Eugene, 99, 139

Dedera, Don, 188, *203,* 207; and Mormon church, 200–201; and Power clemency, 193–96, 198–201, 202, 206–7, 208, 209, 219; and Power pardon, 209–11; and Wootans, 198, 202

Democratic Party, 3, 28, 60; in Graham County, 60, 64, 67, 70–73, 74–76; and Mormons, 65, 67, 70; and the press, 156; in South, 6

depression of 1890s, 27–28

deserters: in Civil War, 16; in World War I, 93, 94, 95, 97, 113, 138–39, 143–44, 175, 176, 250n14, 258n19. *See also* slackers

detectives, 33, 77, 240n43

Dick, W. W., 199, *204. See also* Arizona Board of Pardons and Paroles

Dillon, Joseph P., 92, 94, 100, 248n18; and Power shootout, 123, 124, 146; and Power-Sisson posse, 114, 124, 135, 137, 248n18; and Power warrants, 96, 110, 114, 123–24, 158; and slacker raids, 175

Doan, Fletcher, 42

Doubtful Canyon (Ariz., N.Mex.), 39–43, 51, 135, 234n31

Doubtful Mine, 39, 40–43, 132, 145, 181

Douglas, Ariz., 137–38

Douglas, Walter, 100, 101

draft evasion. *See* slackers

draft. *See* conscription in World War I

Dragoon Mountains (Ariz.), 135

drought: in Aravaipa, 48, 50, 114, 185, 219; in New Mexico, 27, 31, 39; in Texas, 20

DuBois, Harry, 119, 151, 159, 255n3

Duff, James, 14–15

Duncan, John, 33–34, 36, 232n6

Edmunds Act, 64. *See also* polygamy

education: in Aravaipa, 46, 48, 60; and Mormons, 68; of Power family, 3, 4, 5, 8–9, 23, 29, 30, 43, 59, 170, 208

Elliott, Claude, 14

Ellis, Catherine H., 191

Elwood, Richard C., 80, 81, 241n5

embargoes during World War I, 81, 86, 243n20

English, Allen R., 35, 36, 42

Espionage Act. *See under* World War I

Evaders, The (McBride), 213

Eyman, Frank, 193, 208

Faires, Clifford C., 130, 182

Fall, Albert B., 41

Fannin, Paul, 199, 207, 211, 216

farmers, 4, 5, 6, 63; in Aravaipa, 45, 46, 47–48, 52, 53, 219; in Gila Valley, 47, 62–64, 68, 75; and irrigation, 24, 26,

54, 63; Power family as, 4, 6, 7, 8, 9, 18, 24, 26, 29, 37, 39, 53, 54, 55, 85–86, 217; in Southwest, 23–24, 26, 27–28, 39, 45; in Texas, 12, 13, 20; and World War I, 90, 92, 97, 101. *See also* drought

Federal Bureau of Investigation. *See* Bureau of Investigation (BI)

federal prisons, 92, 93, 99, 153, 176–77, 238n13. *See also* Leavenworth military prison

Ferguson, Elliot Lark (alias Pete Spence), 43, 51, 53

feuds, 17, 215. *See also* Power-Wootan feud

Fielder, James S., 40, 148–49; accusations against, 182–83, 260n36; and Power-Sisson trial, 145, 148, 149–52, 157–58, 159, 161–62, 163, 164–66, 167

Fifer, Oren, 207

Filaree (Noble), 213

First Battle of Adobe Walls, 9, 10

First California Cavalry Company, 9–10. *See also* Union Army

Flake, William, 62

Flynn, Thomas, 94, 96, 110, 114, 147–48, 248n25

food poisoning, 108–9

Forest Homestead Act of 1906, 53

forgiveness, 191, 202, 205–7

Fort Grant, 45, 83

Fort Hachita, 141, 142, 144

Fort Smith, Ark., 6–7, 8

Fort Union (N.Mex.), 9, 10

Fountain, Albert Jennings, 27, 41

Fourmile Canyon (Ariz.), 58, 87

Four-Minute Men, 90, 98

Frankfurter, Felix, 101, 200

Fredericksburg, Texas, 12, 13, 17, 18

Freeman, Mary, 198

Freethinkers, 12, 13

freighters, 64, 68

Friendly Pines Camp, 208–9

frontier honor, 32–33, 34, 37, 38–39, 43, 51

frontier regiments, 15, 60

Galiuro Mountains (Ariz.), 44, 49–50, 50, 234n2, 235n12. *See also* Aravaipa Canyon (Ariz.); Gold Mountain mining camp; Rattlesnake Canyon (Ariz.)

Galiuro Wilderness, 219

gambling, 23, 32, 51, 69

Garrett, Patrick F., 41

German Americans: in Aravaipa, 52, 58, 131, 163; Power family as, 3, 131–32; in Texas 12–15, 18, 21; in World War I, 90, 99, 101.

Germany, during World War I, 81, 89–90, 91, 98, 99–100, 102, 139, 184

Gila, N.Mex., 23–24, 26, 29, 39, 43

Gila River, 23–24, 45, 47, 48, 62, 63, 64, 169

Gila Valley, 47; crime in, 43, 62, 63, 66–67, 76, 77, 116–17, 180, 181, 238n13; and Mormons, 47, 61, 62–72, 74, 200; and prohibition, 69–70, 76; views of Power shootout in, 108, 177–78, 179, 183–84, 189, 193, 200–201, 211–12; during World War I, 95–96. *See also* Graham County, Ariz.; Pima, Ariz.; Safford, Ariz.

Gillespie County, Texas, 12–13, 14–15, 18, 20, 52, 195. *See also* Texas Hill Country

Globe, Ariz., 64, 66, 68, 82–83, 215; in World War I, 100, 102

goat ranching, 43, 46, 48, 49, 53, 54, 58, 219

gold mining. *See* mining, placer

Gold Mountain mining camp, 46–47; Power family at, 86, 87, 103, 105–6, 109, 118, 197, 221

Gould, James W., 40–43, 59, 145, 166, 233n25

Graham County, Ariz., 37, 47, 48, 74; military in, 45, 83, 102–3; Mormons in, 64–65; politics in, 60, 64, 67, 70–73, 74–76; slackers in, 94, 95–96; transportation in, 74–75. *See also*

Graham County, Ariz. *(continued)*
  Aravaipa Canyon (Ariz.); Gila Valley;
  San Carlos Reservation
Graham Guardian, 60, 70–71, 116–17
Grand Reef Mine, 46, 48, 74, 75, 80, 82
Grant County, N.Mex, 23–24, 26, 28, 40,
  133
Great Britain, 4, 90, 184
Great Depression, 185, 217, 219
Great War. *See* World War I
Green Corn Rebellion, 101–2, 176
Greenlee County, Ariz., 70, 74, 123. *See
  also* Power-Sisson trial
Gregory, Thomas, 99, 166
grogshops. *See* alcohol consumption;
  saloons

Haby, Gregor (Gregory) and Mary Ann,
  58, 59, 85, 106–7, 108, 127, 131, 163, 218
Haby, Merrel, 59, 108, 183, 217
hangings. *See* vigilantism
Harlin, David, 179
Harrington, Virgil and Pearl, 39, 40, 42
Hayes, Wolcott P., 141–42, 163–64, 252n2,
  253n9
Haynes, Frank, 100, 110–11, 180, 182,
  248n16, 249n7; and federal arrest
  warrants, 110, 111, 113–14, 168, 248n18;
  in Power shootout, 114, 115, 118–21,
  122–24, 125, 127, 135, 148, 249n37; and
  Power-Sisson posse, 111, 112, 114–19;
  testimony of, 124, 129, 130, 133–34, 146,
  149–50, 157–59, 161, 165, 197, 249n7,
  249n32, 250n17, 260n33
Hofmann, Walter, 185, 188, 190, 199, 202,
  204, 206. *See also* Arizona Board of
  Pardons and Paroles
homesteaders, 24, 32, 38, 39, 41; in
  Aravaipa, 45, 46, 49, 52, 53–54, 60
honor system. *See* prisons
Hooker, Henry Clay, 22–23
Hooker's Hot Springs, 33
Houston, Sam, 14

Hughes, A. P., 144
Hughes, Louis C., and Josephine
  Brawley, 65, 69
Hunt, George, 100, 133, 139, 147, 169
hunting, 5, 18, 26; in Aravaipa, 44, 46, 49,
  73, 76, 219

I Bar I Ranch, 56, 57
Industrial Workers of the World (IWW),
  99–100, 101, 157
inquests. *See* coroner's inquests
Inspiration Mining Company, 86–87
International Union of Mine, Miller, and
  Smelter Workers (IUMMSW), 99–100
irrigation. *See* farmers

Jackson, Andrew, 5, 6
Jaynes, Allan B., 156, 163
Jefferson, Thomas, 4
Jehovah's Witnesses, 93, 175–76. *See also*
  conscription in World War I
Jerome, Ariz., 100, 246n31
Johnson, David, 15
Johnson, Hiram, 90
Johnson, William T., 70, 71
Jones, Charles, 86, 126, 243n21

Keith, Jeanette, 99
Keleher, William A., 42
Kelly, Tom, 138–39, 143–44
Kelly, William, B., 156–57
Kempton, Albert, 205
Kempton, Glenn, 191, 196, 205
Kempton, Ira, 238n13
Kempton, Martin, *116,* 201; funeral for,
  134–35; in Power shootout, 120–21, 122–
  23, 125, 127, 128, 129, 132, 139, 145, 146,
  149, 151, 158–59, 160, 166, 168, 170, 181,
  189, 182, 190, 213, 221; as undersheriff,
  76, 77, 95, 96, 114–15, 126, 182, 249n29
Kempton, Nate, 178, 253n14
Kempton, Sena, 76, 115, *116;* civil suit
  against Power family, 171–74

Kentucky, 3–5, 6, 8, 15, 45–46, 55

Ketchum, Black Jack, 148

Kielberg, Emil and Ida, 80

Kielberg Canyon (Ariz.), *50*, 80, *220. See also* Power Mine

Kimball, Andrew, 134

Kimball, Spencer W., 191

Kimble County, Texas, 20

Kino, Eusebio, 44

Kiowas, 9

Kirby, Francis Lee, 53

Klondyke, Ariz., 37, 43, 46–48, 55, 75, 94, 234n4, 240n34; cemetery, 107, 216, 217; Power-Sisson posse in, 117–18, 122, 128, 157, 260n33; post office and store, 48, 81, 196, *212*, 218, 219; saloon, 37, 46, 48, 70, 72, 73, 239n26; schoolhouse, 48, 60; today, 219; Union Church, 48, 88, 89; voting precinct, 72, 73, 76, 88, 91, 94, 185. *See also* Aravaipa Canyon (Ariz.); Sociability Run

Knothe, Ed, 52, 235n17

Korean War, 190

Kountz, Albert, 134, 140, 246n2

labor unions: in Aravaipa, 235n6; and Power-Sisson trial, 157; in World War I, 90, 93, 94, 99–101, 102, 111, 112, 143. *See also* Bisbee Deportation; *names of specific unions*

Laine, Frank, 155, 158, 161–62, 164–65, 167–68, 257n1. *See also* Power-Sisson trial

Lane, Louis L., 148, 150

Latter-day Saints, Church of Jesus Christ of. *See* Mormons

law enforcement: in Graham County, 68; posses, 96, 114–16, 117–21, 245n21; in Southwest, 3, 26, 31, 32, 139, 148–49; in Texas, 17; during World War I, 93–94, 95, 100–101, 102, 111. *See also names of specific lawmen;* Power shootout;

Power-Sisson manhunt; Power-Sisson posse; vigilantism

Layton, Christopher, 64, 65, 66

LCs Ranch. *See* Lyons and Campbell Cattle and Land Company (LCs Ranch)

Leavenworth military prison, 93, 169, 176

Lincoln, Abraham, 15, 153, 216, 228n9, 237n8

Little, Frank, 143

Little Colorado River, 63

livestock inspector. *See* Livestock Sanitary Board

Livestock Sanitary Board, 37, 55, 61, 71, 72, 73, 76, 78, 240n41

Llano County, Texas, 17, 21, 59, 60, 61. *See also* Texas Hill Country

local option laws. *See* prohibition

log cabins, 4, 6, 13, 46–47, 54, 56, 62, 63; at Gold Mountain, 87, 103, 104; in Power Garden, 51, 54, 55, 221. *See also* Power Mine cabin

Longfellow Mine, 47

Long S. Land and Cattle Company, 41–42, 233n27

Long Tom Mine, 52

Long Walk of the Navajos, 9–10

Lordsburg, N.Mex., 39, 41, 77, 83, 133

Los Angeles, Calif., 9, 37

Luster, Ray, 216

Lutherans, 13, 231n19

Lyall, Elmer Archer, 41, 42–43

Lyman, Ed, 81, 86, 126, 258n12

Lynch, A. R., 150, 152

lynching. *See* vigilantism

Lyons, Thomas, 24–27, 28, 30, 33, 38, 51, 59, 231n20

Lyons and Campbell Cattle and Land Company (LCs Ranch), 24–27

Maddox v. United States, 161

Mammoth, Ariz., 37, 46

Mangum, John "Sandy," 98, 162–63, 187

Maricopa County, Ariz., and Mormons, 63, 205

Mason, Patrick Q., 32

Mathews, Lemuel P., 200

Matthewsville, Ariz., 64–65, 69

McBride, Clara Sims, 68, 115, 197; civil suit against Power family, 171–74, 257n9

McBride, Darvil, 68, 180, 191, 198, 202, 213

McBride, Gladys (Stewart), 75, 104, 108, 115

McBride, Howard, 68, 128, 253n14

McBride, Laura Lewis, 65

McBride, Peter, 62–63, 65

McBride, Robert Franklin "Frank," 115; childhood of, 62–63, 65, 68; early career of, 68–69; and federal government, 67, 68, 99; funeral of, 134–35; inquest of, 129; as lawman, 61, 67, 68, 71–74, 76, 77–78, 89–97, 99, 100, 103, 116–17; letter to Jeff Power, 111–12, 124, 126; and Mormon Church, 62–65, 67–68; and politics, 67, 70–71, 74–76, 240n38; and Power family, 78, 87, 96–97, 104, 106–7, 109–12, 113, 124, 126, 248n20; and Power shootout, 119–21, 122; and Power-Sisson posse, 113, 114–16, 117–18, 119, 249n32; and prohibition, 69–73, 75–76, 77, 182, 239n26; and slackers, 89, 94, 95–96, 103, 104; and Wham payroll robbery, 66–67

McBride, Ruth Burns, 62–63, 65, 238n13

McCaleb, Claude, 103, 109–10

McCart, Robert, 141, 142

McCarthy, Joseph, 190, 192

McFarland, Ernest, 192

McSween, Susan, 38

Meade, William Kidder, 66

medical examiner. See coroner's inquests

Methodists, 6, 18, 48

Mexican-American War, 13, 153

Mexicans: in Aravaipa, 45, 47–48; in Southwest, 22, 45, 51; during World War I, 95–96, 101, 141, 214

Mexico: Power brothers' escape to, 185–86; Power-Sisson manhunt in, 136–37, 141–42; and revolutions, 51, 98; and U.S. Civil War, 15; and World War I, 89, 98

Miami, Ariz., 86, 179

Miles, Rye, 135, 137

military forts. See names of individual forts; U.S. Army

Ming, Dan, 45–46, 60

mining, placer, 7, 80, 100, 111; in Aravaipa, 40, 46–47, 52–53, 55, 62, 79–82, 86–88, 133, 209–10, 235n17; equipment, 58, 80, 82, 87, 126, 127, 165, 221, 243n20; in New Mexico, 23–24, 27, 40, 46, 52; during World War I, 81–82, 98, 99. See also California Gold Rush; names of specific mines and mining camps

mining corporations: in Arizona, 46, 47, 52, 82, 149, 153; in New Mexico, 23–24, 27, 52; and Power-Sisson trial, 149, 156–57, 159, 165, 184, 215; and World War I, 82–83, 99, 100, 101, 139, 156–57, 215. See also Bisbee Deportation; mining, placer; names of specific corporations

Mitchell, J. W., 33, 34, 232n6

Molokans, 92, 93. See also under conscription in World War I

moonshiners. See bootleggers; prohibition

Morgan, Amanda Bybee (Wiley's mother), 20, 22, 30, 88, 229n26

Morgan, Amanda Sue Tomlinson (Wiley's wife), 23, 35, 42, 72, 105

Morgan, Bill (son of Will), 203

Morgan, Burt, 56–57

Morgan, George, 33–34, 56–57, 58, 88, 174

Morgan, Ida, 57, 82

Morgan, Joe, 57, 203

Morgan, Seebird "Sebe," 20–21, 22, 23, 33, 97

Morgan, Wiley, 21, 22–23, 32, 33, 37, 39, 55; in Aravaipa, 37, 39, 43, 56–57, 59, 60, 71, 185; in folklore, 36–37, 188; murder charge, 33–36, 127, 232n13; and politics, 33, 37; and Power shootout, 133, 171, 260n33; in prison, 34–35, 169; as saloon owner, 37, 46, 48, 70, 72, 73, 239n26; and World War I, 98, 245n22

Morgan, Wiley, Jr. (son of Wiley), 35, 57, 72, 239n26

Morgan, Wiley (son of Will), 57

Morgan, Will, 39, 43, 57, 82

Mormons, 53; and Aravaipa, 48, 59, 71–72, 74–75, 183–84, 192–93, 200; church leadership of, 8, 62–63, 64–66, 67–68, 69, 95, 183, 201; and clemency for Power brothers, 183–84, 187, 192–93, 197, 199, 200–201, 205; conflicts with non-Mormons, 63–68, 71, 76, 96, 181, 183, 197, 200; in Gila Valley, 47, 61, 62–72, 74, 200; and *Miracle of Forgiveness*, 191; and Mountain Meadows Massacre, 7–8, 201; and politics, 65, 67, 69, 70–73, 74, 75, 193; and polygamy, 8, 63–66, 67, 237n8; in Power shootout folklore, 200–201; and prohibition, 69–73; and United Order of Enoch, 63, 64, 67; and war, 63, 95, 239n15, 245n18. *See also* Wham payroll robbery

Morrison, Robert, 199

Mountain Meadows Massacre, 7–8, 201

Mulheim, James, 86, 243n21

Mullan, Ted, 204–5, 208

Murdock, Catherine Fuller, 53, 152

Murdock, James Jasper "Jay": divorce of, 53, 152; and dying Jeff Power, 127–28, 140, 146, 150–51, 165, 252n46; inquest testimony of, 124–27, 129, 130, 139, 140, 146, 150–52, 154, 250n9, 250n17, 256n15;

and McBride letter, 111–12, 248n20, 248n22; and mining, 52–53, 79; and Power family, 52, 79, 98, 103, 126; and Power shootout, 122, 124–27, 250n9; as source of folklore, 180–81, 192, 197, 253n14, 259n30; trial testimony of, 159–61, 163, 165, 167, 215, 252n46

Murdock, John Maddison: divorces of, 152–53; and dying Jeff Power, 127–28, 162; legal proceedings against, 53, 152–54, 254n36; and mining, 52–53, 79; and perjury, 153–54, 160, 162, 164, 165, 167, 184; and Power family, 52, 79, 103; and Power shootout, 122, 124–27; trial testimony of, 162, 163, 164, 167, 215

Murdock, Martha Charlton, 153

Murdock, Rebecca Jane McBee, 152–53

Navajos, 9–10

Neil, Harry, 81, 86–87, 126

New Braunfels, Texas, 13

New Mexico, 7, 9, 23; during Civil War, 9–10; mining in, 23, 24, 27, 40, 46; Charley Power in, 16, 32, 97, 113, 145, 185, 190, 217, 245n22; Power family in, 21, 22–31, 39, 59, 82, 83, 112, 133, 209; Power-Sisson manhunt in, 135, 138, 139, 141, 142, 144; ranching in, 22–28, 29–31, 32–34, 39, 40; violence in, 41–43, 51, 148–49; in World War I, 89, 101

Noble, Marguerite Buchanan, 199, 213

Oklahoma, 5, 83, 101–2, 176, 179

Old Fort West Ditch Company, 24

Olmstead, Frederick Law, 12

Oracle, Ariz., 53, 133, 196, 251n30

Ouachita Mountains (Ark.), 6, 13

Oxford, Texas, 21

Ozark Mountains (Ark.), 6, 13

Pace Bill. *See* prohibition

Pace, W. W., 70

pacifists. *See* conscription in World War I

Pagán, Eduardo Obregón, 214

Paiutes, 7–8

pardon. *See* Arizona Board of Pardons and Paroles; Power brothers (Tom and John)

parole. *See* Arizona Board of Pardons and Paroles; Power brothers (Tom and John); Sisson, Thomas

Paxton, Ulysses I., 77, 110, 113–14, 150, 158, 248n25, 253n14

Pennsylvania, 3–4

perjury: and John Murdock, 153–54, 160, 162, 164, 165, 167, 184; and Jeff Power, 109, 114, 150; and Tom Sisson, 114, 124, 150

Phelps Dodge Company, 47, 99–101, 156

Phillips, Joseph A., 128

Pima, Ariz.: early settlement of, 63–65; home of McBride, 66, 68, 73, 74, 75; politics of, 74–76; Powers in, 98, 103, 162–63; prohibition in, 69–70. *See also* Gila Valley

Pima (Upper) Indians, 44–45

Pinal County, Ariz., 46, 84, 173, 184

Pinaleño Mountains (Ariz.), 44

Piños Altos Mountains (N.Mex.), 24

Platt, William E.: and lawmen's inquest, 128–29; and Ola Power's inquest, 104, 106–7, 109, 146, 247n9; and Power-Sisson trial, 159, 165

plural marriage. *See* polygamy

poison, 108–9. *See also* Power, Ola May

polygamy, 8, 63–66, 67, 200, 237n8, 238n10

Populism (People's Party): 27–28, 97, 101–2, 214

Power, Charles, "Charley," Samuel, *49, 56*; in Aravaipa, 43, 46, 49, 51, 53–55, 56–59, 82, 83, 85, 236n23; childhood of, 20, 21, 29–30, 196, 213; death of, 217; and Doubtful Mine, 40–41, 42, 132; in

folklore and literature, 192, 264n21; and Power Mine, 85, 173, 209–10; and Power-Sisson trial, 145, 148; as slacker, 97, 113, 157, 174, 185, 242n12, 245n22; and voting, 59

Power, John Grant (Jeff's son), *49, 57, 172, 212*; in Aravaipa, 48–49, 53–55, 56–59, 78, 209–10, 216, 217–18; childhood of, 28, 29–30, 43, 188; conversion to Catholicism, 188; death of Ola Power, 106, 107, 108, 109, 146–47, 217–19; escape attempt, 185–86; final years of, 216–19; gun skills of, 132; injuries of, 125, 142, 143, 144, 147, 253n19; and mining, 79, 82, 86–87, 118, 243n22, 263n5; trial testimony of, 164–65, 257n1; and voting, 50, 215–16. *See also* Power brothers (Tom and John); Power Mine; Power shootout; Power-Sisson manhunt; Power-Sisson trial; Power-Wootan feud

Power, John May (Jeff's uncle), 5, 8, 9, 15

Power, Martha "Mattie" Morgan, 20–21, 22, 23, 28–29, 39, 209, 231n15

Power, Martha Jane "Jane," *49*; in Aravaipa, 53–56, 75, 86, 183; in Arkansas, 11–12; death of, 85–86, 192, 216; and death of Mattie Power, 28–29; depiction in literature, 192; and Doubtful Canyon, 39–43, 132; and education, 18, 29, 43; family of, 11–12, 30; and farming, 24, 26–27, 28, 39, 53–55, 85–86; and frontier honor 37–39, 85; as head of household, 37–38; and legal proceedings, 19, 26, 27, 31, 42–43; marriage to Sam Power, 11–12, 15, 19–21; in New Mexico, 21, 24–31, 37, 39, 41–43, 230n9, 234n31; and Power Mine, 79, 82; and Ola Power, 54–55, 75, 78, 85–86, 87, 103, 107, 108–9; property of, 24, 37, 39–40, 41–43, 86, 234n31; and religion, 18, 55, 85; in Texas, 15,

17–20, 195; and Tom Lyons, 24, 26–27; and violence, 38, 41, 42–43, 85, 132, 166; and voting, 28, 72

Power, Mary Lindsay, 5–9, 21

Power, Ola May, 49, 105; in Aravaipa, 54–55, 75, 173, 180, 183; and cat Tomba, 54, 87, 106; childhood of, 28, 29–30, 43, 55, 188, 234n31; death of, 103–9, 109, 114, 116, 131, 146–47, 162, 164, 184, 216, 217–19, 221, 246n2, 247n7, 247n9, 247n12; in Doubtful Canyon, 41; at Gold Mountain, 78, 87, 103, 108; and the Habys, 58; health of, 97, 103; and Jane Power, 54–55, 75, 78, 85–86, 87, 103, 107, 108–9; in Power-Wootan feud, 195; and voting, 59

Power, Passion, and Prejudice (Wolfe), 215

Power, Samuel (Jeff's great-grandfather), 3–4

Power, Samuel B. (Jeff's father), 5, 7; and alcohol, 19–20; in Arkansas, 11–12; and Civil War, 9, 10, 11–12, 15–16, 21, 97, 228n12; death of, 21, 229n29; and draft evasion, 15–16, 85; marriage to Jane Power, 11–12, 15, 19–21; in Texas, 11, 12, 15–20; and voting, 228n18

Power, Thomas Jefferson "Jeff," 4, 49; and alcohol, 19–20; alleged threats of, 98, 130, 162, 163; in Aravaipa, 48–49, 53–56, 75, 86, 87, 109, 183; burial of, 134, 216, 251n34; and cattle ranching, 24, 38–39, 48–49, 55, 79, 85, 86, 241n9; childhood in Texas, 11, 12, 16, 18, 52, 227n2; and Civil War, 10, 11, 12, 15, 16, 21; and conscription, 92, 97–98, 104, 107, 111–12, 146, 162–63, 195, 214; death of, 122, 127–28, 129, 134, 146, 152, 190, 211, 216; depiction by Don Dedera, 194–95; depiction in folklore and literature, 179, 181, 187–88, 192, 195; in Doubtful Canyon, 39–43, 132; dying declaration of, 128, 140, 150, 161–62, 164; and education, 18, 43;

estate of, 172–74; and frontier honor, 37, 38, 41, 43; and hunting, 55, 59; legal proceedings, 30–31, 40, 41–3, 132, 233n24; and Frank McBride, 78, 104, 107, 109, 111–12, 126, 162, 184, 248n22; and Mattie Morgan, 20, 28, 39; and mining, 79, 80, 81, 82, 86, 92, 221, 241n2, 241n9, 243n20; in New Mexico, 21, 22–31, 39; and perjury, 109, 114, 150; politics of, 18, 28, 38–39, 72; and Jane Power, 21, 38, 39, 54, 82, 85, 86, 87; and Ola Power's death, 104–9; and Power shootout, 118–21, 122, 124, 125, 129, 130, 150, 158, 159, 250n17, 255n10; and religion, 18; and Tom Sisson, 83, 85; and violence, 3, 4, 42–43, 166; and voting, 59, 72, 87; and World War I, 97–98, 104, 107, 126, 130–32, 162–63, 194–95, 214. See also Power shootout; Power Mine; Power Road; Power-Sisson trial

Power, Thomas Jefferson, Jr. (Jeff's uncle), 5, and Civil War, 9–10, 11, 15, 16, 97

Power, Thomas Jefferson, Jr. (Jeff's son Tom), 49, 58, 172, 204, 212; in Aravaipa, 40, 48–49, 53–55, 56–59, 83, 87; as bootlegger, 82–83, 102, 215; childhood of, 28, 29–30, 43, 188; death of, 216; escape attempts, 177–78, 185–86; injuries of 142, 144, 160; and Glenn Kempton, 191, 205; and mining, 82, 86–87; and Morgans, 32–33, 46–47; and Jeff Power, 37, 98, 132; and Ola May Power, death of, 108–9; Shoot-Out at Dawn, 196, 212–13; and true crime magazines, 187, 213; as voter, 59, 215–16. See also Power brothers (Tom and John); Power Mine; Power shootout; Power-Sisson manhunt; Power-Sisson trial; Power-Wootan feud

Power, Thomas Jefferson, Sr. (Jeff's grandfather), 4–9, 10, 21

Power brothers (Tom and John), 12, *172*, *212*; alleged threats made by, 97, 109, 126–27, 129, 146, 162, 165, 166–67, 184; awaiting trial, 145–47; clemency, 177–79, 185, 187–90, 191, 192–207; murder charge, 129–30, 161–62, 171; pardon, 210–11; parole, 208–10; in prison, 168, 169–71, 174, 177–78, 181, 185–86, 187, 188, 199, 210, 253n14, 257n1, 257n6, 259n23; and shootout, 119–21, 122–26, 146, 190, 211; as slackers, 16, 88, 96–98, 102–3, 104, 106, 107–8, 110, 111–12, 113, 130, 132, 146, 150, 174, 184–85, 190, 192, 202, 214, 228n12, 245n22, 248n25, 250n14, 251n28, 258n14; surveillance of, 96, 102, 103, 109–10, 112–13, 126–27, 130–31; warrants for draft evasion, 110–12, 113–14, 124, 171, 248n25. *See also* Power, John Grant (Jeff's son); Power, Thomas Jefferson, Jr. (Jeff's son Tom); Power-Sisson manhunt; Power-Sisson trial

Power Garden Place, *50*, 50–51, 52–54, 55, 79, 80; posse visits, 118, 197; sale of 86, 87, 108–9; today, 221, 265n30. *See also* Rattlesnake Canyon (Ariz.)

Power Hill, 87

Power Mine, 82, 86–87, 103, 109, 180, 241n2, 241n5, 243n22, 263n5; death of Jeff Power at, 127, 134, 216; in folklore, 80, 133, 181, 182, 187, 196–97, 201, 210, 212; lawmen's widows' lawsuit, 169, 171–74, 209–10, 258n12; in Power shootout, 127–28, 134, 157, 164–65, 183; reclaimed by John Power, 209–10, 217; in World War I, 97, 126, 214. *See also* abandoned mines; Power Mine cabin

Power Mine cabin, 118–21, *119*, *220*; as crime scene 148, 149–51, 158–60, 164, 166, 249n37; in folklore, 179, 181–82; today, 221. *See also* Power Mine; Power shootout

Power Road, 83, 85, 87, 180

Power shootout, 119–21, 122, 128, 250n17; aftermath of, 122–33; evidence collection after, 128, 129, 151, 159, 164, 165; in folklore and literature, 122, 133–34, 143, 179–85, 187–88, 191–92, 194–96, 211–14, 215, 218, 221; newspaper coverage of, 12, 123–24, 127, 130–34, 139–40, 146–47, 256n15; Power brothers' version of, 146, 194, 211; and World War I, 213–15. *See also* coroner's inquests; Power, Thomas Jefferson "Jeff"; Power brothers (Tom and John); Power-Sisson manhunt; Power-Sisson trial; Power-Wootan feud; Sisson, Thomas Joseph

Power-Sisson manhunt, 127, 134–43, 146–47, 187, 251–52n4, 252n7, 253n1, 260n33; and airplanes, 138; and bloodhounds, 137–38; and capture, 141–42, 144–45, 123, 249n32, 252n2; and Indian trackers, 137–38; and military, 140, 141–42; reward, 135–36, 144, 242n7, 225n5, 251n35, 253n9; wanted poster, 135, 225n5, 251n35

Power-Sisson posse: federal instructions for, 111, 112, 113–15, 124; McBride's request for, 96–97, 108, 126; rumors about, 181–83, 126, 192, 196, 197, 260n33; trip to the Galiuros, 117–19, 123–24, 126, 157, 163, 182, 183, 192, 248n18, 249n29. *See also* law enforcement; Power-Sisson manhunt

Power-Sisson trial, 141–68, 170–71, 250n21, 256n15, 257n7; and change of venue, 145, 148, 253n14; and circumstantial evidence, 151, 159, 167, 215, 255n3; and dying declarations, 161–62, 164, 167; evidence introduced, 151, 155, 159–60, 164, 165, 250n21, 255n3; jury for, 156–57, 167, 255nn5–6; jury instructions for, 155, 167–68; and mining corporations, 149, 156–57, 159, 164, 184, 215; and motion for retrial,

156, 171, 257n7; newspaper coverage of, 156–57, 159, 161, 163, 164, 183, 255n5, 256n15; and perjury, 109, 114, 124, 150, 153–54, 160, 162, 164, 165, 167, 184; and premeditated murder charge, 129, 151–52, 162, 163, 165, 167, 168; self-defense and, 148–51, 152, 161–62, 164, 165, 166, 167; sentencing, 169, 171, 177, 189, 257n1; transcripts, 155–56, 177, 178, 180, 215, 255n3, 259n24; verdict, 168, 171, 215; warrants for draft evasion, 110, 111, 113–14, 124, 129, 150–51, 157–58, 162, 167, 168, 171, 181, 201, 247n15, 248n25, 259n24
Power-Wootan feud, 192, 195–98, 199, 213–14, 215
prisons, 34, 35, 84; federal military, 92, 93, 99, 176; reform of, 85, 147, 169–70; 253n21, 258n21. *See also* Morgan, Wiley; *names of specific prisons*; Power brothers (Tom and John); Sisson, Thomas Joseph
Progressivism, 69, 85, 90, 100, 139. *See also* capital punishment; prisons
prohibition, 69, 138; in Arizona, 69–73, 76, 82–83, 182; in Texas, 19–20, 229n22. *See also* alcohol consumption; bootleggers
propaganda. *See under* World War I
prospectors. *See* mining
prostitution, 23, 62, 69
Protestants, 4, 64, 67, 69, 188
public lands, 39, 40, 45, 48, 53, 112. *See also* homesteaders; United States Forest Service
Pulliam, Eugene, 198, 216

Quantrill, William, 15
Quinn, James, 74, 122

Randall, Glen L., 193, 199, 201, 203
Rattlesnake Canyon (Ariz.), 48, 50, 49–53, 56, 58, 112; mining in, 46–47,

49, 79–82, 133; today, 219. *See also* Gold Mountain mining camp; Power Garden Place; Power Mine
Rattlesnake Creek, 43, 46, 50–51, 52, 53–54
Rattlesnake Spring, 51, 53, 87, 221
Reconstruction, 12, 16–17, 228n18
religion, 6, 13, 18; in Aravaipa, 48, 71; and World War I, 89. *See also* conscription in World War I; *specific religious denominations*
Republican Party, in Arizona, 156, 193, 196; and Mormons, 65, 67, 76, 193, 193, 199, 239n24; and Power family, 15, 193, 207, 211, 216; in Texas, 16
Richardson, Wilford Rene, 203, 204, 205
"rich man's war, poor man's fight" (slogan), 14, 97, 132
Ridgway, William Ryder, 180
Roberts, Roderick J., Jr., 211–12
Roosevelt, Theodore, 89
Roosevelt Dam, 68
Rose, Peter R., 17
Ross, David, 112–13, 126, 130,

Safford, Ariz., 47, 62, 69–70, 74, 116–17, 134; as county seat, 74–75, 107, 124, 144–45, 160, 216; during World War I, 89, 102–3. *See also* Gila Valley
Salazar, Crespina and Epimenio, 45–46, 48, 57, 59, 164, 218
Salazar, Guadalupe "Lupe," 57, 88, 181–82, 217, 260n33
Salem, Ind., 5, 12
saloons, 12, 13, 19, 23, 47, 52, 62, 69, 138, 187; in Aravaipa, 37, 46, 48, 70, 72, 73, 87, 221, 239n26. *See also* alcohol consumption; prohibition
Salt Lake City, Utah, 62, 65, 95
San Augustine Springs Ranch, 41
San Carlos Reservation, 45, 47, 51, 83, 137, 147
Sanford, John, 122

Santa Teresa Mountains (Ariz.), 44, 49
sauerkraut, 90, 104, 108–9, 131
Scarborough, Thomas, 83
Scarborough, Tilden, 83, 102, 215
Scott, Elizabeth Power, 56
Selective Service Act of 1917. See conscription, in World War I
Shaw, George Bernard, 177
Shenk, Gerald, 175
sheriff. See law enforcement
Shoot-Out at Dawn (Power), 196, 211–12
Shortbridge, Ernest, 156
Shriver, Frank, 141, 142, 144, 253n9
Sierra Bonita Ranch, 22
Silver City, N.Mex., 23, 24, 39, 40, 209, 213
silver mining. See mining, placer
Simpson, Thomas W., 67–68
Sisson, Thomas Joseph, 84; alleged threats of, 162; in Aravaipa, 83–84, 85, 87, 242n14; clemency, 85, 179, 185, 189–91, 193, 215; death of, 191–92, 215; in folklore, 84, 87, 132–33, 143, 191–92; and horse theft, 84–85, 133, 153, 242n17; military career of, 83–84, 133, 138, 178, 191–92, 208; murder charge, 129, 130, 151–52; perjury charge, 114, 124, 150; and Ola Power, death of, 104–9, 146, 218; and Power shootout, 119, 122, 123, 125–26, 127, 129, 132, 133, 151–52, 159–60, 165, 166, 181, 190; in prison, 84–85, 144–46, 169–71, 177–78, 186, 188–89, 193, 257n1, 258n14; and World War I, 98, 113, 131, 132, 133, 168, 251n28, 257n37. See also Power Mine; Power-Sisson manhunt; Power-Sisson trial
slackers: in Civil War, 14, 15–16; McBride and, 89, 94, 95–96, 103, 104; in World War I, 91–98, 176–77. See also Power, Charles; Power brothers (Tom and John); Sisson, Thomas Joseph
Slaughter, Arthur, 145–46, 147, 218
slavery, 4, 7, 13, 14, 15, 16, 63

Smithville, Ariz. See Pima, Ariz.
Sociability Run, 74–75, 85, 104
Socialists, 90, 92, 139, 214
Solomon, Delila "Lila" (Mrs. William E. Wootan), 195–96, 198
Solomon, Lee, 195–96, 198, 199, 203, 205, 208, 213
Solomon, Madge (Mrs. Miller), 195–96, 198, 199
Solomon, Roxie, 195–96, 198
Solomonville, Ariz., 47, 62
Sonnichsen, C. L., 32, 36
Sonoran Desert, 39, 44
Spain, in the Southwest, 44–45
Spence, Pete. See Ferguson, Elliot Lark (alias Pete Spence)
spies. See under World War I
St. Dismas Catholic Men's Club, 188
Steins Pass, N.Mex., 40, 148
Steins Peak, 39, 233n22
Stewart, Brigham "Briggs" F., 76, 142, 144, 145, 151
St. Joseph Stake. See under Mormons
submarines, German, 81, 89, 102
Sulphur Springs Valley (Ariz.), 22, 33, 39, 140, 211. See also Willcox, Ariz.
Sulphur Springs Valley Bank, 82, 241n9

Taylor, John, 64, 65
Taylor Grazing Act, 219
temperance. See prohibition
Texas: American Indians in, 12, 17; cattle ranching in, 13, 17, 18, 19, 20, 21; during Civil War, 11, 12, 13–15, 16, 60; crime in, 17, 18, 60; farming in, 12, 13, 20
Texas Hill Country, 12–13; Germans in, 12–15, 18, 21. See also Power, Thomas Jefferson, Jr. (Jeff's son Tom); Power, Samuel B. (Jeff's father)
Thomas, Bob, 206
Thomas, Norman, 92
Thompson, John Henry, 110, 182

Tombstone, Ariz., 34, 51, 154

Tragedy of the Powers Mine (Wood), 192

true crime magazines, 187–88, 213

Tucker, Commodore Perry, 52, 79–81, 174

Tucson, Ariz., 44, 45, 65, 102, 112–13, 135, 221

Tucson Citizen, coverage of Power-Sisson trial, 156, 161, 163, 164

Tullos, Mrs. Barnes, 141

Turman, Peter, 30

Twain, Mark, 80

Udall, Jesse, 190

Union Army, 8–10, 11, 83, 91, 97, 228n9

Union loyalty leagues, 14–15

United Order of Enoch, 63, 64, 67

United States Army: in Southwest 22, 40, 45. *See also* conscription in World War I; *names of individual forts;* Union Army; Wham payroll robbery

United States attorney for Arizona. *See* Flynn, Thomas

United States Congress, 69, 219; and Mormons, 64, 65; and World War I, 89–91, 98

United States Department of the Interior, 53

United States Department of Justice, 94, 96, 102, 103, 109, 110, 123–24, 166, 171. *See also* Bureau of Investigation (BI)

United States Forest Service, 45, 53–54, 55, 112, 219, 221, 236n23, 253n22, 263n5

United States marshal for Arizona. *See* Dillon, Joseph P.

United States Military Intelligence Division, 130, 182

United States Postal Service, 66, 99, 238n13

United States Supreme Court, 110, 161, 200, 231n1

Upchurch, Al, 117–18, 122, 125, 159, 260n33

Utah, 7–8, 63, 64, 66, 67, 201, 237n2

Vietnam War, 210

vigilantism, 38, 139; and Civil War, 15–17; and Power brothers, 127, 143, 145; and World War I, 99, 100–101, 139, 143, 175

Villa, Francisco "Pancho," 51, 98

Visalia, Calif., 7, 8

Walker, A. G., 76, 77, 178

Weaver, Alva, 191, 203, 205

Webb, Gilbert, 66

Webb, Wilfred, 66–67, 69, 73, 116, 238nn13–14. *See also* Wham payroll robbery

Weber, John F., 116–17

Wham payroll robbery, 66–67, 180, 181, 200, 238n13

Wheeler, Harry: and Bisbee Deportation, 100–101; and Power-Sisson posse, 135, 137–38, 140

Whig Party, 6

Wilhelm II, Kaiser, 100

Willcox, Ariz., 34, 47, 66, 80, 83, 185; Power family in, 39, 43, 108, 234n31. *See also* Sulphur Springs Valley (Ariz.)

Williams, Jack, 210–11, 216

Williamson, Starr K., 153

Willow City, Texas, 18

Wilson, John P., 210

Wilson, Woodrow, 87, 98, 258n19

Witcherville, Ark., 5–6

Wobblies. *See* Industrial Workers of the World (IWW)

Wolfe, Barbara Brooks, 215

Woman's Christian Temperance Union, 19, 229n22

women: in the West, 37–38, 69, 72; American Indian, 10, 45; domestic role of, 5, 46, 54, 105; and frontier honor, 38; legal rights of, 38, 69, 72, and prohibition, 19, 69, 73

Wood, Elizabeth Lambert, 192, 195

Wood, Bob, 201–2

Woodruff, Wilford, 67

Wootan, Joseph Frank "J. Frank," 60, 151, 171, 185, *203*; and Power brothers, clemency for, 197, 199, 202, 203, 207

Wootan, Laura, 61, 76–77, 114, 262n28; civil suit against Power family, 171–74, 197, 262n38

Wootan, Millie, 60

Wootan, Opal (Mrs. Shepard), 114, 198

Wootan, Richard, 72, 88

Wootan, Sarah Chapman, 60, 61, 196

Wootan, Thomas Kane, Jr. (Kane's son), 190

Wootan, Thomas Kane "Kane," 61, 75, 76–77, *117*; death of, 129, 158, 160, 165, 166, 168, 189; financial problems of, 61, 76–77, 114, 173; funeral, 134–35; killing of Jeff Power, 125, 128, 129, 140, 149, 161–62, 194, 199; as lawman, 61, 62, 72, 73–74, 76, 77, 114, 240n41; and Ola Power, death of, 104, 107; in Power shootout, 118–21, 123, 127, 149, 158, 159, 160, 213; and Power-Sisson posse, 114, 117–18, 182, 183; and World War I, 88, 91, 94. *See also* Power-Wootan feud

Wootan, William E. "Black Bill," Jr., 59–61, 196

Wootan, William Lee "Braz," 60

Working Class Union, 101

World War I, 81–82, 88–90, 98, 102, 157, 174–75, 214; in Arizona, 88–89, 93–94, 99–101; and censorship, 99, 156, 162, 184, 253n16; and civil liberties, 92, 99, 101, 156, 162, 175, 177, 184, 214, 253n16; Committee on Public Information, 90; enemy aliens, 90, 91, 101; Espionage Act, 98–99, 114, 177, 245n26, 250n14, 258n20; farmers and, 90, 92, 97, 101; labor unions, 90, 93, 94, 99–101, 102, 111, 112, 143; Liberty (war) bonds, 93, 98, 131; and McBride, 95, 103, 107, 110, 111–12, 113; and Mexicans, 95–96, 101; mining and, 81–83, 99, 100, 101, 139, 156–57, 215; newspaper coverage of, 88–89, 91, 92, 98, 100, 101, 102, 103; opposition to, 89, 90, 97, 101–2, 123, 176; patriotism during, 88–90, 95, 103, 131–32, 134, 184, 214; and Power family, 16, 97–98, 102, 103, 104, 107, 110, 111–12, 113, 130, 132, 146, 174, 184, 190, 202, 214, 228n12, 245n22; propaganda, 90, 98, 102, 108, 143, 184–85; spies and sabotage, 90, 94, 98, 139. *See also* Bisbee Deportation; conscription in World War I; deserters; slackers

World War II, 186, 187–89, 213

Wright, Lorenzo, 203, 205

Young, Brigham, 8, 62

Zimmerman telegram, 89, 90